Coptic Christianity in Ottoman Egypt

Coptic Christianity in Ottoman Egypt

FEBE ARMANIOS

OXFORD
UNIVERSITY PRESS
2011

OXFORD
UNIVERSITY PRESS

Oxford University Press, Inc., publishes works that further
Oxford University's objective of excellence
in research, scholarship, and education.

Oxford New York
Auckland Cape Town Dar es Salaam Hong Kong Karachi
Kuala Lumpur Madrid Melbourne Mexico City Nairobi
New Delhi Shanghai Taipei Toronto

With offices in
Argentina Austria Brazil Chile Czech Republic France Greece
Guatemala Hungary Italy Japan Poland Portugal Singapore
South Korea Switzerland Thailand Turkey Ukraine Vietnam

Published by Oxford University Press, Inc.
198 Madison Avenue, New York, New York 10016

www.oup.com

Library of Congress Cataloging-in-Publication Data
Armanios, Febe, 1974–
Coptic Christianity in Ottoman Egypt / Febe Armanios.
p. cm.
Includes bibliographical references and index.
ISBN 978-0-19-974484-8
1. Coptic Church—History. 2. Egypt—Church history. 3. Turkey—History—Ottoman
Empire, 1288–1918. I. Title.
BX133.3.A74 2011
281'.720962—dc22 2010017993

9 8 7 6 5 4 3 2 1

Printed in the United States of America
on acid-free paper

In memory of Teta Linda,
for her love of learning.

Acknowledgments

Growing up in Heliopolis, I used to sit in my grandparents' living room next to Giddo Hilmy and listen to his spirited stories about the saints. As soon as I learned to read, I devoured all of the books he had authored about the lives of Coptic martyrs and about the saints' miraculous apparitions in Egypt. To us, the saints were real; we talked about them and to them, and their stories and iconography pervaded most aspects of our lives. This book celebrates, in part, my personal heritage but also that of a community whose full history merits greater investigation.

Over the past ten years, I was able to complete my research with generous funding from a number of organizations. My gratitude extends to the Fulbright Commission, the Andrew W. Mellon Foundation, the Philanthropic Education Organization, the Coca-Cola Foundation, and the St. Shenouda the Archimandrite Coptic Society. At the Ohio State University, I am obliged to the Department of History and to the College of Humanities, and at Middlebury College to the Office of Faculty Development and Research for supporting my travels and allowing me to write uninterruptedly for one leave year.

The friendship, collegiality, and intellectual support of numerous individuals have been central to seeing this work to fruition. Of course, any and all errors are solely my responsibility. At Ohio State, I had the pleasure of working with Carter Findley, Amy Shuman, Sabra Webber, Robert Davis, and Joseph Zeidan. I wish to extend special gratitude to Jane Hathaway, whose support, guidance, and conceptual suggestions were instrumental from the earliest stages of this project. I would also like to thank Eve Levin, whose sage advice has been invaluable. I was fortunate to have been part of a lively graduate community and am especially thankful to Kate Heilman, Emre Sencer, Atabey Kaygun, Heather Almer, and Safa Saraçoğlu for great conversation and excellent food. Throughout the years, I have cherished the friendship of Armin Alaedini, Eve Chow, Amy Sordi, Manisha Shah, Alexis Albion, Greg Kaufmann, Ramz Samy, Clare Seelke, Emma Chanlett-Avery, Jeremy Sharp, Jeff Flynn, Ana Garcia, Ian Barrow, Natasha Chang, and Rebecca Bennette.

A number of individuals have offered warm encouragement and critical feedback on various parts of this project. I am grateful to Kristen Stilt, who has been an indefatigable friend and a keen reader. I am especially indebted to Maged Mikhail, Akram Khater, and William Lyster for their meticulous and valuable suggestions on various parts of this book. I am also obliged to the late B. J. Fernea for her warm and enthusiastic support of my research. Thanks to those who have been generous with their time and advice, including Michael Winter, Elizabeth Bolman, Johannes den Heijer, Gawdat Gabra, Mark Swanson, Glenn Bowman, Donald Crummey, Stephen Davis, Karel Innemée, Karen Winstead, Stephen Humphreys, John Voll, Madeleine Zilfi, Anthony O'Mahony, Nelly van Doorn-Harder, Kari Vogt, Tamer el-Leithy, Suraiya Faroqhi, Zuzana Skalova, Elyse Semerdjian, Jim Goehring, Sasha Treiger, Nabil Farouk, Sean Field, and Louisa Burnham.

In the course of my research, I benefited from the expertise and technical support of individuals from all over the world. At St. Macarius Monastery, I am grateful to Abouna Bertie for his kindness and scholarly suggestions. Abouna Wadi Abullif, of the Franciscan Center of Christian Oriental Studies, offered encyclopedic knowledge of Arab Christian manuscripts and inspired me to think more creatively about my sources. This research could not have been completed without the help of Nabih Kamil, historian and librarian at the Patriarchal Library in Cairo; I am grateful for his willingness to open the archives and to answer my queries about the documents. I would also like to thank the librarians at Dayr al-Suryan and St. Mina Monastery, the staff at the Coptic Museum in Cairo, Meline Nielsen at the Selly Oak Colleges in Birmingham, Dona Straley at Ohio State, and the librarians at the British Library and the Library of Congress. Hany Takla at the St. Shenouda the Archimandrite Coptic Society in Los Angeles gave me access to a number of rare manuscripts, without which this book could not have been completed.

At Oxford University Press, I would like to thank Theo Calderara for his patience and support, and Tamzen Benfield, Christi Stanforth, Lisbeth Redfield, and Molly Balikov for their professionalism and meticulousness. The anonymous readers of this manuscript offered rich feedback that was vital for the final writing and revision process. I am also indebted to Elizabeth Lindsmith, Charlotte Weber, and John Tallmadge for their keen editorial eye and thoroughness. The maps were prepared by Bill Nelson. I am grateful to Kathleen Scott and Jaroslaw Dobrowolski of the American Research Center in Egypt for their assistance with the cover illustration. My research assistants—Sheena Christman, Joe Giacomelli, Moritz Remig, Geoff Allen, and Phil Houten—worked diligently and carefully at various stages of this project.

I have valued the encouragement that my family in Egypt and North America has given me over the years. Aida Nashid, Samira DiMitri, Lucy Abouseif, Lilly Elias, Mary-Rose Halim, and Abouna Antuniyus Amin offered enormous personal and intellectual support. My gratitude also extends to Mary Latif, Hany, and Rafik Halim; Amir, Nahed, and Mirey Makariyus; and to Nadia Halim, George Abd al-Malak, and Nancy and Gina Guirguis, all of whom opened their homes and hearts with extreme generosity. I enjoyed delightful meals and conversations with Insaf Armanios and Nevine Farid, whose good humor helped me overcome many challenges. To my parents, Mona and Yousry, and to my sister Mary, your endless love and support motivated me to appreciate and study Coptic history. Finally, I am most thankful to my husband, Boğaç Ergene. Throughout the long years that it took to complete this work, you read countless drafts, gave me invaluable suggestions, and cheered me on at every stage of the process. It is unimaginable that I would have come this far without your care, wisdom, love, and encouragement, and for that I will be always indebted.

Parts of chapter 1 were included in "Patriarchs, Archons, and the Eighteenth-Century Resurgence of the Coptic Community," in William Lyster, ed., *The Cave Church at the Monastery of St. Paul the First Hermit* (New Haven: Yale University Press / The American Research Center in Egypt, 2008).

Portions of chapter 2 were published as part of a coauthored article with Boğaç Ergene, "A Christian Martyr under Mamluk Justice: The Trials of Salib (d. 1512) according to Muslim and Coptic Sources," *Muslim World* 96, no. 1 (2006): 115–144.

Contents

A Note on Transliteration

I have adopted a modified version of the transliteration system used by the *International Journal of Middle East Studies*. All names of individual authors, historical figures, and places, such as Yu'annis, Salib, and al-'Arish, were rendered with 'ayns and hamzas but no other diacritics. Technical terms, book titles, publisher names, and direct quotations were transliterated with full diacritical marks. I have provided the English form of places, terms, and personal names that are commonly used, such as Macarius, Antony, Damietta, and Alexandria. However, the names of Coptic patriarchs, bishops, and laity are given in their Arabic form (e.g., Patriarch Yu'annis XVI rather than Patriarch John XVI).

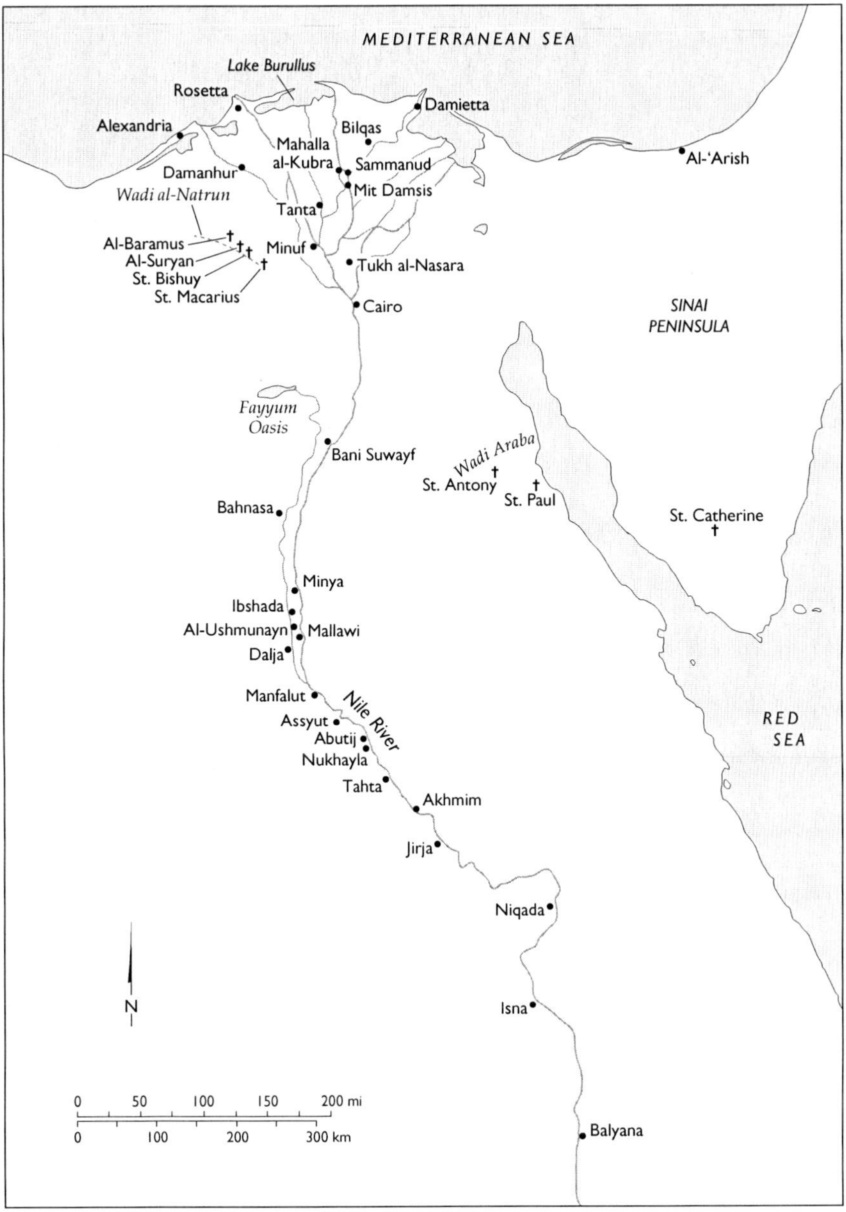

Coptic Locales in Ottoman Egypt

Coptic Christianity in Ottoman Egypt

Introduction

In a rare mention of Coptic Christians, the Egyptian chronicler Ahmad al-Damurdashi inserts a short but telling story about public religious expression in eighteenth-century Egypt. On an otherwise ordinary day in the spring of 1748, the Coptic procession gathering outside the Church of the Virgin Mary seemed particularly loud and boisterous. Clergymen and laypeople, women and children, congregated in one of the narrow alleys of Harat al-Rum. In readying for their pilgrimage to Jerusalem, they loaded camels with specially decorated wooden carriages. Al-Damurdashi notes that once provisions were packed, Patriarch Murqus VII (1745–1769) mounted his mule and was taken to the head of the lineup by a troop of young boys. Behind him rode the Coptic lay dignitaries, or *archons*,[1] dressed in their finest robes, followed by their wives, whose colorful Kashmiri shawls were wrapped neatly over their heads. The archons' wives insisted on traveling by land and were glad to accompany the patriarch on this journey. Coptic leaders had acquired the necessary permissions for the pilgrimage, and everyone sensed that this procession was off to a good start.

The Copts had spared no expense in their planning. Much like the *ḥajj* caravan, their convoy was heralded by a troop of dancers and musicians, while boys guided the pilgrims with their torches. After a short time, however, the hubbub began to disturb the Cairenes, who had gathered to watch the spectacle moving north toward al-Ghawriyya, the old Mamluk neighborhood near the al-Azhar mosque-school complex. As the pilgrims came closer to one of Islam's most revered institutions, all festivities halted. Suddenly the voices of Muslim religious leaders, the *ʿulamāʾ*, were heard from amid the crowds: "How dare they emulate the Muslims?" said one. Others inflamed the crowds by shouting that the procession was an "innovation" (*bidʿa*) and demanded that military officers stop the pilgrimage and seize the Copts' possessions. The pilgrims panicked and scrambled to guard their lives and properties. Coptic leaders sought protection from a high-ranking grandee, who advised them to return to their homes and promised to safeguard their belongings. As the pilgrims fled, they heard news that the Ottoman governor had forbidden all Christians from traveling by land. In this case, the Copts were moderately fortunate. During previous years, they had sometimes been able to make their way out of the city and successfully pay homage to their holiest sites; but on other occasions, they were attacked by angry mobs who looted their provisions and forced them into a humbling retreat. On the scale of successes and failures, as al-Damurdashi reports, 1748 was simply an "ill-omened year" for Egypt's Coptic Christians.[2]

One might conclude that al-Damurdashi's account reveals the occasional act of discrimination against Christians or that it showed acceptance of non-Muslim customs by certain segments of the society but not others. The history of non-Muslim communities in the Islamic world, particularly of Copts, has been often understood within this framework, through the lens of persecution or tolerance.[3] Inevitably, these categories encourage an examination of minorities from the perspective of the dominant culture, and in this context, non-Muslims frequently appear as docile and victimized. However, while the experience and recollection of suffering deserves serious attention, the pilgrimage story indicates that other issues too warrant inquiry, ones that reveal the complex nature of non-Muslim religious practices. For example, in analyzing the above narrative, the historian is left to wonder how Coptic leaders acquired the necessary permits. Why did Copts find it important to hold this procession, knowing that open display of non-Muslim religiosity was forbidden? How and why were religious practices so crucial to Coptic life that they merited such risk-taking? These questions are central to my project, and in seeking to answer them, I will eschew an essentialist representation of a singular voice, of one Coptic identity, and attempt instead to capture snapshots of the religious rituals, writings, and practices that informed a sense of Coptic communality in Ottoman Egypt.

Recently, scholars have begun to examine the political circumstances that shaped Coptic existence under Ottoman rule, but I will maintain that this type of narrative alone tells us little about how Copts experienced their religion. I am interested here in the range of worldviews that emerged within the Coptic community, from high to low, as evidenced by their own writings. Carlo Ginzburg argues in the context of sixteenth-century Friuli that popular religious culture was neither completely isolated from nor totally dependent on the high culture of elites and distinguished clergymen and that in the performative exchange between them one can catch a glimpse of this reciprocal relationship.[4] Similarly, even though most Coptic documents were reproduced under the orders of elite laymen or clergy, "non-elite" actors, peasants, artisans, and lower clergy all actively participated in religious life. Since the majority of sources studied in this book were intended to be read out loud to those audiences, I also view them as a record of the interaction that took place between the church hierarchy and its congregations. By asking what tropes, narratives, and rituals characterized expressions of piety and spirituality among the Copts, I read my sources critically to uncover not only institutional perspectives shared by lay and clerical elders but also clues about the lived reality of the masses.

Issues of acculturation and assimilation will factor into any discussion of Coptic religious life. It has been sometimes argued that in their religious and cultural practices, Copts are indistinguishable from other Egyptians.[5] In the Ottoman period, Copts did share a number of practices with their Muslim neighbors. For example, they circumcised their boys around the age of ten and, following ancient and biblical traditions, abstained from eating "strangled" meat.[6] Likewise, a number of secular and religious festivals in early Islamic, Mamluk, and Ottoman Egypt were attended by all faiths. However, Ottoman Copts also carved out their own social space and occasionally shirked participation in specifically Islamic celebrations.[7] Thus while Egypt's various communities—Copts, Jews, Melkites (Greek Orthodox), Armenians, Syrian Catholics, and Muslims—shared a number of folk practices, Copts generally existed as a separate group with its own devotional rites and spiritual culture. Their distinctiveness is partially tied to an Islamic legal structure that separated religious groups into Muslim believers and *dhimmīs*,[8] and Copts formed the biggest group of dhimmīs in Ottoman Egypt. Ultimately, when it came to holding specific worldviews and to the life experiences that shaped individual attitudes, my research asks what beliefs and practices Coptic Christianity fostered among its adherents.

I have chosen the early and middle centuries of Ottoman rule in Egypt, the "early modern" era (1517–1798),[9] as my primary focus. When it comes to the study of Copts, the early Islamic, Fatimid, Ayyubid, and Mamluk periods, as well as the modern centuries, have received some scholarly attention, but this intermediary and formative period has scarcely been studied. I do not argue, as some have, that the French Occupation (1798–1801) was a moment of liberation and revival for the Christian Copts.[10] In fact, this study will show that revitalization movements arose throughout Ottoman rule, one of the most prominent dating to the late seventeenth and early eighteenth centuries. Still, the French invasion noticeably altered the Copts' status and elevated some to new heights: at least temporarily, one Copt served as a leader of a military battalion and another as a magistrate (*qāḍī*).[11] These developments, as well as the rise of the semi-autonomous Muhammad ʿAli dynasty (1805–1952) and new waves of Catholic and Protestant missionaries to Egypt, so starkly distinguish the Coptic experience at the turn of the nineteenth century from earlier periods that they merit a separate investigation.[12]

The Coptic Church begins its calendar from the rule of the Roman Emperor Diocletian (284–305), when thousands of Egyptian Christians were killed for their beliefs. Their stories were passed down through generations, and today most are recorded in the Coptic *Synaxarium*. Hagiographies of martyrs (or martyrologies) exist as a familiar and living reality within the Coptic collective memory. Historically, the church has also taken pride in having established the institution of monasticism, which is still practiced among the majority of its clerical leaders, including patriarchs and bishops.[13] The ancient monasteries in Wadi al-Natrun, along the Red Sea, and throughout Upper Egypt have served as major pilgrimage destinations since the fourth century. Their remoteness drew those who were seeking the miraculous, the holy, or simply an escape from the mundane. One can argue that the foundations of Coptic faith and practice have been closely tied to traditions of sainthood, martyrdom, and monasticism.

At its height, the church was also an evangelical institution, with particularly successful missions in Sudan and Ethiopia.[14] Its distinctive brand of Christianity, shared with the Armenian, Syrian, and Ethiopian Churches, is worth explaining here. These churches dissented from Rome and Constantinople at the Council of Chalcedon (451) in a dispute over the nature of Christ. Adherents of the Council of Chalcedon argued that two natures (divinity and humanity) united in the person of Jesus Christ, whereas the Copts and other opponents of the council favored defining the person of Jesus as of two natures. The theological dissent had wide ramifications, as each side erroneously understood and consequently condemned the other.[15] In time, Copts separated from Byzantine domination, and after the Islamic conquest of Egypt in 641, they would become doubly marginalized—ostracized by fellow Christians for their anti-Chalcedonian beliefs and estranged as a subordinate religious community. Ensuing historical developments and church policies led to the rise of a relatively insular community that has had, as one scholar writes, a troublesome history of relations "with every other Church in the world, whether Orthodox, Catholic, or Protestant."[16]

The Coptic faith is profoundly ritualistic. At its core are seven sacraments, a rich liturgical heritage, and the strict, nearly vegan fasts that believers are obligated to follow.[17] Official and popular dimensions of the Coptic faith have commonly intersected in the traditions of pilgrimage and the veneration of saints, both of which were nurtured by clerical leaders and patronized by the laity. Veneration preserved the memory of saints and strengthened the church's historical assertion that it was founded on the blood of martyrs. Pilgrimage fostered closer ties between believers and their local churches, shrines, and sanctuaries. Pilgrims were drawn to a shrine not only because they might receive remedies, miracles, or fatherly guidance, but also because of its lively festival, usually celebrated on a saint's feast day (*mawlid*, *mūlid*) or martyrdom date. These festivities were a time when boundaries of prevailing social norms could be overstepped or redefined.

In the decades following the Ottoman conquest of 1517, Egyptians engaged in a kind of spiritual introspection, as seen by the noticeable popularity of Sufism and interest in commemorating mawlids.[18] Some historians have implied that the melancholic atmosphere (or "malaise," as Michael Winter calls it) following the violent conquest triggered an outpouring of religious piety in both urban and rural centers, a feeling that intensified with the rampant plague outbreaks.[19] No doubt these afflictions reinforced Egyptians' sense of misfortune and increased their desire for closer bonds with the spiritual realm; people turned to the supernatural simply to cope with ongoing hardships.[20] Historically, plagues and disease often led people, rich and poor, to make public expressions of penitence and piety, as the afflicted believed themselves to be cursed by God. Life in Ottoman Egypt seems to have precipitated similar sentiments. In addition to disease, however, civil strife dominated Egyptian politics and society: Ottoman governors were regularly deposed or murdered, and violence in urban and rural areas persisted for decades. Thus early modern Egypt also saw the spread of mystical practices as one way of dealing with the bloody outcomes of local political struggles. Among Egyptian Muslims, the attention to popular religion seemed to be part of a desire to find spiritual meaning in an uncertain world and to search, as one scholar writes, for a "compromise between general conformity to performance of prayer, ritual, and formal modes of life prescribed by orthodoxy, and [Sufi] embellishments, interpretations, and beliefs."[21] Egypt's downgrade from an imperial center to a mere province appears to have further encouraged "an apolitical and even other-worldly orientation" among its people.[22]

So how did Copts cope with these circumstances, and in what ways did they use religion to articulate their own concerns? While most Muslim chroniclers and Coptic Church documents avoid this subject, the Ottoman conquest undoubtedly created new challenges for the community. Under Mamluk rule, Copts had faced waves of conversions and attacks against church, property, and life from which they were still recovering in the early sixteenth century. Coptic anxieties intensified in the decades after the conquest because they were forced to contend with the prospect of new rulers. How strictly would the Ottoman sultans and their proxies govern their non-Muslim subjects? How would they enforce existing laws and provisions? No doubt Coptic leaders considered the future of their diminished community as they developed ways to deal with impending challenges. Their impulse for self-protection grew more acute following Catholic attempts at unification in the sixteenth and seventeenth centuries and during direct encounters with Catholic missionaries in the eighteenth century.

In response to these concerns, lay and clerical leaders collaborated, at least intermittently, in preserving communal traditions and supporting forms of religious expression that captured the needs of fellow believers. Martyr cults, for instance, drew on age-old rituals, allayed fears of conversion, and fulfilled the community's needs for local heroes. Other traditions, such as the pilgrimage to Jerusalem, were clearly influenced by the surrounding culture, even to the point where, as al-Damurdashi's story reveals, they provoked the ire of Muslim traditionalists. Still, in coping with these stressful events, Copts generally turned toward rituals that satisfied their own individual desires. On a practical level, differences in how Muslims and non-Muslims expressed their faiths existed not least because the latter were burdened by restrictive rules and laws.[23]

As it fostered an active religious life during the Ottoman period, the Coptic clerical and lay leadership accomplished three tasks that would promote a modest resurgence. First, communal leaders helped write, create, finance, and disseminate texts that represent the collective religious output. Second, clergymen preached homilies and sermons to a lay community (elites and masses) that demanded both traditional and innovative contextually specific stories. Third, lay and clerical leaders organized and supported popular religious traditions, such as pilgrimages and festivals, while engaging in diplomacy with local Muslim leaders. The role of lay elites as well as clergymen in these processes will become central to our discussion. Generally, both were committed to ensuring communal cohesiveness, and both understood that a strong and vibrant community, with defined boundaries, could reinforce their own authority and empower them to act as communal representatives in broader Egyptian society.

Within this framework, my work seeks to fill a void within the scholarly literature on Ottoman Egypt. To date, a few historians have explored non-Muslim involvement in Ottoman Egyptian bureaucracy and society, but most have excluded a detailed discussion of the Copts. The literature on the military organization, trade, literary culture, judiciary, and non-Muslim communities of Ottoman Egypt contains only passing mention of the Copts. Moreover, while we are learning more about Christians in the Balkans and the Levant and about Jews in Palestine and Istanbul—a rich literature that offers important comparisons to the present study—most of this scholarship tends to overlook the Coptic perspective.

Admittedly, archival challenges face anyone who conducts research into non-Muslim communities of Egypt, particularly when it concerns the Copts. On the one hand, there are few available or known documents on Coptic life or religious practices from the Ottoman era. Aside from scattered mentions by chroniclers such as Ibn Iyas, al-Damurdashi, and al-Jabarti, there are almost no references to Copts in Muslim literary sources. At times, and in contrast to their visibility in Mamluk-era sources, one wonders if Copts had simply disappeared from the historical consciousness of Muslim Egyptian writers.[24] An analysis of *sijills*, or court records, which constitute an important source on non-Muslim life in other parts of the Ottoman Empire, could potentially illuminate certain legal and economic aspects of Coptic life. However, sijill-based research is currently at its nascent stages for early modern Egypt, and from what we can gather so far, these records make few references to the Copts' religious worldviews, the topic of the present study.[25] Copts are also mostly absent in Ottoman imperial archives.[26] Unlike their Armenian and Greek correlates, who had active patriarchates in Istanbul, they were primarily governed by local power-holders in Egypt—Ottoman governors, 'ulamā', military households, or their own communal leaders. As such, they scarcely provoked the interest of sultans or their deputies. Finally, most original sources produced by Copts have been deemed either immaterial or inaccessible because they have been safeguarded in closely held archives. Inasmuch as possible, my project focuses prominently on this Coptic-Arabic literature.[27]

Recent studies of early Egyptian Christianity—by David Frankfurter, Stephen J. Davis, and Rebecca Krawiec, among others—have painted a sophisticated picture of Christian life during a formative historical period. They provide a good model for understanding how religious expression was negotiated to meet societal changes and local communal needs. It is remarkable, given the expansion of that field in recent years, that we know comparably little about how Christianity was practiced in the centuries following the Islamic conquest of Egypt. Still, the history of Coptic life—political, social, and religious—during the medieval and Ottoman periods has gradually earned more attention in large part due to historians like Aziz Atiya, Otto Meinardus, and Samir Khalil Samir, as well as to the pioneering, if imperfect, writings of Iris Habib al-Masri, Kamil Salih Nakhla, and Ya'qub Nakhla Rufayla. Among the most recent scholarly endeavors, my book complements Maged Mikhail's research on Coptic identity in the early Islamic and Fatimid periods, as well Tamer el-Leithy's examination of Coptic conversion to Islam under Mamluk rule.

Scholarship on Coptic social and political existence in the Ottoman era has also sprung up in recent years. Muhammad 'Afifi's *Al-Aqbāṭ fī Miṣr fi'l 'Aṣr al-'Uthmānī* (1992) was one of the first to exclusively tackle this subject. His monograph provides an important overview of political and economic life relying, in part, on Egyptian archival sources, and less so on Coptic ones. Alastair Hamilton, moreover, has perhaps written the most important work to date on Western interaction with the Coptic Church. Accessing documents in Arabic and a variety of Western languages, Hamilton elaborates on the struggles of Christian missionaries and European Orientalists in late Mamluk and Ottoman Egypt, revealing their motivations to study the Copts and to convert them to Catholicism or Protestantism. I have used his work extensively, as it divulges documents from European archives that have been heretofore untapped. A growing cadre of Egyptian historians also seeks to expand our familiarity with Coptic culture. Magdi Guirguis, for instance, has explored Coptic legal and communal organization between the sixteenth and eighteenth centuries, relating both, most recently, to iconography in the eighteenth century. His access to a handful of *waqf* (charitable endowment) documents housed in the Coptic patriarchate in Egypt also offers a tantalizing glimpse of potential research in Coptic *waqfiyyāt*, even as the church has placed strict limitations on these valuable sources.[28] Looking to this collective output, one anticipates more research, particularly regarding legal, economic, and art history.

The present study benefits from these important contributions but also steers away from a strict emphasis on political, legal, or ecclesiastical history or the history of Coptic-Western relations. Instead, I focus on a varied understanding of Coptic spirituality and religious practice in relation to processes of identity-formation. Given that, as Bruce Masters notes, religion in the Ottoman Arab world served "as an internalized anchor to each individual's sense of broader community and as the primary signifier of his or her identity to those outside it," I look to faith, piety, and practice to gauge how Copts interpreted their religion and, in the process, how they defined the boundaries of their community.[29]

The Ottoman period has been commonly dismissed as culturally unproductive for all Egyptians, but on closer investigation, we can see that there was a resurgent interest, particularly among Copts, in patronizing manuscript production.[30] Perusing the catalogs of various European and North American libraries, in addition to monastic and church holdings in Egypt, provides only a small glimpse of this prolific output. Original written treatises may have been few in number, but the sheer abundance of documents indicates that there was an enduring literature, supported by a strong belief in preserving a communal heritage and an increase in funds for such conservation projects.

These trends are partially related to the character of Coptic leadership during this period. In the Ottoman world, where dhimmīs frequently visited Muslim legal courts to resolve their social and economic disputes, non-Muslim religious leaders became increasingly trusted with exercising moral authority over their communities.[31] For Coptic clergy, their role was relegated to defining "orthodox" behavior and policing religious rituals. Coptic lay leaders, who were often challenging clergymen over communal authority, recognized that they too could enhance their positions by funding the copying of manuscripts, renovating churches, commissioning icons, and patronizing pilgrimages and festivals. All of these efforts showcased their generosity and could endear them to fellow believers. As such, Coptic religious life and the material culture that preserved it were responsive to the changing nature of communal leadership, to larger political surroundings, and to broader Coptic concerns in Ottoman Egypt.

My research has identified three groups of Coptic-Arabic manuscripts that will be closely considered in this book. The first are chronicles that record communal events, noting momentous occasions such as pilgrimages; even these sparse annals provide evidence of various occasions that brought laity and clergy together in common acts of piety. The second, hagiographies, reveal how copyists reproduced stories of particular saints because they were demanded by and indeed touched the lives of their audiences. Hagiographies were recited to mixed groups of clergy and laity, thus they point to devotional trends among the community at large. The third, sermons, were written with the clear intention of effecting change in communal behavior and therefore serve as a good example of expected moral codes. While focusing mostly on the clerical hierarchy's concerns, they also provide clues to general social and religious practices in this era. Sensitivity toward issues of text-writing, copying, and performance will make for an enriched reading of these sources, which, on initial examination, may appear dull and formulaic. The scarcity of documents might inhibit an analysis of local variations in religious life, but inasmuch as possible, this study attempts to glimpse the worldviews of Egyptian Copts at large.

It is difficult, as will later emerge, to furnish the historical context behind these Coptic narratives, as they rarely make references to their milieu.[32] Moreover, and as has been well established in the scholarly literature, the expression of faith and piety can be tough to gauge with precision, and at times historians are forced to speculate or infer. Realizing these restrictions, I supplement this study whenever possible by turning to the *History of the Patriarchs of the Egyptian Church*,[33] a rich record particularly for the medieval and Mamluk eras. A few choice references to Coptic life in the late seventeenth and eighteenth centuries offer important background information on internal communal dynamics. I also rely on Muslim chroniclers, who seldom mention Copts but still help to furnish some of the broader sociopolitical context. When pertinent, and to help fill the gaps, I closely evaluate and discuss European traveler and missionary accounts, many of which provide detailed, if overly biased, records of Coptic religious life and traditions.

A final note on sources: anyone writing Coptic history from internal community documents must contend not only with the shifting political climate in today's Egypt but also with a reserved church leadership. Untapped and mostly uncatalogued manuscripts are strictly guarded in ancient churches and monasteries. Fortunately, a few of these are exceptionally well organized and more open to critical scholarship. Nevertheless, gaining access to this material still depends, to a great extent, on internal connections, personal relations, and sensitive dealings. Should recent hopes of creating a digital manuscript archive in Cairo be realized, they will surely transform the study of Coptic history.

The patchy nature of sources has shaped this book as a series of roughly chronological "snapshots" of Coptic religious life. The first chapter provides background on the Copts in Ottoman Egypt, focusing on how the conquest affected the community and how the lay and clerical leadership helped to sustain a communal identity during this period. I discuss how Coptic archons benefited from their contacts with Egyptian military households, who had become the de facto political authorities by the seventeenth and eighteenth centuries. As a result of their growing wealth, archons became the financiers of a vibrant religious life. Of course, the masses still relied on clergymen to minister to the community, conduct religious rites like marriage or baptism, and serve, at least symbolically, as communal figureheads. Yet as archons solidified their influence and prestige, tensions brewed over the right to lead. Moments of collaboration or conflict between the two sides shaped religious expression in Ottoman Egypt, which is the subject of later chapters.

Next I move to both a chronological and thematic discussion of Coptic religious life as exemplified in four case studies spanning the sixteenth to the eighteenth centuries. In chapter 2, I investigate the popularity of the martyr Salib (d. 1512), who publicly defamed the Prophet Muhammad and who later refused to convert to Islam in defense of his faith. I examine why Salib's story appeared during this period and suggest that following the tumultuous Mamluk era, Coptic leaders were looking for ways to sustain a fresh interest in their faith. In the sixteenth century, the Roman Catholic Church had intensified its efforts to win the Copts' allegiance through a series of tenuous agreements with Coptic patriarchs. Moreover, written shortly after his death, Salib's martyrology depicts the complex social relations that existed in Egypt right before and soon after the Ottoman conquest and reveals how these relationships were constructed, narrated, and represented to the community. Notably, the text, which relates how a Copt was tortured and executed by Muslim authorities, avoids anti-Islamic invective and focuses, for the most part, on neutral relations with the dominant Muslim culture.

Chapters 3 and 4 focus on Coptic religious practice and rituals. The third chapter examines the popularity of an ancient female martyr, St. Dimyana, whose cult, according to seventeenth- and eighteenth-century sources, was centered on springtime festivities in the Nile Delta. Her written martyrology, which was commonly commissioned by archons and performed at her festival and at local churches, infused discourses of women and gender within the communal consciousness. Echoing earlier discussions of Coptic lay-clerical interchange, a study of this cult reveals complex conceptions of female sainthood and hints to varying notions of gender within Coptic practices. An idealized version of Dimyana as an erudite virgin and vocal devotee was promoted in her hagiography and fostered by the clergy, although it would often be eclipsed by a more popular image of the saint as a beneficent miracle-worker. Dimyana's cult also provides valuable insight into the intersection of religious patronage and communal beliefs during this period.

In chapter 4, I return to the issues raised by the story that opened this introduction and examine the lengths to which pilgrims went in order to make an annual pilgrimage from Cairo to Jerusalem, usually, but not always, with the consent of Muslim authorities. In its particular manifestation during the early eighteenth century, a time of cultural resurgence for the Copts, the pilgrimage illustrates connections to an age-old Christian tradition but also exposes commonalities with the annual ḥajj to Mecca. The pilgrimage, as studied primarily through a historical narrative written by Ottoman-era Copts, shows how lay and clerical elements collaborated to sustain specific rites and to support a Coptic presence in Jerusalem. Moreover, by joining in common religious practice with other Eastern Orthodox communities, the pilgrimage raised Copts' profile among Christians in the Ottoman world.

The overt expression of a distinctive Coptic religious identity becomes clearer by the latter part of this study, especially in chapter 5. An aggressive missionary movement in the eighteenth century prompted Coptic clergymen to mount a moral campaign against "heretical" Catholic teachings. Missionaries had used the pulpit to spread their message among Arabic-speaking Christians, and Coptic leaders responded by disparaging contact with Catholics and scorning their heterodox practices, which were proliferating as a consequence of intermarriage, socialization, or outright conversion. At times, Coptic leaders sermonized for the expulsion of believers who fell outside the lines of moral and spiritual orthodoxy. The intensifying engagement with outsiders also spawned overtly sectarian language and fostered the characterization of an authentic Coptic identity opposed to the perceived depravity of other communities.

By the end of this book, the reader will discern that despite legal and societal prohibitions against non-Muslim religious expression in Ottoman society, popular religion was the glue that held Coptic believers together. The case of Ottoman Copts elucidates how marginalized groups can maintain their claims to self-expression and, in the process, how they can foster a distinctive identity within a dominant religious culture. Forging a communal ethos, both in the early modern and modern eras, often depends on a variety of religious rituals that effectively respond to social and political challenges. Retelling martyrdom narratives, which underscore the otherworldly rewards of suffering, can intensify faithfulness and cultivate belief. Communal ties are also strengthened and preserved in the celebration of festivals and liturgical services. The Copts, in that sense, provide a historical illustration of how belief, spirituality, and politics have commonly intersected.

1

Locating Copts in Ottoman History

The Copts are an acute and ingenious people. They are generally writers and accountants. In business, they accumulate money steadily, without show; long experience having taught them, what the other Christians have yet to learn, that, under an arbitrary government, obscurity is safety. Melancholic in their temperament, but when called into action, industrious and laborious. Otherwise, fond of their distilled liquor, and rather licentious in their amours. The Copts are zealous in their faith and their ecclesiastics are numerous.

—W. G. Browne, *Travels in Africa, Egypt, and Syria from the Year 1792 to 1798*

Most scholars agree that the Mamluk era (1250–1517) left Egypt's non-Muslim communities battered and demoralized. In those centuries, Copts gradually turned into the despised "other," bearing the brunt of the Mamluks' efforts to assert themselves as devout Muslim rulers. The most vehement anti-Coptic descriptions appeared in contemporary Muslim writings: in the late fourteenth century, for instance, the chronicler al-Asnawi made this assertion: "Copts declare that this country still belongs to them, and that the Muslims evicted them from it unlawfully. Then they often steal as much as they can from the state treasury, in the belief that they are not doing wrong."[1] He urged others to act against the Christians and argued that any person who allows Copts "to continue to steal and retain all that is in their power, he is responsible for it in this world, and will have to render account for it on the day of resurrection."[2] To further marginalize Copts, Mamluk authorities limited and in some cases abolished public celebrations of Coptic festivals, confiscated church holdings, and provoked mob violence against Christians.[3] Also, the fervent literary activity spanning the tenth through the fourteenth centuries—the so-called golden age of Arab Christian literature in Egypt—was in steep decline. Thus, in the words of two historians, the fourteenth century dealt a "final blow"[4] to the Copts and was the source of "trauma"[5] for the community. In the fifteenth century, Egypt's non-Muslims faced noticeable decline in their populations and economic status and were targets of frequent harassment and physical attacks.[6] It is easy to understand, then, how by the end of the Mamluk era, the number of Copts had dwindled due to conversions and the destruction of churches, homes, and personal property. Some have estimated that the Coptic population was reduced by half or two-thirds between the fourteenth and seventeenth centuries.[7]

Under these circumstances, one might expect the Ottoman conquest to have brought some measure of hope if not optimism, but in reality, there are few clues as to how the invasion affected Coptic communal life.[8] It is certain that the conquest altered Egypt's long-standing position as the commercial and cultural center of the eastern Mediterranean world. In a short time, Sultan Selim I (1512–1520) unseated the Mamluks, a dynasty that had previously fought off Mongols and Crusaders. During bloody combat with the Ottomans, as the Egyptian chronicler Ibn Iyas reports, at least ten thousand people lost their lives.[9] When the shock dissipated, Egyptians came to realize that their land, center of a powerful empire for nearly three centuries, had fallen to the status of a mere province. New edicts aggravated the somber mood as Ottoman governors temporarily suspended popular religious celebrations such as the festival of the Prophet's birthday (*Mawlid al-Nabī*).[10] The violence and sense of devastation were further compounded by the Ottoman practice of forced exile or *sūrgūn*:[11] manuscripts, buildings, and talented individuals were quickly packed off to the capital city, Istanbul. Among these were notable Copts such as Banub al-Katib, Abu Sa'id, Yuhanna al-Saghir, Yusuf bin Habul, and Shaykh al-Makin al-Skindari and his son.[12] For smaller communities that depended on their best and brightest, particularly during crises, the exile of these men must have been a disturbing development.

Non-Muslims living under Islamic rule were often targeted during times of warfare, and following the conquest, some of Cairo's leading shaykhs and preachers provoked crowds to attack non-Muslims and their properties.[13] Others, such as the popular Sufi Shaykh 'Abd al-Wahhab al-Sha'rani (d. 1565), proclaimed open disdain for Christians and Jews, rhetoric that undoubtedly inflamed tensions.[14] In the first years of Ottoman governance, Egypt experienced severe political unrest and rebellion, but the reign of Sultan Suleyman "the Magnificent" (1520–1566) ushered in a more tranquil era. Military order was restored, the Ottoman governor's position was strengthened, and new laws (*Qānūnāme-i Mışir*) were promulgated to manage taxes and trade. While the Qānūnāme excluded direct references to Jews and Christians, the reinstitution of law and order may have restrained unbridled attacks against non-Muslims.[15]

Policies governing non-Muslims in the Ottoman world were loosely rooted in the Qur'an, reflective of prevailing custom, and derived by scholars and decision makers from the interpretive body of the *sharīʿa*. These provisions have been thoroughly addressed in the scholarly literature and need no major elaboration here.[16] Most historians agree that their enforcement varied over time and place and among different populations. Nevertheless, non-Muslims were essentially, as one historian puts it, "separate, unequal, and protected."[17] As dhimmīs, they received legal protection from Muslim rulers and governments. So long as they followed certain restrictions on their public religious life, outlined in the "Pact of 'Umar,"[18] and paid the requisite poll taxes (*jizya*, *jawālī*), their communities were generally allowed to govern themselves and select their own religious leaders. As individuals, non-Muslims could also pursue a variety of occupations, own property, and follow most of their own religious customs. Although Muslim-dhimmī relations were governed by Islamic law, when it came to intracommunal affairs or to matters of personal status, non-Muslims could seek justice through their own religious courts, if they existed. They could also (and frequently did) choose to resolve issues such as marriage, divorce, and inheritance within sharīʿa courts.[19]

Despite these "protections," Egypt's non-Muslims continued to face many, if inconsistently enforced, restrictions on their public religious life under Ottoman rule. They were generally prohibited from building new or repairing old houses of worship.[20] Limitations also extended to the ringing of church bells, ritual processions, and the display of crosses, banners, or icons. These stipulations reflect an official policy of asserting Islam's superiority; the public display of pomp was reserved for Muslim elites, including the descendants of the Prophet Muhammad, the 'ulamā', and the ruling authorities. Dhimmīs were forbidden from riding horses and from wearing certain types of clothing.[21] In Egypt, the colors blue and black had become associated with Copts and yellow with Jews; in special situations Copts were also required to wear large crosses, especially in places where they intermingled with Muslims.[22] In public, physical segregation from non-Muslims was preferred: the seventeenth-century Ottoman traveler Evliya Çelebi noted that the cleanest bathhouse (*ḥammām*) in Cairo was the one that denied entry to Jews, Greeks, and Copts.[23] Unlike non-Muslims in the Balkans, who came under Ottoman rule in the fourteenth and fifteenth centuries, Egypt's dhimmīs were long accustomed to such restrictions. Nonetheless, all legal codes were open to the arbitrary interpretation of regional and local rulers, and non-Muslims had to be prepared for both leniency and rigidity in their enforcement.[24]

Ottoman rulers in Istanbul appear to have had little interest in Copts or their issues. One imagines that young sultans heard stories about the Coptic involvement in castrating some of the black eunuchs who guarded the inner halls of Topkapı palace and had the sultan's ear.[25] On the whole, though, it seems that the central government preferred to deal with Egypt's non-Muslims through local intermediaries. In Jerusalem, where Copts constituted a small community, the Ottomans recognized them as one of several Christian denominations who owed taxes to the state; Istanbul saw Egypt's Copts similarly, as non-Muslims from whom customary poll taxes would be collected.[26] Sultans are said to have taken special care in collecting the jizya from their non-Muslim subjects. Following earlier traditions, they exempted "children, women, disabled, and blind men, and the unemployed poor"; they rarely farmed out its collection; and for the most part, they trusted magistrates or Islamic judges (qāḍīs) in its administration.[27] In Egypt, however, the 'ulamā' and military officers usually undertook this task.[28] Until the late seventeenth century, villages and towns were officially taxed in lump sum depending on the population of non-Muslims; in practice, however, and at least since the eleventh century, tax collectors estimated the jizya based on each individual's capacity to pay. The money collected, in turn, was bound for the sultan's treasury, mosques, or religious notables.[29]

In 1672, the German traveler Vansleb noted new edicts issued by the Ottoman governor that required all Copts to pay identical amounts and thus "reduced the poor Coptics to despair" and depopulated whole villages.[30] In 1734, in response to new imperial taxes and in the largest recorded Coptic protest during the Ottoman period, one thousand Copts marched on Cairo's Rumayla's Square and clashed with local soldiers; two Copts were killed on the spot.[31] Due to widespread famine and crop failure, many had failed to pay these taxes, but they were ultimately helped by the intervention of Coptic archons, including Nayruz Abu Nawwar, Rizqallah al-Badawi, Banub al-Ziftawi, and others.[32] For these elites, undue taxation was mitigated by their close relationships to Egypt's military officers.[33] The Porte was occasionally informed about corruption in the collection of poll taxes, and during the eighteenth century, special envoys were dispatched to Cairo to rein in exploitation.[34]

In all, the conquest of 1517 and its aftermath did not necessarily mean, as Copts were to discover, that their position would radically transform. Copts remained a minority that existed under special laws and was vulnerable to assimilation, conversion, and, as we will see, internal dissent. Living under Ottoman rule may have liberated them from the chronic oppression they felt in the waning days of the Mamluk sultanate, but it would also highlight their isolation. Within the Ottoman Empire, only a few Copts resided outside of Egypt. The Ethiopian Church, a historical protector of Coptic interests, had been mired in local political struggles since the fourteenth century and became increasingly autonomous from Coptic patriarchal leadership.[35] Under new rulers and during uncertain times, competition would intensify for a place in local patronage networks, employment, and access to limited financial resources. With the exception of Copts, most of Egypt's non-Muslims connected with coreligionists in other parts of the empire or with Europeans to help find their place in this changing milieu.

Among Egypt's Non-Muslim Communities

Copts were Ottoman Egypt's largest non-Muslim community (*ṭā'ifa* or later *milla*). In the absence of census records, their numbers and geographic distribution remain speculative. Nevertheless, extrapolating from European travel accounts, Maurice Martin concludes that Copts constituted roughly 4 to 5 percent of Egypt's population and that most lived between the towns of Bani Suwayf and Jirja.[36] Martin cautions, however, that many sources conflate all Christians with Copts or focus on Cairo's demography, thereby underreporting the broader Coptic population. During the French occupation, the geographer Edme-François Jomard recorded approximately 220,000 non-Muslims in a population of 2,500,000 (around 9 percent), with Copts constituting 10,000 of Cairo's population of 253,210 (around 4 percent).[37] Jomard's actual figures have been credibly challenged by several scholars, notably by Justin McCarthy and Daniel Panzac.[38] But if we take Jomard's most conservative estimates of 4 percent and apply them to McCarthy and Panzac's revised data, the number of Copts in late-eighteenth-century Egypt can be estimated between 153,425 and 180,000. Harald Motzki's calculation of 8 percent, which seemingly accounts for Copts outside Cairo, would yield ranges between 306,851 and 360,000.[39] While tentative, these studies should be weighed against less substantiated estimates that Ottoman-era Copts constituted up to 15 percent of the total population.[40]

In the early modern period, Copts lived side by side with Jews, Melkites, Armenians, and a growing community of Syrian and European Catholics. The terminology regarding these groups merits some explanation here. As noted, since the fifth century, and until waves of conversions to Catholicism or later Protestantism, most Christians in the region were divided into Chalcedonian (Greek, Byzantine) and anti-Chalcedonian (Copts, Armenians, Syrians, and Ethiopians). Historically these terms denoted religious rather than ethnic or national groups. Christians who followed the Chalcedonian doctrine were considered "Greek Orthodox," partly because they retained the use of the Greek language in their liturgies. The latter should be distinguished from anti-Chalcedonian churches that also use the term "Orthodox," as in "Coptic Orthodox" and "Syrian Orthodox."[41] In some

European and Arabic sources, the term for Copts is "Coptie" or *qibṭī* (pl. *aqbāṭ*), respectively. Many Europeans, however, referred to them as "Jacobite,"[42] a term more widely associated with anti-Chalcedonian Syrians.[43] Egyptian sources from this period—Muslim and Christian—speak of a single Copt as *al-naṣrānī al-ya'qūbī* (lit. the "Nazarene Jacobite"),[44] *al-naṣrānī al-qibṭī*, or collectively as *al-ya'āqiba*.

The second largest anti-Chalcedonian group after the Copts were Armenians (*al-naṣāra al-arman*), a community that had settled in Egypt during the eleventh century under the reign of the Armenian Fatimid vizier Badr al-Jamali (1074–1094).[45] Following the Ottoman conquest, Armenians in most of the Arab provinces became subordinate to their bishop and later patriarch in Jerusalem; his correlate in Istanbul did not exercise far-reaching authority until the eighteenth century.[46] As fellow anti-Chalcedonians, Copts and Armenians enjoyed favorable relations.[47] Concentrated in Cairo, many Armenians worked as goldsmiths, jewelers, and tailors.[48] While they were generally among the poorest of Egypt's non-Muslim communities, a few were involved in regional and international trade, since they were part of an "ethnic trading network" that facilitated commercial transactions based on personal relationships with other Armenians throughout the Ottoman world.[49]

Melkites or *al-malakiyyūn* (literally, "the emperor's men," i.e., the Byzantine emperor) were the Chalcedonian "Greek Orthodox" faction that emerged after the schism of 451. The Melkite Church was based in Alexandria, Antioch, and Jerusalem, all of which were subordinate to or at least maintained spiritual ties with the Ecumenical Greek Patriarch of Constantinople.[50] Egyptian court records refer to an individual Melkite as *al-naṣrānī al-malakī* or, more commonly, *al-rūmī*.[51] Despite their geographic isolation from Byzantium, the patriarch of Constantinople was frequently invited to participate in choosing his associate in Egypt, and from time to time, the latter was promoted to the position of ecumenical patriarch.[52] The Melkite Church in Egypt was well connected to its sister churches in the empire and increasingly, in the seventeenth and eighteenth centuries, to the Russian Orthodox Church. Due to their external contacts, Melkites were active in commerce, either running their own businesses or serving as liaisons for European traders, but they also worked in humbler professions such as tailoring or weaving.[53]

Ottoman sources provide more information about the Jewish community than any other, indicating perhaps their high positions in the Egyptian administration.[54] In terms of their employment patterns, Jews and Copts had the most in common. Both were well represented as *ṣarrāfs* (money changers, bankers) and as "financial specialists" (tax collectors, secretaries, or financial agents). Geographically, Jews were concentrated in urban areas, with communities in Alexandria, Rosetta, Damietta, Tanta, Manfalut, and Mahalla al-Kubra. Many worked as butchers, tinsmiths, and tailors. Some were active in the lucrative trade sector as merchants or customs officials, a development helped by their connections to other Jews in the Mediterranean world, as well as their financial and linguistic expertise.[55] However, by the latter half of the eighteenth century, Jews had begun to lose their established positions to Syrian Christians.[56]

The presence of Christian emigrants from Syria grew from the early eighteenth century onward, when Syrian "Greek" Catholics—that is, Greek Orthodox converts to Catholicism from Ottoman Syria—escaped anti-Catholic persecutions and set up as traders in Egypt's seaside towns, especially Damietta and Rosetta.[57] As they prospered and began to associate with Europeans and local power-holders, Syrian Catholics (*al-naṣāra al-shawām*) became a threat to Copts and Jews when they expanded their influence into the financial administration.[58] Their ascendancy was partially linked to the Ottoman system of capitulations. Since the seventeenth century, capitulations to certain European powers including the French, Dutch, Venetians, and later Russians existed in the forms of official documents known as *berāt*s, which bestowed favorable trade status on their holders.[59] European Catholics preferred to give these titles to indigenous Catholics, but Greek Orthodox, Armenians, and Jews also received these privileges, often serving as translators or commercial agents. Berāts were highly coveted, because they allowed their holders to pay reduced tariffs compared to native Muslim or non-Muslim merchants.[60] During the eighteenth century, European consulates sold berāts to the highest bidders; in general, Venetians favored Egypt's Jews, and the French supported Syrian Catholics.

As a consequence of these privileges, among other factors, during the early modern period, Egypt's non-Muslims improved their lots by tapping into various political and economic networks, whether local, regional, or international. For many, the capitulations system in the seventeenth and eighteenth centuries provided access to lucrative employment opportunities with European traders, businessmen, and consular representatives. While there is little evidence to suggest that they either received or were denied berāts, the Copts' geographic isolation likely restricted their ability to participate in international trade. As Thomas Philipp notes, unlike the Jews, Greeks, Armenians, and Syrian Catholics, who were connected to affluent coreligionists outside Egypt, Copts "could never amass the capital needed to acquire tax farming rights over the customs stations."[61] The fact that few, if any, worked within the commercial sector supports this observation.[62] Moreover, Copts appear to have eschewed close connections with Europeans, especially with the French, who, in the Ottoman Empire, had come to represent the Catholic Church, an ideological rival to the Coptic establishment.[63] Rather than ascribing this tendency to mere xenophobia or proto-nationalism, Coptic leaders seemed invested in insulating their coreligionists from foreign ties in order to protect their own power. While the Copts' exclusion from those lucrative arrangements could have been economically detrimental, many derived equal benefit from their connections to Egyptian patrons and their intimate knowledge of local politics.

Coptic Communal Structure

Although Copts were well integrated within the daily rhythm of Egyptian life, they were a distinct community subject not only to Ottoman-Islamic authority but also to their lay and clerical leaders. Even when politically weakened, Coptic clergymen—from patriarchs to low-ranking priests—have traditionally exercised moral authority over fellow believers. Their worldviews both overlapped and competed with those of the laity, a large group that encompassed elite financiers and bureaucrats as well as modest farmers, artisans, and laborers. In discussing Coptic communal organization, it is important to keep in mind that regional, economic, and social variations—which are not always detectable in historical documents—likely made for a heterogeneous community.

Church and Clergy

The Coptic Church consists of a clerical hierarchy made up of patriarchs, bishops, priests, and deacons. The dearth of sources makes it difficult to capture the nature of these posts in the Ottoman period, but based on scattered mentions and on their historical roles, some observations can be made about their functions and influence. After the Arab conquests in 641, Coptic patriarchs—commonly but not exclusively drawn from the monastic orders—were given religious and legal authority over the community and charged with administering canon laws in matters of personal status, including inheritance and marriage, as well as the management of church properties and alms collection. While in the first centuries of Islamic rule, the patriarch was viewed as the "guardian and spokesman of his community," during the Fatimid era (969–1171), caliphs and their advisers regularly intervened in the internal affairs of the church and community, thereby challenging the patriarch's autonomous power.[64] These patterns persisted during the Mamluk period, further diminishing patriarchal authority.[65] Mamluk state policies focused on keeping all of Egypt's Christian communities isolated from outsiders, whether Crusaders, Greeks, or Ethiopians. While Copts were seen as more trustworthy than local Melkites, Mamluk rulers still feared betrayal from Egypt's largest Christian community and followed a policy of "continued isolation" of the Coptic Church. They were concerned, in particular, about the Copts' religious ties to the Ethiopian Church, which had shown active willingness to defend Coptic rights in Egypt.[66] In general, the Copts' isolation persisted in later periods.

Some have suggested that, following the Ottoman conquest of the Arab provinces, Eastern patriarchs submitted to the Greek Church in Istanbul and were forced to solicit the latter's support in political and administrative matters.[67] Others have argued that it was Istanbul's Armenian patriarch who governed his anti-Chalcedonian correlates, although this is improbable, since his reach was limited even among coreligionists.[68] One source from the seventeenth century indicates that the selection of Coptic patriarchs was independent of the center, although it was officially certified by Ottoman governors (pashas) in Egypt[69] by means of documents called *tawqīʿ* (pl. *tawqīʿāt*).[70] Given their community's geographic distance and its localization to Egypt, Coptic patriarchs appear to have had little personal contact with the Ottoman Porte. Consequently, they might have experienced more autonomy to perform their duties and to redefine their office.[71] In reality, and even though they were nominally charged with supervising monasteries and church holdings and expected to minister to their dioceses throughout Lower and Upper Egypt, patriarchs grew increasingly weak.[72] One scholar has suggested that between 1571 and 1656, Coptic patriarchs collected and delivered the jizya to designated Ottoman representatives, but this role may have ended in the late seventeenth and eighteenth centuries, a period corresponding with the archons' increasing power.[73] Moreover, since the early Islamic period, Copts had conducted most of their legal affairs within Muslim courts, a development that further eroded the patriarch's authority over his congregants.[74]

Below the patriarchs, the next rung on the ecclesiastical ladder was occupied by metropolitans (*muṭrān*, pl. *maṭārina*) and bishops (*usquf*, pl. *asāqifa*). In the Ottoman period, metropolitans presided over Ethiopia, Damietta, and Jerusalem, although the Damietta and Jerusalem dioceses often merged into one.[75] In 1714, the Jesuit priest Sicard distinguished the following bishoprics: Niqada, Jirja, Abutij, Manfalut, al-Ushmunayn, Bahnasa, Fayyum, Minuf, and Jerusalem. The metropolitan of Jerusalem was the most powerful, as his jurisdiction extended over the towns of Alexandria, Mansura, Mahalla al-Kubra, Rosetta, and Damanhur, and variably over Damietta.[76] Catholic missionary sources also indicate that in the sixteenth century, Copts appointed a bishop in Cyprus, where a handful of Copts resided, although his status in later years is unclear.[77] While bishops were supposed to be selected "implicitly or explicitly" by their congregants, historically they were chosen by patriarchs, by their predecessors, by miraculous intervention, or simply by purchasing their posts.[78] Bishops held the right to ordain priests but also to enforce discipline, if need be, over lower clergymen. Aside from performing liturgical functions, including the consecration of churches and altars, bishops administered the finances of their dioceses and helped care for the needy. They were charged with collecting alms, and in turn they received a pension appropriate to their rank.[79] The English traveler Richard Pococke believed these functions to indicate that bishops spent "most of their time going round their district officiating in their churches, and collecting the dues that belong to themselves and the patriarch."[80]

A priest (*qiss*, or the higher-ranking hegumenos, *qummus*) was commonly chosen from the deacons and was subordinate to a bishop. In Coptic traditions, priests could be married so long as matrimony took place prior to their ordination. Priests and other clergymen presided over baptisms, marriages, and funerals, events that directly affected the lives of ordinary believers. Allegations of priestly corruption and "ignorance" were widespread throughout the Ottoman period, and complaints were registered both by European travelers and by Coptic clerical leaders. In the seventeenth century, for instance, Vansleb described an incident wherein village priests from nearby Fayyum had hidden a stone idol with carvings of Coptic saints, ostensibly—in Vansleb's view—to curb existing idolatry; however, they later attempted to sell him the idol as a valuable relic in what he interpreted as an extortion scheme.[81] In the seventeenth and eighteenth centuries, Coptic clerical leaders frequently complained about priestly drunkenness and corruption.[82] Still, few doubted that priests exerted great influence over popular religious life. While Catholic missionaries viewed these clergymen as vastly ignorant, superstitious, and obstinate, they admitted that the conversion of a single priest was key to converting scores of Copts.[83] Priests were likely paid for performing common liturgical tasks like marriages and baptisms, and they worked in secular jobs much as they had during medieval times. In the Ottoman era, they also appear frequently as scribes of religious manuscripts, an occupation they ostensibly pursued to supplement their meager incomes.

For the period under study, the least historical information has survived regarding archdeacons (*ra'īs al-shamāmisa*) and deacons (*shammās*, pl. *shamāmisa*), who ranked lowest among the clerical orders. In the first centuries of Islamic rule, deacons were commonly promoted to the ranks of bishops and patriarchs, and the wealthy among them patronized the church.[84] While in the Ottoman era, patronage became mostly the domain of the archons—some of whom were ordained deacons—most Coptic sources refer to those archons using their nonreligious titles.[85] Similar to priests, deacons commonly served as scribes, copying religious manuscripts for lay or clerical patrons. This is unsurprising, since for centuries they had provided administrative services to the church and frequently acted as notaries or witnesses to legal transactions.[86] In some cases, they helped distribute alms, but they also performed liturgical functions, including reading the gospel, assisting in communion, and occasionally delivering sermons. Archdeacons, who ranked slightly higher, organized church services, managed lower deacons, allocated funds to the poor, and maintained liturgical books, instruments, and vestments.[87]

Traditionally, Coptic monks were not considered clergy; most were laymen devoted to a life of seclusion and not ordained to a clerical rank.[88] In the Ottoman era, monasteries were active in Wadi al-Natrun, the Red Sea region, and Upper Egypt. Drawn to their ancient libraries, which housed thousands of valuable manuscripts, European travelers provided disproportionately greater information about monks and monasteries than about ordinary Copts. Although scholars have recently identified a modest revival that took place within the Red Sea monasteries during the Ottoman era, in general monasteries were inhabited by only a few monks; most lived in dire poverty and were forced to rely on the charitable contributions of the laity, the competence of their abbots, or patriarchal benevolence.[89] Coptic monastics were widely admired by travelers for their austerity, fortitude, and hardiness.[90] Those who were ordained supplied the ranks of bishops and patriarchs, and occasionally rivalries arose over the management of monastic holdings. Some patriarchs were suspicious of the power and popularity of certain abbots and were quick to punish these men, justly or unjustly. Sicard described one such incident between Murqus, abbot of the Monastery of St. Antony, and the powerful Patriarch Yu'annis XVI (1676–1718), a former monk from the same monastery:

> It has been four years since the Patriarch visited Bouche and its neighboring monasteries. . . . [Then, the Patriarch had] commanded [Murqus] to follow him to Cairo, but Murqus did not obey. He wanted to remove him from office, but Murqus did not care. One day in the presence of the Bishop of Jerusalem and the principal Coptic clergymen, the Patriarch deliberated in Cairo to force Murqus out, to have him taken by force and delivered into the hands of the provincial governor. I found myself by chance in that meeting, and as I tried to intervene in these violent proceedings by kindly siding with the capable Abbot, the Patriarch suddenly turned to me, saying: "Do you know this Murqus? He is not Christian," he added, "let alone a monk and priest. He is an infidel, an excommunicated demon, a castaway."[91]

Neither Sicard nor Coptic sources clarify the roots of this heated dispute, but the patriarch's language captures the depth of discord that often emerged among higher churchmen. Aside from these internal squabbles, life in Egypt's deserts exposed monks to numerous hardships, including starvation, drought, poverty, and extreme temperatures. The biggest danger, however, came from neighboring bedouin tribesmen and occasional bandits. In what seemed to be a regular ritual in Wadi al-Natrun, monks were forced to hand over food to potential aggressors by lowering a rope from atop the fortified walls of their monasteries; this was carried out to ensure against more serious attacks on their lives and properties.[92]

Lay Archons

During his travels to Upper Egypt in the late eighteenth century, the Frenchman Sonnini wrote that "being the only persons in that part of Egypt who could write and read, [Copts] were the stewards, the superintendents, and the secretaries of the rich and great; and they knew, quite as well as the stewards in any other place, how to avail themselves of the confidence and incapacity of those whose property was entrusted to their management."[93] While archons emerged from a variety of occupations—jewelers, tailors, financial administrators, or bureaucrats—historical sources tend to reveal the most information about individuals, like Sonnini's "superintendents," who worked for Egypt's military and land-owning elites.[94] In this context, our discussion of these Coptic leaders will be tied to broader trends within Ottoman Egyptian society, especially to the ascent of elite households that usurped political power from the Istanbul-appointed governors. For centuries, Copts had been able to dominate certain niches within Egypt's financial and bureaucratic sectors, and they maintained important roles in a variety of key tasks, particularly those related to tax collection.[95] Such expertise was crucial to their personal and communal survival: it tended to distinguish them from other non-Muslims and made them indispensable to their patrons, especially in the Ottoman period.

For the Ottomans, Egypt was a prized conquest. Its strategic, military, and economic value was unmatched.[96] It bordered crucial sea routes and was ideally located to help secure trade and military routes that were needed as the Ottomans competed with Europeans for naval dominance of the Mediterranean and Red Seas. Egypt's proximity to the holiest shrines of Mecca and Medina also allowed Ottoman rulers to organize the logistics of the ḥajj caravans, one of which embarked annually from Cairo and the other from Damascus. Moreover, the taxation and grain derived from Egypt's agricultural lands sustained central and provincial rulers for centuries. To establish the most efficient taxation structures, Egypt was divided into thirteen subprovinces, as it was previously managed under the Mamluks. Initially, salaried officials paid by the central treasury collected taxes in either cash or grain. These agents, or *amīns*, were brought from Anatolia, the Balkans, or other parts of the empire, or were sometimes hired from among the native Copts and Jews.[97] By the early seventeenth century, the Ottomans reorganized the collection of taxes under a system known as *iltizām* (tax farming), with a *multazim* acting as the tax farmer.[98] Under this arrangement, local notables could purchase tax-collection rights at an auction and so, as Jane Hathaway writes, "virtually every significant office, from customs director to the governor of Egypt, came to consist of a tax-farm."[99] The Ottoman Porte favored sales of iltizāms to these bidders, who in turn made direct payments to Istanbul while retaining the right to extort taxes from the local populace.

Progressively, then, Egyptian elites acquired greater political and military autonomy in ruling the province. Rather than meddle with the daily affairs of its most valuable territory, the Porte was generally restrained, acknowledging that Egypt's economy functioned best with minimal interference.[100] These policies had solidified by the end of the sixteenth century, when the empire experienced military conflicts on its eastern and western frontiers and underwent severe financial crises. The flow of silver from the New World, mounting expenses from warfare with the Safavids and the Hapsburgs, and domestic political and economic developments all resulted in the devaluing of Ottoman coinage.[101] Such crises led to a greater and more widespread reliance on iltizām, which ensured a faster and steadier flow of cash. These fiscal and administrative changes would benefit Coptic elites, who were sought after by multazims because of their reliability and their financial skills.

The right to collect taxes was coveted by various local constituencies. Traditionally, the most prestigious iltizāms were held by officials bearing the rank of *sanjak beyi* or *bey*, a group of powerful men who controlled critical political and military posts and occupied seats on the Ottoman governor's *diwān* or council.[102] However, in the early seventeenth century, multazim positions were offered to the highest bidder rather than passed to the beys, and jurisdiction over and management of Egypt's lucrative rural tax farms now fell into the hands of both beys and soldiery, who turned to local Jews and Copts to staff their growing households.[103]

Coptic archons who acquired prominent posts in these households were likely educated, for the most part, within their own communal schools. These institutions were similar in some ways to the Muslim schools known as *kuttāb*s, and they taught religion, writing, and mathematics in efforts to prepare the best and brightest for those lucrative posts.[104] While students would have acquired basic skills, their education was later supplemented by direct mentoring and training into specific professions. Gradually, the most talented found their way into Egypt's administrative and fiscal bureaucracy. They used their influence to enlist other Copts and apprentice them into similar posts, relying on a patronage system that was well established by the Ottoman period.[105]

Thus, the ability to collect taxes in Ottoman Egypt depended, to a great extent, on the expertise of educated and well-trained bureaucrats, who served as financial agents or assistants (*mubāshir*s), accountants (*muḥāsib*s), and scribes (*kātib*s)—all key posts in the tax-collection structure. The high degree of confidence that the Copts enjoyed is shown by the fact that mubāshirs were allowed to keep registers of revenues and expenditures in a special Arabic script that "made it incomprehensible to all but those especially initiated into the secrets of its formation and use."[106] Some also used a "cryptic script," likely combining Coptic with Arabic, to maintain security over accounting and bookkeeping records.[107] Copts were also entrusted as financial agents (*wakīl*s) representing their patrons in business transactions and in various administrative affairs.[108] Similarly, they were visible in the *muḥāsiba* or accounting department of the Egyptian treasury, whose functions included distributing pensions to those entitled to revenues derived from the jizya tax imposed on non-Muslims.[109] Kātibs were used to staff multiple parts of the administrative structure, ranging from participating in cadastral surveys to filling various ranks of the Egyptian treasury. The Ottoman traveler Evliya Çelebi remarked that Copts had an excellent reputation as scribes and mathematicians who "all had the mind of Aristotle" and thus monopolized the "scribal sciences," particularly in Upper Egypt.[110] The Copts' extensive experience would become essential in tasks such as land surveying and tax assessment.[111] Much as it had for centuries, the Coptic calendar continued to determine the general rhythm of life in Egypt, ranging from the calculation of the Nile floods to the celebration of major Muslim festivals.[112]

In these positions, Copts became intimately familiar with the growing factionalism between various beys and military officers. Some even lost their lives to political intrigue.[113] Rivalries were aggravated by the rising inflation, monetary catastrophes, delays in payment to military officers, and soldier revolts.[114] At the end of the seventeenth century, the Ottoman Porte responded by attempting to reestablish its authority over Egypt and dispatched "Turcophone bureaucrats" to staff the local administration.[115] One of the immediate consequences was that Copts were temporarily relegated to secondary positions, but with the reassertion of local households, they would later recover their posts.[116] Increasingly, the Ottoman-appointed governors had a limited stake in local politics and were often confined to Cairo's Citadel.[117] From the perspective of Copts and Egypt's other non-Muslims, this development created further distance and perhaps mistrust between their communities, the local governors, and the imperial court in Istanbul. In these times, Ottoman pashas reaffirmed Islamic prescripts against non-Muslim conduct. Some scholars have argued that this was intended to humiliate minorities and "to gain popularity among the 'ulamā' and the common people."[118] Because of their unstable relationship with the governors during the seventeenth and eighteenth centuries, Coptic elites appear to have grown closer to local grandees and officers in that period.[119]

Besides experiencing demotion from center to province, Egypt on the whole was becoming further destabilized as squabbles and warring erupted between local constituencies and in some cases with the Ottoman Porte. In early years, the central government could usually restore order, but a growing power vacuum provoked new conflict over provincial control. Dissent among the beys throughout the seventeenth century, in addition to the above-mentioned fiscal changes, opened the door for the increased power of military regiments. By the early eighteenth century, political authority had completely shifted from the beys to the Janissary corps, the most powerful and wealthiest of the Ottoman military regiments. Following the civil war of 1711, the Janissaries were dominated by leaders of a rising faction, the Qazdaghlis, who used their powerful positions to gain more clients and augment their household.[120]

In the early eighteenth century, many Janissary officers accumulated wealth by asserting control over customs taxes at Egypt's Mediterranean and Red Sea ports and over the profitable coffee and spice trade.[121] Soon, though, the Qazdaghli household realized that the progressively unstable coffee trade could not sustain its wealth and power. Thus, during the first half of the eighteenth century, they forged, broke, and reforged a series of alliances in an attempt to generate more income for themselves and their clients. A number of Janissary officers tried to assert control over the beylicate and over those stable rural tax farms. Qazdaghli leaders, who were particularly successful in this endeavor, used a combination of negotiation and intimidation, through their household's vast network of patron-client relations, in order to advance their benefactors to the beylicate. By midcentury, as Hathaway writes, the Qazdaghli household "that had evolved within and came to dominate the Janissary regiment infiltrated and came to dominate the beylicate."[122]

Throughout the eighteenth century, most Copts were employed in the households of regimental officers. The close relationship between archons and these households was evident in the former's domination of certain bureaucratic posts. In the late seventeenth and early eighteenth centuries, for example, the Coptic archon Yuhanna Abu Masri (ca. 1704) held the title of *kabīr al-mubāshirīn* (chief of the mubāshirs) and *ra'īs al-arākhina* (head of the archons).[123] Although sources are unclear about the exact meaning of these titles and are unspecific about Abu Masri's employer, he did serve as a mubāshir at the Egyptian Imperial Treasury, specifically within the subdivision known as *Diwān al-Ruznāme.*[124] The treasury administered the collection of taxes and stored the cash assets of the Ottoman Porte in Egypt; hence Abu Masri's position was relatively high-ranking in the financial system.[125] Heading another influential post was Jirjis Abu Mansur al-Tukhi (d. 1718), who followed Abu Masri as the leading archon and who served as *ra'īs al-kuttāb* (chief scribe).[126] Abu Mansur served Murad Katkhuda Mustahfazan,[127] the top Janissary officer in Egypt, so he was likely "chief scribe" in Murad Katkhuda's household. Abu Mansur's successor, Lutfallah Abu Yusuf (d. 1720) was mubāshir for another Janissary officer, Muhammad Katkhuda Mustahfazan.[128] A few years later, another archon named Mercurius Ibrahim al-Fayyumi was mubāshir for 'Uthman Bey Dhu'l-Fiqar, holder of the prominent rank of *amīr al-ḥajj* (leader of the pilgrimage to Mecca).[129] While little is known about Mercurius, his powerful patron 'Uthman Bey rivaled the Qazdaghlis for power, although he was defeated in 1743, driven out of Egypt, and lived out the remainder of his life in Istanbul, where he died in 1776.[130]

Well-known archons would also benefit specifically from the rising fortunes of the Qazdaghli household. Jirjis Abu Yusuf al-Suruji (d. 1737), the highest-ranking archon of his day, served as mubāshir for ʿUthman Katkhuda al-Qazdaghli (d. 1736), leader of the Janissary corps. ʿUthman Katkhuda had taken control of the Qazdaghli faction in 1716, and under his jurisdiction it became the most powerful household in Egypt.[131] Jirjis's brother Yuhanna Yusuf al-Suruji (d. ca. 1757–1758) was also mubāshir for ʿUthman Katkhuda and then for ʿAbd al-Rahman Katkhuda al-Qazdaghli (d. 1776).[132] The latter had inherited the fortunes of aforementioned ʿUthman Katkhuda and was one of the most powerful grandees in the mid-eighteenth century.[133] ʿAbd al-Rahman would eventually give up politics, preferring to devote his enormous wealth to building and repairing pious Muslim foundations throughout Cairo.[134] Many archons, particularly the Suruji brothers, would follow the examples of their prominent patrons and become responsible for (re)building various Coptic churches and monasteries, suggesting not only how archons profited from their political connections but also how they emulated their patrons' charitable activities.

For the remainder of the eighteenth century, the power of the Qazdaghli household was based in the beylicate, while the Ottoman military regiments were reduced to adjunct status.[135] As Hathaway notes, one Qazdaghli *mamlūk*, the ruthless ʿAli Bey al-Kabir (d. 1773), "brought this Qazdaghli hegemony to its peak by killing or exiling all his rivals from competing households. In 1768, he went so far as to assert his independence from the Ottoman sultan, minting coins and having the Friday public sermon (*khuṭba*) in his name."[136] Many scholars regard ʿAli Bey as the founder of a "neo-Mamluk beylicate"[137] that was only disrupted by the French occupation and was finally annihilated by Muhammad ʿAli in 1811 at the massacre of the mamlūks at Cairo's Citadel.[138]

Employment patterns of famous Coptic archons during this period continue to illustrate their influence not only within their community but in Egyptian society at large: the archon Rizqallah (Rizq) al-Badawi (d. 1770) was given the prestigious post of mubāshir al-Ruznāme and scribe; and most important, he served as the direct adviser, "oracle," and personal confidant to ʿAli Bey al-Kabir.[139] His closeness to the latter was disdained by Muslim grandees, who felt humiliated because they were not only forced to "exalt" a Copt but were also obliged to bribe Rizq before making any requests from his patron.[140] Still, his esteemed position offered him (and indirectly the Coptic community) political protection. When Rizq died, his successor and protégé, Ibrahim al-Jawhari (d. 1795), became linked to the Qazdaghli duumvirs Ibrahim Bey (d. 1816) and Murad Bey (d. 1801), the mamlūks of ʿAli Bey and the future opponents of Bonaparte. Al-Jawhari was particularly favored by Ibrahim Bey, who made him mubāshir of his properties and finances.

Both Muslims and Copts admired Ibrahim al-Jawhari for his philanthropy. He helped restore and renovate numerous Coptic churches and monasteries and also patronized the copying of religious manuscripts and icons. Although he was extremely influential both within and outside the community, al-Jawhari was still subject to the whims of Ottoman loyalists, who sought to curb the influence of local Egyptian elites.[141] Due to his absolute allegiance to his benefactors, the chronicler al-Jabarti reports that al-Jawhari's patron Ibrahim Bey "grieved at his death" and walked in his funeral.[142] Jirjis al-Jawhari (d. 1810), on the other hand, served during the short-lived French Occupation, and then briefly in the service of Muhammad 'Ali, although his influence under the latter waned considerably and he died in relative dishonor.[143] Notably, Jirjis supervised the completion of a new patriarchal headquarters in the Azbakiyya district of Cairo. Because of their charitable contributions, the Jawhari brothers are considered saintly figures in the Coptic Church.

The archons' ascent occurred, in part, as they became closer to the centers of power and were included within the "entourages" of influential households.[144] Archons owned slaves, and scattered evidence suggests that some may have even practiced polygamy, like their elite Muslim patrons.[145] In the early part of the eighteenth century, several high-ranking military officers and grandees began to construct extravagant homes in elite neighborhoods such as the southern shore of Birkat (Pond) al-Azbakiyya in western Cairo. By midcentury, the area was dominated by the houses of the Qazdaghlis and their allies, which now displaced the Citadel as the new center of power in Cairo.[146] Historically, the northern shore of the Azbakiyya (al-Maqs) was a humbler neighborhood dominated by Copts, but in the second half of the eighteenth century, archons would build lavish residences, ostensibly to become closer to their influential patrons. The Jawhari brothers alone, by the end of the eighteenth century, owned 167 properties—mostly houses and shops—in the posh Azbakiyya neighborhood.[147] In his eulogy, al-Jabarti remarked that Jirjis al-Jawhari's home was surrounded by a group of "servants and gatekeepers"; the house would be later occupied by Muhammad 'Ali and his son.[148]

The rise of men like Rizq and the Jawhari brothers as advisers to Egypt's top rulers indicates the high level of trust bestowed on archons. The Copts' isolation from Europeans distinguished them among Egypt's other non-Muslims, who were competing to receive economic or political protection from foreign dignitaries. Like all non-Muslims, archons could never directly challenge their patrons' political power, but they were also part of an indigenous community with no external networks and no ties to coreligionists in other parts of the empire. In that regard, archons appeared to be incorruptible confidants to Egypt's local elites.

The "Common Folk"

It is difficult to fully capture the lives of ordinary Copts in Ottoman Egypt, those who constituted the majority but were not included among the clergy or the lay elites. Where did they live? How did they carry out their day-to-day tasks? What occupations were they engaged in? Copts lived in small pockets among Egypt's Muslims, populating urban and rural areas alike. Some remote villages in Upper Egypt were inhabited solely by Copts.[149] In cities, they had a noticeable presence in Alexandria, Mahalla al-Kubra, Akhmim, Manfalut, Mallawi, and Assyut, but historical sources divulge disproportionately greater information about Cairenes. In this geopolitical nexus of Egyptian life, Copts—like other non-Muslims—tended to congregate within religiously mixed districts: for Copts, these were Azbakiyya (especially al-Maqs), Harat al-Nasara, Qantara al-Jadida, and Bayn al-Surayn.[150]

While their economic pursuits varied, the majority continued to be farmers and village craftsmen following the Ottoman conquest. Copts were engaged in traditional agriculture and expressed local variations in their farming and occupations. In the Fayyum region, for instance, where they grew roses, figs, oranges, pears, lemons, and apricots, they specialized in making rosewater and other perfumes.[151] In Isna and other parts of Upper Egypt, they manufactured quality cloths and linen.[152] Throughout urban centers, Copts were well represented in a number of professions, serving as goldsmiths, shoemakers, masons, engravers, and carpenters.[153] Inheritance registers from the early modern period confirm that Cairo's Copts also worked as metallurgists, jewelers, weavers, tailors, furriers, construction laborers, and candle makers, although they were markedly absent in the commercial sector.[154] Copts belonged to a number of religiously mixed guilds, forming a majority in the jewelers' guild and, along with the Greeks, constituting a majority in the tailors' guild.[155] Ordinary laborers earned modest wages, and many died in dire poverty.[156] Of course, some professionals, like the archons, stood out even more as new employment opportunities opened up in the late seventeenth and eighteenth centuries.

Among Copts, the making, selling, and drinking of alcohol, including wine and the anise-flavored liquor *'araq*, were common pastimes, worthy of frequent mention within European travel accounts, Egyptian chronicles and court records, and Coptic religious writings.[157] Coptic farmers tended to vineyards in Fayyum, which they used for producing alcohol, but they also sold their grapes to Muslims, who, according to travelers, reduced the juice into a syrup to sweeten their food.[158] In Cairo, Coptic-owned taverns had long existed near the coastal area known as Khalij, close to Shubra: during Mamluk times, this district generated substantial income from the tax on wine consumption.[159] In the Ottoman period, it was not uncommon for governors to close taverns, along with "places of prostitution," in

Bulaq, Bab al-Luq, Tulun, and Fustat.[160] Many Europeans were surprised at the Coptic predilection toward drinking, perhaps because they had expected stricter enforcement of legal prohibitions against the consumption of alcohol. In 1783, Volney remarked that Copts drank "whole bottles of [ʿaraq] at their supper"; he was astonished that "such excesses do not produce instant death, or at least every symptom of the most insensible drunkenness."[161] Muslim Egyptians also participated in the production and use of alcoholic beverages, but as we will later see, during times of increased religious zealotry Copts caught drinking in public would bear the brunt of criticism by ʿulamāʾ and Coptic clergymen alike.[162]

In Egypt as in other parts of the Ottoman Empire, non-Muslims frequently interacted with each other and with Muslims in courts of law. The sharīʿa recognized that Copts had property rights equal to those of Muslims, including slave ownership for those who could afford it. Coptic men, however, could not marry Muslim women, and Copts were prohibited from testifying against Muslims.[163] Still, all of Egypt's non-Muslims turned to local courts to manage loans, purchases, inheritances, and property rights, as well as all matters related to criminal conduct. Conversions to Islam, while relatively rare in the Ottoman era, were recorded at court, where Copts also registered their marriage contracts and dowries.[164] In the following description from the late eighteenth century, Pococke gives an impression of how Copts, men in particular, were able to simultaneously negotiate Islamic legal codes and church canons on divorce and remarriage:

> The [Coptic] men easily procure divorces, on account of adultery, long sickness, and almost for any disagreements, and, if the party desires it, they obtain leave of the patriarch or bishop to marry again; and if it is refused, 'tis said a priest will notwithstanding sometimes marry either of the parties; but they must, in that case, be excluded from the sacrament for some time: And if their own clergy will not marry them to another, they have recourse to the Cadi [qādi], who will do both.[165]

By using Islamic courts, ordinary Copts could challenge the authority of their own clerical leaders to adjudicate civil matters. In dealing directly with lower priests, they were also skillful in bypassing higher clergymen, who might administer church laws more strictly.[166] There is limited evidence that Christians in the Ottoman world participated in or had regular access to their own legal venues. Still, Pococke's description reminds us that exclusion from religious sacraments and rituals could have been used to dissuade Copts from resorting to Islamic courts and violating church canons. Thus in Ottoman Egypt, the symbolic and at times real force of the church's moral authority should not be entirely neglected.

For Copts, the church functioned as the epicenter of their social, cultural, and, at times, political life. Copts had a few active churches in Cairo, and modest parishes stood in villages and in most urban centers throughout the country.[167] The community would have regularly assembled there for liturgical prayers but also to celebrate religious feasts and weddings. Both men and women attended these rituals, sometimes to raucous effect.[168] In general, the desire for fellowship and spiritual comfort motivated participation in church services, but in poorer communities, Copts also came seeking charity from clerical or lay leaders. In the Ottoman period, Egyptians dealt with numerous calamities: civil and political unrest, warfare, excessive taxation, famine, and disease, among others. The plague, in particular, forced them to habitually confront death, mortality, and an atmosphere of doom: in the period under study, epidemics struck approximately every nine years.[169] These disasters surely ravaged the already vulnerable and starved lower classes more than their wealthy compatriots. The Coptic Church was obligated, so far as it could, to alleviate pervasive suffering, and in this way, like mosques and synagogues, it held enormous sway over the lives of its congregants. Churches became a venue where clergymen could ease the anguish of their parishioners while reminding them of religion's importance in their daily lives.

Shifting Communal Leadership

The churches also became an arena for intermittent power struggles between higher clergymen—patriarchs and bishops—and the archons.[170] At times the relationship appears to have been collaborative, congenial, and productive; at others, competitive or downright hostile. Whenever the clergy felt weakened, they pushed to assert moral and spiritual control over the laity. The oscillation of communal authority between laity and clergy was not new to the Ottoman period. Texts from the eighth to the eleventh centuries suggest a similar breakdown in church authority, with many clergy condemning the laity's role during periods of "decline."[171] While the Ottoman period is characterized by the archons' ascent, some clergy resisted that trend. Moreover, the lines between the groups were frequently blurred. A few patriarchs came from prominent archon families. Others, particularly in the eighteenth century, came out of a strict monastic upbringing and were bold in reasserting clerical authority.

The oft-tenuous relationship between clergy and laity relates to the increased role of archons in choosing patriarchs. As noted, while some form of government approval was needed to implement the community's decision, patriarchs were traditionally chosen through electoral synods that included laity, bishops, and priests.[172] Patriarchs Yu'annis XIII (1484–1524) and Yu'annis XIV (1571–1586) were selected after long deliberations, up to two and half years in the latter case, between "fathers, bishops, and archons."[173] Such drawn-out negotiations suggest entrenched disagreements about appropriate or viable candidates. By the seventeenth century, patriarchs were almost always elected by the highest lay leaders. Yu'annis XV (1619–1629), for instance, was the favorite among the archons.[174] In 1646, a group of archons, guided by their most powerful leader, al-Mu'allim[175] Bishara, fetched the new patriarch Murqus VI (1646–1676) from the Monastery of St. Antony and brought him to Cairo in chains.[176] Patriarch Yu'annis XVI was also taken from the same monastery,[177] and his successor, Butrus VI (1718–1726), was handpicked by leading archon Lutfallah Abu Yusuf. Similarly, Yu'annis XVII (1726–1745) and Murqus VII (1745–1768) from the Monastery of St. Paul were preselected by archons.[178] As time went on, this process depended less and less on the highest-ranking bishops and clergy. The growing influence of Cairo's lay elites was captured by two eighteenth-century travelers: Pococke confirmed that archons or the "principal Copts" dominated patriarchal elections, and Sonnini found it remarkable that monks in the Monastery of al-Baramus received most of their supplies from Cairo's archons rather than from their religious superiors.[179] Financial control over monasteries added to the authority of laymen, who in turn decided which monks to nominate for the patriarchal seat. Archons usually preferred candidates who would be sympathetic to their policies, goals, and interests, and in this way, they altered the leadership structure and influenced internal Coptic affairs.

I do not wish to suggest, however, that power flowed only from archons to patriarchs. It would be more accurate to speak of both competition and interdependency, which certainly increased during the Ottoman period.[180] In the sixteenth century, the clerical leadership was largely intact, albeit weakened from the preceding Mamluk era. In correspondence with the Coptic congregation in Sammanud, Patriarch Yu'annis XIII revealed his vulnerability when reminding his flock that "archons do not control the church. Instead, the church has power over everyone. All affairs should be decided by the church and not by the archons."[181] His successor, Ghubriyal VII (1525–1568), asserted his authority by raising funds to repopulate the long-abandoned Monastery of St. Antony and to reconstruct other edifices.[182] An inscription on the monastery's church walls memorialized the patriarch's spiritual role, noting that Ghubriyal "shepherded God's people with the best of shepherding, and he exerted a successful effort in the rebuilding of monasteries and churches and restoring them."[183] Still, the patriarchs' temporal power gradually dwindled, along with their financial autonomy. In general, patriarchs might have expected to receive income from monastic possessions, parish donations, the performance of certain rituals, and the benevolence of lay elites.[184] One account, however, highlights their vulnerabilities in the economically troubled seventeenth century and their inability to depend on alms (*'aṭṭā'*) and tithes (*'ushūr*) as reliable sources of income.[185] Over time, then, patriarchs increasingly relied on archons to sustain both themselves and the church. In turn, by becoming directly involved with religious patronage, archons seemed to covet, at least partially, the patriarchs' authority, as it provided them with greater legitimacy among cobelievers. Illustrating these trends, one Coptic scribe used the bold title of *al-mawla, al-ra'īs al-dīn al-urthudhuksī* (Lord, Head of the Orthodox Faith) to describe a lay patron of a manuscript dating to 1609.[186] The archons' new power is also captured within wall inscriptions from the early eighteenth century, which praise the laymen's role in financing the renovation of the Monastery of St. Paul.[187] Several years later, these trends became more prominent, as Butrus VI authorized the archon Lutfallah Abu Yusuf to select a new bishop over Ethiopia.[188]

Throughout Coptic history, periods of prosperity among elites often translated into revenue for the church, tangible financial investment within the community, and greater power for the laity. In the Fatimid era, for instance, when many Copts worked for the caliph's government, the church was able to undertake new building projects as well as the renovation of decaying structures, notably in Old Cairo. The few surviving wall paintings in the Monastery of St. Antony also suggest that the medieval period was artistically vibrant and productive.[189] While a paucity of sources limits our understanding of the laity's role during the sixteenth century, it is clear that a cultural resurgence took place in the late seventeenth and eighteenth centuries, when many architectural, literary, or artistic projects were initiated, managed, and overseen by archons rather than by patriarchs. Hundreds of religious manuscripts were copied or restored with these elites' financial patronage. Coptic notables also commissioned dozens of icons, to be hung in churches and in their homes.[190] In 1732 Jirjis Abu Yusuf al-Suruji financed the construction of the Church of St. Michael the Archangel and St. John the Baptist at the Monastery of St. Paul, albeit with the spiritual blessing of Yu'annis XVII.[191] Such endeavors were costly, protracted, and at times daring, yet the archons' commitment is consistent with trends that accorded them greater power. The Jesuit Sicard experienced their burgeoning influence as he planned a visit to the Upper Egyptian town of Niqada in 1714. For his travels, he relied on letters of introduction from the archon Jirjis Abu Mansur al-Tukhi, the "most accredited of Copts in Cairo" and "patron" of Niqada's bishop, whereas only decades before, such missives would have been given by the patriarch.[192]

Within this context, kinship and geographic ties played an important role in shaping communal leadership. In the seventeenth and eighteenth centuries, for instance, the town of Tukh al-Nasara[193] in the Delta province of Minufiyya served as a nucleus for the rise of influential families and networks, from whose ranks would emerge influential lay and clerical leaders. It is perhaps no coincidence that Patriarchs Mittawus III (1634–1649), Mittawus IV (1660–1675), and Yu'annis XVI, as well as the archons Dawud al-Tukhi and his prominent nephew Jirjis Abu Mansur, were all from this town; their families were likely associated through friendship and marriage. Moreover, marriage further strengthened ties among the leading archon families and fostered closer relations with patriarchal families. Two known cases illustrate this tendency: the archon Lutfallah Abu Yusuf was married to Yu'annis XVI's niece, which may have enabled him to influence the selection of Yu'annis XVI's successor Butrus VI (1718–1726).[194] Another by the name of al-Mu'allim Jirjis Abu Shihata, a widower, married the sister of al-Mu'allim Lutfallah during the reign of Butrus VI.[195]

The complex relationship between archons and patriarchs is most evident in the figure of Yu'annis XVI, whose well-documented reign exemplifies the political, economic, geographic, and personal ties that shaped lay-clerical relations in the Ottoman period. As a layman, Yu'annis—or Ibrahim, as he was known before he was consecrated—was on his way to becoming a successful archon, yet instead he chose a life of seclusion in the Monastery of St. Antony. Indeed, it appears that his former ties to wealthy archon families in Cairo led to his selection as the next patriarch: he was chosen from the familiar ranks of the archons, most likely by Jirjis Abu Mansur, and in that sense, his Tukhi origins also facilitated his upward mobility. The situation of mutual interdependence between patriarchs and archons became more visible when Yu'annis transferred the supervision of important communal properties from Coptic artisans into the hands of leading archons, who became *nāzirs*.[196] In doing so, the patriarch relied on the archons' political connections to help restore decaying properties.[197] As a previously rising archon, Yu'annis XVI appreciated the scope of their power and thus solicited their influence and resources for communal revitalization. Their collaboration was also visible in upholding religious practices and rituals. In 1703, for instance, this partnership was on display in the preparation of the Holy Mayrūn (Chrism).[198] As revealed in Coptic Museum MS Liturgy 128, the eminent archon Abu Mansur led the revival of this long-forgotten and costly ritual.[199]

The archons' increasing public confidence would enrage some Muslim leaders; in particular, it drew the ire of the Ottoman governor Kara Muhammad Pasha (r. 1699–1704), who attempted to end the budding Coptic resurgence. Nevertheless, due to their positions of influence, archons "who were undertaking the service of the great of Egypt" were able to pursue their projects, of church and monastic renovations in particular, despite the governor's opposition and legal restrictions.[200] During this period, archons successfully attained *firmāns* (Ottoman imperial decrees) and challenged Islamic prescripts against public processions. Because the Coptic community was larger than any other non-Muslim group in Egypt, their leaders were perhaps more daring and therefore more willing to oppose authority.[201]

At times, the archons' boldness provoked retaliation. On Easter Eve in 1728, a fire broke out at the recently renovated Church of the Virgin in Harat al-Rum (at the Patriarchal Headquarters), and an investigation by the Ottoman governor and his soldiers revealed that most of the church had been burned and looted.[202] Copts also faced obstacles in executing renovation projects. In 1739, a venerable Muslim religious leader, Shaykh al-Damanhuri, was prompted to write a treatise on the legality of Christians' building new churches. He wrote that "dhimmīs began the construction of a church in Cairo, in the neighborhood of Hin Street, causing a great agitation among Muslims"; he was appalled that Copts no longer observed Muslim prohibitions intended "to deter the infidels, the enemies of the faith," from building or renovating their houses of worship.[203] In 1786, as they became caught in the conflict between Ottoman authorities and local rulers, harsh taxes were imposed on Egypt's Christians; according to al-Jabarti, "each person, high or low, [paid] a poll tax of one dinar in addition to the poll tax," and slave girls belonging to wealthy Christians were forcibly bought for 40 riyāls per slave.[204] Regardless of their successes, Copts and their powerful leaders could still be held liable under strict interpretations of Islamic law, and archons were limited in protecting communal interests when the situation turned dire.

The rise of Egypt's archons echoes other developments in the Ottoman world that help explain, at least partially, why lay elites spent their wealth on philanthropic endeavors. Examples of the Greek Phanariots and Armenian *amiras* are particularly instructive here.[205] By the early seventeenth century, the Greek patriarchate in Istanbul, located in the Phanar (Fener) district, was mostly managed by Greek elites also known as "archons" and later as Phanariots. The Phanariots' power came primarily from a tax-farming arrangement, whereby they would pay a lump sum to the government and in return acquire the right to collect lucrative land taxes or customs on seaports. With their economic stature, Phanariots saw themselves as inheriting the Byzantine emperors' legacy of "defending Orthodoxy," a role they displayed by holding special ceremonies at the patriarchate that bestowed them with princely titles.[206] By the end of the seventeenth century, Istanbul's Phanariots chose patriarchs and administered the internal affairs of their church. While the Greek patriarch gradually became "the pensioner of the Phanariots" and was vulnerable to their agendas and policies, the Phanariots preserved his clerical authority, since it legitimized their own status as protectors of Orthodoxy.[207]

Similar patterns surfaced among Istanbul's Armenian community. As early as the sixteenth and seventeenth centuries, a class of Armenian lay elites known as amiras influenced the Ottoman Porte's decisions in selecting patriarchs. Many had gained their fortunes within the financial sector and became known philanthropists, showcasing their riches in the renovation of monasteries and churches.[208] But their philanthropy, according to Hagop Barsoumian, was not simply an act of "piousness and selflessness"; rather, it was motivated by a political desire to gain loyalty from their Armenian coreligionists and, in time, to assert control over the entire community.[209] By the late eighteenth century, the amiras' power had grown to the extent that in official church records, their names were mentioned ahead of clergymen's. The Ottoman Porte also recognized their status, and they were granted tax exemptions and employment posts usually reserved for Muslim elites.[210] Ultimately, their financial authority, their status as communal benefactors, and their increasing clout over the clergy gave them virtual control over coreligionists. As Barsoumian notes, whatever power these laymen lacked within the Ottoman political structure, "they found ample opportunity and almost complete freedom to exercise" authority within their community.[211]

Throughout the Ottoman world, then, Christian lay elites became respected (and sometimes feared) by coreligionists, for they formed a crucial conduit between those who were politically marginalized and the active centers of power. In Egypt, the improved fortunes of Coptic archons and the religious revitalization they undertook allowed them to augment their position. A stronger and more vibrant community reflected well on these emergent leaders and strengthened their position in the eyes of local political and military authorities. As we shall see, some Coptic clergymen in the late eighteenth century would raise concern over these developments.

Summation

Following the Mamluk period, Egypt's Copts were few in number, scattered throughout the country, and generally insular in their relations with outsiders. Distant from and mostly unfamiliar to the new sultans in Istanbul, they were left to fend for themselves. Patriarchs became detached from the center of governance and would gradually lose most of their political functions. In the context of Egypt's rising military and political households, archons became integral within the growing financial bureaucracy. Their ascent symbolizes, in part, the historical trust invested in Copts by local rulers. These laymen would contribute large portions of their wealth to charity and to religious endeavors, and with impressive political skill, they transformed themselves into effective communal leaders.

In this context, religious practice would become relevant not only for pious consumption but also for its political implications. Martyr cults in the sixteenth and seventeenth centuries reveal the intersection between the laity's financial patronage of religious life and the clergymen's ongoing attempts to exert moral authority over the community. Traditions such as the pilgrimage to Jerusalem illustrate not only lay-clerical collaboration but also the increased confidence of archons in showcasing their power and prestige. By the end of the eighteenth century, at a time when the teachings of Catholic missionaries and local converts appeared to challenge what it meant to be a "Copt," higher clergymen turned to the pulpit, delivering sermons that outlined acceptable versus deplorable conduct. With a new moral program in hand, they sought to reestablish themselves as the Copts' true leaders. All of these practices would leave their mark on future generations, particularly in an increasingly refined expression of a Coptic identity. What follows is an attempt to understand the space—loosely termed "popular religion"—that unified Copts: a space where the laity and clergy negotiated, cooperated, and collided with one another in the course of sharing their worldviews and expressing their collective beliefs.

2

Championing a Communal Ethos

The Neo-Martyrdom of St. Salib in the Sixteenth Century

[Copts] pay religious veneration to the images of saints and in this they surpass all nations living under the sun. They have, as we said, some particular places wherein they set their images. On Holy-days they light up candles and lamps before them, and if any adversity at any time happens, or imminent danger appear, they apply themselves to them, and with great devotion ask their assistance, bowing down to the ground, and beating their breasts with their fists, and also shedding of many tears. But they have nothing graven, because they think that an idol, but only images of wood, pictured according to the manner of the Greeks, neither do they use any new images as the papists do, but only those of the Virgin Mary, and some doctors of the primitive church as of Georgius, Theodorus, and also of martyrs, as Antonius Marcus, and of Holy Fathers. The Images of God the Father or of the Holy Ghost, they have not; but that of Christ, and of the Virgin, they have painted together in their private houses which they do worship with great devotion.

—Yusuf Abudacnus, *The True History of the Jacobites, of Egypt, Lybia, Nubia, etc.*

This chapter and the next will investigate how Coptic leaders looked to familiar religious traditions, centered broadly on martyr cults, to create a more cohesive community in the early Ottoman era. Following the tumultuous Mamluk period, varying Coptic factions, particularly from the clerical ranks, sought to dissuade coreligionists from converting to Islam and to discourage unification with the Roman Catholic

Church. The writing, reproduction, and performance of martyrologies served as a reminder that loyalty toward one's faith was model Christian behavior.[1] However, the pervasiveness of martyrologies within Coptic literature of this period also indicates that the earliest days of Ottoman governance were unpredictable, that the numbers of Copts had diminished, and that defections from the faith, while in all probability few, seemed real. These stories both entertained and consoled believers, while showcasing the bravery of local heroes. Set in late Mamluk Egypt and popularized in the early Ottoman era, the martyrology of St. Salib, focus of the present study, relates how a defiant if at times reckless Copt upheld his faith before Muslim authorities. The choice of words, the meticulous description of Salib's surroundings, and the narration of his judgment and execution render this source invaluable for understanding Coptic religious life. There is little doubt that Salib's story, and others like it, would help preserve a distinct Coptic ethos during the first centuries of Ottoman rule.

Background

The sixteenth century was a period of transition and uncertainty for the Coptic community. By this time, Copts had become overwhelmingly Arabized and had abandoned their own language in daily use while preserving it in liturgical ceremonies as a way of validating "their religious tradition in response to conversion and assimilation."[2] During the Mamluk era, thousands of Copts had converted to Islam, and most converts no longer felt socially or economically obligated to former coreligionists.[3] To combat these trends, in the fourteenth century, martyrdom was purposely sought by dozens of Cairene Copts, who hoped that their sacrifice would set a moral example for fellow believers.[4] Still, conversions persisted and by the sixteenth century, Copts were left to reevaluate their place, and their leaders forced to consider tactics that could ensure their own viability and preserve their dwindling community. A religious worldview grounded in martyrdom would endure as an integral part of the battle to protect communal boundaries and maintain a coherent identity.

During early Ottoman rule, the church and community faced major social and political challenges that heightened the appeal of martyrdom narratives. For one, plain apprehension lingered over the community's survival as incidents of undue violence against non-Muslims persisted. For instance, in the year 1521, three Coptic notables became publicly drunk and subsequently engaged in a cursing match with a local qāḍī, defaming him and the Islamic religion. The qāḍī had them arrested, and they were tried by the justices of the four Islamic schools, three of whom concluded that their crime was punishable, although not by death, since intoxication made the culprits unaware of their actions. Displeased by the qāḍīs' leniency, however, some Janissary soldiers captured the offenders and hacked two of them to death. Their bodies were burned under the windows of al-Madrasa al-Salihiyya.[5] Terrified at what he had seen, the third Copt immediately converted to Islam and was protected from retaliation.[6] In a graphic description of a Jew and a Copt, condemned to death in 1522 for debasing coinage, the chronicler Ibn Iyas reveals that the Copt was executed (through impalement) by Janissary mobs even after he had converted to Islam.[7] In another incident wherein some drunken Copts fought with and cursed a Muslim shaykh, one Copt was captured and then threatened with execution by burning; the suspect converted to Islam, and his conversion was publicly celebrated as he was paraded in Cairene streets wearing a white skullcap.[8]

Aside from susceptibility to coerced conversion or violence, restrictive provisions against non-Muslims issued by two Ottoman governors, Khadim Hasan Pasha (1580–1582) and Sharif Muhammad Pasha (1596–1598), also aggravated the Copts' sense of anxiety, as did financial hardships and uneasiness about paying requisite (or arbitrary) taxes.[9] In 1584, for instance, local soldiers rebelled against the ruling Ottoman governor because of rising inflation. The extortion that followed, as committed by the soldiery, was particularly harsh for Egypt's peasants and non-Muslims.[10] Adding to these pressures, Coptic religious leaders began to discern that their authority was waning. In the sixteenth century, Copts were turning to Sufi leaders and holy men to grant them blessings and miracles. On one occasion, they sought Shaykh ʿAbd al-Wahhab al-Shaʿrani—ironically, an outspoken detractor of Christians and Jews—and asked him to "write a blessing on amulets for their children and for sick coreligionists," but when the shaykh inquired about the seeming lack of reverence toward their own clergy, "they declared that they believed in him more than in their patriarch and other religious leaders."[11] Whether real or exaggerated, Coptic leaders were likely aware of these practices and looked for ways to cajole coreligionists into remaining loyal to their authority.

Moreover, during this period, the Roman Catholic Church made vigorous attempts to coax Coptic patriarchs into unification. These efforts paralleled the growing Venetian and French influence within Ottoman borders, which, among its many privileges, allowed missionaries to travel with greater freedom and to preach among Orthodox Christians.[12] Tempted to improve their lot in this era of uncertainty, a few Coptic patriarchs welcomed Rome's protection and were convinced to sign professions of the Catholic faith.[13] Although the Coptic Church never fully ratified these agreements, in the long run, debating the merits of Catholic protection was a painful process that at times jeopardized communal unity. Among other concessions, unification demanded that Copts denounce "heretical" theological beliefs, accept the Council of Chalcedon, reform religious practices regarding marriage and fasting, and recognize the Roman Catholic pope as head of the Coptic

Church. All of these issues would be disputed within the community throughout the early modern period.

In general, Ottoman Christians, especially their highest-ranking leaders, considered union with Rome during times of hardship or plague, or when the jizya was deemed exorbitant.[14] Here, the reign of Patriarch Ghubriyal VII (1525–1568) typifies these sorts of problems as experienced by the Coptic leadership. In 1561, Ghubriyal had welcomed Catholic emissaries and entertained discussions over unification.[15] However, the breakdown in talks would pain the patriarch, since in 1568, the Ottoman Sultan Selim II (1566–1574) reportedly demanded an additional tax from Egypt's non-Muslims.[16] Ghubriyal must have been enticed to acquire the Catholic pope's political support and, more important, to benefit from his riches, but he feared conceding core Coptic beliefs, particularly anti-Chalcedonianism. Above all, he wished to appear loyal to local authorities and to his own community, many of whom had suspected him of extortion and financial corruption. Demoralized, the patriarch escaped to the Monastery of St. Antony, where he allegedly died from emotional duress.[17] Anxieties over internal disunity as well as external pressures by Muslim authorities and missionaries left the clerical leadership with few options for maintaining its influence.

In general, more conservative Copts, clergy and laity, shied from unification out of concern for appearing disloyal to local military or political authorities. At times, the difference in opinion—whether to receive Catholic protection or remain insular—turned violent. Yu'annis XIV (1571–1585) was allegedly poisoned by an opposing faction just before agreeing to unification. Standing against this agreement were monks and clergy who expressed concern over the loss of communal autonomy.[18] Union was almost achieved during the reign of Ghubriyal VIII (1586–1601), but his successor Murqus V (1602–1618) "lost all enthusiasm" and effectively ended serious talks for a settlement.[19] Consequently, a group of pro-Catholic, pro-union Copts (based in Damietta) allied with the French consul in Cairo, had Murqus stripped of his office, and chose an alternate candidate named Kyrillus to take his place.[20] Allegedly, according to a letter written by the French consul to the Vatican, Murqus was captured by Ottoman soldiers, severely beaten, and imprisoned by order of the Ottoman governor.[21] Coptic sources allude to these events but couch Murqus's troubles in terms of a conflict over the rights to practice polygamy and divorce that took place between Copts in Cairo and Upper Egypt, on the one hand, and in Damietta, on the other.[22] Magdi Guirguis transcribes a marginal note from a manuscript that allegedly captured the complaints of the dissenting Coptic faction as made to local political authorities: apparently, they mocked Murqus's religious duties by noting that "he sits on a high chair and he commands people to bow to him. They spray incense on him as if he were a god. He forbids the consumption of meat and milk and allows the consumption of alcohol."[23] Their words, which are cleverly phrased to rouse the anger of Muslim authorities, suggest that recurring hostilities—occasionally inflamed or even adjudicated by external parties—had the potential to agitate the entire community.

In this climate, clergy and laity would turn to stories that glorified their religion and celebrated Coptic valor. Martyrdom tales implicitly and explicitly criticized those who were unable to persist in their faith, frowning on (potential) converts' inability to act as witnesses for Christ despite trial, tribulation, or even the threat of death. Here, the Copts' approach was similar to that of Arab Christian communities living under early Islamic rule as well as Balkan Christians in the Ottoman world, who used hagiographies and religious art to help sustain a sense of "historical consciousness" among their ranks.[24] What follows is a close reading of how a martyrology could foster confessional unity and how it might reveal contextual concerns related to the Copts' place in late Mamluk and early Ottoman Egyptian society. In discussing Salib's story, it will be important to consider the exaggerated nature of hagiographic texts, as well as issues related to their authorship, their intended audience, and their value as historical sources.

Neo-Martyrdom as Coptic History

In general, Coptic annals are scarce for the sixteenth century, reflecting trends in Egyptian historiography at large.[25] On religious life, the most abundant manuscripts are Arabic-language hagiographies and martyrologies, the majority reproducing familiar stories of ancient saints. In some cases, these texts document the lives and deaths of "neo-martyrs" and reveal how Coptic communal leaders focused on preserving saints' cults of all varieties—ancient and contemporary. Neo-martyrs were Christians who died for their faith following the seventh-century Islamic expansion into the Middle East and Europe.[26] In the Ottoman period, these tales continued to spread throughout Egypt.[27] For Copts, they no doubt provided diversion and solace from common burdens such as sectarian attacks, civil unrest, disease, and financial hardships.

Two versions of Salib's story have survived—one Muslim, the other Coptic—and both relate how Salib allegedly blasphemed the Islamic religion, and specifically its prophet, and was killed for his crime.[28] While the famous Egyptian chronicler Ibn Iyas penned the short Muslim excerpt, the Coptic-Arabic martyrology was recorded by an unknown author in the first decades of Ottoman rule. Within Coptic archives, there are six known manuscripts related to Salib's hagiography or life; the earliest used here (hereafter cited as *M.Salib*) dates to 1550.[29] Because of the rarity of historical narratives from this period, *M.Salib* provides a valuable portrait of Coptic life. Signaling their commitment to the cult of this saint, when Yu'annis XIII died in 1524, community elders chose to bury him under Salib's newly constructed shrine at the Church of the Virgin in Harat Zuwayla.[30] Many patriarchs would be similarly interred close to Salib's remains.

Historically, neo-martyrdoms were prolific among Arab Christians in the early Islamic centuries and among Orthodox Christians in the Ottoman Balkans (including Greeks, Serbs, and Bulgarians). The scholarly literature on both offers good comparisons for the present case. During difficult times, neo-martyrdoms represented an important source of authority for church leaders. In the early Islamic context, for example, they functioned as part of an "apologetic" literature that signaled to believers and potential defectors that "Islam was not the one true religion."[31] In the Balkans, they were used as part of a sermonizing "resistance" literature that bestowed greater authority on increasingly ineffectual clergymen.[32] As Eleni Gara notes, Balkan Orthodox churchmen promoted martyr cults with great pride in order to deal with "the criticism of Roman Catholics who regarded with disdain Christians living under Ottoman rule."[33] I will read Salib's text similarly by looking at why it might have been written and endorsed by Coptic leaders in the sixteenth century. On the one hand, conversion to Islam continued to be an attractive alternative to Copts seeking to alleviate their dhimmī status; Salib's story, in this context, epitomized Coptic bravery against daily and extraordinary burdens.[34] On the other hand, partisan groups that opposed unification with Rome would have been attracted to martyrologies because they highlighted themes of sacrifice and communality. In effect, Salib's neo-martyrdom took a familiar, ancient genre and presented it in a contemporary way so that it could inspire its Ottoman-era audiences to preserve their faith.

The issue that historians most often confront when dealing with neo-martyrologies (or hagiographies in general) is that of their authenticity. For the most part, scholars have accepted the basic facts and dismissed redundant motifs: the words and emotional states of the martyrs as well as the forms and phases of persecution. For the early Islamic period, Sidney Griffith remarks that it is difficult to corroborate these texts because "non-Christian sources and in particular no Islamic text [confirm] any one of them."[35] For the Balkan context, Elizabeth Zachariadou goes so far as to say that their corroboration is immaterial, since a neo-martyr's "vita is an expression of the attitude of the [church]; it matters little whether the stories are true or false."[36] Few would dispute that martyrologies are often exaggerated by a clerical hierarchy seeking to promote its authority, though with this approach, a martyrology such as Salib's—filled with colorful subtexts intended to rouse its audiences—could be simply dismissed as an allegorical tale embellished by an overzealous writer.

Despite their problematic nature, another approach could provide alternative readings of these texts. For one, many martyrologies appear hyperbolic because they were intended to be performed and read out loud. In his study of neo-martyrdoms in the early Islamic centuries, for instance, David Vila notes that the use of repetitive, emphatic phrases transformed these traditional stories into dramatic "hagiographical sermons," to be shared and heard by the broader Christian community.[37] In Mamluk Egypt, audience approval was sought by public orators, and spectators were quick to criticize the efficacy of storytellers and Muslim preachers by cursing or threatening to stone the performer in question.[38] For the Ottoman Egyptian context, Nelly Hanna argues that public storytelling was a form of entertainment in the seventeenth and eighteenth centuries and that some of the most engaging repertoire recounted heroic deeds of the past.[39] Other historians have noted that, in general, Ottoman writers and chroniclers appreciated the diversity of their audiences, as evidenced by the choice of language—colloquial or formal—that they employed.[40]

Many Coptic-Arabic texts from the Ottoman era appear to have functioned similarly, and while relevant details such as the author's identity are often missing from a Coptic hagiography, it is still possible for a historian to infer how a text might have been used. Within *M.Salib*, rich colloquialisms, dramatic descriptions, entreaties to audiences, and references to local places and events imply that it was intended for public consumption.[41] These details allow the researcher to appreciate a story's dynamic value, even if it is "contaminated"[42] by the author's faulty memory or his literary embellishments. This approach echoes that of scholars of European history who have come to understand religious texts not only as readable but also, and more important, as fully audible and performable.[43] Here, I also look to David Frankfurter's approach toward reading early Christian hagiographic texts, situating myself between those who reject their historical validity and those who embrace them with minimal criticism.[44] That is, my reading of *M.Salib* as reflecting the church's historical memory in early Ottoman Egypt will be critical, varied, and at times conjectural. Ultimately, few would dispute that martyrologies could be used to rally a community during adversity. For Copts who were experiencing fragmentation, coercion, and internal conflict, *M.Salib*'s ability to be performed time and again could inspire loyalty among future generations.

Salib's Martyrdom: The Muslim Account

In recent years, Ottoman historians have begun the process of checking the accuracy of neo-martyrdoms against other historical documents and have exposed the limitations of this endeavor primarily because of the weakness or inaccessibility of sources. Phokion Kotzageorgis, for instance, has argued that while the field would benefit from a comparison of authentic Muslim and Christian documents, few neo-martyrdoms were preserved in Ottoman records, partly because the central government took heed of offending Christians only when they acquired a mass following.[45] Eleni Gara has looked to court records (sijills) to corroborate some of the numerous tales that exist in Balkan church narratives; finding few, she points out that either cases of blasphemy or apostasy—the most common charges against these martyrs—were rare or they may have vanished.[46] Moreover, she notes that existing sijill narratives can be deceptive, since the goal of court scribes, in contrast to church writers, was to present how a case conformed with Islamic law and not necessarily to give "an account of what happened."[47]

The small number of known Coptic neo-martyrologies from the Ottoman period, as well as the limited access to most texts from Coptic archives, has made such comparative research quite challenging. For the present study, then, the historian feels fortunate that a single Muslim chronicle made a brief but important reference to Salib's martyrdom. Ibn Iyas's *Badāʾiʿ al-Ẓuhūr fī Waqāʾiʿ al-Ḍuhūr* is a distinctive account of late Mamluk and early Ottoman history.[48] The section relating Salib's story allows an exploration of history in a way that is impossible with many other martyrologies. For Ibn Iyas, Salib's death was a passing incident he deemed significant enough to record. His description is concise, straightforward, fairly linear, and short enough to include here in its entirety. Ibn Iyas begins his description by referencing a "strange incident" that took place on Monday, 20 Ramadan, in the year 918 AH, or 29 November 1512 CE:

> [On this day] There was a Christian person who was called ʿAbd al-Salib. He was from the area of Dalja in the southern regions.[49] It was said about him that he insulted the Prophet, peace be upon him, with vulgar words. A group of people witnessed this and wrote a record [*maḥḍar*] of it, which was authenticated by the judge [qāḍī] of the area. When they brought the Christian before the sultan and he confessed to what he said against the Prophet, peace be upon him, they offered him conversion to Islam, but he refused. The sultan sent him to the house of Amīr Tumanbay al-Dawadar, and he convened an assembly [*majlis*]. [ʿAbd al-Salib] confessed what he had spoken before the judges [*quḍāt*] and insisted upon this. He pledged not to change his religion, so the judges condemned him to death. Representatives of the ruler bore witness to this [confession]. So they mounted him on a camel while he was nailed,[50] and they displayed him in Cairo until they brought him to al-Madrasa al-Salihiyya. They beheaded him under the windows of the school. The public then brought fire and wood and burned his body in the midst of the market [*sūq*]. When nighttime fell, the dogs came and ate his bones, and his matter ended.[51]

The chronicle *Badā'i'* was written by someone who was highly invested in the Mamluk regime, and Ibn Iyas includes this story as one of many that took place during al-Ghawri's reign.[52] In the scheme of things, this incident likely meant little to Ibn Iyas and his relatively well-educated audience, although the fact that the accused stood before the sultan and was offered reprieve made the story worth retelling. By the same token, the chronicler likely referenced Salib's death in order to reflect on the justness of a Mamluk regime that he admired, in comparison to the new Ottoman establishment, and to convey his and the community's repugnance toward a Copt who had overstepped his bounds. There also seems to have been a deliberate effort by Ibn Iyas to foreshadow Tumanbay's importance as the last Mamluk sultan who stood up against the Ottoman onslaught.[53]

In all, Ibn Iyas's description was one not of a heroic martyr but rather of a criminal.[54] It will later emerge that Ibn Iyas and *M.Salib*'s narrator attribute different values to Salib's death, each according to his perspective and to his intended audience. Since I am primarily interested in the significance of this story to Coptic audiences, however, I focus most of my analysis here on *M.Salib*. Ibn Iyas's chronicle allows the historian to make more accurate presumptions about the reliability of *M.Salib* but offers few clues about the conceptualization of martyrdom, per se, in sixteenth-century Egypt.

Salib's Martyrdom: The Coptic Version

Even if *M.Salib* is far longer than Ibn Iyas's account, filled with elaborate details and rhetorical flourishes, and prone to exaggeration, it can still be probed for historical details and for its meanings to Coptic Christians. At times, this might require a historian to "read the silences" and hypothesize about how the martyrology was heard and understood by its audiences.[55] From the first pages of *M.Salib*, the hagiographer seeks not only to evoke images of heroism and bravery but also to arouse a personal connection to the story. To achieve this goal, the Coptic-Arabic text was partially modeled on known Coptic martyrologies, and in fact, the narrator appears to be especially familiar with the story of John of Phanijōit, a thirteenth-century Coptic convert to Islam who retracted his conversion and was eventually executed.[56] Salib's story is also quite similar to Diocletian-era hagiographies, as it includes a voluntary confession of faith followed by arrest; questioning by a ruler; apparitions of an angel; a journey on a ship along the Nile to be tried before a different ruler; and torture and execution.[57] By using more recent historical events as its starting point, however, *M.Salib* calls on believers with divergent interests and backgrounds to rally and unite in the face of external pressures. At the same time, it expresses differences within the Coptic collective, depicting distinct viewpoints and ideals on issues such as asceticism, marriage, and sacrifice.

From the outset, audiences become aware of Salib's origins and his Christian credentials. Salib was born to a devout family from the town of Ibshada in the Upper Egyptian province of al-Ushmunayn.[58] His parents raised him with the virtue of purity and gave him a most esteemed name, Salib ("cross"), the name that represented the sign of "worldly redemption."[59] Both parents worked as modest carpenters. Christian hagiographic texts generally reflect a desire to present a martyr as one who strove to mimic the life of Christ (*imitatio Christi*), in this case, possibly his profession. Salib's parents also taught their son the customs (*adāb*) of the Coptic Church. One day they decided that Salib should be wed to a relative, hoping that his marriage would bring offspring who could assist in the family business. But they made these plans without Salib's consent, and Salib vowed not to "lie with [his wife even for] one day," because his body was pure and without sin.[60] According to the narrator, Salib was defying his parents to heed the words of the gospel, which he had heard so frequently in church and which advised him to be virtuous and chaste.

To escape his marital responsibilities, Salib spent most of his time visiting the numerous monasteries and churches that dotted Upper Egypt and listening to the "divine word." These actions so enraged his parents that they shackled their son, but to their dismay, his chains miraculously broke and the saint was freed by the "power of Christ."[61] During these hardships, Salib appealed to the Virgin Mary, asking her to bestow on him the crown of martyrdom so that he could join Christ in heaven. On one of his usual wanderings, he encountered some "non-Christians," and without provocation, it seems, he insulted them by uttering something that was "not appropriate to be heard" (*shay'un lā yalīqa bi samā'ihi*). The offended group was angry and captured him, but they later released him as a "courtesy to his parents" (*ikrāman li wālidayhī*). However, Salib spewed more insults, so they—having lost their patience at that point—took him to the governor of Upper Egypt or al-Sa'id (*al-mutawallī bi'l-ḥukm fī bilād al-Sa'īd*). As he stood before this official, Salib did not deny the charges and "confessed" in public, before a large crowd. Consequently, he received much abuse for whatever it is that he had said (the narrator omits these words). He was tied up and stoned, but miraculously the Archangel Michael shielded him from harm.[62]

The governor then ordered Salib imprisoned. During the day, the jailer witnessed Salib's chains breaking miraculously. At night, the jailer's wife saw that the saint was praying to an "illuminated woman" who foretold that he would receive the crown of martyrdom in the name of her son. On witnessing these events, the jailers offered to help Salib escape, but he refused. Thus the next morning, Salib stood before the local qāḍī, who ordered that he be sent to Cairo. Just as he was being taken away, Salib's parents and brothers arrived to bid him an emotional and tearful farewell. Aboard the ship, absorbed in prayer, Salib declined to eat or drink, while his guard witnessed more conversations between Salib and the illuminated woman. In Cairo, the commander of the guards approached a group of Christian "believers" and asked them to give the martyr some money, as he had nothing; the group complied and also offered to feed the saint.

The guard then took Salib to meet his sister, who lived in Cairo. During this encounter, the sister pleaded with her brother to abandon his quest for martyrdom, but Salib stood firm by his position. He was then taken to *al-ḥākim*, an amīr, and the written evidence against him, in the form of letters that recorded what he had said in his hometown, was also presented. Salib was confronted with these accusations and asked about their veracity. Threatened with torture if he did not respond truthfully, at that moment the saint was gripped by the "Holy Spirit," and "he confessed the noble confession," confirming the accusations.[63]

The next morning, the amīr ordered that Salib be taken to the "king of Egypt" (*malik Miṣr*), presumably Sultan al-Ghawri. At this point, as in other parts of the text, the hagiographer interjects the martyr's thoughts, noting his state of mind, his disposition toward martyrdom, and his recollection of scripture that strengthened his resolve to die. According to the narrator, Salib was unimpressed by the splendor and glory of the sultan's court and showed little fear of the sultan's soldiers or the torture with which he was threatened. The sultan asked him to recant what he had said, promising that if he converted to Islam, Salib would be forgiven for those inappropriate utterances. But Salib responded, "Everything that they said and wrote about me, and sent to you, is true. There is not a single word in it that is false. Everything that I uttered was from my heart and from all of my senses. I declare publicly that I am a Christian!"[64] One would assume that this self-incrimination would have sent Salib directly to his death, yet the sultan asked that judges be invited to hear the accused's statement and to judge him according to Islamic law. Before those judges and other witnesses, Salib confessed once more, claiming, "Not only was everything that I spoke true, but I would even add more to what I have said."[65] Consequently, on seeing the face of the accused and hearing his words, the judges condemned Salib to death.

Salib was nailed to a wooden plank in the shape of a cross and then mounted on a camel. A crowd paraded him in Cairo's streets, repeating the words with which he had blasphemed Islam, although the offending words are once again omitted from the text.[66] The saint was pleased that the hour of his death neared, the hour when the promise made to him by the Virgin Mary would be fulfilled. In one of the most emotional parts of the text, the narrator speaks directly to Salib about how his suffering affected the surrounding community:

> When they raised you upon the cross over the camel's back, how much sadness fell upon the Christians while they were stoning and shaming

> you, yet you were riding joyfully without your body being affected with weakness. Rather you were like a lion with your mind lifted to heaven abandoning all earthly things and all pleasures of the world. The Archangel Michael had been protecting you until you completed your good perseverance. After they paraded you in all of Cairo's streets, they took you down from the cross, from the wood on which you were crucified. They propped you up where they were accustomed to performing beheadings. Rejoice and be glad, oh great martyr of the eleventh hour, he who has earned a full day's wages.[67] You became counted with all martyrs. Blessed are you oh martyr of Christ because you attained what an eye has never seen, what an ear never heard, and what a man's heart never conceived.[68] Blessed are you oh great martyr because powerfully, courageously, and patiently you had the courage. Christian assistance came to you from the Pantocrator,[69] since none of the Christians happened to be shamed and crucified on a camel but you alone. While in the flesh, you became higher than all of them, and when they made you stand to cut off your neck, you turned your face toward the east with joy and happiness.[70]

At those final moments, Salib was brought before the executioner and a qāḍī; the latter offered him one last reprieve, saying, "'Salib, recant your opinion and I will keep you alive [lit. "restrain your bloodshed"] and allow you to go on your own.' So he increased his outcries with the loudest voice and said, 'I will not die except as a Christian in the name of Christ!' When the judge heard this noble confession from the martyr, he immediately ordered that his holy head be taken off."[71] After his death, the Virgin Mary "took his soul," "wrapped it in sheets of light," and presented it to her son in heaven. Salib's body was burned in the midst of the city, but miraculously, according to the hagiographer, it withstood the fire for three days without damage or theft by "unbelievers." Finally, a group of "believers" claimed his body and brought it to the patriarchal headquarters in Harat Zuwayla, which remains the main shrine for the saint to this day.[72] From there, the saint's relics were dispersed to various churches in Egypt and became the source of numerous miracles and healings. His martyrdom date according to the Coptic calendar is 3 Kiayhk, 1229 AM, which matches the date recorded by Ibn Iyas.[73]

In Ottoman Egypt, Salib's martyrology would have introduced a sense of drama that only a local and recently martyred saint could stimulate. In matching the Coptic version with Ibn Iyas's brief account, we find that the story alludes to familiar people, scenes, and places, the most notable being the site of Salib's execution at al-Madrasa al-Salihiyya, which was close to Bab Zuwayla in the southern wall of Fatimid Cairo, near the city's commercial center.[74] In the sixteenth century, listeners to Salib's story may have been eyewitnesses to his death, or they may have heard about these events from parents and grandparents. In all, a text rich in colloquialisms, vivid social interaction, and references to familiar sites was no doubt widely popular.

Among a Christian Family

From the progression of Salib's martyrology, it becomes clear that one of the factors that may have led him to profess his disdain for the Islamic religion and to insult the Prophet Muhammad was frustration with the conventionality of his life among his family and local community. Salib saw himself as achieving more spiritual or material fulfillment than could be provided by the life of an ordinary carpenter. To some audiences, his restlessness likely echoed their daily frustrations of being part of a marginalized community bound by various legal and social limitations. Salib's spiritual exploration and his single-minded drive toward martyrdom began when he received distinctly contradictory messages from his family, on the one hand, and from his church, through the gospels, on the other.[75] While his parents raised him to be a proper Christian and to serve God, they also wished him to marry, procreate, and conform to a conventional life. For Salib, these expectations violated his goals to be virtuous, and according to the narrator, religious obligation outweighed filial duty.

When his parents ignored his wish to remain single, he became frustrated at having to abandon a life of solitude and was faced with the horror of losing his chastity by "touching his wife." Salib had few options but to escape, seeking comfort in nearby hills and monasteries. Although this trope echoes stories of itinerant ascetics from the Coptic monastic tradition and even evokes widely circulating tales of wandering Muslim dervishes in the Ottoman world, the narrator does not directly address the issue of whether Salib wished to become a monk.[76] Salib's later exhortations (or insults) before a group of Muslim observers suggest that he was searching for an audience or that he may have even viewed himself as a preacher of the Christian faith. Nor does the narrator editorialize about the parents' response to his acts of rebellion. In passing, he notes that they had chained their son in order to prevent him from evading his duties and obligations as a husband, duties that he presumably owed them and his wife.

Could we read the parents' actions, their attempt to limit his spiritual quest, as a subtle critique of the ascetic life? Is it possible that some church leaders were so concerned about the demographic demise of the community that, betraying its own traditions of monasticism and asceticism, they advocated and upheld married life, particularly for men, over sexual abstinence? Perhaps, although the hagiographer could also have been drawing on motifs from early Christian martyrologies, which commonly focused on the tensions between a family's desire for offspring against a martyr's goal of preserving his virginity and serving Christ.[77] Salib, here, can be viewed as a "male virgin martyr," distinguished from ordinary Copts by his physical sacrifice. In his deprivation from sexual pleasure and his renunciation of a normative family life, he represented a specific paradigm of sainthood for fellow believers, one congruent with early Christian traditions.[78] In all, Salib's bravery in the face of familial pressures, before sexual temptation, or later in front of a Mamluk sultan legitimize his path to salvation and the church's own message of perseverance. Even if family stood in his way, a true martyr would not back down from his religion.

While the hagiographer eschews criticism of the parents' harshness toward Salib, he replaces Salib's earthly parents with a "heavenly family." The martyr's chastity was protected from his wife's sexual advances by the Archangel Michael, depicted here as an overseer or even as an older brother.[79] The saint's new and more powerful mother was the Virgin Mary, and the overarching father figure was God himself, whom the saint longed to meet and join. This heavenly family guides Salib's actions and quietly comforts him. In an emotional scene, written in strikingly colloquial Arabic, Salib meets his sister and emerges as resolute in his pursuit:

> She was wailing and said while crying: "Woe to me my brother and the light of my eye." She kept wailing like that saying to him, "Recant this act, for perhaps you will be saved from this punishment and from the chains with which you are bound." When she had said this, he accepted her words with great difficulty and bid her the farewell of someone who was ready to endure death. She continued to wail and said, "How long am I going to miss you my brother, the iris of my eye? Your absence, your separation and your being away from my eyes will be so long." After he bid his sister farewell, he departed.[80]

This scene is depicted with consideration to the social setting in which the story occurred and to the everyday relationships that constituted this saint's life. The sister was begging and imploring her brother to change his mind, yet even though it pained him, he calmly sustained his quest. Once again, *M.Salib*'s author emphasizes that an earthly family becomes secondary to a martyr who has chosen the path of Christ.[81]

On the other hand, a powerful motif within *M.Salib* is the portrayal of familial decisions as pronouncements made by both parents. It was their combined decision to name him Salib, to raise him in proper Coptic traditions, to betroth him to a relative, and to insist, through punishment, that he conform to his expected societal roles. Even the passersby before whom Salib spoke his insults were reluctant to punish him, out of respect to his parents. Here, one detects moralizing undertones within the text and subtle suggestions about the church's stance on marriage. In the Ottoman period, divorce was not easily authorized by the Coptic Church.[82] Throughout the empire, Christians and Jews frequently turned to sharīʿa courts to adjudicate their divorces, which, particularly for Orthodox Christians, were more difficult to acquire through communal channels.[83] Aware of increasing violations to its canons, the church made greater efforts to preserve marital sanctity; as suggested in the martyrology, joint parental decisions and harmonious relations were posited as expected, normative conduct among the faithful.

So while the narrator highlights the hero's courage in the face of Muslim harassment—an element of the story that likely roused his audiences—the coded subtext of Salib's Christian family, their internal disputes, and the integrity of his parents' marriage emerge as noteworthy. Indeed, perhaps as much as his commitment to Christ, it was Salib's desire to escape the burden of familial and social expectations that led him to seek his own death. Salib could not imagine abandoning devotion to his heavenly family for a mortal existence restricted by societal demands. Conversely, his parents could not forgo their desire to have offspring who would help sustain their customs and livelihood. These intrafamilial tensions complicate the assumption that a martyrology written during a period of presumed oppression would be inclined to glorify all Christians and disparage all Muslims. The protagonist's decision to seek martyrdom was shaped by pressures, reminiscent of the daily burdens felt by Copts as they attempted to preserve their faith and community. Ultimately, Salib's fortitude represents defiance to such challenges.

Muslim or Christian? Fluid Identities

According to Mark Swanson, the lines dividing Christians and the "other" are often clearly drawn within Arab Christian martyrological literature.[84] In that sense, one of the more remarkable elements of Salib's hagiography is the virtual absence of moral judgment in the narrator's descriptions. As the story progresses, many individuals are introduced without reference to their religious affiliation or comment on their actions.[85] Audiences are left to decide how to react to generic terms like "believers" and "nonbelievers." If a character is Muslim, even an official representative, he or she is not intrinsically portrayed in a negative light. These characters serve as witnesses to the life, death, and mission of the saint and to the supernatural powers that backed him.

The mob in Salib's hometown, before whom he pronounces his initial defamation, are the first group of such witnesses. The narrator refers to them as "non-Christians" who were passing through, either on a military campaign or a mission (*ḥamla*). Their behavior is perplexing. Although they first capture Salib because of his offensive insults, they immediately release him. However, as Salib utters more insults, they become possessed with a "satanic jealousy" (*ghīra shayṭāniyya*) and decide to take him to the local ruler.[86] One could read the narrator's phrase "satanic jealousy" as indicative of malicious intent, yet it seems that for a time these observers were willing to give Salib the benefit of the doubt. They have allegedly witnessed a crime under Islamic law, yet they act with noticeable restraint. Only when he reiterates these insults in front of the ruler and numerous other witnesses is he physically attacked by surrounding mobs.[87]

Shortly thereafter, the narrator introduces the jailer and his wife; they are the second married couple in the text. One assumes that they are Muslim, although no mention is made of their religion. The couple witnesses the miraculous powers working through this seemingly ordinary man. The jailer chains Salib, only to repeatedly find his chains broken and the martyr walking about his cell. The idea that this martyr could not be tied down by earthly shackles is reintroduced in prison, much as it was noted when he was chained by his parents. As for the jailer's curious wife, she sneaks a peek at the prisoner during the night and observes him talking to an illuminated woman (presumably the Virgin Mary). Although it is stated that the jailer's wife had no comprehension of their cryptic dialogue, she was nevertheless deeply moved by this vision.

From these details, one detects that the narrator consciously split the couple's two experiences. Each was privy to different aspects of the martyr's supernatural abilities, thus their conversation is unusually dramatic. As the couple shares their encounters, in awe and amazement, the husband concludes that their prisoner is a magician (*saḥḥār*).[88] Consequently, and possibly out of fear of his powers, the jailer and his wife are emboldened not only to offer Salib his freedom but also to reveal their intentions of escaping. He rejects their offer, however, for he seeks spiritual freedom, the freedom that would unite him with his heavenly family. In contrast, the jailer and his wife seek a different kind of freedom. Trapped by their societal roles, facing a powerful sorcerer, and perhaps feeling confined by their own (read Muslim) religious values, the couple, as the story subtly implies, were tempted to "escape" to Christianity. They had been quite moved, according to the text, by his miracles and were persuaded by the divine power backing him. In its entirety, this trope mimics—to a large extent—New Testament passages detailing the imprisonment of Paul and Silas, and their interaction with a jailer and his family, who adopt Christianity on account of witnessing the miraculous.[89] While the words "Muslim" and "Christian" are never used in *M.Salib*'s subplot, these witnesses' reaction reveals the narrator's and perhaps his audience's conviction that, particularly in face of a Copt's paranormal skills, nonbelievers can act with kindness and compassion, and that they are "redeemable."

A similar exchange occurs when the officer in charge of Salib on the boat trip from Upper Egypt to Cairo witnesses apparitions and conversations between the martyr and the Virgin Mary. Here, the narrator implies that it is this experience that moves the officer to ask a group of believers to aid Salib on their arrival in Cairo.[90] Not only does the officer approach these Christians; he also makes a persuasive plea on behalf of his prisoner, reporting his lack of financial means and support. Indirectly, the guard's kindness is juxtaposed with that of the helpful Christians. The narrator describes the Christians as joyous in receiving Salib and kind in their generosity toward him; they are widely praised for their charity. Immediately, in another act of compassion, the guard takes Salib to see his sister and bid her farewell. It is only after these episodes are concluded that the guard finally brings Salib to face his judges.

In these passages, no negative words are used to decry the passersby, the jailer, his wife, or the officer. Their behavior, whether motivated by kindness or supernatural forces, seems remarkable in a narrative where the protagonist is ultimately condemned by Muslim state officials. An intentional separation exists between those who make the judgment of death and incite violence against the martyr and those ordinary individuals (fictive or real) who carry out their duties in the most compassionate way.[91] Furthermore, through a careful representation of most Muslim characters, the homiletic intonations of this text become clearer. While the church signaled to believers that they must be willing to sacrifice themselves for their faith, this text indicated that they should also be conciliatory toward the majority of Muslims, toward nonbelievers, who are represented (if not idealized) as humane.[92] *M.Salib*, in this regard, appears typical of earlier Arabic (as opposed to Greek) neo-martyrdoms, which, according to Sidney Griffith, not only "edify, but [instruct] Christians in how they should think about the religious challenges of Islam which daily confronted them."[93] In effect, through these tropes, the church may have been suggesting survival tactics for Copts living in this dominant Muslim culture.

Prosecution or Persecution: Conflicting Views of Martyrdom

Much like Peter of Capitolias, an Arab neo-martyr killed under the Umayyad Caliph al-Walid (705–715), Salib sought his own death by provoking Muslim passersby and insulting their faith.[94] Still, *M.Salib* depicts a Copt who presumably lived under the rule of an oppressive Islamic state but experienced no confrontation with a Muslim individual or official prior to his arrest. This lack of direct, antagonistic encounters is generally typical of the Arabic neo-martyr genre, as opposed to its Greek and Balkan counterpart, in which Muslims often seek out Christians to victimize.[95] Indeed, the lines between Muslims and Christians become clearer only when *M.Salib*'s narrator introduces characters who are part of the judicial system.[96] Moreover, almost to the letter, the description of Salib's treatment within the Mamluk legal structure is identical in Ibn Iyas's account and in *M.Salib*. After the initial offense was committed, Salib was taken to either a ruler (*M.Salib*) or a judge in his local district (Ibn Iyas's version). There, he was confronted with his crime, and he confessed. Subsequently, he was sent to Cairo for further hearings, first facing a ḥākim, as he is known in the Coptic-Arabic text (Amīr Tumanbay al-Dawadar in Ibn Iyas's account), then the sultan, then back to the amīr. At the residence of the latter, a meeting of judges was convened to determine Salib's fate.[97] The judges concurred that he should be executed, and the execution is recounted in similar fashion by both *M.Salib* and Ibn Iyas. As such, it is more than likely that the sequence of judicial steps accurately reflects how a criminal accused of blaspheming Islam was treated in this historical context.[98]

The presumption in Salib's martyrology, moreover, is that the accused actually and even willingly committed the crime without any sabotage by his accusers. This, once again, stands in contrast to most Balkan accounts, wherein neo-martyrs are either falsely accused of insulting Islam or of blaspheming the Prophet Muhammad, or tricked into publicly professing their Christian faith.[99] These coincidental martyrs were in the wrong place at the wrong time, but their bravery is nevertheless applauded.[100] On the whole, the neo-martyrdom genre embellishes the courage of its heroes and, in the process, insists on detailing the judicial processes used to condemn them. Neo-martyrs, including Salib, gain more credibility when they must defend themselves multiple times before numerous Muslim judges and rulers. In a manner reminiscent of antique and late antique martyrologies, these narratives illustrate the tenacity with which true Christians hold to their faith.

Here, Salib's life story and his exchanges with accusers evoke their sixteenth-century setting as well as the biblical trials of Jesus. In a stylized manner, Salib's life represents *imitatio Christi*: he is named "Cross"; he is a carpenter; he is nailed to a cross; he is judged in front of multiple arbitrators. Conversely, the depiction of the Muslim judicial system is relevant not in its brutality, per se, but in how it lends authenticity to Salib's story. The narrator, for instance, knows that his audience is aware of an Egyptian judicial system that includes a "sultan" or a "king" and sharīʿa judges. His audience no doubt was also familiar with the fact that in the Mamluk period, Copts or Coptic converts found guilty of violating Islamic law were sometimes executed by crucifixion. Thus historical and contemporary images are prominently contrasted, and the depiction of verbal exchanges in *M.Salib* both resembles and diverges from the trials of Jesus.[101] In biblical and hagiographic narratives, witnesses are brought forth, and the accused is asked to respond to the charges. However, while the Bible emphasizes Jesus' innocence in the face of false accusations, the narrator of Salib's hagiography, as noted, never casts doubt on the martyr's guilt:

> And they brought [Salib] to one of the rulers in the land of Egypt and they stood him in front of the ruler and brought to him [the ruler] the books and letters which they had written regarding what the pure one had spoken in the lands of al-Sa'id and he asked him, saying, "Oh Christian one, did you truly speak those words that they have alleged against you? Tell me the truth or else I will bring upon you the harshest of tortures." Upon hearing these words, the martyr derived strength from the Holy Spirit and made the noble confession, saying courageously and with little fear of the torture with which they had threatened him, "Everything they have spoken about me regarding the religion of Christ is true, for there is no God in heaven or on earth, except Jesus Christ."[102]

Whether this dialogue actually took place or whether a modest carpenter would have been so defiant in the presence of a Mamluk official cannot be known. Ibn Iyas's chronicle certainly does not give any indication of such an exchange. Once again, it is not the accuracy of the encounter but its dramatic retelling that was important to Coptic audiences. The story is consistent with similarly emotional encounters related in the Bible and in other hagiographies, all of which intended to signal specific reactions among listeners familiar with the genre.[103]

Following the above exchange, Salib was sent to the sultan and offered reprieve in exchange for his conversion to Islam. Salib's refusal prompted the sultan to send him to the judges so that they could hear his testimony and make a ruling.[104] In this scene, by forcing Salib to another confession, the biographer foretells the martyrdom of the saint in the most conclusive way, thereby fulfilling the expectations of his audiences. In many regards, these contests between the saint in one corner and the Islamic judicial system in another, retold in colloquial language, are more striking than later descriptions of torture and death.

In these encounters, Muslim authorities ask Salib to recant his "inappropriate" words, but Salib stands by his words, upholds his Christian faith, and even refuses the sultan's entreaties to convert to Islam. Curiously, then, the mystery of Salib's precise offense lingers in the Coptic-Arabic text. According to Ibn Iyas, Salib's crime was speaking "criminal words" against the Prophet Muhammad; conversely, Salib's "confession" in the hagiography does not necessarily vilify the Prophet (*sabb al-rasūl*) but entails what Muslim jurists call "associationism" (*shirk*), tantamount to "vilification of God" (*sabb Allah*).[105] Could this discrepancy be accidental? Salib's statements in the martyrology would have been considered an act of apostasy—a crime punishable by death—if made by a Muslim, yet it is not clear in the sources whether dhimmīs were supposed to be punished for uttering such words.[106] Could it be that Salib was executed merely for professing his Christian faith? This too is unlikely. A careful reading of Salib's martyrology and Ibn Iyas's narrative shows that the two accounts do not actually conflict regarding the nature of his crime; rather, each text concentrates on different aspects of the event. Ibn Iyas focuses on Salib's crime and punishment. The martyrology, on the other hand, calls attention to Salib's bravery, to those utterances that are inoffensive to Islam, and to his steadfastness in remaining Christian, particularly in his resistance to offers of conversion. *M.Salib* explicitly acknowledges that Salib spoke inappropriate words but does not specify these words; rather, the author depicts Salib's "confession" through statements that illustrate his religious devotion.

This choice indicates that the narrator had a significant degree of awareness about the type of "crime" that Salib committed and its possible consequences. It also suggests—along with the colloquial tone of the text—that the narrator anticipated that the martyrology would be read aloud in churches throughout Egypt, and sanitized the language accordingly. This was certainly the case with earlier Coptic-Arabic texts.[107] Here, Salib's ambiguous words can be contrasted with those of Greek and Balkan neo-martyrs who were portrayed, by their hagiographers, as vehement defenders of Christianity against Islam and its Prophet. One known example is of the Greek Orthodox martyr-monk St. Michael, from the Mar Sabas Monastery near Bethlehem: standing before the Umayyad Caliph 'Abd al-Malik (685–705), Michael pronounced that the Prophet Muhammad was "neither an apostle, nor a prophet, but a deceiver."[108] In an Ottoman-era case of a Bulgarian monk who faced charges of blaspheming Islam, the accused shouts, "Your false Prophet Muhammad is a teacher of perdition, a friend of the devil, and an apostate of God. His teaching is satanic and you unprofitable servants have believed in him and are destined for hell unless you believe in Christ the true God."[109] The absence of such invective within *M.Salib* clues the reader to an unusual tension between the martyr's actions and the narrator: while elaborate dialogues between the accused and his judges are provided, the goal of the narrator seems neither to praise Salib's crime nor to encourage his audience to commit illegal acts.[110] Rather, the narrator provides one albeit Christian depiction of the incident in order to recapture select images of Salib's heroism. Care is taken to avoid insulting the Prophet Muhammad or his mission, thus *M.Salib* achieves a balance of testifying to the Coptic faith without rousing intercommunal hatred or conflict.

Partisan literature, both in the early Islamic and Ottoman eras, proliferated among Christians because it signified a sense of "liberation" from an oppressive, dominant culture.[111] However, *M.Salib* seems much more open to constructive or at least neutral relations with Muslims. In sixteenth-century Egypt, it made little sense for the church to foment hatred against a dominant religious group and jeopardize their community's already fragile security. Moreover, communal leaders were generally conservative when it came to relations with outsiders, as they feared provoking local rulers. The Coptic case offers an interesting foil to the Balkans of the sixteenth and seventeenth centuries, where an "age of conversion" was ongoing and where approximately 40 percent of the population had adopted Islam.[112] The Greek, Serbian, and Bulgarian Orthodox Churches saw daily conversions from within their ranks and experienced a gradual erosion of their dominant demographic status. As such, their neo-martyrologies needed to be far more potent and persuasive. Gruesome descriptions of torture, the venomous words used to insult Islam and Muslims, and the grisliness of deaths by hanging, dismemberment, impalement, stoning, burning, drowning, stabbing, and shooting all warn their audiences against conversion to Islam and against displaying any consideration toward this "heathen" religion and its practitioners.[113] In Salib's story, set several decades after the Copts' own "age of conversion," there is no overtly diabolical Muslim. The narrator intentionally distinguishes between those who incite violence and make the judgment of death and those regular folk who carry out their duties. While the text hopes to discourage conversion by promoting a glossy picture of Coptic heroism, the narrator also realizes that ordinary Copts—who are already committed to their faith—need encouragement and guidance in their day-to-day dealings with Muslim neighbors.

Conclusions

The only point on which *M.Salib* and Ibn Iyas markedly differ is the fate of Salib's burned body. The martyrology insists that no harm came to the corpse during the burning. This was a true miracle to Coptic audiences, one that validated his suffering and sacrifice. Ibn Iyas's chronicle, however, indicates not only that the corpse was burned but also that its remains were subsequently "eaten by dogs," another degradation that he claims Salib (or, rather, his body) had to endure.[114] What is interesting in this context is that, although the two accounts make different claims, both narrators regard the corpse's fate as an affirmation of their own perceptions. The legacy of Salib's body—desecrated in Ibn Iyas's account, but, in *M.Salib*, divided into relics to be distributed throughout Egypt—shows how one man was remembered as a criminal by one community and considered a hero by the other.[115] For Copts, this martyrdom reflected the continuous commitment of one of their own to Christ, in death and in the hereafter.[116] Together, the oral performance of Salib's martyrology accompanying the dissemination of his relics to churches throughout Egypt, to be held and touched by the believers, offered a powerful validation of the Coptic faith.

Read within its historical context, *M.Salib* reveals important, if indirect, clues about the Coptic Church's intent to counter Roman Catholic propaganda in the early Ottoman period. Copts and their Eastern Orthodox cohorts were frequently deemed by European missionaries as lesser Christians or simply as heretical. Their religious practices appalled Catholic missionaries and, in later centuries, their Protestant counterparts, who questioned everything from Coptic circumcision to their customs of fasting and baptism.[117] The Jesuits Eliano and Rodriguez, who led most of the Catholic expeditions to Egypt in the sixteenth century, seemed "inflexible and inquisitorial" toward Copts and generally inconsiderate of their local needs and problems.[118] Perhaps the missionaries' contempt elicited a defensive reaction within different Coptic ranks, particularly among the clergy. Copts took pride in their history of martyrdom, and this recent story had great potential to liven stale ones. Although there are few Coptic reports of their encounters with the Catholics, *M.Salib* hints at the potential relationship between martyrdom and the Copts' resistance to external religious assimilation.

The story can be especially appreciated in an era when the idea of any Copt acting in defense of his or her religion would have seemed virtually unthinkable. Two centuries earlier, in 1320, following the mob burning of churches all over Egypt, a group of Coptic monks decided to avenge these acts by plotting the destruction of Cairo. A number of Cairene districts were burned in the catastrophe that followed, and the long-term consequences for Copts were grave.[119] By the mid-fifteenth century, most churches in Egypt had been defiled or destroyed; thousands had been killed or had converted to Islam. So the combined motifs of bravery (or, at times, apparent foolishness), showmanship, and defiance made Salib a timely hero. In other words, Salib not only inspired Copts to be better Christians but also personified the best aspects of the Coptic character at a time when the church was ostensibly worried about defections. In emphasizing this point, Salib is presented as purposely seeking his death, an act that enhances his steadfastness.[120] Clerical (and later lay) leaders—through their promotion of various religious texts and practices—sought a stronger formulation of confessional characteristics. Their goal of communal unity is apparent even though the multiplicity of perspectives represented within Salib's neo-martyrdom also suggests that church ideals on marriage, sexuality, and celibacy may have been contested.

Salib's story exemplifies how martyrologies, which are inherently structured to memorialize suffering and persecution, can be indicative of a more complex historical context. However, to perceive this story simply as a form of opposition to Roman Catholicism or to the threat of conversion to Islam perhaps overlooks what Abudacnus attempted to capture in the epigraph to this chapter: the emotional attachment to particular saints and the complex nature of religious belief.

Ultimately, the overall efforts to preserve the faith would bear some fruit in the late seventeenth and early eighteenth centuries, when attention to Coptic religious life became more prominent and productive, to be seen in our discussion of the cult of St. Dimyana and the pilgrimage to Jerusalem. By that point, though, clerical authority had begun to wane with the rise of archons as the main patrons of Coptic religious life.

3

A Female Martyr Cult in the Nile Delta

Dimyana and the Forty Virgins

The relationship between the divine and mortal, the supernatural and mundane, clearly surfaces in the cult of the saints, whether in the context of Christianity, Judaism, Islam, or Buddhism. Believers have historically brought questions about family, health, relationships, fertility, and even politics to saintly intercessors. What made saints remarkable was the perception that they formed a special conduit to the divine, a status lacking in other mortals. In early Christian times, martyrs were deemed model saints, but after Christianity was officially embraced by the Roman Empire, notions of asceticism, self-sacrifice, sexual purity, and abstinence took root as the new standards of piety.[1] In due course, saints' cults grew and were reinforced through material and spiritual patronage. Relics, including clothing, weapons, body parts, and—in Eastern churches—icons, were valued as a link to the supernatural. Apparitions and healings raised a saint's profile, and although miracles were understood to come from the divine, holy objects and holy places were believed to exude divine power.[2] Patronage of religious shrines further supported popular devotional practices. Pilgrimages became annual events that drew the community into collective acts of worship. Festivals emerged as a vehicle for political, economic, and cultural exchange, and as a place where scriptural authority intersected with popular conceptions of piety. As a space for the "chaotic and liminal," they allowed for social and physical boundaries to be trespassed and for spiritual authority to be challenged and altered.[3] Moreover, a saint's hagiography came to be seen as a reliquary of her literary body.

Hagiographies may initially have been written to record historical events or to promote local cults, but over time, they also became active texts capable of transforming listeners and of being transformed by them.[4]

More "recent" stories like Salib's were by and large uncommon in the Ottoman era, since the Coptic Church traditionally favored martyrologies from the antique and late antique periods. From the sixteenth to the eighteenth centuries, dozens of these familiar tales, set during the rule of Roman Emperor Diocletian, were commissioned for copying by Coptic clergy and archons, filling church, monastic, and private libraries throughout Egypt. What follows is an analysis of Dimyana, a female saint ostensibly martyred during Diocletian's rule whose cult became noticeably popular in Ottoman Egypt. By investigating how the church expressed its social and religious mores through her hagiography and by examining the involvement of the laity at Dimyana's annual festival, I explore how piety and intracommunal relations intersected through the act of veneration. I focus on Dimyana here because more historical information about her hagiography and cult than about any other saint has survived, allowing us to construct a fuller picture of Coptic religious life.

Expanding Lay Authority in the Seventeenth Century

Otto Meinardus was the first to recognize the emergence and spread of Dimyana's cult in the early Ottoman period, during what he called an "unproductive time in the history of the Coptic Church."[5] The earliest evidence of Dimyana's festival and written hagiography does stem from the seventeenth and eighteenth centuries. As opposed to Meinardus's characterization of stagnancy, however, this period saw dynamic transformations in Coptic leadership and in communal priorities. In general, scholars of Ottoman Egypt have described the political landscape of this era as chaotic: soldier revolts from other parts of the empire regularly spilled onto Egyptian soil, and the decentralized tax structure undermined Istanbul's hold on Egypt while empowering local figures.[6] Frequent rebellions also took place against Ottoman governors in Cairo. In 1605, a mutinous faction killed Ibrahim Pasha, who posthumously earned the nickname "al-Maqtūl" or "the Slain." Leaders of another rebellion in 1609 named an "alternate sultan," which signified Egypt's growing detachment from the Ottoman center. At the restoration of order, this event was dubbed "the second Ottoman conquest of Egypt."[7] In the mid-seventeenth century, rivalries between ranking beys instigated conflict over political influence and, of course, over Egypt's lucrative resources. During this time, as we recall, Coptic archons had become the wealthy clients of rising military households.

In this turmoil, the Coptic clerical leadership fared poorly. Earlier examples revealed how in disputes over Catholic influence and marital rights, Murqus V was challenged and imprisoned and an alternate patriarch was named in his place. Perhaps not coincidentally, this mutiny coincided with the 1609 rebellion against Egypt's Ottoman governor. Murqus's successor, Yu'annis XV, was allegedly poisoned in 1629 by a wealthy archon from the town of Abnub in Upper Egypt, who became angered at the patriarch's rebuke of his polygamous practices.[8] The reign of another patriarch, Murqus VI (1646–1656), was also tumultuous. Animosity between this patriarch and a powerful archon, al-Muʿallim Bishara (ca. 1650), weakened the patriarch's position among coreligionists. Moreover, in his first few years, Murqus VI issued an order that Coptic monks abandon their practice of living outside designated monasteries. In resistance, one monk wrote a letter to the Ottoman governor accusing the patriarch of committing physical abuse and even homicide against the monks. The patriarch was arrested but later released after a group of "elders of the state" (*akābir al-dawla*, ostensibly archons) paid his suretyship; he would move to Upper Egypt and spend years "forcing Copts" to give him donations, seemingly to repay his debts.[9] Although the patriarch was accused of hoarding his wealth, an inheritance deed later showed that he was indebted to *Diwān al-Jawāli,* the Ottoman government's local arm for collecting the jizya.[10] When he died, as one Coptic manuscript reports, a number of believers wondered, "Who needs patriarchs?"[11] The highest clerical seat would be unfilled for the next four years, hinting at a serious vacuum in clerical authority.

New waves of Catholic missionaries and fresh meddling from European powers further highlighted the vulnerability of indigenous clergymen in the Ottoman Empire. In 1657, for instance, the Greek patriarch of Istanbul, Parthenius III (1656–1657), was executed when Ottoman authorities became concerned about his "suspicious" contacts with Russian and Romanian princes.[12] Throughout the seventeenth century, Franciscan and Capuchin missionaries began to establish permanent bases in Egypt, provoking more dissent over unification and conversion.[13] As Coptic sources indicate, during the second half of the seventeenth century, "bishops, priests, and laity" frequently rebelled against the patriarch's authority.[14] Over time, patriarchs became more isolated and paranoid: in 1672, when the German traveler Vansleb visited Mittawus IV in his Cairene headquarters at Harat al-Rum, his virtual house arrest seemed scandalous:

> I went to visit the Patriarch of the Copties, one of my best friends; and because I had often intreated him to come and dine with me, I reiterated the same intreaty now again, but he answered me, that he had not been out of his house a year before for fear of the Turks. He complained that all the Patriarchs of the other sects had the liberty to go about the town,

> without fear of being disturbed by any, to visit whom they pleased, and to travel whither they lifted [*sic*]; but he was so narrowly observed by the Turks, that he could not so much as go out of his house, nor talk with any of the other nations openly, much less travel into any other place, but he must give them a jealousy of plotting against the state, by this means his life would be in danger.[15]

Progressively, and partially to fill in the gap left by a weakening clerical leadership to which Vansleb alludes, archons became more involved in every aspect of Coptic religious life. Philanthropy was generally expected from Christian believers, particularly from the wealthy, and almsgiving was frequently deemed an "obligation" (*farḍ*) for Copts; but by financing and helping to organize religious rites, archons would also create new opportunities to influence popular piety. While one scholar has suggested that Ottoman-era archons supported a "nonreligious" culture within their community, one that curtailed the Coptic faith, this description errs in distinguishing between the "religious" and "secular" in this historical context.[16] Most archons never shied from supporting religious life, and some were even ordained deacons. As this chapter and the next will illustrate, by investing in pilgrimages, festivals, or manuscript reproduction, archons sought, much as their Armenian correlates did, to safeguard the "integrity and specific religious-cultural profile of their [community] because their own function within the multireligious and multiracial empire was predicated on their role as intermediaries between the state and [coreligionists]."[17] In a sense, through their patronage, archons matched and at times superseded clergymen in their religious and temporal authority. Before exploring these issues, however, I will first ask who Dimyana is and how her hagiography became prominent, as the answers to both questions help to explain why the laity in general and the archons in particular were drawn to her cult.

Sharing Dimyana's Story in Ottoman Egypt

Dimyana's hagiography was among the most widely copied during the Ottoman period, and her annual festival one of the most popular. When heard by Coptic men and women, this story of a nobleman's daughter surely evoked images of valor and heroism. The Coptic Church recognized only a handful of new saints in the centuries following the Islamic conquest of Egypt, and of these, few, if any, were female. To fill this void, Copts drew from earlier stories such as those of saints Barbara, Febronia, Marina, the Virgin Mary, and Dimyana. In the seventh and eighth centuries, the church had translated many Greek and Coptic hagiographies into Arabic, and in the process, stories were altered, modified, and embellished to suit their new milieu. Coptic-Arabic texts came to emphasize their Egyptian landscape, include familiar places and locales, and even echo, at times, "orientalized" themes.[18] It was during those early Islamic centuries, according to Arietta Papaconstantinou, that the Coptic Church increasingly adopted the epithet of "Church of the Martyrs" and saw its roots in the Diocletian era as useful for preserving the Coptic faith within an Islamicizing culture.[19] It is unsurprising, then, that stories like Dimyana's continued to be popular in the early centuries of Ottoman rule; for one, they would have been spiritually uplifting for Copts who feared their community's demise under new rulers. But they also highlighted culturally familiar themes—such as, in Dimyana's case, gender segregation—which in effect drew attention to a lifestyle that was associated both with Coptic traditions (i.e., monasticism) and with Muslim practices.

There is surprising consistency and uniformity in the reproduction of hagiographic texts in the Ottoman period, suggesting that they were copied from a single source, perhaps the Cairene patriarchal headquarters or the Monastery of St. Antony.[20] From there, manuscripts would be distributed to churches or patrons who requested them from all over Egypt, and this mode of cultural transmission seems typical of this period. In Ottoman Anatolia, for instance, Muslim pilgrims traveled to the convent of Haci Bektaş and, on receiving the blessing of his shrine, visited the convent's impressive library to copy texts for their personal use; along their journey or back home, they shared these copies with other libraries.[21] The wealth of manuscripts produced in early modern Egypt among both Copts and Muslims might be related to the affordability of paper and to the existence of large numbers of copyists.[22] In the monasteries of Egypt, like those of other regions, scribes abounded, as monks commonly passed their days immersed in this activity.[23] Among the copies of Dimyana's hagiography that I have examined, little textual variation appears, indicating constancy in and supervision over its reproduction, and reflecting what Lucy-Anne Hunt calls a "chain of authoritative copying."[24] In these ways, the church partially (and perhaps indirectly) controlled her veneration by choosing which written version would be disseminated to the public.

However, in the Ottoman era, hagiographies were commissioned not only by or for clergymen but also quite often by archons.[25] These elites, by making available Dimyana's hagiography, facilitated the spread of her cult and her renown throughout Egypt. Among their patrons, hagiographies were recognized as a medium for preserving religious and cultural traditions. Ostensibly, the circulation of more copies meant that more people heard them, as public readings would have taken place at local parishes in addition to the saint's festival. There, a hagiography became part of a public performance wherein the community, as a whole, partook in the collective remembrance of this revered saint.[26] Over time, then, the story could serve as a vehicle for transforming established mores, and its repeated performance made it possible for official and folkloric or lay understandings of this saint to overlap.[27]

What was it, though, that drew people to her story? What made Dimyana an especially accessible model of piety to Ottoman Copts? The search for answers begins first with the Coptic-Arabic text that preserved her life during this era. According to her hagiography (hereafter cited as *M.Dimyana*),[28] Dimyana was the only child of Murqus, Roman governor of the Nile Delta province of Burullus, Za'farana, and Wadi al-Sisban.[29] Murqus loved his daughter dearly, for she was well mannered and "extremely beautiful in appearance" (*hasnat al-ṣūra fi'l-ghāya*).[30] When Dimyana was one year old, he had her baptized at a local monastery. Her family saw this as such a joyous event that a three-day feast was held to serve the poor and destitute. Although the text does not specifically mention Dimyana's mother, as is often typical of female virgin martyrologies, it notes that "*they* [my emphasis] raised her in the best way and taught her to read."[31] At the age of fifteen, contrary to her father's wishes, she refused to wed, declaring that she had promised herself to Christ. Murqus consented and also granted her request to build a "pleasant place" outside the city where she could live an ascetic life. Dimyana desired this retreat not only for worship but also to shelter herself from the ostensibly lustful eyes of young men (*urīdu maḥallan astatir fīhī 'an a'yun al-shabāb*). To satisfy his daughter, Murqus ordered the construction of a luxurious palace, built in only a few days, according to the text.[32] As soon as she settled in, along with forty of her closest female virgin companions, Murqus posted guards to protect them.[33]

Shortly thereafter, Diocletian promoted Murqus to governor of al-Farama, another Lower Egyptian province.[34] Meanwhile, Diocletian had begun his notorious persecutions against the Christians. His first act was to summon government officials and ask them to prove their loyalty by praying to the Roman gods, an order with which Murqus complied.[35] At this point, *M.Dimyana* begins to situate itself within other Coptic hagiographic narratives: allegedly, while Murqus bowed to Diocletian's orders, others refused and were punished accordingly, through torture and martyrdom. These dissenters—a venerable troop of Coptic saints—included Theodore (Tadrus) Stratelates, the Roman general; Theodore the Eastern (al-Mashriqi); Justus (Yustus), son of King Numerianus;[36] Victor (Boqtor, son of Diocletian's vizier Romanos);[37] and Claudius (Iqludiyus).[38] Their presence shows that *M.Dimyana*'s author made a deliberate attempt to situate her life within its "authentic" Diocletian-era context.

When news came of her father's betrayal, Dimyana and her companions marched to al-Farama and persuaded Murqus to retract his breach of faith. Before long, Murqus headed to Antioch and reprimanded Diocletian for his pagan beliefs. The emperor, unnerved at the betrayal of his "dear" friend (*kāna a'az al-aṣḥāb*), consulted his vizier Romanos about an appropriate punishment. Romanos, whose son Victor had been earlier executed for a similar crime, recommended that Murqus be swiftly beheaded for re-professing his Christianity.[39] The faithful vizier later informed Diocletian that Dimyana was to blame for his friend's disloyalty and, therefore, for his execution. On hearing this news, Diocletian sent a military battalion to punish the unruly daughter. The hagiography then describes the severe tortures and multiple deaths that she experienced; as typical of Diocletian-era Coptic hagiographies, the saint was resuscitated through divine intervention following each gruesome death.[40] Finally, she and the forty virgins were beheaded, along with thousands of bystanders who had converted to Christianity after being inspired by Dimyana's example.

The text then discloses how Dimyana's shrine came to be constructed in the Nile Delta by order of Emperor Constantine (274–337). Allegedly, Constantine was so moved when he heard Dimyana's story that he sent his mother, Empress Helena (ca. 250–330) to Egypt.[41] Helena found the bodies of Dimyana and her companions to be unharmed and uncorrupted, so they were collected, wrapped in linens, and stored in a crypt that was locked with Constantine's seal. Dimyana's shrine was then built atop her former palace, which was demolished under Helena's orders. After its completion, the shrine was consecrated by the Coptic Patriarch Iskandarus I (312–328).[42] It should not be lost on the reader that this patriarch defended Christian "orthodoxy" against Arianism in the fourth century and was closely backed in this endeavor by Emperor Constantine.[43] Once again, his inclusion in the hagiography reveals that special care was taken to validate the historicity of Dimyana's story and to vouch for the people involved in building her shrine. In this way, later believers would be assured that her tomb was authentic and blessed by the church.

Generally, Dimyana's story is comparable to other Coptic martyrologies and features a marked tension between family, violence, sexuality, and religion.[44] Unlike most martyrologies set in the Diocletian era, however, hers has no known Coptic or Greek-language counterpart; that is, her story was available to Ottoman-era audiences and is available to us only in Arabic. The language used is predominantly Egyptian colloquial, which would have made the story easily accessible. Her hagiography was allegedly transcribed from Coptic to Arabic by Yuhanna, Bishop of Burullus, possibly a fourteenth-century figure; his motivation—to revive Dimyana's story and cult—is detailed in the prologue:[45]

> I was Bishop of Burullus and I had always attended the Church in Za'farana. I saw that it was in ruin because of the passing of time and the neglect of people. Thus it came to my mind that I should investigate the lives of the martyrs of this church. After some time passed, as I thought more about this matter, I came up with an idea which is that I sought to see the hagiographies of the martyrs who inhabited this church and to

> know their story [*qaḍiyyatihim*]. More time passed and I was unable either to eat or sleep because of my preoccupation, when a saintly monk from Dayr al-Mayma[46] came to me. He carried old and damaged books from that church. . . . He said, "Father, take these books in order to prepare the orders of the church since you are our father and have authority over this church." . . . I searched the books and found the orders of the church, in both Coptic and Arabic. While I searched, I [also] found the desired story [*al-khabar al-maṭlūb*], the hagiography [*sīrat*] of the chaste and pure martyr-saint Dimyana. . . . I began to transcribe it, as it had been written in the handwriting of a boy [*ghulamān*] from the slaves of Julius al-Aqfahsi, whose name was Ikhristodolo.[47]

Here, the reference to Julius al-Aqfahsi and his slave hints to the story's possible origins and reveals that the hagiography may have once existed in Coptic or Greek. Coptic martyrdoms are often grouped within the same literary cycle, since they share plotlines, including the martyrs' "superhuman fortitude under torture," and the repetitive mention of the same characters.[48] In the Diocletian-era or "Antioch" cycle, this common character is often Julius, a "sympathetic scribe" with access to a martyr's private thoughts who was eventually martyred himself.[49] His inclusion indicates the hagiographer's familiarity with Julius's status in parallel stories and confirms, as Saphinaz-Amal Naguib points out, that authors of Coptic and Coptic-Arabic hagiographic literature paid great attention to textual "authentication"; during this process, "original" texts were attributed to recognized (if invented) authors whose presence added "authority and credibility" to later hagiographies.[50]

Another important clue to the origins of Dimyana's text stems from the frequent mention of Diocletian's vizier Romanos. The Coptic *Martyrdom of Victor the General*, arguably the most central hagiographic text in the Antioch cycle, confirms that Romanos was Victor's father and that the father had ordered his own son's death.[51] This trope was used by *M.Dimyana*'s author, although the latter diverges slightly from the original story, wherein Victor was prosecuted and tortured in Antioch but killed in Egypt.[52] References to various Nile Delta monasteries within Dimyana's hagiography also hint to a post-Constantinian authorship date. Although asceticism had been practiced in Egyptian deserts since the earliest decades of Christianity, formal monastic communities were unknown before the fourth century. Rich clues as these may be, ultimately it is difficult to draw reliable historical information from Diocletian-era legends, as they copied freely from one another, and generally scholars have concurred that their most historically reliable contributions were usually geographical—that is, a description of where in Egypt the martyr cult existed.[53] A close hagiographic exegesis, in all cases, is deserving of separate investigation and is beyond the scope of our current discussion. My hope here is that with this backdrop, we can better understand how Dimyana's story might have been heard and interpreted by Ottoman-era audiences and how the repeated transcription of her Arabic hagiography reflects her popularity.

Dimyana and the Forty Virgins: Life and Parable

Dimyana's story opens a window into conceptions of gender, family, and sacrifice, particularly among Christians in the Ottoman world. In general, we know little about Christian piety in the Ottoman Empire, especially as it relates to women. Suraiya Faroqhi has offered preliminary observations on the Greek Orthodox nun-saint (Philothei) in sixteenth-century Athens, and the life and legacy of the eighteenth-century Maronite nun Hindiyya 'Ujaymi has received some scholarly attention.[54] Recently, Akram Khater has undertaken an important project that explores the religious worldviews of Aleppan female devotees in the eighteenth century, focusing on activities that were partially prompted by Catholic missionary movements in the Levant.[55] However, in contrast to these real women who shaped events in their own times, and in a handful of cases left behind self-authored documents, Dimyana influenced popular beliefs through her "ancient" hagiography and at her shrine. Coptic devotees left few records of their attitudes toward this saint; thus an investigation of her hagiography and later of her festival allow us to surmise why her story was promoted by clerical and lay leaders and how it may have been heard by Ottoman audiences.

As glimpsed from earlier discussion, at the start of the hagiography, Dimyana is a self-assured young woman who appears to be in absolute control of her destiny and, arguably, of all those surrounding her. This type of female empowerment traditionally seen in Christian virgin martyrologies, as Gail Ashton argues, reveals the inherent "fissured and unstable" nature of hagiographic texts: they tend to embody both the authorial and patriarchal male voice and a "feminine voice that reveals itself differently," putting pressure on the masculine narration.[56] Hagiographies upheld a model of virtuosity and chastity, but they also painted their heroes and heroines as assertive and confident in their pursuit of martyrdom. Among female saints in particular, the Christian hagiographic tradition has often found ways to curb this potentially unbridled autonomy. Medieval European stories, for instance, advocated the ideal of an "enclosed" woman, whereby a male character (usually a father or suitor) attempts to restrict, imprison, and disable the saint and her female sexuality.[57] Some Coptic female martyrologies, like St. Barbara's, follow this model: Barbara's "pagan" father, who is arguably the "anti-Murqus," secludes his Christian daughter in a tower, hunts her down when she attempts to escape, and delivers her to her torturers and executioners.[58] But in Dimyana's case, Murqus readily accepts his daughter's desire to stay celibate. He not only agrees to build her a sanctuary for prayer but also allows her to live in a homosocial environment with forty female companions, an arrangement that openly rejects the desire or need for male presence. In this way, her story contrasts with Barbara's and also—on some level—with normative expectations of female dependence on patriarchal authority within the Ottoman cultural milieu. Moreover, her story, seems to parallel those elucidating the roles and expectations of Coptic nuns and monastics, rather than martyrs. Murqus, by financially supporting Dimyana, allows her to lead a life of piety, free from his charge and independent from any "husband-provider."[59] Isolated among her companions in a fortified palace, this heroine rejects marriage and stands forceful against male domination. Today and rather unsurprisingly, Dimyana and the forty virgins represent the dominant archetypes of female monastic practice within the Coptic community.

While the text depicts Dimyana as the typical Coptic protagonist who bravely faces the persecution of the evil Diocletian and his lackeys, in the course of her suffering and eventual martyrdom, she transforms into a more complex and dynamic heroine. Ultimately, she champions her faith through her verbal authority.[60] Her speeches and commentary pervade the text, highlighting strength in conversations with her virgin companions, her oppressors, and her father. Tempting as it may be to read Dimyana's eloquence as reflective of a contemporary reality, a historian must be careful in presuming that virgin-martyrologies mirrored existing patterns of female autonomy and empowerment. Representations of women's speech in hagiographies usually served as a reminder that heroines were "exceptional as well as exemplary for their audience," and Dimyana's exceptionality stems from the efficacy of her words.[61] As Maud McInerney maintains, "virgins are the most argumentative of all martyrs," and Dimyana tends to win all arguments, particularly those with her father.[62] Her speech is reinforced by the presence of the forty companions, who follow her loyally wherever she goes (even to the death), acting as a mostly silent Greek chorus.[63]

Still, diverging from other martyrologies, Dimyana's hagiography minimizes the emphasis on her virginity, a cultural ideal that would have been presumably valued by Ottoman-era audiences.[64] It appears secondary to the relationship with her father, a relationship that becomes a disruptive subtext within an otherwise typical narrative. Virgin martyrologies tend to depict a triangular struggle between the martyr, her male oppressor, and Christ. Often, the oppressor is not only the evil ruler who aims to soil her (metaphorical and literal) virginity but also a pagan family member: in the case of St. Barbara, a father, who has alternate plans for the aspiring heroine. However, rather than tormenting his daughter, Murqus acts as a loving parent. In fact, from the start of Dimyana's life, he places her in the path of faith and righteousness. At her request, Murqus leaves his daughter to enjoy her relationship with Christ and to abandon expected responsibilities like marriage and procreation. Thus competition for the virgin's attention emerges between a benevolent father and Christ.

To our modern sensibilities, Dimyana might appear as rather thankless toward a father who had given her unbridled autonomy to live as she wished. But a closer reading shows that Dimyana desperately sought balance between her faith and family. She questions Murqus's betrayal because she sees herself as Christ's bride and messenger first and earthly daughter as a close second. As we see below, while her supplication to Murqus demonstrates her role as a vessel of the divine, their dialogue seems like any ordinary rapport between father and daughter.[65] If understood purely as a literary ploy, the following scene, in which Dimyana successfully reconverts Murqus to Christianity, constitutes one of the most profound aspects of the story:

> And when the news [of Murqus's bowing to the idols] reached his daughter the Lady Dimyana, she leapt up hurriedly, accompanied by the forty [virgins], . . . and headed to al-Farama. She met with her father, who, on seeing her, rejoiced greatly, since it had been a while since he had departed from her. After he greeted her, she told him, "Father, what is this news that I heard about you, which put fear in my heart and hindered my slumber?" He responded, "What is it, my daughter?" She said to him: "I heard that you have left the religion of Christ, the strong God who has created and raised you, and that you prayed to the blind idols which are not worthy: [those] stones made by hands. . . . Look above, my father, and raise your gaze. Stare at the joy of the heavens and the beauty in the arrangement of the sun, the moon, and the stars and at how the heavenly dome filled with divine wisdom exists without support and above which the hosts of angels [roam]. . . . How did it cross your heart to do this? Know my father, that if you continue in this state of being, then I shall be a stranger to you in this world and in the next world, on the Day of Judgment. I shall deny you in the Valley of Jehoshaphat[66] in the midst of the dreaded judgment, and you will have no part nor share in the eternal birthright. This is my final word to you." On hearing this, her father came to consciousness as if he had been drunk and revived. At once, he screamed and cried, saying, "I am a sinner for what I have done, for I made the stones as my yoke and in Satan's house I prayed to them. Blessed be the hour that I saw you, my blessed daughter!"[67]

Their conversation becomes notable when placed in the context of this mostly fantastical martyrology, and it is followed by Murqus bidding his daughter farewell before he confronts Diocletian and faces eventual death. For Dimyana, the ultimate sacrifice is to save her father from eternal doom by, in effect, persuading him to die for his Christian faith. This act is selfish in that Dimyana thinks only of her commitment to Christianity but, at the same time, selfless in that she will soon lose her earthly father. Intentional or not, this narrative deemphasizes the story's mythic elements, such as Dimyana's elaborate tortures and multiple deaths, bringing audiences intimately closer to the saint. To find resolution for her most difficult dilemma, Dimyana convinces Murqus to join her in death. One important moral of this hagiography, then, to put it crudely, is: a family that dies together stays together, at least in the afterlife.

In essence, Christ dictates the dynamics of family relations. Dimyana's eloquence, boldness, and strength, while inspirational, all result in her death.[68] In a hagiography filled with hints of empowerment and agency, it is a male figure, Christ (and implicitly, here, the church acting with Christ's authority), who determines the limitations of female action and who brings about Dimyana's downfall. Hence, while it exudes one woman's empowerment, it is likely that a woman's speech and authority were being validated in the only viable means: as bound to her religious duties and obligations. In a poignant reminder, Robert Mills notes that a virgin martyr's agency should not be seen as a "force totally separate from the [patriarchal] order it opposes."[69]

Still, in the cultural context of Ottoman Egypt, where female authoritative speech was generally stifled, the representation of Dimyana's eloquence and valor cannot be easily dismissed. Significant here is Dimyana's role as a witness to her faith within a church that had few religious functions for women and in a society where non-Muslim women were often marginalized because of their gender and religion. Dimyana's story reflects a literary space for both men and women, but it may have also sanctioned an alternative role for women in broader society. As Leslie Peirce has shown for the Ottoman legal context, which strictly regulated the speech of female witnesses, women often looked to different and creative approaches to ensure that their voices were being heard.[70] In eighteenth-century Egypt, the period in which Dimyana's cult was notably popular, women increasingly participated in public economic roles.[71] In a sense, then, a popular hagiography infused with a strong female voice may have privileged if not partially legitimized women's involvement in society, even if channeled through a male scribe's writing and the church's agenda. In Dimyana, as we will later see, Coptic women could see a defiant role model, and although the hagiography reveals some of the church's traditional concerns regarding female chastity, one cannot presume that these ideals were the only ones embraced by the masses.

Roots of Dimyana's Cult

While the hagiography alleges that Dimyana's shrine was constructed by Empress Helena in the fourth century, Meinardus might be correct in assuming that her cult became widely active in the early Ottoman period. The seventeenth century is the earliest period for which there is evidence of her festival. Still, Dimyana's shrine was probably known to Copts as far back as the Mamluk era. The chronicler al-Maqrizi mentions a "Dayr Gimyana"[72] as part of a cluster of four Coptic monasteries in the Nile Delta.[73] As René-Georges Coquin notes, after the destruction of the nearby Dayr al-Maghtis in the fifteenth century, a popular destination in the Delta, pilgrims may have shifted their attention to the Dimyana shrine.[74] Another source alleges that a thirteenth-century quarrel over Coptic regional festivals took place between priests at the Delta town of Mit Damsis and those at the convent of St. Dimyana; the latter faction was disturbed by the popularity of a Fatimid-era neo-martyr, Mari Jirjis (St. George) al-Mizahim, whose relics were kept at their church, and apparently agitated for the removal of his remains to another parish.[75] That Dimyana became widely popular in the Ottoman era, however, is supported by the fact that at least one church in the Upper Egyptian town of Akhmim, dating to the sixteenth or seventeenth century, was named after the saint. There is also evidence of an ancient monastery near Balyana that adopted her as its patron saint sometime after the fifteenth century.[76] Since both churches were located far from the Nile Delta, their existence illustrates the breadth of her cult. As will be noted, icons of St. Dimyana also became noticeably popular during the Ottoman period.

Earlier, I alluded to the appeal of martyrdom narratives at a time when Coptic leaders looked to promote local saints who upheld and captured their communal identity. Indeed, some have suggested that Dimyana's story was invented following tensions between Copts and Melkites; her cult was possibly bolstered in order to counter the Greek Orthodox cult of St. Catherine, whose shrine was based in the Mount Sinai monastery.[77] A few similarities exist between the hagiography and iconography of Catherine and Dimyana, and in fact, one nineteenth-century traveler confused the two saints.[78] It was common for earlier Coptic hagiographies to indigenize Greek saints, depicting them in more recognizable terms.[79] Although sources do not divulge any disagreements between Copts and Melkites in the Ottoman era or hint at specific quarrels that might have prompted the creation of a new Coptic cult, non-Muslim communities were often embroiled in competition and sought to routinely distinguish themselves from one another in the eyes of Muslim political authorities.[80] Still, this theory is not well substantiated, since for the most part, the stories of Catherine and Dimyana have little in common beyond torture, martyrdom, and chastity—tropes that are a general hallmark of this genre.

The rise of Dimyana's cult appears more closely tied to residual Coptic-Muslim tensions from the Mamluk period. For one, it looks to have rivaled the cult of the female Muslim saint Sayyida Nafisa bint al-Hasan (762–824), the Prophet Muhammad's great-granddaughter who was buried in Fustat (Old Cairo) and whose veneration became particularly prominent during the Fatimid era (909–1171).[81] Mamluk-era miracles recorded for Sayyida Nafisa recount her successful intercessions on behalf of Coptic devotees, particularly barren women, and these stories were often used to strengthen the dominant Islamic religion against Coptic religious practices.[82] Nafisa's cult continued to be popular among Egyptians, and local saints and scholars were sometimes buried at or near her shrine.[83] In his lifetime, the known philanthropist ʿAbd al-Rahman Katkhuda al-Qazdaghli (d. 1776) renovated her mausoleum along with those of notable female saints Zaynab and Ruqayya.[84] Perhaps in challenging the Nafisa cult and in reinforcing their religious beliefs, Copts revived the story of a local girl—born, baptized, and raised on Egyptian soil—and promoted pilgrimage to her shrine in the Nile Delta, far from Nafisa's in Cairo.

Moreover, Mamluk-era tensions over the practice of an ancient springtime festival may have pushed Copts to discover an alternate geographic focus for their festivities. Until the fourteenth century, Copts observed the Festival of the Martyr (*ʿĪd al-Shahīd*) along the banks of the Nile in Cairo, on the eighth day of the Coptic month of Bashans (16 May). In this ancient celebration, the finger of a male Coptic martyr, symbol of a sacrificial gift, would be thrown into the river to assure the Nile's prosperity.[85] However, the festival's excessive revelry alarmed Mamluk officials, who, while profiting from taxes collected from the sale of alcohol, faced outrage from conservative ʿulamāʾ. This festival ended in 1355 when officials took the finger of the martyr, burned it, and threw its ashes into the Nile.[86] These events occurred at a time when Copts still constituted a visible part of the Egyptian population. Following the waves of Coptic conversions in the fourteenth century, many Coptic festivals died out, were suppressed, or remained confined to churches or homes.[87] Dimyana's feast occurs on the day commemorating the consecration of her church (12 Bashans / 20 May) rather than her martyrdom date (13 Tuba / 21 January) as was customary with most other saints, illustrating a deliberate decision to observe these festivities in the spring.

It was logical that Copts would move such a large, bustling, and potentially disruptive festival to a remote territory, at a distance from the eyes of conservative Muslim clerics. In the medieval period, many jurists had leveled criticisms against Christians, specifically Copts, accusing them of corrupting Muslims with their seemingly heterodox rituals.[88] Increasingly, Copts sought to disassociate many of their practices from Muslims in order to avoid censure or retaliation. Moreover, even for Muslim pilgrims, the veneration of saints outside major urban centers had become the norm. Christopher Taylor echoes this development in his study of the Qarafa cemetery-shrine, where he has shown that in Mamluk Egypt, this space—located just outside of Cairo's walls—allowed pilgrims to intermix openly, away from the eyes of the orthodox religious establishment.[89] Dina Rizk Khoury shows a similar pattern of "peripheralization" in eighteenth-century Ottoman Mosul, where there was also a gradual move toward the veneration of mausoleums near outer city walls.[90]

In Egypt, shared Muslim-Christian festivals continued to be observed; some celebrations centered on the Nile took place under the supervision of the Ottoman governor.[91] Gradually, however, Copts moved major festivals beyond the capital city. Further confirming these developments, Vansleb notes that an annual celebration for the flooding of the Nile, which coincided with the Coptic Feast of the Holy Cross (17 Tut / 27 September), was displaced against the wishes of the patriarch. He writes that the patriarch "was wont to perform this ceremony with great pomp and state; but because the Mahometans suffer them not to go in procession about the cities publicly, their priests observe this custom every one in his own village."[92] The Copts' self-policing in this particular case helps to explain why, by the Ottoman period, the Dimyana cult at its rural and remote Nile Delta destination had become one of the most significant Coptic festivals.

A Springtime Festival

Evidence for Dimyana's festival is somewhat sparse, and in scrutinizing the sources, one must be cautious in formulating definitive conclusions about annual traditions. For one, the perspectives of Coptic believers toward religious practices in the early modern period have rarely been self-documented. Details about the festival are mostly furnished by memoirs of European travelers, some of whom were Catholic missionaries attempting to convert Copts and, in the post-Reformation milieu, were generally biased against popular religious practices. Still, since they open a window onto little-known traditions, their writings should be carefully considered. It is my contention here that the laity were able to use Dimyana's festival for channeling an alternative veneration of this saint, one that was mostly independent of clerical supervision. Her annual celebration and cult also hint that the archons' financial contributions and political connections helped sustain Coptic religious life.

Historically, Coptic religious celebrations were notorious for their rambunctious practices. Pilgrims often came to a shrine because of its bustling festival, thus the Coptic Church has customarily attempted to exercise some control at these occasions.[93] To this end, a martyr's feast usually included a more structured or liturgical side. It was common that a homily would be read by a leading preacher, recounting the saint's sufferings and even describing miracles performed at her shrine.[94] A festival also featured the chanting of hymns in praise of the saint or of psalms whose words were believed to have healing powers.[95] These practices continued in Islamic Egypt, as evidenced by examples from the ninth century when at one active shrine, pilgrims chanted designated texts at various stations in the sanctuary.[96] Rituals performed in earlier centuries, in addition to new ones that were continuously added, became part of what defined a Coptic martyr festival in the Ottoman era.

In the medieval and Ottoman periods, most Muslim, Jewish, and Christian believers were too poor to make the pilgrimage to Mecca or Jerusalem, and thus they frequently visited nearby locales to partake of their blessings and to share in common celebrations.[97] This would also be the case for Copts, but aside from their proximity and their renowned celebratory atmosphere, what drew the faithful to local shrines like Dimyana's was a belief in those saints' supernatural ability and in the effectiveness of their intercessions. Through prayer and vow-making (*nadr*), believers hoped that the most powerful of these saints would intercede on their behalf and help them in times of need. Made daily, weekly, monthly, or annually, depending on geographic location, a pilgrimage was a journey to the "homes" of saints who were considered to be "extended family members" or patrons of whom one can ask favors.[98] The believers, in essence, took their concerns, problems, and offerings to the saints rather than (or in addition) to the divine.[99] This inherent heterodoxy embedded within the cult of the saints has been the point at which official and scriptural authority intersected and sometimes collided with popular practices.[100] Clerical leaders may have been divided about promoting cults like Dimyana's: on the one hand, veneration upheld the memory of these martyrs and strengthened the church's authority, but on the other, the lack of regulation allowed the laity to have open contact with the saints. Moreover, while saints' cults often reinforced the power of elites, who usually organized and funded them, for ordinary believers these "invisible companions" served as more powerful protectors from daily afflictions and social abuses.[101]

Risking danger in the course of traveling to a saint's shrine intensified a pilgrim's experience, and reaching Dimyana's church in Bilqas, a relatively remote area in the Delta, represented the first such challenge. The Delta was a popular pilgrimage destination during the earliest centuries of Ottoman rule and still is today for Copts and Muslims.[102] In 1762, the German-born traveler Carsten Niebuhr observed, "The eastern part of the Delta, which has been, as yet, but little frequented by the European travelers, is not less rich in antiquities than that which is better known. The frequency of robbers and the looseness of the police, in that remote district, deter the curious. Yet one might visit those parts without danger, by accompanying the Copts, of whom great numbers go every year, in pilgrimage to an ancient church, near *Gemiana* [Dimyana]."[103] The shrine's isolation explains why few travelers ventured to this festival, considered to be one of the greatest among Copts.[104] But Niebuhr's comment alludes to the fact that Bilqas had become, at least once a year, a special Coptic space. Its remoteness discouraged most passing travelers, but in the company of Copts, who had a close agreement with local authorities and inhabitants, this journey was made safer. Much as in early Christian times, in the Ottoman era pilgrims came from great distances. In 1672, Vansleb remarked on the preparedness of oarsmen and bedouin to help pilgrims in making this journey, which took a lengthy five days from Cairo.[105] The readily available transportation indicates, in part, the festival's economic benefits for Delta locals. In the early Ottoman centuries, the Gharbiyya Province, which administratively included Bilqas, was home to a number of thriving Sufi lodges and to the annual festival for Sidi Ahmad al-Badawi in Tanta. Bedouin leaders played a prominent part in these celebrations, and in keeping with this tradition, Coptic organizers of the Dimyana festival communicated with villagers and bedouins to ensure their own successful event.[106]

While difficult to reach, the shrine was located in a fertile and lush region, a picturesque scene for the weary traveler. Vansleb mentions that it was surrounded on the east and the west by branches of the Nile, which rendered it bountiful. Writing a few decades later, the Jesuit Sicard described this area as a plain, covered all year with vegetation as the Nile waters flooded and fertilized it, creating a suitable grazing ground for oxen and sheep that were kept by herdsmen.[107] Even from a distance, the Church of Dimyana was an impressive sight. In the seventeenth century, Vansleb remarked that the church was "not yet finished," possibly indicating that renovations to the shrine were ongoing. The beautiful structure was architecturally asymmetrical, its twenty-five arches or domes unequal in size.[108] The church had one chapel and one altar, and windows were located in every arch.[109] By all accounts, this complex, made of white limestone and situated in the midst of green pastures, was striking.

In general the festival itself lasted between eight and fifteen days; the final day was the martyr's feast.[110] As pilgrims arrived and settled into encampments surrounding the shrine, there was a discernible and infectious energy. Believers visited Dimyana's tomb, bringing their offerings or making supplications to the saint. Both profane and religious rituals marked the collective celebrations. Christian and Muslim visitors swarmed, and the festival's highlights were the miraculous apparition of Coptic saints inside the church and the performance of the equestrian exercises (*furūsiyya*) by bedouin horsemen. Sicard notes that "the Javelin, the lute, the dances, [and] the feasts were the common occupation of both religions."[111] Traders and vendors sold their wares. Meats and fish were peddled in great quantities; water and wood were readily available. Later accounts mention that "numbers of merchants usually go and hold a bazaar, in which they sell food, drink, sometimes clothing, ornaments, perfumes, rings, handkerchiefs, sticks, etc., and especially wooden and brass crosses imported from Jerusalem."[112] Religious celebrations have historically functioned in this way: as a space for ritual and an occasion for trade and economic exchange.[113]

In order to sustain a festival for so many days and with such a large number of people, it was necessary for Coptic leaders, Ottoman officials, and bedouins to forge an agreement.[114] At the onset, armed bedouins gathered at the church and awaited the customary hospitality for the duration of three days, which was funded by donations collected from archons and the laity. Vansleb reported that "the custome of feeding the Arabians there-abouts is very ancient" and that "it comes from their pretending to be the Lords of the Country round about where this Church is built, and therefore for this consideration they hinder not the Christians, as they are able, from coming to this festival."[115] Copts exchanged hospitality for freedom from harassment, and the task of supplying these bedouins fell to the church's treasurer, most likely a high-ranking lay leader or an archon,[116] who was required to care for their livestock and furnish them with food and drink. Moreover, the bedouins performed their games, their warlike exercises, entertaining the numerous crowds. On the third and final day of this arrangement, bedouins were served dinner and were expected to leave within two hours of finishing their meal. If any bedouin was present thereafter, he would be severely punished by the Ottoman official representative, the "lieutenant governor,"[117] who also attended the festivities.

In relating the hospitality of its organizers and showcasing the financial resources expended by Coptic pilgrims and their leaders, Vansleb also told of a great feast thrown by the church treasurer, describing it as an "extraordinary banquet" where he ate "meat [that] was to be torn in pieces between the fingers, according to the custome of the country."[118] This special banquet honored esteemed guests, including local officials as well as lay notables and clergy. Afterward, however, the social prescripts of generosity dictated that the treasurer must feed the populace, who were gathered around the tent. Vansleb mentions that after the distinguished guests finished dining, "out of the [treasurer's] tent a long skin of leather was spread on the ground for the ordinary people, where they were very well treated."[119] The fact that it was being funded, at least partially, by lay donations and seemingly coordinated by lay leadership showcased the centrality of Coptic elites in facilitating this event. Indeed, a modern account of the festival says that pilgrims donated large amounts of jewels, money, and gold and silver plates.[120] These donations would have supplied the bedouins, fed the masses, and paid for an alcohol tax to authorities in attendance.

For Coptic archons, such visible acts of organizational and public charity would have created an important opportunity to legitimize their leadership. Charity as a means of achieving political prestige has been well studied in the Ottoman context. We have already noted its role among the Greek Phanariots and Armenian amiras, and acts of generosity and benevolence had long existed as a cornerstone in the public policies of Ottoman sultans and local provincial elites as well. Following his conquest of Egypt, for instance, Sultan Selim I is said to have distributed alms to the poor following Friday prayers to demonstrate the benevolence of a new regime and ingratiate himself to the conquered.[121] During crises, supporting popular festivals, pilgrimage, and religious infrastructure helped maintain if not strengthen Ottoman authority in Egypt.[122] In Jerusalem, through the waqf system, elite women and men constructed soup kitchens, public baths, and schools in order to gain new clients and expand their political networks.[123] In places that lacked "sultanic charitable activity," like Salonica, local notables built new shrines, mosques, and prayer spaces in hopes of using "charity to foster patronage networks and to bolster their own image."[124] Maronite Christian leaders in Lebanon, particularly from among the laity, used religious endowments as a way to reinforce their economic and political power within the community.[125] Thus Coptic archons were surrounded by various models of beneficence in Ottoman society; many of their own patrons in Egypt went to great lengths to showcase their generosity.

The Ottoman security presence further suggests the role played by the archons in organizing this festival and intimates that there were close connections between archons and local military households. Claude Sicard reported that this "lieutenant governor" of the province actually owned a large home near Dimyana's shrine. Familiarity with the military regiments and ties to their various local leaders would allow archons to communicate easily with Ottoman authorities and to relate concerns over security and order. The lieutenant governor, in turn, asked his "cavalry" (*sipāhī*)[126] to be present during the festival and to contain "the Arab inhabitants of the desert."[127] The sipāhī were dispatched to prevent potential havoc, quarrels, and robberies, as noted by Vansleb:

> There is here no danger of being robb'd; for the Lieutenant of the Bey of the Mohelle [Mahalla al-Kubra] is also at this festival with a good guard of Spahins [sipāhī] to prevent disorders, quarrels, and robberies which might happen among rude and barbarous people: so that in this place one may be with as much safety as at Cairo in a house. On this account there happen'd a pleasant accident; a poor Arabian had taken from a Christian a handful of Barly to give it to his ass, he was taken on the fact: the Christians immediately dragg'd him with a great noise, to the Beys Lieutenant to have him punish'd: Whiles they were leading him a great

> tumult of people ran to see him; some upbraided him with his boldness and impudency to steal, without apprehending the punishment of the saints that appear'd in their church, and did so many great miracles; another ask'd him whether he did not fear that God would punish him? At which words he answer'd, Ane Baaref rabbene; that is, What, do I know that there is a God? Or, I know not what is God. This caused me to wonder, both at the Copties settled persuasion of the real apparition of their saints, and at the ignorance of the Arabians, seeing that some of them know not that there is a God. At last this wretch was shut up in a cage, and I know not what happen'd to him afterward.[128]

While there existed a popular belief that "Sitt Dimiana can prevent thieves from stealing, or from escaping with what they have stolen,"[129] the cavalry nevertheless enhanced the feeling of security. Guards were also called to monitor the gathering at the Church of Dimyana during the saints' apparitions. In these times, large crowds crammed inside the small chapel, and guards gathered out of curiosity and to supervise the crowds' excitement at the apparitions.

Although European travelers viewed the apparitions of Coptic saints as fraudulent, the miracles astonished the pilgrims and reinforced their faith.[130] In fact, it is in their most opinionated descriptions that Vanslcb and Sicard furnish a fascinating commentary on Coptic lay practices. What emerges here is how crowds, in a random and oft-violent fashion, decided the identity of the saint they were observing and the emblems by which he or she was recognized. The assortment of saints and their specific manifestations distinguished these apparitions from others during this period.[131] Vansleb described his experience as follows:

> During three days I examined this apparition, and the causes from whence it proceeds as exactly as I could possibly; and found it to be nothing else but the reflection of the objects that went by the church at a convenient distance, which being carried into the chappel, by the air, through the two windows that give light. It represents, over against upon the wall, the shadow which is like the object that goes by: for example, when a horse-man goes by, there is to be seen upon the wall, in a confused manner, a shadow of a man on horse-back. If it be a woman that hath a child in her arms, one may see the shadow of that appearance; and so is it with all other things. Now the people being superstitious and of a dull apprehension, not knowing how this happens, fancy that the saints appear to them. They know and distinguish them, according as they are painted in their churches: for example, when they see the shadow that represents a cavalier, they say it is S. George; for the Copties, as well as the other people of the east, represent him as a man

> on horse-back, killing a dragon. When they see a woman carrying of [*sic*] an infant in her arms, they say that it is the blessed Virgin, because they see her thus represented in the pictures of their churches. When they see the shadow of a man on foot of a reddish colour, they say that it is S. Menna, because they paint him with a red habit. They distinguish the other saints in the same manner. They are so much bewitch'd with the fancy of the reality of these apparitions, that if any person should offer to deny it, he would be in danger to be knock'd on the head. . . . only by chance these shadows have appeared, and been taken notice of. This apparition continues three days following; in which time there is such a great concourse of people, that one is ready to be stifled. . . . When they saw some shadows upon the wall which had a relation with those saints that are painted in their churches, they cry out for joy, in their language, Selam lak Kaddis Filan; I salute you o saint N.N. To this they add an Hymn proper to the saint, and prayers, tying upon the wall some little crosses of wax. Of all the saints that their church worships, I have heard none called upon but the blessed Virgin, S. George, S. Menna, and S. Porter [*sic*].[132]

Vansleb's narrative provides a portal into the worldviews of the masses: for Copts, like other pilgrims throughout the region, the saints were touchable and tangible, but in illustrating the distinctiveness of Coptic rituals, the experience of believers was fully informed by their familiarity with their specific religious traditions.[133] Visions were contested; each spectator, man or woman, saw saints in various colors and shapes, yet all attributed their familiarity to hagiographic and iconographic images.

How these apparitions were interpreted shows the intersection of the church's scriptural and pictorial authority with lay beliefs. "The opinions are all divided," noted Sicard, but "everyone shouts, disputes and sings hymns; it is an appalling hullabaloo caused by the ignorance and the superstition of Copts, but which brings pity upon those who believe it."[134] What inspired "pity" for Sicard was in reality a source of blessing (*baraka*).[135] Standing among the audience, Sicard wrote that "I was not however able to speak, because I was not in safety in the midst of a mob unaware of its insane behavior . . . but the Turkish and Arab soldiers who were there in great numbers . . . [challenged] the gullibility of the Copts, and by sometimes blocking the window of the dome of the Appearances, sometimes separating the masses on top of the platform, they tried to convince the Christians that the alleged passages of the Saints dispersed naturally."[136] Soldiers clearly believed these apparitions to be a farce, but it is likely that Copts saw them as a way to legitimize the supremacy of their Christian faith. The crowd's mob mentality ensured that these miracles would go mostly unchallenged; even when soldiers tried to discredit them, pilgrims stood unmoved. Indeed, the apparitions indicate the pilgrims' conviction to generate their own religious experience, one that was "more informal and more personal" than common rituals.[137]

Remarkably, Coptic clergy took a minimal part in these events and offered neither argument nor support to these apparitions. Sicard, as a Catholic priest, was taken aback by their apparent ineptitude and offended by their disregard and laxity toward proper liturgical traditions.[138] His objections intensified when village priests from the Delta region joined the crowds in their tents for eating, drinking, and merrymaking; the priests, in turn, resented Sicard because he had turned down their anise-flavored liquor 'araq in favor of water.[139] His dismissals of the apparitions, in addition to criticism of the role that Coptic priests should play, illustrate how the festival was interpreted by post-Reformation Europeans: as a space for popular (and profane) practices for the masses.

The Coptic laity, on the other hand, drew what they wished from Dimyana's festival—her locality, the prominence of her shrine, her supernatural abilities. During the apparitions, Dimyana's hagiography loomed large, but it was her miraculous powers that attracted pilgrims each year. While church texts cast her as a chaste and erudite Christian heroine, her popularity was decided by raucous masses determined to express their opinions without direct pastoral instruction.[140] At her shrine, Dimyana rewarded visitors with food, festivity, miracles, and promises of protection. Echoing this point, during his travels in Upper Egypt in the early eighteenth century, Claude Sicard captured the words of a Coptic archon who spoke of his pilgrimage to another shrine, that of the martyr Mari Jirjis (St. George) in the town of Baba. The archon indicated that he had sent a "present of candles to Mari Jirjis in order to obtain his protection and his intercession before God."[141] Dimyana's and other saints' acts of generosity, in turn, corresponded to private and public acts of lay benevolence. Dimyana's annual festival in Bilqas would be financed through their donations and facilitated by notables, whose political connections ensured the success and continuity of her cult.

Women at the Festival

The legitimation of a female voice and even of a separate female space is arguably one of the most important parts of Dimyana's hagiography.[142] According to her story, Dimyana lived with her forty female companions in homosocial isolation. This trope can be read, in part, as a nod to the Coptic female monastic tradition. During the Ottoman period, archons financed the renovation of various monasteries, although it is not known whether Coptic convents experienced a similar revival. Perhaps, as Bernard Heyberger has argued for the eighteenth-century Levant, daughters of Christian elites had an easier time convincing their parents to let them enter a convent because their families "revered the ideal of the consecrated virgin."[143] But aside from monasticism, which would have affected only a few women, sexual segregation was customarily practiced among urban or wealthier women in Ottoman Egypt. Dimyana's story, then, may have appealed to some audiences—specifically women—because they could identify with her lifestyle.[144] By popularizing Dimyana's hagiography, community elders reinforced expected mores and encouraged women to maintain their restrictive social boundaries.[145]

This makes sense in the early modern period. Medieval Muslim jurists had commonly censured women's practices at religious shrines and characterized them as *bid'a* (innovation) or as *fitna* (social unrest), since they generally saw women's public presence as morally corrupting.[146] Muslim religious scholars in Ottoman Egypt similarly insisted that women retain their modesty in all public spaces. Jurists went so far as to suggest that women "be kept out of sight of the public" or at minimum that "married women be secluded."[147] Yet Egyptian women frequently transgressed their prescribed boundaries, and at Dimyana's festival, women felt free to roam and even to display their femininity.[148] Scanty historical references from the early modern era restrict our analysis of women's practices at Dimyana's festival, but later sources offer possible glimpses into these earlier customs. One description comes from a nineteenth-century American Protestant missionary, who set up a tent in order to distribute Bibles and other wares and who noted that "the women, who at home would never appear even to near relatives uncovered, were unveiled; and the strange phenomenon was explained to me by the popular belief that in this region, which is under the special protection of 'Our Lady Damiane,' and during the week of her Mulid, the wanton glance is inevitably punished with blindness, and the illicit embrace with even heavier inflictions."[149] Other accounts confirm that there was a general laxity in attitudes by and toward women and that female visitors walked about with audacity, knowing well that men would lower their gazes because of the protection provided them by Dimyana.[150]

Vansleb, Sicard, and Niebuhr make few references to female pilgrims, and Coptic sources are equally silent on this topic. However, one could reasonably infer that some of these later practices were already established, given that Ottoman-era celebrations reveal parallel attitudes toward gendered participation. For example, in Ottoman Egypt, Muslim women commonly joined in popular festivals and even led certain Sufi gatherings (*dhikrs*).[151] In Istanbul, at an imperial circumcision in 1582, which was attended by members of the religious establishment, women were fairly unrestricted in their behavior and movement, and many were unveiled.[152] In Mosul, the veil did not inhibit women, and in fact propelled them into the public sphere, as they overtook festival spaces, pushing male observers to the back.[153]

Sometimes women's behavior at religious festivals was deemed indecent by outside observers. During the seventeenth century, the Spanish priest Antonius Gonzales recorded a strange story of a springtime pilgrimage that allegedly took place in the western Nile Delta, somewhere between Cairo and Rosetta. Gonzales was appalled that during this festival, which was devoted rather inexplicably to a "prostitute-saint," men allowed their wives to be sexually brazen.[154] Gonzales relays this story from a secondhand source, and there is little historical evidence to corroborate his bizarre tale.[155] However, a comparison with Dimyana's "eastern Nile" festival shows that—in popular practices or even in folkloric consciousness—both men and women ignored strict rules of gender interaction, and their violations were widely tolerated. Therefore, it is possible to argue that Dimyana's Ottoman-era festival represents a case, among many, in which religious ritual created an alternative female space, where pilgrims could defy dominant and orthodox interpretations of what constitutes proper behavior, and where they could even express themselves in nonconventional ways.

Along with the apparitions, another known miracle bestowed by Dimyana may have been her promotion of fertility and the protection of young children. A modern account describes women as coming to Dimyana's festival to seek her power of granting "fruitfulness to women, or long life to the children of a woman who has lost many in infancy."[156] Women pilgrims bought souvenirs at the festival to take to their native villages, believing that they conveyed a "blessing from Sitt [Lady] Dimiana," hoping that their requests for health and fertility would eventually be fulfilled. Throughout the Middle East, as in other parts of the world, there has been a long-standing association between saints' shrines and barrenness.[157] While references to Dimyana's status as a fertility saint derive from later accounts, they offer comparisons to other saints, notably to the Christian martyr St. George. Particularly in the Ottoman Levant, barren women visited St. George's shrines (or among Muslims, those of Khidr) to beseech him for offspring. His feast day in the spring, like Dimyana's, also evoked the fertility not only of women but also of the land, marking the beginning of the agricultural cycle.[158] As with their Levantine counterparts, the daily activities of most Coptic pilgrims, especially women, would have been centered on agricultural labor. Springtime festivals were so popular among Copts and Muslims that in 1787, when local authorities attempted to control public order, they explicitly banned all women from attending the Shamm al-Nasīm celebrations.[159] In addition to its timing and physical setting, other symbols of fertility pervaded Dimyana's festival: for example, one type of food, *fissīkh*, which was also associated with *Shamm al-Nasīm*.[160] All of these tactile symbols, associated with fertility, likely enhanced the pilgrims' experience.

Without presuming that later traditions reflected widespread practices in the early modern era or that her hagiography mirrored the reality of gender roles or expectations in Ottoman Egypt, Dimyana's story somehow reverberates within these practices. In her isolation with the forty virgins, gender segregation would have been reinforced, and female monastic orders were also validated. Dimyana lived in a separate palace so that young men's gaze could be averted, and presumably men knew not to stare at unveiled women during her festival. In that regard, it seems that Dimyana's autonomy and independence (rather than or in addition to her segregation) held meaning for audiences, and for women in particular. She represented a female icon at a time when few such models existed.[161] Her martyrology, its interpretation, its reproduction and oral performance, and the rituals at her festival infused discussions of gender into Coptic and Egyptian worldviews and further bolstered the participation of women alongside men in public religious life.

Conclusions

As a saint who was born, raised, and martyred in Egypt, Dimyana held great importance for local villages, which benefited politically and economically from her shrine and accompanying festival. This "locality" would transcend a specific region as her hagiography was transmitted, reproduced, and made accessible to many Copts.[162] Few were literate in the Ottoman period, yet her story was heard at various churches and monasteries throughout Egypt. Ordinary people sought comfort and reassurance through their relationships with the saints, a relationship that transcended the temporal world.[163] At her festival, Dimyana gave Copts an important connection to a distant, fantastical past; the martyr lived on through her apparitions, and pilgrims could take her blessings home. Moreover, pilgrims enjoyed a loosening of rules that ordinarily governed everyday behavior—between Muslims and Copts, laypeople and clergy, men and women.

Here one can see that Coptic archons may have used some of their connections and their financial resources to bolster Dimyana's popularity and to bring together the community at a time when clerical leaders were unable to dispel economic or political challenges. Archons repeatedly commissioned the copying of Dimyana's hagiography and helped to spread her cult. Moreover, in this period various archons would show their ongoing patronage of this special martyr by commissioning her icons for private and public use.[164] Competition among lay elites within the realm of religious patronage may have encouraged financial donations and helped support what was likely an expensive festival. The clergy, according to traveler accounts, occupied a secondary place at this annual event; lower-ranking priests were mostly content with feasting alongside the masses, and the sources omit mention of participating bishops or the patriarch. An organized, well-armed, yet fairly relaxed security contingent, made up of Ottoman officials and soldiery, hints at the close relationship between archons and emergent military households in the late seventeenth and early eighteenth centuries. One cannot determine precisely how the clergy felt about these developments. On occasion, as the next chapter illustrates, they seemed accepting of the archons' (and, in general, the laity's) increased role in supervising certain dimensions of Coptic religious life. In fact, some collaborated with archons in upholding traditions such as the pilgrimage to Jerusalem. At others, as the later discussion of clerical sermons reveals, their frustrations with burgeoning lay power became more apparent.

4

The Miracle of Pilgrimage

A Journey to Jerusalem in the Early Eighteenth Century

Pilgrimage to Jerusalem constitutes one of the most important and public manifestations of Christian religious expression within the Ottoman world. The execution of this practice among Copts in the early eighteenth century—costly and precarious as it was—reflects a moment when lay and clerical leaders negotiated with each other and with local religious and political authorities in the course of preserving this ritual. The close ties between archons and Egyptian elites, cultivated throughout the seventeenth and eighteenth centuries, helped sustain Coptic religious practices even in the face of laws curbing their public expression. In this context, seeing their power progressively diminish, some patriarchs developed a closer relationship with lay elites. Their partnership resulted in a communal renewal, whose specifics are still being investigated by historians.

In the context of Dimyana's cult, archons may have looked to religious patronage as one way of solidifying their political position within the community. By the eighteenth century, many churches in Cairo had been renovated under their guidance, and important religious centers, such as the Monastery of St. Paul, had been repaired and repopulated with the cooperation of lay and clerical interests.[1] Likewise, several scholars have studied Coptic religious art and icon production during this era and have linked both to lay beneficence.[2] It is possible that for their philanthropy, archons turned to examples of patronage by local Muslim grandees, relied on their own experiences, or looked to broader models of charitable practice within the Ottoman world. Since the pilgrimage to Jerusalem existed in earlier periods, what is remarkable is not the act but rather the ability of Coptic communal leaders to finance an elaborate ceremony with specific (and extremely public) processional practices close to those performed during the Muslim ḥajj. After the seventeenth century, the funding, organization, staffing, and execution of the annual ḥajj became a priority for the Ottoman Porte.[3] The ḥajj constituted an important source of legitimacy for Ottoman sultans as well as local military and political leaders in Cairo and Damascus, where the caravan was organized and launched each year.[4] One might reasonably infer that archons, seeing the heightened attention to this ritual in Egyptian society and among their Muslim patrons, were inspired to follow the trend.

In the Ottoman period, pilgrimage to Mecca or Jerusalem was characterized by collective planning and constituted a shared religious practice. Muslims and Christians both displayed pageantry en route to their destinations. Both valued returning pilgrims, bestowing them with venerable titles and honors. At their destinations, however, pilgrims participated in rituals that reinforced their religious distinctiveness. For Muslims, this included the circumambulation of the Kaʿaba, and for Copts, the climax took place on Easter eve inside the most revered Christian shrine, the Church of the Holy Sepulchre, where Orthodox Christians gathered for the miracle of "Holy Fire."[5] Through pilgrimage, Coptic clergy, in particular, participated in ceremonies that demonstrated and enhanced their authority. Archons capitalized on their political connections and emerged as financiers and facilitators; their influence was welcomed (or tolerated) by clergymen because it was seen as the best way to preserve Coptic communality.[6] In the eighteenth century, then, clergy and laity worked in complementary ways to preserve religious life. Moreover, the Jerusalem pilgrimage would allow Copts to see themselves—even for a brief period—in a different and perhaps more empowering light than was commonly afforded them.

Background and Sources

Despite the popularity of innumerable shrines all over the Christian world, Jerusalem has always retained extraordinary meaning for worshippers. In the fourth century, Emperor Constantine had reconstructed the city in order "to give visible topography to the legends, sacred books, and developing liturgy," and the later devotion spawned by this "physical theatre," as David Frankfurter calls it, gave birth to multiple "imitative 'liturgical Jerusalems.'"[7] While pilgrims visited this city for similar purposes and agendas, they each had separate, preexisting visions of the Holy Land derived from lore, liturgy, and iconography.

Jerusalem offered a sensory connection to the biblical life of Christ. There, believers could attempt to transcend barriers between their physical selves and the ethereal Christ, between the material and spiritual worlds. By praying atop the Mount of Olives, at Gethsemane, or at Christ's sepulchre, they could "touch" the divine.

Copts were not alone, of course, in valuing this pilgrimage; European and Near Eastern Christians, Jews, and Muslims regularly visited the city and its surrounding holy sites.[8] Historically, some Muslim jurists—notably the fourteenth-century puritanical scholar Ibn Taymiyya—condemned the Muslim pilgrimage to Jerusalem, fearing that it rivaled the more legitimate and religiously sanctioned ḥajj to Mecca.[9] But for Copts, the pilgrimage was easily integrated within existing religious traditions, and it would come to serve two distinct purposes: to venerate religious shrines in Egypt, en route to the Holy Land; and to visit sites associated with Jesus' later life in Palestine. The latter culminated at the Church of the Holy Sepulchre with the celebration of Christ's Resurrection. In the Gospel of Matthew (2:13–18), Egypt was mentioned as a place of refuge for the Holy Family. Herod (37–34 BCE), "King of the Jews,"[10] had sought to kill the Christ-child, hailed as the future King of the Jews, by massacring all male infants in Bethlehem. Mary, Joseph, and Jesus stayed in Egypt, according to the gospel writer, until it was safe to return to Nazareth after Herod's death. In time, the memory of a visit that reportedly lasted more than three years had materialized in Coptic rituals, literature, and art, even though the Bible is silent about its details.[11] Local traditions surrounding the visit and the miracles performed by the Holy Family constituted the basis for a pilgrimage map.[12] Copts traveled to Jerusalem not only to fulfill a simple vow or get blessings from its shrines but to see the extension of a landscape in which their native Egypt had played part.[13]

During the early modern period, however, most would be unable to afford this journey. Financial hardships, in addition to the threat of bedouin attacks in rural and desert areas, were a chronic concern for all pilgrims, Muslims, Christians, and Jews alike.[14] Adding to these challenges, Copts could not depend on the leniency of governors and 'ulamā' in granting them permission to perform their rituals. In certain years, pilgrims were attacked for ostentatiously parading in Cairo's streets and were restrained from making their journey. Moreover, many were dissuaded from traveling because they could conveniently visit sacred shrines in Egypt. Copts already had access to a living part of Jesus' life in their own lands in addition to local sanctuaries of countless saints and martyrs. For all these reasons, the pilgrimage in its Ottoman-era manifestation was a fluid rather than predictable ritual, and for Copts, it was subject to changing relationships and negotiations between their communal leaders and various political interests. This, of course, contrasts with the ḥajj, whose organization and makeup were fairly consistent, since the ritual reflected directly on the political and religious legitimacy of its patrons, the Ottoman sultans.[15]

The unpredictability means that, in contrast to Muslim and Western narratives, hardly any sources detail Coptic practices during early Islamic centuries or in the Ottoman period. In fact, pilgrimage narratives written by Christians living under Islamic rule are generally uncommon.[16] Some Ottoman Egyptian chroniclers like al-Damurdashi and al-Jabarti point out "failed" Coptic pilgrimages and describe the intercommunal tensions that resulted from overly boisterous processions. Many Western travelers note the Coptic presence at the Church of the Holy Sepulchre, verifying that pilgrims made the journey from Egypt, but few indicate how they arrived to their destination or how they organized their travels. Only a handful of contemporary historians have studied the relationship between Copts and Jerusalem in the early modern period.[17] In his monograph on Christian sites in seventeenth-century Jerusalem, Oded Peri has helpfully recorded the demographic history of the small Coptic community in Jerusalem but has not described their specific rites and rituals.[18] My study here focuses on the act of pilgrimage itself, relying predominantly on a lengthy manuscript from the Coptic archives (Coptic Museum, Liturgy 128) written by an eyewitness and a participant in this event, the scribe ʻAbd al-Masih, who describes a successful pilgrimage from 1709.[19] The author's ideological motives are difficult to determine, but it is clear that those who commissioned the manuscript intended for their experience to become part of Coptic communal memory.

In my analysis here, I will look in particular to Glen Bowman's study of the medieval Catholic experience in the Holy Land, which, although recorded by elites, was disseminated to all believers through processions, souvenirs, and storytelling.[20] Scholarly investigations of Muslim pilgrimage narratives are also helpful; in the Ottoman era, pilgrimages to Mecca bolstered travelers' sense of geographic identity by allowing them to see themselves as more superior, moral, and upright in comparison to other pilgrims.[21] In many ways, the Coptic pilgrimage would function similarly: as a public ritual to be shared by fellow believers during the journey and as a source of communal pride for Copts who encountered various groups and denominations along the way. It should be noted that pilgrims' accounts are often filled with literary embellishments and are generally less concerned with reality than they are with testifying to the piety of their patrons.[22] Our Coptic manuscript, while free of most flourishes, provides a descriptive account that also functions as a tribute to pilgrimage organizers. Because of its richness of detail, I read this text both as a snapshot of pilgrimage performed by elites and of broader religious life during the early eighteenth century.

Pilgrimage in the Ottoman Era: Regional and Local Trends

It is difficult to pinpoint when Copts began making pilgrimages to the Holy Land or established satellite churches there. Most likely, they were among the earliest Christian pilgrims in the fourth and fifth centuries. By the ninth century, they had established a small community in Jerusalem, and Patriarch Ya'qub (810–830) had ordered the construction of the Church of the Magdalene.[23] In the tenth and eleventh centuries, Copts abandoned pilgrimage altogether due to the political instability of the region, which was heightened in 1008 by Fatimid Caliph al-Hakim's (996–1020) order to destroy churches in Cairo and Palestine, ban pilgrimages, and, more consequentially, demolish the Church of the Holy Sepulchre.[24] The Christian Crusader kingdom (established in 1099) was even more restrictive, limiting access to holy sites for indigenous Christians. After an initial prohibition, however, Crusaders allowed back most Eastern Christians, although Copts were explicitly forbidden from performing the pilgrimage, since they were deemed particularly heretical.[25] One traveler in 1165 and another in 1172 reported that Copts resided in Jerusalem, and Copts regained their pilgrimage rights when Salah al-Din al-Ayyubi (1171–1193) reconquered the city in 1187, as he also lifted road taxes that had been placed on various Christian pilgrims.[26]

The instability of the Coptic diocese in Jerusalem and the fear that other ambitious sects might seize their holdings prompted Patriarch Kyrillus III (1235–1243) to appoint a permanent metropolitan in Jerusalem (Basilyus I, 1236–1260) who monitored community possessions and cared for visitors.[27] A capable and well-established diocese was also needed to withstand the pressures placed—mostly by other Christian communities—on Coptic churches, chapels, and shrines in the Holy Land. The extent to which the Egyptian mother church intervened in the affairs of its Jerusalem diocese is not always clear. In later periods, Jerusalem may have fallen under the management of the bishop of Damietta, who would annually visit the city before Christmas, remaining there until Easter time.[28] Some sources indicate, however, that it was Damietta that fell under Jerusalem's control.[29] Perhaps the administration regularly changed hands depending on the particular metropolitan in charge.

In the years following the Ottoman conquest of Arab lands, travelers speak of an established Coptic diocese in Jerusalem. A letter from Germanus, Greek patriarch of Jerusalem, to Russian Tsar Ivan IV ("the Terrible," 1553–1584), cites the dismal state of his own sect as compared with the Armenians and Copts.[30] During his reign, Murqus V (1602–1618) visited the Holy Land, when he reportedly ministered to his congregation and surveyed patriarchal properties, appointing Qummus (Hegumenos) Ya'qub in charge of Coptic possessions.[31] The incorporation of the metropolitan of Jerusalem into the ceremonial consecration of Coptic patriarchs in

Cairo can also be dated to the early Ottoman period. The first known incidence of his participation took place during the reign of Metropolitan Zakariyus I (1575–1600), who administered the proceedings for Patriarch Ghubriyal VIII (1586–1601).[32]

There is little doubt that for Copts, the preservation of the pilgrimage and, by extension, of Coptic properties in Palestine depended a great deal on the attitude of Ottoman authorities at the central and provincial levels. In general, Ottoman rulers wished to maintain Christian and Jewish pilgrimages, since both financially benefited authorities in Istanbul as well as lesser power-holders: the bedouins, the suppliers of food, lodging, and transport, and the provincial and district governors.[33] On the other hand, there was some sense among religious leaders throughout the empire that Christian rites should not detract from the predominantly Muslim character of the region.[34] Ottoman authorities were prudent in dealing with intercommunal conflicts, and they generally managed to protect the rights of Christians while also upholding Islamic tenets.[35]

The difference between Ottoman and local Muslim attitudes toward Christian religious practices is noteworthy. Muslim "guardians" of the faith—the 'ulamā' or sometimes zealous Sufi dervishes—sought to defend traditional prohibitions against non-Muslims, protesting their public rituals, ostentatious processions, and church renovations. Ottoman authorities (sultans, governors, military representatives, magistrates) usually leaned toward appeasement, particularly in Palestine, a volatile region that was home to multiple religious groups historically susceptible to European influence. Politically, the Porte benefited by protecting Christian religious sites in Palestine and the pilgrimage: for one, parallel Christian and Muslim structures reinforced their image as heads of the dominant but tolerant Islamic religion. More importantly, as Peri has argued, as European and Catholic influence increased within their territories, Ottoman rulers worried that a decline of Christianity in Palestine would disturb relations with foreign Christians.[36] To facilitate pilgrimage, the Ottomans safeguarded the roads into Jerusalem, which also benefited Muslims who came to visit the third holiest site in Islam, often in conjunction with their pilgrimage to Mecca.[37]

While central and provincial attitudes shaped how regularly the pilgrimage could be performed, in Jerusalem, the Greek and Armenian sects dominated smaller Christian communities and competed for the right to perform important religious functions. In the late seventeenth century, the Greek Orthodox constituted nearly 70 percent of Jerusalem's Christian population.[38] The Armenians ranked second and were followed by the Roman Catholics (specifically the Franciscan order) in terms of property rights and political power.[39] By maintaining close relations with Istanbul, Greeks and Armenians were able to win the government's favors in building up their communal properties. Armenian patriarchs of Jerusalem traveled to the capital regularly in order to acquire permissions for renovating their churches or to persuade the sultan to reverse negative rulings made against them by local governors.[40] For these communities, business with the Porte could be conducted with relative ease and gave them an edge over other Christians, like Copts, who had no patronage networks in the capital city. Occasionally, the Ottoman government directly intervened to restore order and balance. In the eighteenth century, violent struggles between Greeks and Catholics prompted Ottoman authorities in Istanbul to more clearly delineate the properties of Christian groups in the Holy Land in an effort to bring calm to the region.[41]

Nevertheless, protection for influential Christian communities did not necessarily exempt them from burdensome payments, and in Christian annals Ottoman authorities are accused of levying excessive taxes on all pilgrims. Copts had to pay a number of taxes during their journey and at their arrival to Jerusalem, including the road tax (*ghafar*) charged at particular checkpoints according to rates determined by central administrators in Istanbul.[42] On the other hand, the policy of levying taxes on pilgrims entering the Church of the Holy Sepulchre was decided locally and based on their place of origin. Among pilgrims from Europe, Anatolia, Armenia, Iran, Iraq, and Syria, Egypt's Christian pilgrims paid least of all.[43] Still, the financial demands hindered ordinary believers' ability to make the journey. Beyond official checkpoints, pilgrims were forced to deal with arbitrary and random stops, where some bedouins extracted additional fees.[44] At times, unexpected charges became so numerous that many arrived stripped and penniless.[45]

Despite these expenses, an average of one hundred Christian pilgrims traveled annually from Egypt to Jerusalem in the late sixteenth century, although we cannot presume that all were Copts.[46] Evidence suggests that the tradition also continued even during the widespread economic crises of the seventeenth century. For instance, Abudacnus describes in some detail the Coptic motivation for the pilgrimage at that time:

> The Jacobites [Copts] are used to go on Pilgrimage upon a Religious account: for to say in a word, there are many places in Egypt, where the Bodies of Saints, and Images of the blessed Virgin are kept, which they believe to perform many extraordinary Miracles. But about the middle of Lent for the most part, they are wonted to travel to Jerusalem and because the Road is infested with Thieves and Arabs, they use all to gather together in the Metropolis of Egypt whether Jacobites, Greeks, or Europeans, Merchants or Artisans, Pilgrims, etc. and there join in one Body, or Caravan, as they call it, and the number of Pilgrims is so great that it sometimes exceeds sixty thousand men.[47]

While the estimate of sixty thousand seems exaggerated, the organization and planning behind the pilgrimage, by multiple communities in Egypt, indicates a determination and financial capacity for making this journey. Still, there does appear to have been some overall decline in this ritual during the late seventeenth century, one paralleled by a decline in Coptic residents in Jerusalem. The latter's numbers fell from 326 in 1526 to 113 in 1691.[48] The welfare of Jerusalemite Copts was directly linked to the status of their mother community in Egypt, which supported the former with gifts, supplies, and financial donations.[49] As Ottoman control of Egypt waned in this period, internal chaos threatened road security, and negotiations with powerful bedouin leaders became taxing. Egypt's bedouins often attacked pilgrims and travelers out of their frustration at being mistreated by governors or local military officers.[50] At the same time, special taxes were also placed on Copts and Ethiopians on account of a monastery that they owned in the vicinity of the Church of the Holy Sepulchre (probably Dayr al-Sultan).[51] Travelers report that by the late seventeenth century, Copts living in Jerusalem were quite destitute and present only in small numbers.[52]

Tensions between Catholics and Greek Orthodox over property and prayer rights at the Church of the Holy Sepulchre further disrupted the pilgrimage. Between 1689 and 1696, these disputes prevented all Orthodox pilgrims from entering the church and hindered them from participating in the Holy Fire ceremony.[53] Still, European travelers confirm that by 1697, despite their dwindling numbers and the Greek-Catholic conflict, Copts were still included in rituals performed during Holy Week.[54] As will be seen, by the start of the eighteenth century, Copts would make a successful attempt to resume their traditions. Their confidence, or at least that of their wealthiest ranks, had risen, reflecting that this was a time of increasing economic prosperity in Egypt in general and among Copts in particular.[55]

Motivating Pilgrimage among the Believers

In practice, then, while fulfilling an important social and spiritual function, pilgrimage was also encouraged as part of the Coptic Church's attempt to fund-raise and help maintain its properties in Palestine. During the Ottoman period, the church faced mounting pressures from local Muslim interests in Jerusalem and from more powerful Christian communities. In the wake of a cultural renewal pervading their community in the late seventeenth and early eighteenth centuries, various Coptic leaders invested time in enhancing religious life not only in Egypt but also in Palestine. To this end, Coptic clergymen likely turned to the familiar genre of sermons and promoted this ancient ritual among parishioners.

Two sermons remind us of the different ways that the clergy historically encouraged believers, particularly the wealthy, to make the journey to Jerusalem. In a thirteenth-century sermon, the well-known Coptic jurist and theologian Abu

Ishaq al-Mu'taman ibn al-'Assal (d. last quarter of thirteenth century) urges his congregation to make the *ḥajj 'ila al-Quds al-sharīf* ("the pilgrimage to the noble Jerusalem," an epithet common in Arabic-Islamic literature). He entices his audience with a description of Jerusalem as the place of biblical tales and exploits. Could congregants forget, implores Ibn al-'Assal, that it was in nearby Bethlehem that Jesus was born, or that the Holy Land was the stage for Jesus' miracles, where he cured a blind man, a leper, and a paraplegic, and commanded the wind and water to calm their force? He pleads: "Let us proceed to [God's] holy city like bees hovering to pick fruits so that you may pick from the palm trees of paradise [which are] ripened with spiritual [fruits]."[56] Ibn al-'Assal finally justifies the journey in the most practical terms by noting that whatever funds they spend in making this trip will be recompensed one hundredfold here on earth and in heaven, where they will receive eternal life.

In another text from Coptic archives, likely dating from the seventeenth century, the writer maintains that anyone who can afford the journey, unless he or she has a binding excuse, must visit the "sites of our Master's suffering and look on the place of his death and know that everything is true and right."[57] Beseeching his parishioners, the author states that those who cannot make the journey (despite its being a farḍ, an obligation) should at minimum contribute by making "offerings" (*qarābīn*). This rhetoric of farḍ echoes the requirement of daily prayers, almsgiving, the Ramadan fast, and the pilgrimage to Mecca as obligatory practices in the Islamic faith.[58] That the Coptic orator presents the pilgrimage to the community—particularly to its notables—as compulsory hints at the depth of cultural influence between Muslims and Copts during this period.

Hoping to win his audience's sympathy, the author also paints a dismal picture of communal properties in Jerusalem and of an impoverished congregation whose status depends entirely on the contributions of Egyptian coreligionists. He requests items such as gold, silver, clothes, iron, copper, and liturgical instruments—items that only the rich could afford to supply. The pilgrimage or any donations would yield a generous blessing for the benefactors, he insists, since they are considered to be "a good practice in front of God" (*sunna ḥasnā' quddām Allah*).[59] Aiming to persuade those who are indisposed, he couches his request as "good" and its neglect as "evil," dismissing the congregation with the final warning that anyone who disobeys these orders (which are delegated by God) risks being a violator of God's law (*namūs*) and being cast aside as a heretic and Satan's agent.[60] In contrast to earlier sermons, this writer is harsh, reproachful, and quick to judge and condemn. Taken together, these sermons suggest that most Copts could not afford the pilgrimage and that at times wealthy elites had to be coaxed to support the ritual. They also recall how preaching was one of the most important vehicles used by clergymen to exert their authority over lay congregants. Whether the congregants heeded such demands, however, cannot be always determined.

In encouraging pilgrimage during the Ottoman period, Coptic clerical leaders, like their Armenian counterparts, appear to have relied on functionaries, whose main duty was to travel among different parishes, reading similar pleas from the patriarchate and raising funds for the pilgrimage and for the Jerusalem metropolitanate.[61] Another sermon, this time from Patriarch Yu'annis XVIII (1769–1796), includes this type of request, in this case seeking contributions to repair the Monastery of St. George in Jerusalem.[62] In this text the patriarch claims that "local Muslim rulers"[63] in Jerusalem were threatening the community and that if Copts did not rebuild the monastery, it would be turned over to other Christian sects (read, Greeks or Armenians) or converted into a mosque. Such fears were based in reality: a court case from September 1564 reveals that some Muslim Jerusalemites questioned Coptic property rights to that same monastery. After the presentation of official documents, Coptic ownership was proven, and the qāḍī declared that "no one should undertake any steps that might interfere with the full and unimpeded exercise of Coptic rights in their place of worship in Jerusalem."[64] Still, Copts could not always expect favorable rulings, as Ottoman authorities in Jerusalem had earlier seized Franciscan and Greek Orthodox churches and turned them into mosques.[65] Once again, the sermon's intent was to protect communal properties: the patriarch urges congregants to donate money and entices them with familiar words, declaring that the spiritual rewards for their charity would be as great as those received for participating in the pilgrimage.[66]

Inasmuch as they were able, clergymen encouraged pilgrims to make the journey or, if that was not feasible, to contribute funds in order to sustain the Jerusalem diocese and other Coptic properties. Such donations became indispensable to the church, and by the eighteenth century, laymen had assumed most of the responsibility for organizing this tradition, bearing its costs, and, apparently, for preserving the Jerusalem diocese. While the participation of lay elites can be easily contextualized within their ongoing rise as communal leaders, they may have also been persuaded by the oratory of Coptic clergymen. These sermons underscore one basic point: clerical leaders constantly contended with unpredictable variables in the maintenance of church rituals and properties, but some found greater security by seeking an alliance with archons willing to finance their plans. In this way, clerical leaders still had an important function to play at the pulpit and, as will soon emerge, as ritual overseers and interlocutors to other Christian leaders.

Pilgrimage in the Eighteenth Century: Attempts, Failures, and Successes

Following its apparent decline, Coptic pilgrims in Egypt—laity and clergy—struggled to maintain this tradition throughout the eighteenth century, and at times they succeeded. The pilgrimage of 1709, the focus of our study, appears within Coptic annals as a triumph for the community. I will argue that this achievement was due in part to the fact that clergy and archons worked to solidify a network of cooperation from various parties and at each step of the journey, whether in Cairo, in the Sinai deserts, or in Palestine. By drawing on sources that offer comparable examples from 1748 and 1751, I examine the organization and the earliest stages of the Coptic pilgrimage. I do not wish to conflate these later pilgrimages with that of 1709. Yet these events, mostly recorded in the annals of Muslim chroniclers, allow us to see how Copts were informed by Muslim practices during the eighteenth century and how they dealt with challenges to their own travels.

Echoing the inconsistency with which this ritual was performed in preceding decades, the first pages of Coptic Museum, Liturgy 128, provide a marginal note remarking that "blessings such as the renovation of the Hanging Church [al-Muʿallaqa] and the visit of the father Patriarch Yuhanna 103 [Yu'annis XVI][67] to Jerusalem [in 1709] occurred close to each other in time and God eased the way for them and yet they do not represent the norm; hence they are considered as miracles."[68] Aside from miraculous intervention, what was the impetus for making this pilgrimage, and what steps were taken in planning it? The immediate and most obvious reason is feasibility. The scribe notes that for several years, Copts were forced to take the sea route, traveling alongside merchants heading to Palestine.[69] This situation posed some problems, however, as it seemingly limited the number of pilgrims. Thus once the roads were cleared, the idea for the pilgrimage originated with al-Muʿallim Jirjis Abu Mansur, who at the time was the head of the Coptic community and held the honorific title of "head archon" (*al-arkhun al-ra'īs*).[70] Abu Mansur had obtained information that, after twelve years of insecurity, the road from Cairo to Palestine was now safe: Ismaʿil Kahya Mustahfazan[71] received letters from Muhammad Pasha,[72] governor of Gaza, and from bedouin leaders (*shuyūkh al-ʿarab*)[73] verifying these developments.[74] This was likely a reference to the events of 1708, when local attacks against the Janissaries resulted in the Porte's banishment of several Muslim notables, including the *muftī* of Jerusalem.[75] Despite risks associated with ongoing violence, the planning began in December 1708 and was carried out by Abu Mansur, who notified Yu'annis XVI that he would accompany him to Jerusalem. Earlier, I discussed the collaboration between Yu'annis and Abu Mansur, which holds an important place in Coptic life during the early eighteenth century. Aside from their known partnership in renovating numerous churches and monasteries, in 1705, a procession was organized from Cairo to the Monastery of St. Antony and then to the Monastery of St. Paul, which culminated in the consecration of the Church of St. Mark in the latter. These events were led by the patriarch, several clergymen, and the archons, as supervised by Abu Mansur.[76] Only a few months before his pilgrimage to Jerusalem, Abu Mansur had spent some of his fortunes on the renovation of al-Muʿallaqa Church in Old Cairo. His supervision of this latter project—including personal attention to building, carpentry, and painting—was praised by fellow Copts in a commemorative manuscript, which described his fine managerial skills (*ajmal niẓām*) as well as his influence and prestige within the community and without.[77]

The pilgrimage narrative similarly highlights Abu Mansur's skills, knowledge, and authority. He instructed the patriarch to send letters to all Coptic bishops in Upper and Lower Egypt, informing them of the trip and asking the community for contributions (*indār*). The patriarch quickly complied, and the letters were sent only two days later. Soon after, other notables began to offer expertise and resources in preparing for the journey. The archons and patriarch elected a monk named Ishaq, who had come to Cairo from the Monastery of St. Antony, to help administer the planning.[78] An archon named Karamallah Abu Fulayfil (ca. 1708) knew, from past pilgrimages, which provisions were needed, and in a meeting at the home of another prominent archon, Lutfallah Abu Yusuf, the exact planning for the pilgrimage was determined. Even though Abu Yusuf did not intend to accompany the caravan, he volunteered to gather supplies for the trip, specifically to furnish the liturgical instruments used for the ceremonial blessing of the Church of the Holy Sepulchre. These might have included the censer; a cross to be held by the patriarch, bishop, or priest during prayers; a cruet for holding sacramental wine as well as chrism oil; the eucharistic bread basket; a gospel that was to be used in liturgical prayers; and possibly an incense box. That they had to be taken from Cairo to Jerusalem indicates that specially decorated objects, perhaps made of fine silks and metals, were utilized only during Easter services and that these tools had to be regularly replenished over the years.[79]

Abu Yusuf also obtained an order from the Ottoman governor (Husayn Pasha, r. 1707–1710) that ensured the safety of the patriarch and the caravan. In addition, he acquired letters from regimental officers and beys in Cairo, which were addressed to the custodians of different fortresses along the road and to bedouin leaders.[80] Such missives were not expected only from Christian travelers; Muslim pilgrims to Jerusalem also acquired them to guarantee their safety and plan for their accommodations.[81] After gathering these assurances, Abu Yusuf sent gifts and provisions to bedouins at Damietta and al-ʿArish.[82] These procedures were nearly identical to the general preparations undertaken for the ḥajj.[83] For over two months, Abu Yusuf collected the necessary supplies, and in that regard, his job compared closely to that of *amīr al-ḥajj* or "caravan commander."[84] The monk Ishaq, on the other hand, assisted with these efforts but had few of the political and financial resources necessary to prepare for the journey.

When it came time to depart in the spring of 1709, during the second week of Lent, the travelers, many from Upper Egypt, gathered in Cairo. Although it is difficult to discern the exact size of the caravan, it was large enough to have separated into two smaller convoys.[85] The Coptic narrative does not describe where pilgrims initially congregated and what ceremonies took place on their gathering. We can look to the accounts of later pilgrimages to help fill these gaps. In this book's introduction, I noted al-Damurdashi's description of the pilgrimage of 1748, a caravan led by Patriarch Murqus VII that departed from Harat al-Rum. Pilgrims lined up according to their social standing and the functions they served, although, as the reader may recall, the outcome was disastrous for Copts:

> We turn to the incident of the Coptic Christians. Their patriarch wished to visit *al-Qimāma al-Qudsiyya* [the Church of the Holy Sepulchre],[86] to celebrate the Saturday of Light [*Sabt al-Nūr*], and to visit Bethlehem. So he sent agents [*mubāshirīn*] to the bedouins to persuade them to allow the patriarch to visit Jerusalem. The wives of the agents said, "We will accompany the patriarch by land." Thus some of them purchased camels and provisions. They constructed wooden carriers, decorated them, and prepared their provisions. They sent them [the provisions] to al-'Adiliyya,[87] along with supplies, tents, and equipment. Young boys [*ghilmān*] led the camels and the patriarch, who rode a mule. Behind them were the agents, 'Abd al-Malak, the clerk for the imperial granary, and others, [as well as] the women who covered their heads with Kashmiri shawls. In front of them were the dancers [*jenk*] and behind them a Turkish band, and young boys with torches wrapped in *zardakhān* towels.[88]
>
> They departed from Harat al-Rum to al-'Aqqadin[89] and to al-Ghawriyya[90] with this procession, where our masters, the 'ulamā', saw them and said, "[This sight] is an innovation [bid'a]. How dare they emulate the Muslims?" They obtained a firmān from the *qa'im maqām* addressed to the Janissary agha so that he would prevent them from traveling by land and take possession of all that they were carrying. He gave them the firmān, and the Janissary agha as well as the *wālī* [the chief of police] departed for al-'Adiliyya. 'Uthman Bey Abu Sayf was sitting in charge of Sabil 'Allam [at that time] and the Christians went to him and begged him to help save their possessions, and he did. When the agha and the wālī arrived to al-'Adiliyya, they found no Christians. They announced that no Christian would travel by land and that he who violates [this order] would deserve whatever happens to him. They returned to Cairo. It was an ill-omened year for the Coptic Christians.[91]

Clearly, the procession violated Islamic prohibitions against public religious display by non-Muslims, but the presence of women added insult to injury. Muslim religious scholars frequently "objected when a woman went on pilgrimage to the Holy Cities for the sake of sight-seeing and pleasure."[92] The raucous procession in addition to the inclusion of women lent an air of frivolousness to the Coptic endeavor, which further upset the sensibilities of the 'ulamā'. Moreover, the similarities between Coptic and Muslim practices were simply too many, as the procession of 1748 also diverted from customary roles.[93] Major Coptic festivals and rituals had long been conducted out of public view, and this ostentatious display seemed to challenge, disrupt, and to some extent threaten established traditions.

Through their study of French consular documents, both André Raymond and Muhammad 'Afifi provide a different version of the 1748 story as recorded in French archives. In this narrative, Ibrahim Jawish al-Qazdaghli[94] received a bribe from the Coptic patriarch in exchange for guaranteeing the communal right to make the pilgrimage; however, Ibrahim Jawish was reportedly so greedy that he forced every pilgrim to pay an extra surcharge for the right to travel. On hearing this news, the Azharite shaykhs were infuriated and refused to allow Copts to parade in a caravan so closely patterned after the ḥajj.[95] Because of their protests, the situation ended with Copts and Muslims clashing, the death of a dozen Copts, the dissolution of the pilgrimage caravan, and the use of soldiers to restore order. The patriarch was also forced to give the shaykhs 30,000 dinārs in order to secure protection from further retaliatory actions against Copts.[96]

These reports are supported by another account—this time by al-Jabarti. In 1751, the Coptic pilgrimage was similarly spoiled by Muslim protesters, but al-Jabarti's version adds novel details.[97] The chronicler refers to the Copts' leader at the time, al-Mu'allim Nayruz Abu Nawwar, as "the elder among them" (*kabīrahum*) and as the driving force behind the pilgrimage. Abu Nawwar informed the famous Azhari Shaykh 'Abdallah al-Shubrawi[98] of the intended pilgrimage and also gave him a "gift" of one thousand dinārs. Thereupon al-Shubrawi issued a legal judgment (*fatwa*) declaring that Christians were not to be hindered from making their pilgrimage. When it came time for the trip, al-Jabarti reports that the Copts formed a grand procession and marched with their women and children through town, and with them were drummers and the *zumūr* (reed musical instrument) players. They also paid bedouins to escort and protect them.

When news of this commotion spread to other religious leaders, al-Shubrawi was asked to defend himself. After initially denying charges of corruption, he was confronted by 'Ali Efendi, brother of his close friend Shaykh al-Bakri,[99] who warned of brewing anger among the Muslim populace. Al-Jabarti recounts 'Ali Efendi's confrontation with al-Shubrawi: "'[W]hat is happening, O shaykh of Islam?' said the sick man reproachfully, 'How can you agree to give the Christians a fatwa and permit them to carry out these activities just because they have bribed you and given you gifts?'"[100] Al-Shubrawi denied that he had accepted this bribe, but his accuser continued: "Nay, they bribed you with 1,000 dinārs and gave you a gift. And so this will become a custom with them. Next year they will march out even more pompously. They will make themselves a *maḥmal* [palanquin], and people will talk about 'the Christians' ḥajj' and the Muslims' ḥajj."[101] Furious and humiliated, al-Shubrawi announced to the public that they were free to loot the caravan. Thus the inhabitants of the neighborhoods near al-Azhar surrounded the Copts, stoned them, beat them with sticks and whips, stole their belongings, and even plundered a nearby church. As al-Jabarti concludes, somewhat sympathetically, "the Christians' fortunes suffered a great reversal in the incident; everything they had spent was lost and scattered."[102]

A preliminary reading of these narratives might support the notion that Copts were grossly mistreated. However, both situations reveal complexities beyond the persecutory treatment of Copts. For one, the attacks against Copts mirror earlier violence against Muslim pilgrims to Mecca in 1699. On that year, a group of North Africans (Maghribis)—who were known for their strong religious zeal—physically assaulted and humiliated scores of pilgrims as they marched out of Cairo.[103] The pilgrims' crime was smoking, which the attackers viewed as disruptive to acceptable moral conduct. In that case, however, the crowds fought back, and the Maghribi instigators were incarcerated by Janissary guards.[104] In another case, from 1778, Europeans partaking in a lavish procession through Cairo's streets were verbally abused on their way to the Ottoman governor's residence in the Citadel.[105] Such incidents, whether against Muslims, Europeans, or Copts, took place periodically when certain groups felt that public practices contradicted acceptable religious and social standards. In fact, objections to the Coptic procession in 1748 and 1751 could be seen as a form of political protest by different factions within the Egyptian 'ulamā' against each other and against their Ottoman overlords, primarily because the latter had failed to stop this pageantry and protect the Islamic character of Egyptian society.[106]

The timing of their objections was hardly coincidental. A revival among the 'ulamā' was taking place during the eighteenth century, a period that saw a growing interest among the Muslim religious establishment with issues of public morality as linked to spiritual growth.[107] Within a cultural context where political power was frequently showcased through a strict enforcement of Islamic mores, one of the quickest ways to increase political legitimacy was to renew restrictions against non-Muslims.[108] Ottoman governors may have acquiesced to the 'ulamā''s actions, since, at the time, Egypt was succumbing—even if partially—to the influence of regional puritanical movements and to sectarian sentiment. In 1743, Egypt's Ottoman governor briefly outlawed tobacco smoking at a time when the sultanate was not only dealing with the Wahhabi influence in Arabia and nearby regions but was also fighting Shiʿi shahs in Persia. In these times, Ottoman rulers were upholding their role as protectors of the "true" Sunni faith, an attitude reflected in their decrees and policies.[109] Thus in mid-eighteenth-century Egypt, Coptic mechanisms for ensuring a successful pilgrimage likely fell prey to local and regional forces beyond their control. In 1709, on the other hand, archons may have understood their surroundings and the social divisions within Egyptian society and exploited them for their own benefit. But they were also quite lucky: on that occasion, their plans worked.

From Egypt to Palestine: Archons, Clergy, and Communion with Other Christians

Once challenges within Cairo were overcome, pilgrims were eager to visit shrines in Egypt and to reach their destination, where they would perform their customary rituals. These rituals—votive offerings, informal and formal prayer, and socializing with fellow believers—played a central role in instilling cohesiveness among the pilgrims. They became the medium by which the pilgrims affirmed their personal beliefs but also collectively discovered different dimensions of their faith. Between Cairo and Jerusalem, the archons acted as the principal organizers of the caravan, ensuring the pilgrims' safety by providing hospitality to local bedouins and offering gifts to administrative leaders along the way. At Jerusalem, on the other hand, pilgrims looked to their patriarch for guidance and leadership. Our narrative reveals a platform for this exchange between pilgrims and patriarch, as well as the ceremonial interplay between members of the Coptic caravan and external groups.

After journeying out of Cairo, the pilgrims traveled from Cairo to al-ʿAdiliyya, where supplies and equipment were sent in advance; al-ʿAdiliyya also served as a point of congregation for the ḥajj during the Ottoman era.[110] Two caravans moved from al-ʿAdiliyya to al-Matariyya,[111] the first led by Jirjis Abu Mansur and the second by Yu'annis XVI. In Matariyya, pilgrims visited sites associated with the Holy Family's journey and took blessings from them. Many locals gathered, old and young, notables (*aʿyān*) and archons, to greet the patriarch and his entourage and wish them well on their journey.[112] Following this exchange, they traveled to al-Khanqa "al-Yaraqutsiyya,"[113] a meeting point for travelers, merchants, and pilgrims going to Jerusalem. The text takes special care to note that as they readied to leave al-Khanqa, more crowds came to greet the pilgrims: old and young, men and women, priests and laypeople from all over Egypt.

Next, they headed toward Bilbays, approximately thirty miles northeast of Cairo, where they set up camp. Bilbays was a significant stopping point along a main courier route between Cairo and Damascus in the Ottoman period. But more important, Copts believed that the Holy Family stayed there during their sojourn in Egypt and that the infant Jesus miraculously raised a dead man.[114] Pilgrims partook

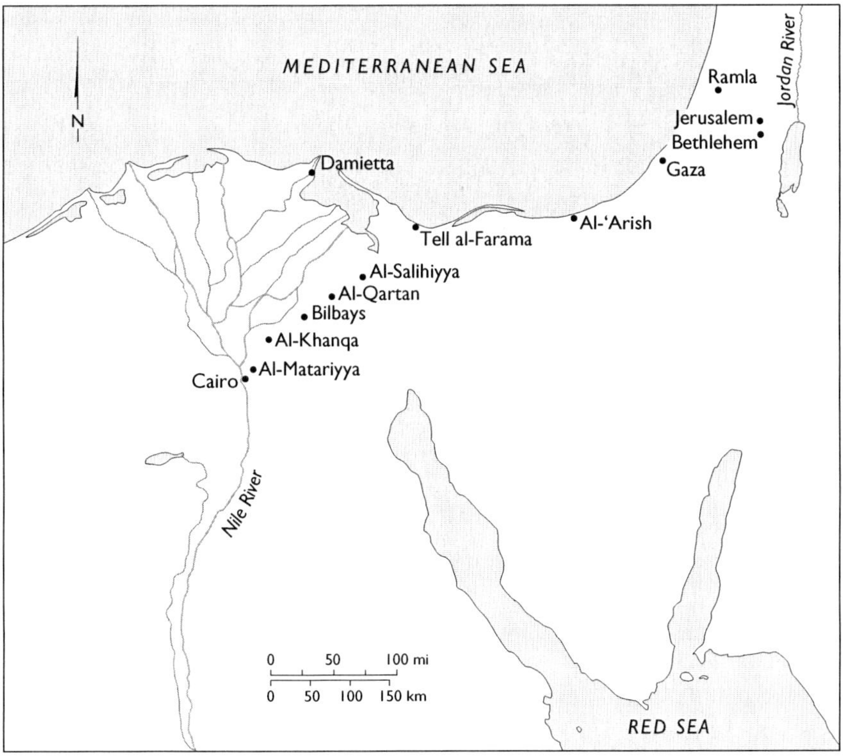

Major Stopping Points for Coptic Pilgrims to Jerusalem in 1709

of the blessings associated with this site. From Bilbays, they moved northeast to al-Qartan, where they camped, and then the next day to al-Salihiyya,[115] where they remained for two days. During these stops, more people congregated, including not only Copts from the Delta region but also bedouins, who apparently gathered out of tradition to receive the hospitality of the pilgrims, as seen at Dimyana's festival. Abu Mansur, as well as his brother, the archon and deacon al-Mu'allim Ibrahim Abu Sa'd, provided food and drink for the masses. They were also forced to fend off the bedouins who insisted on receiving more reward for their acquiescence to the caravan.[116]

The caravan's leisurely pace and its many stops indicate a philanthropic side to this pilgrimage, one that allowed the patriarch and communal leaders to minister to the broader community. This may have been one of the few times, if any, that Copts living in those areas would meet their patriarch. More notable, perhaps, is the fact that bedouins had to be appeased along the way, implying that negotiations continued to take place in order to ensure the caravan's safety. While this particular account notes the ease of the pilgrims' travels and the congeniality with which they were received by locals, the pilgrimage, as we recall, is referred to by the Coptic scribe as a "miracle," the miracle being, perhaps, success in traveling from Cairo to Palestine. Archons, it seems, were partially responsible for this wondrous act, as they placated bedouins and local officials throughout the journey.

A few days after it had departed, the metropolitan of Jerusalem, Ghubriyal, joined the caravan. Although the text omits mention of where they met, Ghubriyal could have brought along supplies from Damietta, where they had been sent earlier and where, as I noted above, the metropolitan of Jerusalem occasionally resided.[117] The caravan may have even visited Holy Family shrines in Tell al-Farama, along the Mediterranean Sea, and at al-ʿArish, where provisions had also been sent. On reaching Gaza, Abu Mansur inquired about meeting with Muhammad Pasha, governor of that district, but the pasha was in Ramla, so instead Abu Mansur met with the governor's lieutenant (referred to as *katkhuda* here), his deputy governor (*qāʾim maqām*), and the chief of the Arab tribes (*shaykh al-ʿarab*).[118] He gave them all appropriate gifts, and they provided him with assurances of safe travel. Once again, Copts negotiated for their safety and bought their caravan's protection. These negotiations raise an important point: while the ḥajj caravan traveled with armed guards to ensure its protection, the Coptic caravan may have had fewer or perhaps less reliable guards. Thus the possibility of violence from local tribes or rulers existed at each phase, and political and financial resourcefulness were needed to secure safe passage. While Egyptian chroniclers highlight the violence facing Copts in Cairo, these later stages were perhaps the most difficult for pilgrims: outside Cairo, their political networks were less established, and archons used skill in coping with unexpected challenges and in patching fragile agreements that were made in advance of their travels.

After a brief respite, the caravans arrived in Ramla and set up camp. Exhausted from their travels, Abu Mansur and the pilgrims quickly accepted an offer of hospitality made by monks from a nearby Armenian monastery, where they stayed for four days.[119] The generosity of local Armenians is significant, as it indicates the necessity of intercommunal cooperation and social exchange during the course of the pilgrimage, and indeed the Copts and Armenians would consolidate their friendship by celebrating mass together. Later, Coptic leaders met with the aforementioned Muhammad Pasha and presented him with fittingly lavish gifts. With all logistics completed, the road to Jerusalem was finally cleared. On Monday, at the beginning of the sixth week of Lent, the patriarch's and Abu Mansur's entourage headed out of Ramla and entered Jerusalem.

Despite their long journey, as soon as pilgrims arrived in Jerusalem, they opened their churches for prayer. Near the Church of the Holy Sepulchre, three chapels were made accessible: the Church of the Four Incorporeal Beasts, the Church of the Angel, and the Church of St. George. All of these were inside Dayr al-Sultan, the ancient Coptic monastery that would serve as their main lodging in

Jerusalem. Also, a meeting was quickly arranged between the Coptic Patriarch Yu'annis XVI and the Greek patriarch of Jerusalem.[120] As noted, the Greek Orthodox were the most influential of all Christian groups; by the end of the seventeenth century, they had secured from the Ottoman Porte, through Phanariot elites, the greatest influence among Ottoman Christians.[121] This meeting ensured that the Copts were in their good standing. Indeed, following the lead of the Greek patriarch, the Armenians and Roman Catholics were generous in their treatment of the Coptic patriarch. At the same time that the patriarch met with his clerical counterparts, Abu Mansur also bestowed gifts on local notables, the elders (*akābir*) and the qāḍīs in Jerusalem.[122] In all, Copts had to ingratiate themselves with Ottoman officials, Muslim notables, and distinguished Christian leaders. For a group that was generally marginalized from the Ottoman center, a successful pilgrimage depended on an array of deferential gestures to higher-ranking communities. Such ceremonial "paying of respects," among an array of Ottoman Christians, seems to have taken place exclusively in Jerusalem.

Some days later, and following customary practice, the Greek patriarch opened the doors of the Church of the Holy Sepulchre. The narrator describes the order in which Copts entered the church, which reflects the distinct social hierarchy within the community. First came Abu Mansur, along with the metropolitan, Ghubriyal. They were followed by Yu'annis XVI and a number of priests, dressed in their ceremonial clothing (*baranīs*).[123] An impressive total of eighty deacons and priests, holding icons and singing hymns of praise, preceded the patriarch as he entered the church holding the censer in his hand. They processed around the interior of the church until they reached the Coptic chapel near the tomb of Christ, where they celebrated the Eucharist. Afterward, all pilgrims received the blessing of Christ's Sepulchre, and for the remainder of the day, as well as for the duration of Holy Week, they visited shrines all over Jerusalem. These included a stopover at 'Ayn Silwan,[124] where they drank from the holy water; another at Bir Ayyub (Job's well);[125] and a climb up Jabal al-Su'ud[126] (the Mount of the Ascension), where the footprints of Jesus are reportedly imprinted on a rock. Later, they visited the sepulchre of the Virgin Mary in Gethsemane, where they prayed the liturgy.

In the final days of Lent, Palm Sunday celebrations were held inside the Church of the Holy Sepulchre. The narrator explains that Copts prayed early that day and then, after communion, partook in the traditional Pascha[127] litanies associated with Holy Week. The sacred functions of the pilgrimage are revealed within these descriptions, as the community of Christian pilgrims from all over the Ottoman Empire participated as a single group in unified ritual. In the late morning of Palm Sunday, worshippers congregated for another procession led by the Greek patriarch, who circled the outside of the church with his entourage thrice and then entered to pray. The Greeks were followed in order by Armenians, Copts, and Syrian

Orthodox. Yu'annis XVI wore special vestments, as did the accompanying priests, and they held in their hands palm branches and Bibles.[128] At the conclusion of these rituals, Holy Week had officially begun. On Monday and Tuesday, the Coptic patriarch led pilgrims to the Jordan River to receive the blessings of the water in which Jesus was baptized. During that week, they also conducted traditional services in their own chapels, until the Church of the Holy Sepulchre was reopened for communal prayer on Good Friday.

For the Coptic patriarch, these rituals in and outside Egypt provided him with an opportunity to increase his social standing within the community. On leaving Cairo, he had direct access to Copts in other parts of Egypt and to Christian communities in the broader Ottoman domain. His role along the journey, at least those elements of it that drew the scribe's attention, differed considerably from that of the archons. While archons focused on the dispensation of material philanthropy, the patriarch bestowed prayer and blessings on those who gathered to greet the caravan. He also represented the community in meetings with notable Christian leaders. Through the dignity of his office and his liturgical role, the patriarch enhanced the prestige of the Coptic delegation to Jerusalem. In these ways, the pilgrimage cannot be simply reduced to a story of archons dominating or triumphing over clergy. Their interdependence proved crucial to the realization of this important ritual.

Holy Fire: Orthodox Christians on Easter Eve

Religious rites on Easter eve receive a great deal of attention within our Coptic-Arabic text and make explicit the centrality of these events to all pilgrims, both Copts and other Orthodox Christians. By Saturday (referred to by Copts as the Saturday of Light or *Sabt al-Nūr*), the scribe notes that preparations were being made for the "Miracle of the Holy Fire." In contrasting the Coptic description of this tradition with Western accounts, one detects the varying attitudes of post-Reformation European Christians versus Eastern Orthodox toward the miraculous, the former highly skeptical and the latter fully devoted. Moreover, it becomes clear that certain religious rituals among Ottoman Christians, not unlike the apparitions of the saints at Dimyana's shrine, were partially intended to impress Ottoman soldiers and officials with the supernatural power of the Christian faith.

While Crusaders had once reveled in the dramatic ceremony of the Holy Fire, beginning in the thirteenth century after the reconquest of Latin territories by Muslim rulers, Europeans—whose access to these holy sites was now limited—saw it as a "forgery."[129] Ottoman-era Western accounts exhibit a similar attitude; in addition to general reservations about the religious practices of Eastern Christians, many raise suspicion toward this alleged miracle. Abudacnus, the seventeenth-century Coptic convert to Catholicism, describes the custom as follows:

> But on the Sabbath day they assemble all together in the Church of the Sepulchre and hear Mass; which all the Bishops that are present celebrate in so many several Chappels. In the Chappel of the Sepulchre only the Patriarch of the Jacobites [Copts], if he be present, otherwise his Vicar [the Metropolitan of Jerusalem], with some of the Abyssine Churches, upon whom, they say, a Light shineth out of the Sepulchre. But the Turks, that are Keepers, extinguish all of the Lamps and Candles set up that day in the Church, which are again lighted by the Divine Light springing out of the Sepulchre. But many esteem this to be a fiction; and in truth it is so: it is possible, and many testifie, that this might anciently have been, when those that professed the Christian Religion were very rare, but now the Faith being displayed through the whole World, we have no need of any such Miracles. But that the Turks may have good esteem of the Christian Religion, they are wont to deceive the credulous minds of the simple with such Arts, as may bring no damage to the Christian Faith, feigning the Lamps, to have been kindled by a light shining out of the Sepulchre, when indeed they have a Lamp suspended out of the Sepulchre, with which the Priest lighteth up again all the rest that were extinguished. And this is done by the Ethiopians, or the Jacobites, because they alone, as we said before, celebrate mass in the Chapel of the Sepulchre. Many Europeans believe this, but to impose upon the Greeks and Chaldeans[130] in this matter is a thing impossible.[131]

One line immediately stands out within this description: the Eastern Christians perpetuated this ritual so "that the Turks may have good esteem of the Christian Religion." The miracle functioned, in this context, as a means for spiritual and political legitimacy. It not only helped believers take pride in their own religion but also allowed them to participate in a ritual that conveyed the superior qualities of their faith. The honor wrought by this ritual was so coveted that the right to lead this ceremony was frequently contested among different sects. In the early seventeenth century, it was the Greek patriarch who entered the tomb and then emerged with glowing candles. However, in 1634, the Armenians challenged the Greeks, and in 1657, a compromise was reached whereby the two patriarchs would enter side by side.[132]

Subsequent rituals at the sepulchre are described in detail by Antoine Morison, a French Catholic priest visiting Jerusalem in 1699. First, he relates how all of the communities processed around the sepulchre, with twelve or fifteen banners carried around by the various "schismatic" Christian denominations and different clergymen donning their most glorious robes, studded with gold and precious jewels. Next, the Greek and Armenian patriarchs were locked inside by four Janissary guards, where they remained for an unspecified period as a multitude of believers waited.[133] On their grand exit from the tomb they passed around this "miraculous fire," which was used to light the candles of approximately two thousand people occupying the church. Shortly thereafter, according to Morison, the stories of "false miracles" began to circulate, which, in his opinion, were intended to impress the Ottoman Janissaries. Morison contrasts the "chaos" with the orderly and spiritual Catholic Easter celebrations completed weeks before, and he laments the disrespect for Christ's sepulchre shown by these schismatic ceremonies.[134] Similarly, in the eighteenth century, the missionary Sicard focused on the bustle outside the church's doors. Because pilgrims were unable to enter, tensions erupted and punches were thrown. Sicard notes:

> The crowd and the confusion increase on Saturday morning; for throughout the day a multitude of young people, workers, and villagers are not able to enter into this vast Church, so that they spend their time running, screaming, singing, and dancing around the [Holy] Sepulchre. The quarrelers begin to form and to beat each other with big blows of fists and feet. The Turk arises to control the mayhem, striking right and left with a big baton. The disorder stops and then recommences at an instant, just as the Procession ceremony begins.[135]

Rather than fixating on the pandemonium perceived by Western travelers, the Coptic-Arabic narrative focuses on the awe it inspired in all the participants. In this version, Christian sects prayed together on Saturday night, until dawn Sunday, when reportedly the light came out of the tomb. The communities decided which pilgrims had the right to purchase the Holy Light and the sequence in which each would receive it. Copts had bought the spot of the Syrians so that the light would be passed from the Greek patriarch to the Armenian patriarch, then to the candles of the Coptic patriarch, and then to al-Muʿallim Ibrahim Abu Saʿd, one of the most esteemed archons and Abu Mansur's brother. In a strange scene that seemed to break with Coptic traditions and that reveals, yet again, the archons' burgeoning influence in religious ritual and ceremony, Abu Saʿd, an ordained deacon, was made to dress in traditional liturgical vestments, some of them reserved for priests (including *al-akmām*, *al-badrashīn*, and *al-burnus*),[136] so that he could properly assume his spot next to the patriarch.[137] Significant here is the deviation from traditional ecclesiastical order, which is usually from patriarch to bishop, priest, deacon, then laity. The text in this section makes no mention of other clergy: Abu Saʿd stands right next to the patriarch and receives the light from him, seemingly superseding all other clergy in attendance. Following a particular order, Abu Saʿd passed the light on to the candles of Coptic pilgrims, who had prepurchased their place in line. A long procession was conducted afterward, in the customary order of Greeks, Armenians, Copts, and Syrians.[138] Once the celebrations finished, the traditional Easter greetings were exchanged among celebrants.

In all, the success of this ceremony reflected positively on the Christian leaders. From these descriptions, one wonders whether the dramatic performance, even as occasionally heightened by infighting, was timed precisely to make an impression on the Ottoman political and military representatives in attendance or whether it aimed to reinforce the faith of thousands of pilgrims. There is enough evidence to support both perspectives. Europeans saw this tradition as chaotic, and their observations highlight how Western travelers in this period focused much more on a pilgrim's quiet and meditative experience of the sacred.[139] Among Eastern Orthodox, however, this ritual was defined by communality and occasional unruliness. While there were some personal dimensions to this journey, the spotlight was on shared travel and collective ceremonies.[140]

According to the manuscript, the miracles did not end with the Holy Fire ceremonies. In the following week, Coptic pilgrims visited additional sites, including shrines in Bethlehem, but on the first Saturday after Easter, Jirjis Abu Mansur decided to return to Egypt; thus that evening, the doors to the Church of the Holy Sepulchre were opened, and the pilgrims entered to pray one last time. Following liturgy and after most of the congregation had been dismissed, a private ceremony took place in which the patriarch and some of the archons visited Christ's tomb for one final blessing. They departed on 7 May 1709, retracing their earlier journey. As they neared Cairo, news regarding infighting among Ottoman soldiers nearly ruined their perfect pilgrimage. Abu Mansur had learned that Isma'il Kahya, *amīn al-jawālī* (supervisor of jizya) and the multazim of the province of Bilbays, was coming to al-Khanqa, where the caravan was halted, in order to raid the Coptic pilgrims. However, when they arrived in Bilbays, the fighting among the soldiers had ceased, and Cairo's gates were opened. The caravans were directed to al-Matariyya, where the patriarch and Abu Mansur disembarked. They ordered the camels and baggage sent to Cairo and once again visited local Holy Family shrines. At these sites, many locals gathered to serve them and to hear their stories. No doubt the miracle of the Holy Fire and the miracle of their successful travels were shared with fellow believers and would become part of their communal memory.[141] Finally the pilgrims returned to Cairo and completed their journey.

Conclusions

It is difficult to generalize about the Coptic pilgrimage to Jerusalem for the entirety of the Ottoman period, as the ritual was changing and historically contingent. Still, the pilgrimage in the early eighteenth century reveals an institution that simultaneously worked to glorify the Coptic religion, to challenge restrictions against public processions, and to link Copts to dominant Christian communities in the Ottoman world. Copts were more empowered to perform their rituals during this period, as many of their communal elders held important jobs in the households of Egypt's political and military leaders. The pilgrimage sometimes reflected the archons' confidence that they could evade attacks; on those occasions, processions became public entertainment that included dance, music, and a dramatic ceremony through Cairo. These practices, however, were likely circumscribed when Copts feared or expected challenges to their endeavor. In all, leaders of this community learned to be adaptable and recognized which strategies to employ in order to uphold their religious traditions. On a successful year, archons negotiated with local power-holders, supplied necessary provisions, gave alms to the poor, and paid requisite fees. The patriarch, in his spiritual capacity, blessed villagers, led the community in prayer, and interfaced with his Christian correlates in Jerusalem. On his return to Egypt, he may have even been inspired to exercise greater authority. William Lyster has suggested that following the pilgrimage of 1709, Yu'annis XVI ordered the impressive artistic renovations within the Cave Church at the Red Sea Monastery of St. Paul, motivated by the grandiose churches he saw in Jerusalem.[142]

Pilgrimages, in Victor Turner's classic characterization, are acts of communal fraternity; they can be voluntary or obligatory; they are life-changing "rites of passage" transporting believers from the familiar to the foreign and back to the familiar; they allow pilgrims to surpass both spatial and temporal limitations in the course of their journey.[143] Undoubtedly, for Coptic Christians, the pilgrimage to Jerusalem rejuvenated their faith and allowed them to experience this sense of communality. The oral traditions that likely accompanied their return created the context for a kind of "secondhand" pilgrimage, one that was passed down orally, literally, and physically.[144] In its entirety, the pilgrimage illustrates nuances in Coptic religious practice. The caravan, for one, focused on philanthropy, attracting bystanders who wished to speak to the travelers and to benefit from their blessings (both material and spiritual). When a Copt returned from Jerusalem, he or she would have been recognized as *muqaddas* or *muqaddasa* (derived from "al-Quds," the Arabic name for Jerusalem), a title comparable in prestige to the *ḥajj* and *ḥajja* returning from Mecca. Pilgrims shared their relics with family and friends: all cherished candles that were lit in the ceremony of the Holy Fire, and perhaps some showed off their tattoos. Historically, Coptic pilgrims chose to inscribe on their skin the figure of the cross (the "Jerusalem cross"), which commemorated the occasion and protected the bearer, or the year of the pilgrimage.[145] Along with candles, rosaries, and pictures, tattoos became keepsakes that continued to commemorate this event.[146] And in Coptic homes, where amulets or icons were displayed, the Jerusalem relics were a reminder of God's grace and of the protection he bestows on pilgrims, who now received recognition, status, and influence within their community.

In these ways, the pilgrimage provides a snapshot of how Copts, while informed by Muslim rites, developed their own distinctive practices. Moreover, it shows how they shaped their own fortunes. Communal leaders devised proactive strategies in order to make their journey. Different actors collaborated to strengthen the Coptic community, perhaps helping it to endure during tumultuous times. This example, however, might point to a false norm of lay and clerical concord. As the next chapter reveals, by the end of the eighteenth century, the potential vulnerability of Coptic believers to the teachings of Catholic missionaries challenged communal cohesiveness and created new rifts.

5

Weapons of the Faithful

Defining Orthodoxy through Sermons

A missionary must not repel at the attachment Copts have toward their traditions. On the contrary, he must work closely and patiently with them; often invoke the gospel, for which they have great respect; and repeat to them the same truth frequently, in order to overcome little by little the obstinacy in their ignorance, without ever giving them grounds for believing that he has contempt for them.

—Claude Sicard, *Oeuvres* II

Despite the preceding example of intracommunal cooperation, it is more accurate to characterize the archon-clergy relationship as one of intermittent collaboration and contention. One case of friction between both sides, if subtle, is documented from the late eighteenth century. At that time, higher clergymen grew concerned about Catholic influence over Coptic believers. They saw it necessary, first, to defend their community against external threats, and second, to reassert themselves as its true leaders. To counter missionary sermons that censured the Copts' "deviant" practices, religious leaders preached against spiritual and moral degeneration among coreligionists. Their sermons suggest that they were frustrated with an inability to control priests and lower clergymen as well as with their declining position in relation to archons. Heterodoxy among the masses added further insult to the injury of their weakening power. In this chapter, I will argue that through sermons, Coptic clerical leaders, of the highest ranks, stylized themselves as guardians of orthodox Christianity. In their oratory, they posited the idea of an anti-Chalcedonian, Orthodox, and Coptic identity to contrast the Catholic label adopted by new converts, and in this way, they signaled the religious and cultural uniqueness of Egypt's largest Christian community.

What follows is an examination of three sets of sermons that capture, at least partially, the encounter between Copts and Catholics in late-eighteenth-century Egypt, the resulting intracommunal tensions, and the growing need for clerical leaders to define religious boundaries. The first set dates from 1772 and was authored, in Arabic, by an unknown Catholic Copt who was ostensibly preaching to potential converts in Egypt; the other two were written by Patriarch Yu'annis XVIII (1769–1796) and Bishop Yusab (r. 1791–1826). The exact dates for Yu'annis's and Yusab's sermons are unknown, but based on the clergymen's reigns and on the events surveyed within their homilies, they were likely completed in the last quarter of the eighteenth century. Comparing these texts with other, coeval Coptic homilies and tracing changes in clerical attitudes would have been beneficial, but our inquiry is limited by the scarcity of sources. Still, the sermons at hand are notable for dealing with issues of identity, a concept referenced more overtly in these texts than in other communal records from this period. Coptic rhetoric was not necessarily innovative in this regard; the effects of Westernization on other Middle Eastern Christians could be seen as their faith became "more standardized, better controlled by [their] institution[s], and at the same time more internalized."[1] As Christian leaders distinguished their communities from others, conversion was discouraged through the branding of converts as traitorous. It is difficult to judge whether Coptic polemical sermons prevented conversion or strengthened the community in any way. Still, the texts reveal how higher clergymen perceived popular practices and, accordingly, how they used preaching to delineate sectarian boundaries.

Catholic Missions to the Middle East

From the time of the Crusades in the thirteenth century, Franciscans had guarded sacred sites in the Holy Land and also conducted missionary activities among indigenous Christians. In the Ottoman period, they moved into Cyprus, Egypt, Greater Syria, and Istanbul, albeit with limited success.[2] As discussed, in the sixteenth century, the Catholic Church had made several attempts to unify with Eastern Christians, including Copts, but most of their efforts ended in failure. The Protestant Reformation, however, motivated Rome to spread its influence and gain new converts. In the seventeenth century, missionaries resumed their activities, backed in their endeavors by France, the dominant Catholic and European power in the eastern Mediterranean.[3] France's position had grown considerably during this period as Frenchmen came to monopolize the lucrative Levantine trade, particularly of cloth; correspondingly, their consulate held significant political and economic leverage over the Ottoman Porte. In time, as one scholar puts it, the French government "used its patronage to buy local souls."[4] To reward conversions, French consuls—working in parallel with missionaries—offered incentives to indigenous Christian merchants, including protection for their ships as well as berāts that gave them legal and diplomatic protection in addition to trading privileges.[5]

In 1665, through its connections with the Hapsburg ambassador, and in 1690, through the French ambassador in Istanbul, the Catholic Church acquired sultanic decrees that were directed to provincial governors and allowed missionaries to preach freely in Ottoman territories; the 1690 edict indicated that "the Jesuits and other French priests who were teaching the principles of the Christian faith to the people of the Rum, Armenian, and Coptic sects (*mezhebler*) were to be left alone. Neither government officials nor members of the other Christian religious communities would be suffered to interfere with their work."[6] Notwithstanding official policies or lack thereof, conversion was becoming an attractive option among Ottoman Christians, as it afforded them new ways to acquire a desirable socioreligious and economic identity. In Aleppo, for instance, missionaries succeeded in converting the majority of native Christians, including three-quarters of that city's Syrian Jacobite community.[7] Still, the Levant should be distinguished from other parts of the Ottoman Arab world. For decades, it was home to scores of European merchants who maintained extensive commercial networks, particularly with local Christians. The latter, long familiar with Europeans and their religion, seem to have accepted conversion more readily, knowing that it offered valuable political connections, language skills, and a good education.[8] In time, many became protégés of foreign merchants, traders, and dignitaries. Conversion was also prompted by less material motivations; missionaries in the Levant were known to be effective teachers, offering a straightforward and practical education, and they were particularly willing to allow the laity—especially women—greater involvement in their own parishes.[9]

These transformations, however, wrought upon Eastern Christians an array of legal, political, and intra- and intercommunal challenges. New converts looked to Rome rather than to local clergy for patronage and protection, but in most cases they also maintained their traditional customs, praying in their own languages and observing their traditional rites.[10] The closeness in religious practices among converts and orthodox evoked conflict not only between clergy and laity, as might be expected, but also between or within different sects. In Ottoman Syria, for instance, tensions with Orthodox Christians contributed to an exodus of Catholics to other parts of the empire, especially to Egypt.[11] In Palestine, Catholic friars clashed over the lucrative alms that came from Eastern converts, who were accustomed to paying their priests for religious rites.[12] Initially, Ottoman authorities disregarded what appeared to be local squabbles among their Christian populations. So long as missionaries eschewed contact with Muslims, following Islamic prescripts prohibiting conversion, they would be allowed to conduct their affairs with little intervention.[13] However, in the late seventeenth and early eighteenth centuries, subsequent to the negotiation of new capitulations treaties, many native Christians working for European patrons were exempted from paying the jizya and were allowed to pay lower customs taxes than their Muslim counterparts.[14] Over time, the Ottoman center became troubled by these privileges and by the missionaries' increasing influence. New orders were issued throughout the eighteenth century, the first in 1722, restricting missionary teaching and in essence negating earlier decrees that had tolerated their activities.[15] These orders were erratically enforced, however, and in provinces like Egypt where Ottoman control had waned, missionaries were monitored mostly (and rather superficially) by local rather than central authorities.

In all, Catholic missions in the early modern Middle East saw successes in places where Christians benefited tangibly from commercial and political ties with Europeans. By the end of the eighteenth century, Catholics had succeeded in converting pockets of Christians in Istanbul, Aleppo, Damascus, and Palestine. As Bruce Masters has shown, the long-standing presence of European merchants and French consuls in most of those areas, combined with the ambition of urban Christian laity to assert greater control over their churches, facilitated conversion. An economic transformation among new converts was accompanied by changes in their social and cultural mores. Educated and upwardly mobile Christians had become disillusioned with traditional orthodox hierarchies, so they more easily identified with the Catholic Church and its seemingly accommodating leadership.[16] Their new churches, called "Uniates," maintained familiar religious practices and customs but also allowed members to connect with Catholic communities within and beyond the empire.[17]

The situation would differ in Egypt, where European missionaries would have few options but to target the largest Christian community, the Copts, if they were to see their efforts bear fruit. In the short run, since most Copts lived in rural areas or worked in urban sectors outside trade, they saw few immediate benefits to adopting Catholicism. Still, the idea of entering into a wide patronage network would eventually become attractive to some, and missionaries in Egypt found modest success among those who were eager to leave the confines of the Coptic Church and its leadership.

Catholics and Copts: Conversion and Confrontation

When studying the history of Coptic-Catholic relations in the eighteenth century, one can scarcely imagine that there was a time when Coptic patriarchs were amenable to improved relations with Rome. Yet in 1440, at the Council of Florence, a Coptic delegation sent by Yu'annis XI agreed to unification and denounced the Copts' long-standing opposition to the Council of Chalcedon. These agreements, however, were never formally ratified. Alistair Hamilton has suggested that for Copts, abandoning "a millennium of traditions" was simply too much to bear.[18] Still, missionary efforts continued after the Ottoman conquest. As noted in chapter 2, Ghubriyal VII initially welcomed negotiations with a Jesuit mission. However, following months of failed dialogue he told them, in so many words, that the Catholic pope "was only the head of the Franks, just as the patriarch of Constantinople was the head of the Greeks and he himself was the head of the Copts."[19] In 1561, Pope Pius IV invited Ghubriyal VII to participate in the Council of Trent, where the Catholic Church would come to establish most of its Counter-Reformation mandates. While Ghubriyal insinuated that he would send a representative to the Council, the Coptic bishop of Cyprus, in the end no one turned up.[20] Another mission by the Jesuits in 1582 was equally ineffective. Initially, when one delegation succeeded in convincing Ghubriyal VIII to unify with Rome, he showed his reverence to the Catholic vicar by addressing him as "honored sir, great proprietor, head of the priests of the world, vicar of Saint Peter, the greatest among the apostles, the Father Sixtus the Fifth"[21] and also spoke of the two churches as "a single fold and a single faith."[22] However, beyond these formal pronouncements, this mission too would ultimately fail; at that point, Catholics began to focus on conversion of rather than unification with Copts and on establishing a more permanent missionary presence in Egypt.

In the sixteenth century, the Franciscans of the Custody of the Holy Land had built a hospice in Old Cairo and were permitted by the Coptic leadership to pray at the Church of St. Sergius.[23] In 1622, to help manage its missions in the Middle East, Pope Gregory XV (1621–1623) founded the "Congregation of Propaganda Fide" in Rome, which devised a specific program to convert native Christians; among other things, the latter were pressured to accept Chalcedon, the use of unleavened bread, and belief in purgatory. Moreover, "matrimony was proclaimed indissoluble: adultery, heresy, and other obstacles could lead to separation, but never to new marriages."[24] The Propaganda Fide would succeed in creating a more permanent Catholic presence in Egypt. In 1630, the Capuchin order[25] founded a mission in Cairo, and the Reformed Franciscans followed in 1687, with centers in Cairo, Fayyum, Rosetta, and Damietta.[26] At first the Coptic clerical leadership submitted to these developments, justly believing that the Catholic mission was too small and ineffective to threaten its own affairs. It is even reported that in the mid-seventeenth century, Copts allowed missionaries to use the monasteries of St. Macarius and St. Antony for language instruction.[27] In a move that may have haunted later clergymen, Mittawus III (1634–1649) also permitted Catholic priests to preach in Coptic churches. When a new effort toward unification emerged, however, the "immoral conduct of the Catholics residing in Egypt" was cited as a main reason for its failure; reportedly, Mittawus III complained that "the Roman Catholic Church in this country is a brothel."[28] Ultimately, most Coptic laymen and clergy were insular in their religious outlook and, throughout the sixteenth and seventeenth centuries, showed limited interest in unification or conversion. The French consul in Egypt wrote a report in 1692 indicating that missionaries had "tried everything, but the only way of making a convert from the Copts is to take a child almost from birth and separate him entirely from his own people."[29]

In 1697, the Franciscans succeeded in founding a new mission of Upper Egypt, Nubia, and Ethiopia (based in Akhmim); Jesuits also established a permanent center in Cairo.[30] Initially, the Akhmim mission was slow to gain converts even though in the eighteenth century, missionaries had proliferated due to the French's rising influence in Egypt.[31] In 1703, Father Jacques d'Albano reported to Rome that after five years, he had obtained very few conversions.[32] Some years later, the Jesuit priest Sicard wrote with suggestions on how to change the situation: "The sole conversion of one Coptic priest, which the Lord allows, is the key to a great number of conversions; because to convert one Coptic priest, that is to convert with him several others of his nation. The gross ignorance of Copts is such that they blindly follow all that their priests do."[33] Adjusting missionary tactics apparently worked, as sources in the 1730s report that at least one hundred Copts in Upper Egypt alone were converting each year; by 1750, there may have been up to thirteen hundred Coptic Catholics.[34] Copts were also converting outside Egypt. In Jerusalem, one metropolitan, Athanasius, adopted Catholicism in 1739, and between 1768 and 1856, the conversion of 189 Jerusalemite Copts was recorded within Franciscan archives.[35] These conversions, many from prominent individuals and families, created new boundaries between former coreligionists.[36] Without minimizing the complexities behind processes of conversion, one could argue that some Copts became aware of and tempted by the stature enjoyed by Catholics, especially by the immigrant Syrian Catholic population.[37] New converts opened themselves to an important network that included European and Near Eastern Catholics, one that allowed them to receive benefits such as an advanced education and, if they desired, trade connections.[38] As noted, throughout the Ottoman Arab world, orthodoxy had come to represent traditional clerical interests, and conversion to Catholicism symbolized an antiestablishment stance.[39] In Egypt, new converts could detach themselves from a seemingly regressive church leadership and from the restrictive dominance of archon power. In all, even if conversions were few in number, they were enough to fracture the Coptic community, for the first time, into Orthodox and Catholic.

In this context, both communities became vocal in outlining confessional boundaries. Franciscans demanded that Coptic converts destroy their old books, and many missionaries "actually ridiculed and misrepresented the Eastern rites, tradition, and customs."[40] Mutual distrust and, at times, loathing would be reproduced in their rhetoric and writings. A letter sent to Rome by a missionary in Cairo describes the increasingly antagonistic position which emerged during the reign of Coptic patriarch Butrus VI (1718–1726):

> We have had a very cruel persecution on the part of the Coptic nation and the Patriarch [Butrus] of this same nation; but then I say that the Patriarch is not so much guilty, since I know him well, and between us there is a great friendship, and he himself has sworn to me his not wanting to consent to the words of his Copts; but by force and because of fear of not being recognized and of being proclaimed like a Frank, he agreed with them and they wrote Letters of excommunications and maledictions for all the Coptic Catholics and they wanted to have them read publicly in their churches and to deliver all these Catholics in the hand of the tyrants.[41]

The text stresses Butrus VI's fear of "being proclaimed like a Frank" and of being denied recognition within his own community, among "his Copts," a likely reference to influential laymen. Here, one wonders if the patriarch's qualms extended only to coreligionists, or whether they reflect worries about his relationship with Muslim authorities, who—in a tumultuous political climate—likely frowned on the formation of an indigenous Uniate church.[42] To illustrate his loyalties toward the Ottoman governor and local power-holders, the patriarch not only repudiates the idea of "Frankness" but also delivers those "Franks" to "the hand of the tyrants," presumably to local officials.

With increased tensions, the missionary movement intensified its battle on two fronts: in Cairo, through its attempts to win the allegiance of the patriarch, and in Upper Egypt, through its mission in Akhmim. Consequently, Coptic clergymen grew uneasy toward European Catholics and new converts alike. Conflict erupted over the recruitment of Coptic boys in Akhmim to be educated in Rome.[43] Also, several priests secretly professed their allegiance to the Catholic faith but continued to serve their Coptic congregations.[44] In response, Patriarch Yu'annis XVII "threatened to excommunicate all those who would have become 'Franks,' [and] prohibited all 'Franks' from entering the house of a Copt and vice versa, under penalty of losing all their goods."[45] He also ordered his priests to serve wine made from "dried grapes," as was the custom in Coptic traditions, and to read in each church the excommunication edict against priests who had become Franks.[46] To Coptic clerical leaders, conversion implied adoption not only of the Catholic faith but of a new, alternative, and entirely foreign identity.

During these tumultuous times, it appears that most archons continued to be loyal to the Coptic Church and committed to preserving their community. Archons had followed this policy for some time, since, with a more coherent and defined community, their own positions as its interlocutors to Egypt's local military and political leaders grew stronger. In 1778, a European traveler to Upper Egypt confirmed how some archons' allegiance to their faith resulted in persecution of and retaliation against new converts:

> Among the number of the Coptic inhabitants of Tahta, there were several Catholics. The Copts, it is well known, are one of the sects which the Roman church condemns as heretical. I frequently visited the most respectable among them, and, to my great satisfaction, I there found their vicar an Egyptian who had passed fifteen years in a seminary in Rome. He spoke Latin and Italian pretty well; and I took a pleasure in conversing with a man whom I considered as an European. He informed me that the Egyptians attached to the Roman church were cruelly harassed and tormented by those of their numerous countrymen who followed the heresy with which they were infected, and that their most determined and implacable persecutor was the very man [the Coptic archon Murqus] in whose house I resided. Enjoying the confidence of the kiaschefs [*kāshif*s], he thence arrogated to himself an authority to impose extortions on those of his nation who had adopted a religious doctrine preached by foreigners, in consequence of which they were often obliged to collect considerable sums in order to avert the effects of his animosity.[47]

Through these discriminatory actions, archons were likely working to ensure that their community persisted as the dominant Christian sect and that they, instead of the Catholic leadership, would be recognized as its principal leaders. Their position also signaled to their Muslim patrons that Copts were dependable and that they were autonomous and resilient against external pressures. This, in effect, strengthened their trustworthiness and further ingratiated them to local patrons.[48] In the eighteenth century, Europeans were frequently blamed for corrupting the moral fabric of Islamic society, particularly by spreading habits such as smoking and drinking.[49] By maintaining their faith and even at times persecuting the Catholics, archons outwardly showed their fidelity.

However, intermarriage and cross-religious interaction perpetuated heretical practices and promoted unsanctioned social and religious exchange. As they worked to preserve fragile communities of new converts, Catholic missionaries took a stronger stance. For decades they had complained about the most sacrilegious practices among Copts: divorce, concubinage, underage marriage, the use of magic, and the neglect of one of the most important sacraments—confession.[50] Such grievances were certainly not restricted to the Coptic Church, as missionaries frowned on the behavior of other "schismatic" believers throughout the Ottoman Empire. Missionary sources are plentiful regarding incidents of misconduct and apparent resentment of the infiltration of Orthodox practice into Catholicism and more generally of Islamic practices into Christian culture.[51] In their writings and sermons targeting Copts, missionaries used rhetoric consistent with the Counter-Reformation movement, which found popular religious practices to be particularly abhorrent. It is difficult to determine the reactions of local inhabitants toward these missionaries and their oratory. In general, fewer documents detail the perceptions of Orthodox communities. As such, the critiques made by Coptic Church authorities, to be discussed later, will provide an important contrast to known Catholic discourses. In attempting to understand the specific nature of Coptic counter-preaching, however, we first explore a treatise written by a Coptic convert to Catholicism that was formulated to win over Orthodox believers.

Catholic Exhortations against Copts

In the seventeenth century, missionaries in the Middle East experienced many difficulties, especially in mastering the Arabic language. Some in Egypt had grumbled about the "ridicule they received from the Copts when pronouncing [Arabic] badly or for not knowing the correct theological terms and concepts necessary for the work of conversion."[52] Yet by the eighteenth century, missionaries not only exhibited a better mastery of local languages but had succeeded in training a number of indigenous converts in theological and doctrinal matters. A handful of these converts were Copts, including Yustus al-Maraghi (d. 1748) and Rufa'il Tukhi (d. 1787). Both had traveled to Rome in 1736, studied at the Vatican, and returned to Egypt to preach, although Tukhi would later go back to Italy, where he became known as a translator of Coptic liturgical books.[53] Later Coptic sermons were part of an organized reply to those missionaries and their convert protégés, whose writings and sermons had been circulating throughout Egypt in the late eighteenth century.

One of the most eloquent, forthright, and representative of Catholic critiques of Orthodoxy is *Kitāb al-Istifhām ba'd al-Istibhām* or "The Book of Asking Questions after Being in Doubt" (hereafter cited as *MS.KI*). This theological work was written in 1772 by an anonymous spokesman from the Coptic Catholic community.[54] The manuscript is divided into twenty chapters and a conclusion. Its tone and language suggest that the intended audiences were Copts, elites and commoners alike, who were considering conversion to Catholicism but had questions regarding the differences between the religious practices of the two faiths. Although filled with colloquialisms, the language of this treatise is generally lucid and straightforward. This text enables an appreciation of later Orthodox counter-sermons and provides the unique perspective of an individual who straddled two identities as a Copt and as a Catholic.

The author's attention to issues like sectarianism, the Frankish label, clerical ineptitude, and factionalism confirms that the ideological rift between Copts and Roman Catholics centered on identity and socioreligious behavior. In a sense, the thoughtful, targeted, and persuasive tone within *MS.KI* represents the formidable intellectual challenge that Copts faced in dealing with the missionary movement. From the outset, it is clear that the author of *MS.KI* aims to counter negative rhetoric against the Franks. He focuses on the supreme role of the Catholic pope and the unity within Catholicism as compared to the multiple divisions among Orthodox churches. He refers to Copts as followers of the "Jacobite"[55] sect and argues that the disunity among Orthodox sects is indicative of the falseness of their beliefs:

> We see that all the sects which are opposed to your [Coptic] faith refute your opinions, do not follow your orders, and do not obey your patriarch. So you cannot prove that your church is the one holy catholic apostolic church because it is alone, isolated, and its teachings are opposed to the truth, opposed to each other [other churches], and opposed to what is written in your theological and scientific books. You dismiss the Rūm [Greek Orthodox] and call them heretics because they believe in two natures and criminalize Dioscorus,[56] and they call you heretics [as well]. Yet you say about them that upon their hands appears the light of Christ at the Sepulchre on the Great Saturday . . . so the conclusion of your talking is that their faith is more correct because of the miracle which occurs upon the hands of their patriarch since the miracle is a sign from God. . . . If the Greek Orthodox hold the truth because of the light, then *you* are wrong because of the difference of belief from them![57]

The miracle of the Holy Fire in Jerusalem has been discussed in chapter 4, but our author here reveals a novel critique of intra-Christian relations that might have appealed to his readers. If Copts were so interested in preserving their own communal identity, he argues, then why do they hold the Greek patriarch in such high esteem? Here, *MS.KI* appeals to sectarian feelings among Copts by attempting to sow discord with the Greek Church. This may have caused some knowledgeable Copts to question the practices and teachings of their own church, and to further consider conversion to Catholicism.

Still, the stigma of being labeled a Frank, a foreigner, or a non-Copt deterred potential converts, and *MS.KI* seems particularly attuned to this point. The author attempts to explain to his audiences what the term "Frank" actually signifies:

> You must learn that in truth, those [Catholic] monks and missionaries are not of the Frankish race because the true Frank, to whom this name applies, is the Frenchman such as the foreign [*khawājāt*] French merchants who live in Cairo; they are truly Franks. But others are from different races; among them are those from Rome, Austrians, those from Naples, Portuguese, Venetians, French, and others. These are all worldly races, just as in the East there are Greeks, Armenians, Syrians, Copts, Abyssinians, Nubians, Sudanese, and others. These races do not signify faith but the origin of nationality. So if all of these sects believe in the Orthodox faith, then we are all one in Christ through faith, not through race. Not each person who is a Catholic is a Frank; we [for example] are Catholics by faith and Copts by race. We are like you in all things spiritual and physical, except in the heresy and teachings [of the Coptic Church].... [We are like you] in the material things such as food and clothes. We are enslaved like you are, and we pay the sultan's jizya just like you do.[58]

To the best of his ability, he differentiates between the Catholic religion—the system of belief adopted by converts—and the Copts as an ethnic group. According to *MS.KI*, missionaries and converts had been misrepresented by the malicious epithets used among the Copts: they were defamed and called "new Jews" and "non-Christians," when in fact indigenous converts were "Copts by race."[59] This was a novel idea: reminding audiences that they could continue being Copts—with all of the advantages and disadvantages that this entailed—even after leaving the Coptic Church. To counter these arguments, Coptic clerical leaders would repeatedly maintain that these two identities—faith and race—were completely inseparable and accused anyone who converted to Catholicism of abandoning their Coptic identity.

Beyond decrying heretical beliefs, however, the author of *MS.KI* attacked some of the most inconsistent and seemingly backward practices among Copts, which were the outcome, in his opinion, of ignorance among and lack of guidance from church authorities. On the subject of fasting, for example, the author reveals that Copts in Cairo diverged from their counterparts in Upper Egypt in their interpretation of when to follow the core fasts of the church. Whether or not this division reflected the historic divide of Lower and Upper Egypt, it was vital in illustrating disarray within the Coptic community:

> I speak to you about the differences in the ritual [of fasting] between the Roman Catholic Church and the Copts. . . . In the Coptic Church itself, it differs between the city of Cairo and Upper Egypt, even though this is one sect, following one ritual, and under the leadership of one patriarch. In Cairo, the Christmas fast is twenty-eight days beginning from the first of the month of Kiyahk [November/December]. But in Upper Egypt, it is forty-three days, which is the last half of the month of Hatur [October/November], fifteen days before Kiyahk. . . . This [situation] is the same for the Apostolic fast. In Cairo, they fast fourteen days before the feast of Saints Peter and Paul. . . . In Upper Egypt, they fast from the Pentecostal Feast, which is the fifty days known as the *Sajda*, and this makes the fast, following Easter, up to forty-nine days long.[60]

In his own sermons, Patriarch Yu'annis XVIII would criticize laymen who were neglecting the church's fasts. He would be less worried, however, about the spiritual welfare of the community than about portraying a negative image of Copts to outsiders, which they could and apparently did use to criticize the church. Copts throughout Egypt practiced different interpretations of fundamental church rituals, evoking an image of disunity and of a weakened church hierarchy that Catholics could manipulate while persuading Copts to change their faith.

The author of *MS.KI* considered Coptic clergy's inability to control a wide array of practices to be one of their gravest errors. Underage marriage proliferated, as the rule of waiting until boys had passed the age of fourteen and girls passed the age of twelve was commonly neglected. This practice, as such, turned a holy sacrament, whose goals were procreation, into unbridled sexual lust.[61] Similarly, the author was appalled by the disorderly conduct that took place at Coptic weddings. He writes, "[There is] gossip, mockery, inappropriate finger pointing, and sinful language against purity since the people believe that marriage is only for sex and do not consider it as a church sacrament. So they wink and laugh when the priest orders the groom and bride to love one another!"[62] The church was a space for quiet prayer and meditative worship; the raucousness at weddings offended his Catholic sensibilities. Once again, these attitudes, reminiscent of travelers' descriptions of practices at Dimyana's festival and at the Church of the Holy Sepulchre, reflect Counter-Reformation teachings whereby the church, as Elizabeth Tingle argues, was no longer the epicenter of social life but rather an orderly space for "holiness and prayer, where mingling and gossip were inappropriate. Silence and contemplation were to be enforced."[63] Lastly, the widespread practice of divorce, made easier by Coptic recourse to sharī'a courts, was shunned as an act of adultery and heresy.[64] Of course, Copts had long been negotiating most of their legal disputes within Islamic courts. Still, in his view, recourse to Islamic justice showed the downfall of a Coptic ecclesiastical hierarchy that had failed to enforce its canons. It is worth noting that the focus on women, interspersed throughout his discussion of social reform, suggests that missionaries viewed Coptic women, much as they saw their correlates in other parts of the Middle East, as "central to the process of edifying and uplifting the local population."[65]

In general, the author disparages the incompetence of Coptic priests in ministering to their congregants. These men, he writes, "praise" those believers who use magical practices and astrology to resolve their problems.[66] They assume their offices through nepotism; priesthood is passed down from generation to generation solely because of hereditary rights, not because of aptitude.[67] Once again, he is indignant at how, during liturgical prayers, priests fail to control unruly congregants among whom the men "speak with one another about worldly news and such, and the women about the news of their men, their children and their clothes."[68] To add insult to injury, none of the believers can understand the Coptic-language hymns that are being sung, including the priests who are themselves singing. Moreover, like "animals," priests and their congregants spend most of Sunday—the day of the Lord—feasting, eating, and drinking ʿaraq.

Finally, in attacking the most detestable practices, the author criticizes priests' inability to preach, which was, in his view, due to sheer "stupidity." He writes, "They have been raised in ignorance, like you, and the Bible says that 'if a blind man leads another, both of them will fall into the pit.'"[69] He directs his words to laymen who believe that they are part of a "flock" that must blindly follow its "shepherd"—that is, its priests—and then notes that "a layman says 'I am a sheep and not a shepherd; thus I believe that the sheep which does not follow the *good* shepherd will be lost, found by the wolf, and will suffer.'"[70] By arguing that these shepherds are too inept to lead believers to salvation, this writer asks his audience to rebel against their religious leadership and join a community where salvation is a closer reality. He reminds them to look at model Catholic missionaries in Egypt, at their learned traditions and at their efforts to study the Coptic language in order to "correct" all of the wrongdoings of past generations. His words echo other Arabic Catholic sermons from this period, which viewed a priest's role primarily as caring for Christian souls through "preaching, teaching, advising, and censuring."[71] Catholic preachers roused their Arabic-speaking flocks with visibly partisan language: in one collection of eighteenth-century sermons targeting Aleppan, Jerusalemite, and Cairene audiences, a priest praises the sacrifices made by Catholic heroes and martyrs and rallies his followers with the cry that "we are Christian Catholics. We are believers of the Roman Church and nothing in the world could persuade us to leave this faith. . . . our blood, money, lives, and everything is a sacrifice for our faith!"[72] Such rhetoric helps to explain why Coptic clergy may have interpreted missionary rhetoric as hostile to their leadership and to communal integrity.

In replying, they would seek to rouse their own parishioners but would also attack those same failings in an attempt to restore order and regulation within their community.

The Coptic Response to Catholic Missionaries

From the start of the eighteenth century, high-ranking Coptic preachers sought to deal with this overheated language and perceived threats to their community, but two men in particular stood out: Yu'annis XVIII and Bishop Yusab.[73] Yu'annis was originally from the town of Fayyum, where he resided until he joined the Monastery of St. Antony at an unknown date. In 1735, Yusab was born to wealthy parents from Nukhayla, a province of the Upper Egyptian town of Assyut. He joined St. Antony's around 1760 and would serve, from 1791 until his death in 1826, as bishop of the Upper Egyptian diocese of Jirja and Akhmim.[74] It is more than likely that the two men's tenure at the monastery overlapped.[75] This seemingly isolated Red Sea destination was quite influential in shaping the Coptic patriarchate during the Ottoman period.[76] Monks were frequently exposed to outsiders, as the monastery attracted eclectic visitors and residents from other religious sects.[77] One of its main draws was an impressive library, rebuilt, along with the monastery itself, during the early Ottoman period and eventually restocked with large numbers of manuscripts. St. Antony's pluralistic setting might explain Yu'annis and Yusab's apparent familiarity not only with Coptic theological teachings but also with Catholic rhetoric. In a society where Christians had little access to education beyond local religious schools (kuttāb), St. Antony provided a stimulating intellectual environment for these clergymen.[78] The young Yusab, in particular, was immersed in researching and studying all matters related to theology. Because of his apparent devotion, compatriots named him librarian and charged him with the care of valuable manuscripts;[79] his intellectual prowess also earned him the nickname "al-Abbaḥ," literally "the Hoarse" (from speaking) but commonly translated as "the Eloquent."

There is little doubt that their monastic upbringing and their struggles to battle Catholic missionaries constituted the basis for Yusab and Yu'annis's lasting friendship.[80] In 1767, Yu'annis left the monastery and proceeded to lead the community as patriarch for a lengthy and tumultuous period of Egyptian history. Not many details are known about his reign or his personal life. It is clear, however, that Yu'annis took seriously the threats posed by missionaries. In 1791, when he recalled Yusab to Cairo, he asked him to fill a post that had been abandoned decades earlier by Antuniyus Fulayfil, a high-ranking bishop who converted to Catholicism in 1758.[81] Yusab went to Akhmim at a time when tensions had reached their height. On arrival, he perceived his diocese as being engaged in some of the most syncretic practices.[82] Seeing his role as that of a shepherd, Yusab was intensely committed to bringing the flock back to the true faith. One of his first tasks was to build a large church that would serve as the center for his bishopric.[83]

In time, however, both clergymen turned to sermons in order to outline their concerns; they presented an alternative vision of appropriate conduct for Copts, one that excluded contradictory and foreign customs. For his purposes, Yu'annis responded to missionaries by turning to a genre new to the Ottoman period, that of the *Adrāj* ("decrees" or "letters").[84] The *Adrāj* were intended to guide the Coptic community in proper behavior, but also to clarify a practical and accessible theology. Addressed from a father to his children, the sermons cover a wide range of topics, many of which were similar to *MS.KI*: they discuss basic principles of proper belief, make a plea for funds to support the Coptic community in Jerusalem, and rebuke those who participated in acts of greed and in drunken behavior.[85] His narrative is repetitive, as the patriarch frequently recycled his most effective speeches. Since his reign spanned nearly three decades, any subject of significance during his office received mention in the *Adrāj*.

Yusab's sermons, on the other hand, were titled *Silāḥ al-Mu'minīn* or "the Weapon of the Faithful," and his "weapons" were directed at the "loose" morals of a lay community seemingly corrupted by the influence of outsiders.[86] The *Silāḥ* circulated widely throughout Egypt, and today manuscript copies are found at the Patriarchal Library in Cairo, the Monastery of St. Macarius in Wadi al-Natrun, and the Bibliothèque Nationale in Paris, among others. Like *Adrāj*, these sermons range from purely theological matters, such as the incarnation of Christ, to issues of popular behavior and misbehavior, including the practices of dancing at banquets held in honor of a martyr's feast and gambling in church.[87] From his writings, it is easy to detect the bishop's struggle to teach his congregants the "true" beliefs of the church.

In contrast to *MS.KI*, these sermons are distinguished by an often obscure, overly colloquial, and at times indecipherable writing style.[88] Still, it is clear that both clergymen recognized that the situation in late-eighteenth-century Egypt called for a specific type of pastoral guidance. Bishops were converting to Catholicism; priests were becoming corrupt in their management of traditional sacraments; and the laity was immersed in a "popular religion" that distanced them from core Coptic beliefs. The *Adrāj* and *Silāḥ* exhort congregants but are also tender and respectful. Yu'annis began most of his sermons with the following phrase: "To the blessed sons, to the beloved and chosen ones who are obedient to the Orthodox religion, the fervent archpriests, the faithful priests, the glorified deacons, the elders and the venerable archons, and the estimable scribes [*kuttāb*]." For Yusab and

Yu'annis, the prospect of losing the faithful, whether through intermarriage with Catholics, heterodoxy, or outright conversion, prompted new approaches. Preaching was a form of censure, but beyond having the immediate intent of curbing immoral habits, it was also designed to correct Coptic practices and to strengthen the clergymen's moral authority over their community.

The Sermons of Yu'annis and Yusab

To give a sermon in the Coptic Church is a highly regarded duty. The orator is generally a clergyman—a priest, a bishop, or the patriarch himself—or an esteemed layman known for his skills and for his talent in rousing audiences. As he steps to the lectern, he brings to life the words that he has committed to paper (or to memory). Sermons, which differ from other religious literature in that they contain a message of moral or spiritual improvement, are usually given during a liturgy, but they might also be delivered at funerals to console mourners, or sometimes at weddings to counsel newlyweds. Homilies are also a regular part of commemorative feasts and saints' festivals. In a church deeply rooted in cyclical and ritualistic oratory, the weekly sermon is perhaps the only opportunity for the speaker to explore the demands of his community and to give moral and religious guidance suitable for his day and age.[89] In this context, language can reveal a great deal about the performed aspects of a sermon. As discussed in earlier chapters, colloquialisms and emphatic repetitions can indicate how a writer intended a text to be recited. Sermons and their delivery represent that performative encounter between a speaker and his audiences. In Ottoman Syria, for instance, Catholic missionaries noted that believers challenged their preachers and noisily expressed their approval during sermons.[90]

Coptic clerical sermons in the eighteenth century appear to have been influenced by various sources: from the church's long-standing traditions; from a broader Ottoman context in which oratory was utilized to instigate political action or promote good morals; and, of course, from missionaries who were using sermons to win converts. Before printing presses, which were not widely available in the Middle East until the nineteenth century, public oration was one of the most effective means to shape popular opinion. In the midst of the 1711 struggle between religious zealots and Egyptian 'ulamā, a Turkish preacher effectively used the pulpit to criticize popular rituals among Sufi dervishes in Cairo, including practices associated with the cult of the saints, and thereby provoked attacks against the offenders.[91] This incident echoed the puritanical Kadızadeli movement, which had popularized preaching in Ottoman Istanbul and targeted common vices such as drinking alcohol and coffee, smoking, and dancing.[92] In Cairo, large crowds gathered to hear another Turkish preacher named Ahmad Efendi (d. 1748). They were drawn to "the sweetness of his words and the beauty of his eloquence," although his vehement scolding of local military leaders nearly cost him his life.[93] Within the Ottoman Empire, then, Coptic clergymen were not alone in attempting to define acceptable moral behaviors for their community or in criticizing those of other sects. Their goal was to reform the church and lead believers toward the path of salvation, but implicitly it was also to protect the Coptic community and to preserve their own authority over coreligionists. While the sermons under study here reflect their Ottoman Egyptian milieu, they were intended first and foremost to combat missionary activities. In Ottoman Syria, Catholic preachers struggled to compete with talented Orthodox orators, but as missionaries learned local dialects and converted native preachers to Catholicism, their sermons grew more effective.[94] Coptic clergymen knew that sermons had become a favorite missionary tool, and they developed counter-preaching as a defensive means.

On the Rules of the Church

Many of Yu'annis's and Yusab's sermons can be subsumed under the heading of church rules or doctrines, and one of the most discussed violations was the underage marriage of Coptic girls and boys, a practice that had been widely criticized by missionaries. This topic received special attention by Yu'annis in his thirty-first sermon:

> In years past, we have written to you sermons, out of our love, on the marriage of immature [*ghayr mudrikīn*] girls so that no one should marry immature girls nor immature boys. Because of the long time that passed, you have forgotten what we have written to you, and how we explained to you that this act creates an excessive harm. He who marries immature girls trades joy for sadness and happiness for hatred, and [creates] a bond with evil, as well as other things that are too elaborate to address here. All of you know, one by one, that marriage is one of the sacraments of God . . . and God's laws do not permit the marriage of those who are immature.[95]

He goes on to discuss how this type of marriage "ruins" young girls. Lust was the sin of the biblical Sodomites, Yu'annis proclaims, and will draw a similar punishment if uncontrolled. The patriarch does not command the abolition of this practice, however; rather, he pleads passionately for its end ("We *beg* of you with our love that you stay away from all of these habits").[96] He also blames the mothers of these girls: "If a woman is asked about her daughter, 'Is your daughter mature?' and she confirms her maturity although [the girl] is not mature, this woman will be held responsible under the laws of the church."[97] Immediately, these words challenge an existing perception that Christian women in the Ottoman world were excluded from attending liturgical services within their respective churches.[98] Indeed, the sermons repeatedly address audiences of men and women, echoing an established oratorical tradition within Coptic and Egyptian society.[99] More important, perhaps, Yu'annis viewed women as central to the process of eradicating abhorrent practices by exercising authority over their daughters. Although he is silent on what the church dictates as a penalty, he implies that punishments outlined in the Old Testament might apply. Thus while the patriarch employs tender language as he solicits an end to this custom, specifically by invoking mothers, he resorts to punitive threats to stir fear among congregants.

Yusab also addressed the ways that the community had gone astray from the church's core teachings. Here, the bishop was determined to remind congregants of their duty to observe obligations of their faith, such as confession and fasting. Catholic missionaries had long noted that few Copts practiced confession, which was viewed to be particularly heretical. Coptic clerical leaders focused on the same problem, and not surprisingly, in their opinions, the trouble also stemmed from poor pastoral leadership. Yusab asks, "How can you, the priest who does not confess his sins, teach the people to confess their sins?" He goes on to refer to priests as "spiritual doctors" and condemns their lack of wisdom in dealing with congregants' sins (ills) and in prescribing remedies. Ultimately, he advises priests to "search for each person, among men and women, and to attract them to repentance through preaching, teaching, confession, and communion."[100] Yusab characterizes this action as an obligation: priests must uphold the vow that they took during the rite of ordination and bear responsibility for their congregants' souls. If they fail, their congregants will be damned.

The topic of fasting, which is not a sacrament but a duty in the Coptic tradition, also drew the clergymen's ire, as it was inconsistently practiced among the laity. Traditionally, fasting assumed two forms: one was the total abstinence from food, and another was the abstinence from animal-derived products such as eggs, milk, and meat. It was expected that a total abstinence would be incorporated until a certain hour of the day during predetermined fasts, such as Lent. However, in Yusab's view, laymen appear to have redefined this practice in their own terms:

> I have seen among our Christian children disgusting [*damīma*] habits to which they have grown accustomed. Through these customs, they have come to decide whether to carry out or go against the fasting on Wednesdays and Fridays, and [also] the Forty Days Fast [Lent]. They arise early in order to smoke and drink coffee. Then they come up with empty excuses, [saying,] "My head hurts," or another says, "If I do not

> drink coffee I cannot open my eyes," and another says, "The smoke helps expunge the phlegm which is upon my chest." . . . Oh, how meaningless are these bonds? Bonds which have tied the Christian children and [even] the most renowned among you, those who are employed in the dīwāns,[101] the archons, and the masters [al-mu'allimīn].[102]

The bishop goes on to explain that self-denial of food, drinking, and smoking must be followed at least until three in the afternoon. It is likely that this criticism was falling, for the most part, on deaf ears. If an archon claimed that without coffee he was unable "to open his eyes" and was subsequently incapable of performing his duties at the administrative council, then it is doubtful that a bishop's words would have effected much change.[103] In the Ottoman period, the laity were known to be raucous in their demands for more lenient rules regarding fasting. An anonymously authored manuscript from the Coptic Patriarchal archives dated to 1699 rebukes their lack of self-control and suggests that men follow abstinence not only from certain foods but also from conjugal relations with their wives.[104] During the eighteenth century, the traveler Pococke noted that Copts practiced an "odd ceremony" where, in the attempt to acquire permission from the patriarch to break their Lenten fast, "it is said they take him in a chair, and ask him if he will give them leave; on refusing it, they ask if he will be thrown down; and repeating these questions three or four times, at last he consents to give them leave to eat eggs in Lent."[105]

In criticizing similar practices, Yu'annis further admonishes those who randomly followed the church's dictums. He is less worried about spiritual welfare, however, than about giving outsiders ("the enemy") an impression of factionalism and disunity, which they can then use to attack the church. The Coptic way of fasting, particularly abstention from meat, was admired by Muslim writers in the early Ottoman period, and its dilution potentially damaged the perception of Copts within broader Egyptian community.[106] As Yu'annis remarks,

> You should all fast according to the guidelines and the laws of the church for fasting. Do not give to the enemy a way through which he may enter among you. The breaking of church laws might allow us to be pillaged by those outside nations, who would say, "What is the state of those people? Some of them fast and some do not. Perhaps they do not have any beliefs in their church, particularly those who are clerics, or those who are educated or those who are notables." . . . When the lower classes regard them [those who break the fast] while they are being careless in their gluttony, conquered by [their] love of lustfulness, they [too] will quickly fall.[107]

Both Yu'annis and Yusab were threatened by the lack of uniformity with respect to church doctrines and rules.[108] That this theme is recurrent throughout their sermons reveals concerns over communal integrity and over the clergymen's leadership. Their own orthodoxy was being challenged by missionary teachings, thus the eradication of heterodox behaviors and the emphasis on correct and proper doctrine became their most pressing concerns. In response to missionary ridicule of the pastoral establishment, Coptic clergymen focused on a new program that defined, to clergy and laity, the church's traditions and rules.

"Frank and Foreign" versus "Copt"

As they fought foreign influences, which were commonly deemed "Frankish" (*Ifranj*), Coptic clergy accused their opponents of introducing heretical behavior and corrupting believers.[109] They disparaged the "other" in order to discourage conversion and assimilation. Coptic sermons reveal fears of Frankish plots to overtake the church, critiques of Frankish morals and habits, and a demonization of non-Coptic mores.[110] In late-eighteenth-century Coptic writings, "Franks" appears as a reference not only to French and other European merchants in Egypt but also to the missionaries who were ubiquitous in Cairo and in Upper Egypt. Franks were rejected because their ideas and teachings not only contradicted those of the Coptic Church but also aimed to devalue its leaders. Through their emphatic use and demonization of this term, Yu'annis and Yusab attempted to delineate new boundaries between Copts and Egypt's other religious communities.

The two men suggested that Catholic activities had opened the doors to unregulated religious practice and created an environment in which heterodoxy proliferated. Seeing missionary activities as an obstacle to the church's survival, Yusab tackles converts to Catholicism with a most aggressive approach. In his eighth sermon, titled "From the Sayings of Bishop Yusab on Those Followers of the Franks Who Left the Coptic Community," he writes:

> Tell me, you follower, you Coptic believer of the Chalcedonian Council . . . if you were asked about your faith, you would have no answer other than "I follow the pope and the Western church." I want you to tell me: what good have you seen in *their* church? What wisdom have you witnessed from *their* missionaries, or what kind of truth have you seen? How have *we* misled you? What have you seen within us, in terms of heresy? . . . Could you possibly answer that you have seen the truth and the correct belief among them?[111]
>
> I also ask you: are you Copts by race or Franks? You must answer that we are Copts and our forefathers are Copts.[112]

As evident, the question of conversion went beyond adopting another faith: it threatened communal boundaries and challenged the collective "we"—that is, "the Copts." Conversion endangered the fundamental unity of the Coptic identity and prompted the question "Are they better than us?" At least for a time, publicly criticizing the Franks succeeded in deterring a large number of conversions and in maintaining a cohesive community, but Coptic leaders still struggled with the threat of religious syncretism. Another sermon reveals Yusab's state of mind on arriving in Akhmim in 1791 and how it had changed over time:

> When we arrived to the seat [of the bishopric,] we found you committing customs which are not according to the laws [canons] of our church, such as your intermixing with the Franks and your marrying your sons to their daughters and your daughters to their sons. You were committing these acts without insight and we know that previously our church has forbidden these acts. We were informed that most of you returned to the laws of our church, and this pleased us.[113]

However, those who displeased the bishop were harshly criticized. Yusab conveys his disgust at the fact that "mixed couples," of Catholic and Coptic backgrounds, prayed in separate churches. He condemns this behavior not just as a minor error but as a sin worthy of eternal damnation and threatens that "if the husband and wife do not return to pray in one church [i.e., Coptic] and take communion from one cup, I absolve myself of their behavior."[114]

The idea that conversion divided families existed widely throughout the region.[115] To combat such trends, Yusab acknowledged that the unity of the Coptic family stems from the spiritual agreement of husband and wife. Both must strive to preserve the integrity of their family and, by extension, of their community. In his concern over intermarriage between Copts and Catholics, Yusab asked Yu'annis for guidance. Their correspondence is included in the *Adrāj*, and Yu'annis's reply is predictable: he condemns intermarriage with "nonbelievers" and the separation of husbands and wives who pray in different churches. His pedagogical style and choice of words are worth noting here:

> If a person was married to a woman who is a nonbeliever [*ghayr mu'mina*] and she wished to live with him, he should not leave her. If a nonbelieving [*ghayr mu'min*] man wished to live with a believing woman, then she should not leave him, or else their children would be defiled. These words were true in the days of the missionaries, when the mission was new and the wonders were plentiful. The Apostle Paul said this: that a male believer should attract the nonbelieving woman to the faith, and the believing woman attract the nonbelieving man to the faith.[116]

> But today, it is not the case. The nonbelieving man attracts the believing woman to his sin and to his nonbelief. And the nonbelieving woman attracts the believing man to her ill belief. The man perhaps listened to the woman until she fed him the fruit of disobedience. This situation exists today in the case of every man who obeys his wife, particularly if the person [the man] loves temptation, and his hands are loose, and his organs are controlled by the runny moisture. . . . If [the man and woman] are divided in their belief, there is nothing worse, for the kingdom that is divided will be destroyed.[117]

Aside from its sexually charged language, this passage is striking for what it reveals about the patriarch's rhetorical approach. First, he clearly reinterprets apostolic teachings by dissuading intercommunal marriages. Second, he appeals to women, who are seen as equally tempted by "nonbelieving" men as the men are by "nonbelieving" women. Coptic marital practices were commonly derided within missionary rhetoric, yet most missionaries viewed a stable marriage and home as the basis for a healthy Christian life. Clergymen could not sidestep these discussions and emphasized the church's expectations of normative marital relations. Yu'annis's and Yusab's sermons include women, since the latter's role was viewed as central in the process of conversion and reconversion—that is, as vital in preserving the place of male members in the community and in keeping them "Coptic."[118] The Catholic faith was posited as the downfall of the male believer. Yu'annis argues that it is because of her "impurity"—that is, because of her religious faith—that a Frankish woman will bring about the demise of a believing and faithful Coptic man. The Frankish woman is likened to Eve, the temptress who feeds Adam (the Orthodox man) the "fruit of disobedience" (the metaphorical "apple" of Catholicism), a taste of which could lead to damnation.[119] By appealing to women, the church expressed concerns that the Catholic mission endangered the propagation of future offspring. The Coptic leadership, therefore, sought to battle the mission at the heart of its domination, inside the home. That the struggle against intermarriage continued for years to come is evidenced in the sermons of Yu'annis's successor, Murqus VIII (1796–1809). In anger against the wealthy for allowing their daughters to marry notable Muslims or non-Coptic Christians, the patriarch blamed those priests who continued to officiate the wedding ceremonies despite longstanding prohibitions.[120]

On Drinking and Its Vices

Modern discourses of guilt and shame can "serve to protect the integrity of individual identity and also protect the social order by ensuring conformity" in thought and behavior.[121] On some level, Yu'annis's and especially Yusab's writings against drinking appear to have been constructed with similar goals in mind. Both were concerned with reestablishing religious conformity and imbuing Copts with a sense of responsibility in order to immunize them against criticism from outsiders. Here, their sermons parallel Muslim rhetoric, which shunned public drunkenness in general. Earlier, we saw how Copts who were publicly drunk and disorderly were often lynched in punishment for their behavior. In one description from 1799, al-Jabarti remarked that Egypt's local Christians, including Copts, "lost all self-control [and] discarded all decency" by riding their boats "in the company of their women and whores, drinking and displaying publicly the vilest laughter and derision, blasphemies and mockery of the Muslims."[122] Coptic clerical leaders must have been aware of existing critiques against their congregants, particularly those leveled by members of the Muslim religious establishment. Indeed, Yusab's and Yu'annis's sermons illustrate an acute awareness of the Copts' minority status and signal the clergy's mission to clarify expected codes of conduct not just to their parishioners but to Egyptians at large.

Drinking (especially of 'araq) figures prominently in these sermons, and Yu'annis uses one of his favorite tropes, women, in addition to some racially tinged remarks, to illustrate its "ugliness": he writes "[When the drunkard appears in public,] he is laughed at. His rotten drool is dribbling from his mouth and he stinks of that hateful smell of alcohol. . . . This drunkard is like a free woman in the arms of a Berber who is of a strange race, who is ugly in appearance, and who attacks her dignity."[123] In another homily, which was meant to reproach priests for disregarding the prescribed Wednesday/Friday fast, Bishop Yusab digs from within the church's archives and lifts motifs—almost verbatim—from an earlier sermon composed by Patriarch Benjamin I (622–661).[124] In doing so, Yusab not only relates an evidently fictive (but nonetheless threatening) story that illustrates the community's problem with drinking and its lack of respect for "the house of God" (*bayt al-rabb*) but also indicates the punitive action that he might be willing to take against drunkards:

> Believe me, my brothers, I saw a group of people who went to church while they were carrying alcohol in their containers. I do not want you to reproach me so I will not tell you this individual's name and that individual's name. After the liturgy ended, they held a feast and then drank alcohol. They thought by doing this that they would be happy and joyful. But I saw them . . . and the devils were playing with them. The [state of] drunkenness and those madmen[125] led them to being angry toward each other. The anger led them to beating each other until finally I took them to the local ruler [ḥākim].[126] Some of them were beaten and

> humiliated; others were fined. Look, my brothers and my beloved ones, to the outcome of drunkenness! From now on, do not carry alcohol to the house of God, ye who seek prayers and repentance for your sins. Do not make up empty excuses and say, "I have habits that I cannot stop and so I will take a little bit and drink it outside the church." Tell me . . . what is the benefit of your going to church? If you say that it is for prayer and repentance, I would reply to you, which sin is greater than drunkenness? For the Apostle Paul said that the drunkard and the adulterer do not inherit the kingdom of God. Ye who seek repentance, prayer, and supplication in the house of God [also] bring alcohol to the house of God. . . . Do not allow this anecdote to be your story, nor these deeds to become your deeds. Let your life be moral and good in a way that is fitting to the sons of Christians.[127]

Even if the story was exaggerated or invented, it is clear that drunkenness was not taken lightly. The bishop's threat to engage outsiders within internal problems reveals the gravity of the situation and perhaps indicates his desire to be seen as an upright leader who not only criticizes widely deplorable conduct but also works to curb it.

The task of reprimanding Coptic laymen and of managing their spiritual well-being was supposed to fall on church pastors. In one of his sermons, Yu'annis prompts priests to coax their congregants (both men and women) into confessing their sins (e.g., drunken behavior) prior to services and to "teach and discipline" so that believers attend church with the "fear of God in them."[128] The patriarch also emphasizes that priests themselves should be without any obvious faults and should set an example for the community. He specifically mentions that a priest should be "the husband of [only] one woman," the "other woman" likely a reference to priests' dependence on alcohol rather than the rare but not completely unknown practice of polygamy practiced among elite Copts.[129] He warned that if any priest failed to follow these rules and to do his job, he would be "defrocked" and removed from his office.[130]

The fact that priests were unable to exercise self-control, particularly when it came to drunkenness during liturgical prayers, infuriated the patriarch.[131] In his sermons discussed below, we hear the implicit question "What shall the Muslims think of us?"[132] How despondent the patriarch's words seem as he tries to encourage moderation in these popular practices. Perhaps out of a realization that a prohibition against alcohol was unenforceable, Yu'annis warns them at least not to drink on the day before or on the eve after holding mass:

> If a priest came forth to offer liturgical prayers, then he must not drink 'araq or liquor, or any alcoholic drinks in the evening of the day in which

> he will make the offerings nor in the day prior to that. . . . The smell of ʿaraq during that evening will not disappear from the breath of the person who drank it and also [will not disappear if he drank it] the day before. How could it be that you, while your mouth is filled from the devil's cup, can spoil your mouth [before drinking] the true cup [of communion], that with which your sins are forgiven? How is your state of being while you are embracing that magnificent cup [of Christ's blood], which was sacrificed on behalf of the world for their sins, while your mouth smells of the horrific smell of ʿaraq? . . . How could you teach others so that they learn to fear approaching [the communion cup] when they are unworthy?[133]

One can only imagine the public embarrassment that drunken priests caused; their habits were commonly derided by Catholic missionaries, as noted in *MS.KI*. While Yusab threatened to involve local authorities in disciplining disorderly laymen,[134] the patriarch was more forgiving toward clergymen. Yu'annis firmly rebukes but does not threaten his subordinates. In the end, both clergymen's attitudes were summarized best by Yusab: "He among you who wishes to drink should drink in the hidden corners of his home [and not in public spaces]."[135] In a sense, these comments underscore how Yu'annis's and Yusab's concerns were not with alcohol, in and of itself, but with conspicuous drinking. While they condemn its physiological effects (diluting the senses, altering the mind, or distracting attention from prayer), they are also concerned with the smell of alcohol, the possibility of public intoxication, and the actions that could be openly perceived by outsiders. Implicitly, Yusab and Yu'annis might have turned a blind eye to drinking if laymen and priests could have controlled their public revelry and preserved the Coptic image within broader society.

On Feasting, Merrymaking, and the Practice of Magic

Popular festivals had of course been a prominent feature of the Egyptian socioreligious landscape since ancient times. It is not surprising, then, that Yusab addresses the topic of excessive revelry among Copts, particularly on the occasion of martyrs' feasts. This behavior, however, extended beyond large festivals to the smaller and more private affairs held by wealthy notables, often in their homes. Yusab was displeased at lavish and decadent celebrations of any kind: first, he derided the immoral practices that inevitably arose during these feasts; second, he cautioned against the arrogance of revelers who splurged on food, drinks, and entertainment while their impoverished brothers and sisters languished; and finally, he appeared most concerned about the public perception of archons within broader society:

> If one of you makes a vow or throws a dinner party in the name of a martyr, then he should ask about the widowed, the orphaned, the impoverished, the blind, and disabled. He should send the mercy [feast] that he made and distribute it among them in their homes. This should be done in secret. . . . [But] I have seen one of you make a feast in the name of one of the martyrs. He invited all of the priests and all of the clerical orders, all of his beloved ones, men and women, [who were] his rich neighbors. I was at a nearby house. I heard many different sounds. The priests were singing church hymns, and others—deacons—were praising with chants in honor of the martyr. And then they drank alcohol and began to perform the poetry of the Arab Abu Azyad[136] and the women were bellowing with their well-known sounds [that they make] at weddings. Others became very drunk so they began to quarrel and to beat one another.[137]

Here, the festivities was held in honor of a Christian martyr, and the attendees were fellow elites ("rich neighbors"), respected clergymen and deacons, but the celebration was a mishmash of popular syncretic practices. Church hymns were sung; the martyr was honored; then disorderly drinking ensued and (profane) Arabic poetry was recited.[138] While the sermons discussed earlier criticized pricsts and lower clergy, this homily, perhaps more so than any other, admonishes the archons' practices. After all, the archons were the effective leaders of the Coptic community, and their behavior was unbecoming of their esteemed role. They were, moreover, corrupting lower clergymen with their actions.

In the bishop's view, lewd practices went hand in hand with stinginess toward the poor.[139] Charity was expected from the archons, and their lavish and wasteful spending was condemned as pure arrogance and selfishness. One wonders if references to economic inequity were also intended to rouse the anger of impoverished congregants toward the wealthy. The sermons pay particular attention to wastefulness and overspending at the expense of "ordinary Christian persons." In a combined critique of injustice and immorality, Yusab suggests that revelers were more willing to pay money for sexually charged entertainment than to help a needy person:

> I have heard that on the days of your weddings you participate in games that are inappropriate to believers. You invite to your weddings adulterous women. You defile your eyes with adulterous sights. You defile your ears with words inappropriate among believers. You savor their [the women's] depraved songs, and then you adorn them with gifts and money. And if a Christian person came upon you [at that moment] and asked you for something in the name of Christ, not only do you throw

> him out but you also hurl curses at him! . . . Tell me, my beloved children, is this a habit that you found in the laws of our Church? . . . I have also heard that [among you] at weddings and occasions, you play strange games. I believe that you have learned them from those who are outside of our faith because such things should not be mentioned among the faithful in Christ.[140]

The origin of these habits, then, lay outside the Coptic community: "you have learned from those who are outside of our faith," writes the bishop. Playing games and excessive celebrations involving "adulterous" women are blamed on an "outside" culture—most likely, here, an ambiguous "Islamic" culture—whose vices had infiltrated the Coptic community.[141] The sexually charged activities of the laity emerged as particularly abhorrent. If church leaders were promoting images of pious and sexually innocuous women (like Dimyana), then the laity's behavior directly violated those teachings. Of course, other Christian and Muslim moralists commonly condemned debauchery within their own ranks. Nearly identical complaints were made by pious writers against the Armenian amira class in Istanbul; the former were "scandalized" by the "lavish festivities that the amiras organized in their houses, some of which apparently had an oriental character and were marked by self-indulgence, with professional entertainers to amuse them."[142] And, at the end of the seventeenth century, the Egyptian Hanafi Shaykh Muhammad Safi al-Din attacked those "who mixed games and dancing with their religious rites, and used to turn in the circles of *dhikr* moving their hands backward and forward and shaking their heads up and down, right and left imitating the Christians in their game called 'the running of the cock' (*rakd al-dīk*)."[143]

In the late-eighteenth-century Coptic context, popular games such as *al-dāʿ* (dice) and *al-fanājīn* (foretelling the future by reading coffee grounds) further encouraged immoral conduct and did not befit "the faithful in Christ"; as Bishop Yusab reports, they brought out the worst in people, causing them to use foul language and curse. Some games were more serious, as they went beyond frivolous amusement and bordered on experimentation with the paranormal. Alchemy, magic, and astrology were popular and ancient practices not only among Copts but also among Egypt's Muslims and Jews. In the spring of 1735, for instance, a panic spread among Cairenes who believed millennialist rumors that were allegedly spread by Jews or Copts, the latter deemed authentic experts in "numerology and astrology."[144] Among Copts, practices of the occult were not restricted to the "masses" but were also found among the clergy and notable archons.[145] Coptic bishops had habitually engaged in these customs, at least in the first half of the eighteenth century, and seemingly without repercussions from church authorities.[146] In the late eighteenth century, the widespread use of magic was seen as undermining the "pure Christian" values of the Coptic community. Patriarch Yu'annis, in his forty-sixth sermon, firmly explains why these practices are akin to worshipping idols and threatens his congregants with the ultimate punishment available to him:

> There are those [individuals] who attract people to their evil habits which anger God: [these habits are] magic and astrology. Those who behave like such people, who say their [magical] words, or act in a way that leads to evil intentions, [should know that] the magician is a slave of something other than God, which is Satan. For the Bible says, let there be none among you who is either a fortune-teller or a follower of fortune-tellers. Do not ask them [the fortune-tellers] for anything lest you get defiled by them. He who follows fortune-tellers and allows them into his house or goes into their houses will bring upon himself my severe anger and he will be banished from my people.[147] . . . He who . . . speaks about the Book of Birthdays or the Book of Astrology, or who predetermines the outlook of a coming day, saying, "This day is blessed" or "This day is impure," and also the hours, [will be condemned]. None of you should visit the ponds and the wells in which the devils live because they mislead people. All of these things we have mentioned are the remnants of idol worshipping. . . . Any man, woman, or child from the Coptic Church who practices any of [these habits] will be excommunicated. He will be forbidden from entering the church and no offerings will be accepted from him. He cannot take communion, nor can he interact with the other faithful. If he died in this state of being, without remorse for what he has committed, he will not be prayed over, nor will he be memorialized, nor would offerings be made on his behalf.[148]

The fact that Yu'annis brought up excommunication shows the gravity of this practice. Exclusion from communion (and the community) was normative canon law for a number of other offenses, but as seen from above examples, the patriarch handled the punishment of priests' drunkenness with a more moderate approach.[149] Alchemy and fortune-telling had the potential to rival the church's own teachings of the miraculous and the divine. It remains unclear whether Coptic clergymen would have aggressively preached against these habits had Catholic missionaries not raised the issue. Catholic missionaries, articulating a Counter-Reformation worldview, drew sharp distinctions between magic and religion. In Europe in this period, "magic" was distinguished by methods that were intended to manipulate supernatural powers for solving tangible, day-to-day problems. On the other hand, "religion" functioned by explaining the unknown, by comforting believers, by defining a moral agenda for its adherents, and, most important, perhaps, by criticizing those believers who fell out of line.[150] In the eyes of clerical leaders, "good" Copts should know better than to practice the former: they were expected to be faithful churchgoers and to allow only its true teachings and doctrines to guide their spiritual needs.

Conclusions

In the late eighteenth century, clerical leaders revealed a growing anxiety over their status within the community. Anti-Coptic discourses and sermons had become pervasive as Catholics in Egypt sought to strengthen their mission and win new converts. In time, higher clergymen blamed intracommunal dissent on that which was foreign, using "Frank" as a catchall for offensive behavior stemming from Coptic interaction with outsiders. Heterodox practices weakened "authentic" Coptic traditions, blurred the outlines of the community, and threatened the clerics' authority. By articulating the outlines of a Coptic Orthodox identity in contrast to "Frankishness," Catholicism, and even against the dominant Islamic culture and by invoking heated language that could galvanize popular support, the clergy rallied Copts to preserve their faith. As they specified which qualities were inherent to a Coptic believer and what behaviors, social mores, habits, and values defined Coptic-ness, Yusab and Yu'annis stylized themselves as *the* protectors of a core Coptic identity.

The clergy were particularly conscious of what constituted appropriate behavior for Copts within a predominantly Muslim society. In an attempt to reassert their influence, they sought to show outsiders that they could sway parishioners to act within acceptable moral boundaries. Through preaching, higher clergymen offered a rigorous moral program that protected church traditions on marriage, fasting, and prayer and that attempted to revamp the priesthood. Moreover, with their sharp rhetoric they indirectly challenged the archons' leadership and communal standing. Historically, preaching and the pulpit represented a clerical domain, and at least in churches where these sermons were delivered, archons would have been restricted in their immediate response against the clergy.

Charged with the care of a small but influential community, Yusab and Yu'annis felt an urgent need to establish their community's independence; as the largest non-Muslim group in Egypt, and the most vulnerable to mass conversion, the Copts had the most to lose. And in a sense, many of the core issues they faced were not fully resolved in their time—whether to solicit Western protection or to invoke the interference of Muslim leaders within internal matters, or whether laymen or clergy should ultimately decide the future of the community. These questions continued to be a major site of contention within the Coptic community over the next two centuries.

Conclusion

St. Dimyana acts through God's power, not human power; therefore she is increasingly loved in the hearts of the people. We are unsurprised to see people's love toward St. Dimyana . . . [such as] those who seek to take the blessing of her icon during a procession, and who crowd at us, tugging right and left, until we are nearly thrown on the ground. But we say that all is forgiven for the sake of the love of St. Dimyana.

—Anba Bishuy, as quoted in *Muʿjizāt wa Ẓuhūrāt al-Shahīda al-ʿAfīfa Dimyana*

These words of a contemporary bishop, overseer of the Convent of St. Dimyana, serve as a reminder of her ongoing popularity. Believers persist in showing devotion to this saint by seeking to handle her relics and icons, often to the point of violence. Today, the demand for anthologies of her miracles abounds, as the saint is believed to heal, cure, and comfort her followers. Martyrdom narratives like Dimyana's and Salib's have become ubiquitous within the community largely because of increased political tensions between Muslims and Christians. Over the past three decades, bloody confrontations with Islamist radicals have made Copts acutely apprehensive about their political status, and in response, they have turned to the church, particularly to martyrdom tales, for solace.[1] Clerical leaders have assuaged the laity's concerns by widely promoting these stories of suffering, fortitude, and eternal salvation.

Religion has always represented a vital force in day-to-day Coptic life, forming a space where believers could defend and contest their fundamental convictions as well as seek relief from their despair. In the early modern period, Copts turned to their own set of devotional acts so that they could feel closer to the divine and the miraculous. Pilgrimages, visits to martyrs' shrines, and offerings of appropriate restitution, whether in spiritual or financial terms, all reflected a sense of active piety among the populace. Sermons related clerical concerns and aimed to transform practices that contradicted existing teachings. In all, within a restrictive political and legal context, religious life emerged as the primary arena for the articulation of a Coptic voice, allowing coreligionists to heed and give advice, provide moral guidance, determine ethical conduct, and express their views on social relations. Coptic writings of this period reveal not only how believers engaged with their milieu but also how they drew boundaries between themselves and other communities.

The multiple interpretations of religion in Ottoman Egypt, whether in official or popular realms, hint at some insecurity about the present and future. Recurrent plagues, civil discord, and random violence pushed believers toward rigorous if, at times, unorthodox religious observance. Consequently, both Muslim and Coptic clerics dealt with increasing challenges to their authority. Especially during the eighteenth century, in an atmosphere of political decentralization and conflict, Egypt's 'ulamā' worked to protect the integrity of Islam by curbing popular Sufi practices, such as smoking, drinking coffee, or venerating the shrines of other faiths. But they also faced criticism from more puritanical groups who objected, in particular, to anyone who turned a blind eye toward deviant practices. Coptic leaders found themselves entangled in similar challenges. On sensing the community's vulnerability to heterodoxy and to assimilation by external groups, they sought to instill uniformity in religious practice. But ordinary Copts did not always follow clerical prescriptions: they developed their own worldviews and found their own explanations for everyday problems.

The cases explored in this book highlight nuances in the Coptic experience, particularly in the consistency and flexibility of religious expression. One quickly learns that in Ottoman Egypt, legal obstacles against non-Muslim practices could be navigated with political connections, financial stature, and good providence. In the cult of Dimyana, for instance, Copts relocated a major spring festival to the Delta region, away from orthodox 'ulamā' in Cairo, and their leaders negotiated with bedouins and military regiments to ensure pilgrims' safety. Dependence on local grandees in various facets of Coptic religious life reveals that non-Muslims living under Islamic governance occasionally accepted external involvement within communal affairs. Aside from soliciting immunity to make their pilgrimage to Jerusalem, Copts asked Muslims to arbitrate their internal dissent and some clergymen made threats to involve Muslim political leaders in curbing immoral behavior among the Coptic faithful. In some of their writings, Coptic authors distinguished between their Muslim neighbors and perceived malefactors. The martyrology of Salib, a story intended to provoke a remembrance of suffering, shows a deliberate attempt to represent day-to-day Muslim-Christian relations in their full complexity. Even when Coptic leaders blamed debasement of religious practice on other groups, one still detects quiet influences among Egypt's various communities, as seen in their mutual veneration of the saints and parallel pilgrimage practices.

While Coptic beliefs were shaped by their encounters with Muslim and Christian neighbors, their religious life was also fashioned by the dialogue between patrons of religious culture and its recipients. Clerical and lay leaders made ongoing efforts to preserve core traditions, and they channeled their time and wealth into community-building strategies. Despite an intermittently hostile environment and legal prohibitions against their actions, elites showed immense interest in building churches, repairing monasteries, and funding literary and artistic projects. Here, revivalist efforts by archons, particularly in the eighteenth century, draw attention to the nature of communal authority in early modern Egypt. Archons patronized religious life to foster collectivity and, in turn, to augment their power. Progressively, patriarchs depended on archons to retain control over their positions and preserve communal integrity. While they found some of the archons' personal habits suspect, they also found them difficult to challenge.

Still, in face of ongoing pressures to convert or assimilate, the laity were increasingly expected to know, respect, and practice the basic tenets of their faith. By the eighteenth century, clergymen like Bishop Yusab and Patriarch Yu'annis eschewed formulaic homilies in favor of original sermons that addressed practices such as fasting, marriage, avarice, drunkenness, lewd behavior, and noncompliance with church rituals. In the process, they characterized a specific Coptic identity and distinguished a pure Coptic morality from the perceived vices of other communities. They spoke to men and to women, the latter seen as central in rearing children who would preserve the church's teachings and doctrines for posterity. Their sermons also hinted at the church's disapproval of members' wasting money on drunkenness or excessive festivities rather than investing in community or church.

One might be tempted to read a nascent Coptic or even Egyptian patriotism within sermons that were written, at least on the surface, to discourage conversion to European Catholicism. Such is the anachronistic interpretation often seen in communally authored histories of the Ottoman period.[2] While it is easy to dismiss this line of thinking, we cannot ignore the fact that as Copts sensed rivalry from other religious groups, they turned to a religio-ethnic discourse (broadly defined) to anchor their own beliefs.[3] Here, my work challenges those scholars tending to view religion as a secondary marker of identity among Ottoman non-Muslims. Bernard Heyberger, for instance, warns that the breakdown of Eastern Christians into categories such as Coptic, Maronite, or Armenian is a "modern construction, characteristic of the nationalist era," and that while religion played an important role in early modern societies, Christians "essentially shared the mentality of their [Muslim] compatriots, including their perception of the sacred and their religious practices."[4] Molly Greene notes that seeing Christians and Jews as distinct from each other and from Muslims could potentially "[enlist] the community in the service of nationalist historiography."[5] To this end, in the Egyptian context, some historians have minimized the role of religion—Muslim or Christian—within intellectual and literary life in the early modern period, presuming that this progressively modernizing society was also "secularizing."[6]

In many of these discussions, religion has been equated to later ethnonationalist markers or seen as a negative force in the lives of Ottoman peoples who were seeking to compete economically and intellectually with a secularizing West. Rather than argue against this paradigm, I have maintained throughout this book that religion worked in extremely complicated and often constructive ways to satisfy spiritual, social, and individual needs within the Coptic community. The popularity of homiletic literature, for example, hints at the search for coherent instruction in face of fracture and heterodoxy. But religion also served as a conduit for articulating those inimitable characteristics that separated Copts from other communities. Acts of suffering, as documented in historical and coeval martyrologies, were repackaged to inculcate communal pride among new generations. In their sermons, clergymen feared the dangers posed by unguided popular practices, and blamed Catholics and occasionally Muslims for inhibiting their community's potential. Here, once again, the Coptic experience paralleled emerging trends in the Ottoman world. In the wake of increased contact with Europeans and the rise of Muslim puritanical movements in the eighteenth century, debates over internal reform or renewal (*tajdīd*) began to acquire a sectarian tinge. For instance, various Muslim writers in Ottoman Iraq used a language of "exclusion and inclusion" as they attempted to deal with outside influences and "the 'corruption' of ritual and legal practices."[7] Dina Khoury calls this development a shift toward a "public political language," one that was infused with religious symbolism and intended to appeal to the masses. This characterization rings true for other regional discourses promulgated by Muslim and non-Muslim writers, which emphasized the basic tenets of one's faith, affirmed core virtues, and dissuaded corrupting habits.[8] Using the case of the Levant, Akram Khater suggests that individual (if at times sectarian) interpretations of religion were "at the *center* of earlier modernizing projects in the Middle East."[9] In the late eighteenth century, he notes, pious expression among Christians, specifically among Aleppine nuns, reflected a desire to enforce their agency vis-à-vis traditional power-holders as well as European missionaries, and would allow them to carve out their own place in a changing and modernizing milieu. All of this should remind us, as Bruce Masters has maintained, that religious identity was "both primary and primordial" within the Ottoman world.[10]

This discussion helps us to better understand Coptic reformist impulses from later centuries, especially ones that have looked to faith and practice as their starting point. Two examples—one from the nineteenth century and the other from the twenty-first—show continuities with and diversions from early modern developments. After the defeat of the French, the reestablishment of Ottoman rule in 1801, and the rise of the Muhammad ʿAli dynasty (1805–1952), new reforms were instituted with the goal of eradicating the dhimmī system in Egypt. Muhammad ʿAli openly allowed Christians and Jews to build synagogues and churches and to conduct public religious processions; his son, Saʿid Pasha (r. 1854–1863), abolished the jizya in 1855. These changes likely took place because Egypt's ruling governors were keen on opening the doors to European economic and political influence and on gaining European favor. Parallel developments were also unfolding at the Ottoman capital, Istanbul, in the guise of the Tanzimat reforms. For the Egyptian context, little evidence exists that Muhammad ʿAli or his successors were personally interested in advancing the Copts' status or that they viewed Copts as "more than good tax collectors and accountants."[11] Copts were excluded from student missions to Europe and from receiving a government education, and some sources suggest that the ruling family preferred to employ other Christians, like Europeans or the Western-educated Syrians and Armenians.[12]

In light of increased economic competition, Copts turned to missionary schools to advance their skills; many would adopt the religion of their American and British teachers. Missionary activities were once again deemed threatening by the Coptic Church, but this time, clerical leaders were more prepared. In response, Patriarch Kyrillus IV (1854–1861), who is dubbed "Abu al-Iṣlāḥ" (Father of Reforms), made communal revitalization a top priority. In 1853, he commissioned the building of the Great Coptic School in Cairo, near the new Azbakiyya cathedral. Instructors were recruited to teach Coptic, in an unprecedented revival of this language, and to educate students in proper chanting and ritual.[13] Kyrillus hoped to address the Copts' economic worries and to curb criticisms of religious backwardness that had been raised by Westerners. He worked on improving pastoral leadership and mandated the schooling of priests, requiring them to study theology and doctrine and to participate in weekly debates, which he closely oversaw.[14] Kyrillus's focus on reviving the Coptic heritage, and on instruction for priests and deacons, recalled homilies that had exhorted clergy to police communal practices.

Within this mid-nineteenth-century modernizing milieu, however, Kyrillus also developed practical approaches to help advance the Copts' status. His school offered a Western-style curriculum that included languages such as English, French, Italian, and Turkish, as well as instruction in history, geography, fine arts, and music. Kyrillus purchased Egypt's first privately owned printing press in 1860, with the primary goal of preserving Coptic religious manuscripts.[15] Reform continued after Kyrillus's reign, and a lay council (*majlis millī*) called the Coptic Communal Council was established in 1874 to oversee further transformations and manage the church's religious endowments.[16] Some scholars have seen this council as the fulfillment of the archons' political roles in the early modern period.[17] It has been long thought that Kyrillus's reign inaugurated modern Coptic history, yet the patriarch's policies and the resurgence of lay power reflect both well-established trends from the eighteenth century and innovative responses to intercommunal rivalries within a transforming context.

These developments would set the stage for reformist movements in the twentieth and twenty-first centuries,[18] and our second example draws on the contemporary revival of martyrologies. Among Copts, stories of ancient martyrs have historically symbolized the persevering Christian believer living in a hostile society. Today, martyrologies are being retold using modern tools such as film, television, and print media. Sectarian friction has made Copts apprehensive about their future and skeptical about the possibility of coexistence. Martyrdom tales, in this context, represent a renewed Coptic identity firmly based on steadfastness and sacrifice. The popularity of these narratives also reflects the religious zeal pervading Egyptian society in recent years. A rising tide of Islamic revivalism that promotes the inclusion of Islam in all public realms has motivated Copts to find alternative channels for communal expression. Since 2005, for example, the Coptic-owned satellite channel Aghapy TV has aired films on martyrs and saints, liturgical services, and other programming intended to champion religious life and to counter Islamist-leaning media outlets.

In this context, martyrdom films, or video hagiographies, have transformed seemingly mythical figures into realistic, colorful, and living personalities. Coptic believers can closely identify with heroes and heroines who are portrayed by recognizable Coptic actors, by their own people. On-screen, martyrs appear empathetic: their dress, their body language, their physical expressions, and their spoken Egyptian dialect seem current and familiar. The distant martyr's tale—once heard occasionally in churches and at festivals—has become a real-life drama, an expanded television serial embodying the tangible concerns of this minority. On satellite networks, these films can be easily accessed by Copts and non-Copts, thus regularly placing communal stories, for the first time, within a broader public arena. As in early modern Egypt, when neo-martyrdom reminded Copts of allegiance to their Christian faith, today's films provide alternative tellings of traditional stories. Both represent testimonies to an idealized past, and both allow audiences to become participants and co-owners of these traumatic-consoling events.[19] New, however, is the interaction between audience and media, which can easily take place in the comfort of one's home. In this intimate setting, an opportunity has been created for a different, perhaps more individual, understanding of an ancient tradition.[20]

The modern era offers many colorful examples of the changing relationship between piety, ritual, and religious expression among Egypt's Copts. Of course, in studying Ottoman Copts, the historian is limited by a narrow source base; manifestations of Coptic Christianity in the early modern period surely exceed the few case studies presented in this book. Still, on different levels, I have attempted to draw a complex picture of religious life and to note the Copts' flexibility in dealing with ongoing social, political, and economic challenges. The Copts' historical experience is relevant in that the possibility of coexistence between different religious sects appears increasingly fragile in today's Middle East. Gradually, the voices of non-Muslims—often Christians—are being subsumed, inadvertently or not, by a hegemonic Muslim culture. The case of Ottoman Copts can help us understand how the seemingly marginalized can carve out their place in relation to dominant religious and political actors. More important, perhaps, it reminds us that in seeking to write an inclusive history of the Middle East, we must embrace the multiple and diverse voices of all its peoples.

Notes

INTRODUCTION

1. "Archon" (Arabic, *arkhun*, pl. *arākhina*) is the ancient Greek word for "official," "magistrate," or "ruler," but since the early Islamic conquests of Egypt in the seventh century, it has been used to refer to influential Coptic notables.

2. This is my rewording of the story in Ahmad Katkhuda 'Azaban al-Damurdashi, *Kitāb al-Durra al-Muṣāna fī Akhbār al-Kināna*, ann. 'Abd al-Rahim 'Abd al-Rahman 'Abd al-Rahim (Cairo: Institut Français d'Archéologie Orientale du Caire, 1988), 347. The exact story, in its original and complete version, is discussed in chapter 4.

3. In the study of Jews under Islamic rule, the former has been dubbed the "neo-lachrymose theory" and the latter the myth of "interfaith utopia." Both views have been criticized as oversimplifications. See Mark R. Cohen, "Islam and the Jews: Myth, Counter-Myth, History," *Jerusalem Quarterly*, no. 38 (1986): 125–137. For a general discussion of these debates in the Ottoman context, see Bruce Masters, *Christians and Jews in the Ottoman Arab World* (Cambridge: Cambridge University Press, 2001), chapter 1; and Karen Barkey, "Islam and Toleration: Studying the Ottoman Imperial Model," *International Journal of Politics, Culture and Society* 19, no. 1–2 (2005): 5–19.

4. Carlo Ginzburg, *The Cheese and the Worms* (Baltimore: Johns Hopkins University Press, 1980); on this approach toward popular religion, also see Natalie Zemon Davis, "Some Tasks and Themes in the Study of Popular Religion," in *The Pursuit of Holiness in Late Medieval and Renaissance Religion*, ed. Charles Trinkaus (Leiden: E. J. Brill, 1974), 307–336; and Peter Brown, *The Cult of the Saints: Its Rise and Function in Latin Christianity* (Chicago: University of Chicago Press, 1981).

5. Masters, *Christians and Jews*, 50, notes that shared practices among Ottoman Copts and Muslims "blurred the cultural divide between the two communities." In the modern context, another scholar concludes that in most of their religious practices and rituals, Copts and Muslims "are almost identical to each other." See Airi Tamura, "Ethnic Consciousness and Its Transformation in the Course of Nation-Building: The Muslim and the Copt in Egypt, 1906–1919," *Muslim World* 75, no. 2 (1985): 103.

6. Charles Thompson, *Travels through Turkey in Asia, the Holy Land, Arabia, Egypt and Other Parts* (London: J. Newberry, 1767), 247. The abstention from strangled meat is one of the few Christian dietary laws and derives from the New Testament (Acts 15:20).

7. In the seventeenth century, for instance, the German traveler Johann Michael Vansleb indicated that when Egypt's Muslims celebrated *'Īd al-Aḍḥa* (Feast of the Sacrifice), a three-day festival, Copts "buy no Victuals from the Mahometans, nor bread, wine, flesh, coffee, nor water. By this they discover their abhorrency of that religion, for thereby they shun all occasions of communicating with them." See Vansleb, *The Present State of Egypt; or A New Relation of a Late Voyage into That Kingdom Performed in the Years 1672 and 1673* (London: R. L'Estrange, 1678), 230.

8. Copts, like all Christians and Jews in the Islamic world, lived for centuries under the *dhimma* (protection) system, which is frequently referred to as *millet* in the nineteenth-century Ottoman context.

9. There are some limitations in applying this phrase, as derived from European history, to the study of the Middle East. But I find it instructive for discussing Coptic religious life here, since the latter was progressively interlinked to early modern transformations affecting the Catholic Church in Europe. For a discussion of this term in the context of Ottoman history, see James Grehan, "The Great Tobacco Debate in the Ottoman Middle East (Seventeenth and Eighteenth Centuries)," *American Historical Review* 111 (2006): 1353–1354.

10. For instance, Otto F. A. Meinardus writes that "when Napoleon Bonaparte and his thirty-seven thousand soldiers disembarked in Alexandria on July 1, 1798, the Coptic Church had reached its lowest ebb." See *Two Thousand Years of Coptic Christianity* (Cairo: American University in Cairo Press, 2002), 66.

11. This is in reference to the judge Malti and to Ya'qub, the commander of a small military battalion. On Malti, see 'Abd al-Rahman al-Jabarti, *'Ajā'ib al-Athār fi'l-Tarājim wa'l-Akhbār*, 4 vols., ed. Moshe Perlmann and Thomas Philipp (Stuttgart: Franz Steiner Verlag, 1994), 3:35–38, 3:149, 3:302, and, on his execution, 3:375. On Ya'qub and his battalion, see al-Jabarti, *'Ajā'ib*, 3:139, 3:167–169, 3:254, 3:276, and, on his escape to France, 3:288. Also see, in general, Anouar Louca, "Ya'qub et les lumières," *Revue des Mondes Musulmans et de la Méditerranée*, nos. 52–53 (1989): 63–76.

12. On Protestant missionaries in Egypt, see Heather J. Sharkey, *American Evangelicals in Egypt: Missionary Encounters in an Age of Empire* (Princeton: Princeton University Press, 2008).

13. The founder of monasticism is generally considered to be St. Antony, an Egyptian hermit who lived in the Red Sea desert in the third and fourth centuries and is viewed as having established the first monastic communities.

14. For centuries, the Coptic patriarchate in Egypt was accustomed to sending a bishop to Ethiopia in order to oversee the satellite church. However, this practice ended in 1955, when the Ethiopian Orthodox Church declared itself independent from Egyptian administration.

15. Copts, like other opponents of Chalcedon, define Jesus' nature as composite, rather than singular. For this reason, they reject the label "monophysite," preferring "anti-Chalcedonian" instead. For an overview of the historical usage of this term and its various meanings to Copts and non-Copts, see Maged S. A. Mikhail, "Egypt from Late Antiquity to Early Islam: Copts, Melkites, and Muslims Shaping a New Society" (PhD diss., University of California–Los Angeles, 2004), 30–40. For more on Copts and the Council of Chalcedon, see Stephen J. Davis, *The Early Coptic Papacy: The Egyptian Church and Its Leadership in Late Antiquity* (Cairo: American University in Cairo Press, 2004), chapters 3 and 4. It should be noted that in 1973, the Coptic Patriarch Shenouda III (r. 1971–) came to an agreement with Catholic Pope Paul VI (r. 1963–1978) over previously disputed Christological formulations. See Meinardus, *Two Thousand Years*, 125.

16. Dina El Khawaga, "The Political Dynamics of the Copts: Giving the Community an Active Role," in *Christian Communities in the Arab Middle East: The Challenge of the Future*, ed. Andrea Pacini (Oxford: Clarendon Press, 1998), 172.

17. These are baptism, chrismation (anointing with holy oil), communion (the Eucharist), confession, marriage, priesthood, and the anointing of the sick.

18. J. W. McPherson, *The Moulids of Egypt (Egyptian Saints-Days)* (Cairo: Nile Mission Press, 1941), lists 150 mawlids that were commonly recognized by Christians and Muslims in Egypt.

19. Michael Winter, *Egyptian Society under Ottoman Rule* (New York: Routledge, 1992), 130.

20. Ibid., 235.

21. Susan Jane Staffa, *Conquest and Fusion: The Social Evolution of Cairo A.D. 642–1850* (Leiden: Brill, 1977), 360. Also see Gamal el-Din el-Shayyal, "Some Aspects of Intellectual and Social Life in Eighteenth-Century Egypt," in *Political and Social Change in Modern Egypt: Historical Studies from the Ottoman Conquest to the United Arab Republic*, ed. P. M. Holt (London: Oxford University Press, 1968), 124–125.

22. Winter, *Egyptian Society*, 130.

23. Masters, *Christians and Jews*, 17.

24. Indeed, this is the point made by Bruce Masters when discussing Ottoman-era Muslim chronicles. See *Christians and Jews*, 16–17, 28.

25. Scholars have noted the limitations of court records for the study of religious practices among Ottoman non-Muslims. See, for instance, works by Eleni Gara, Rossitsa Gradeva, and Najwa al-Qattan. A socioeconomic analysis of Coptic life in the Ottoman period, using court records, has been attempted by Muhammad 'Afifi, *Al-Aqbāṭ fī Miṣr fi'l-'Aṣr al-'Uthmānī* (Cairo: al-Hay'a al-Miṣriyya al-'Āma li'l-Kitāb, 1992), especially 191–247. Unfortunately, 'Afifi mostly summarizes the contents of his sources and provides few citations to the documents used in his lengthy discussion. As such, his work must be consulted with care.

26. Winter, *Egyptian Society*, 199.

27. Hilary Kilpatrick has noted the general neglect of literature written by Christians and Jews in Ottoman lands, particularly for the Levantine context. See "Brockelmann, Kahhala & Co: Reference Works on the Arabic Literature of Early Ottoman Syria," *Middle Eastern Literatures* 7, no. 1 (2004): 33–51.

28. Guirguis has published one of these waqf documents, dating from the year 1740, in "Idārat al-Azamāt fī Tārīkh al-Qibṭ: Namūdhaj min al-Qarn al-Thāmin 'Ashr," *Annales Islamologiques* 33 (1999): 45–59.

29. Masters, *Christians and Jews*, 5.

30. On the "decline" of Islamic learning in Egypt, see in general el-Shayyal, "Some Aspects of Intellectual and Social Life." On the Coptic community, see Tito Orlandi, "Literature, Copto-Arabic," *Coptic Encyclopedia* 5:1460–1467; and Aziz S. Atiya, *History of Eastern Christianity* (Notre Dame, IN: University of Notre Dame Press, 1967), 100. Ottomanists have challenged the "decline" thesis in different ways. See, for example, Jane Hathaway, "Rewriting Eighteenth-Century Ottoman History," *Mediterranean Historical Review* 19, no. 1 (2004): 29–53.

31. Amnon Cohen, *Jewish Life under Islam: Jerusalem in the Sixteenth Century* (Cambridge: Harvard University Press, 1984), 48–49, analyzed by Najwa Al-Qattan in "Dhimmis in the Muslim Court: Legal Autonomy and Religious Discrimination," *International Journal of Middle East Studies* 31, no. 3 (1999): 431.

32. For much more on this point with reference to the Ottoman context, see Derin Terzioğlu, "Man in the Image of God in the Image of the Times: Sufi Self-Narratives and the Diary of Niyāzī-i Miṣrī (1618–94)," *Studia Islamica* 94 (2002): 139–165.

33. I will be relying on *History of the Patriarchs of the Egyptian Church, Known as the History of the Holy Church*, vol. 3, part 3: *Cyril II–Cyril V (1235–1894 AD)*, trans. and annot. Antoine Khater and O. H. E. khs-Burmester (Cairo: Société d'Archéologie Copte / Institut Français d'Archéologie Orientale du Caire, 1970). Hereafter, I will refer to this edition as *HPEC* III/3.

CHAPTER 1

1. Moshe Perlmann, "Notes on Anti-Christian Propaganda in the Mamlūk Empire," *Bulletin of the School of Oriental and African Studies* 10, no. 4 (1942): 847.

2. Cited in ibid., 847.

3. Taqiyy al-Din Ahmad ibn 'Ali b. 'Abd al-Qadir al-Maqrizi, *Al-Mawā'iz wa'l-I'tibār fī Dhikr al-Khiṭaṭ wa'l-Athār*, 4 vols., ed. Ayman Fu'ad Sayyid (London: al-Furqan Islamic Heritage Foundation, 2002–2004), 4:1070–1076; in general, see Huda Lutfi, "Coptic Festivals of the Nile: Aberrations of the Past?" in *The Mamluks in Egyptian Politics and Society*, ed. Thomas Philipp and Ulrich Haarmann (Cambridge: Cambridge University Press, 1998), 254–284.

4. Tamer el-Leithy, "Coptic Culture and Conversion in Medieval Cairo, 1293–1524 A.D." (PhD diss., Princeton University, 2005), iii.

5. Mark N. Swanson, "The Monastery of St. Paul in Historical Context," in *The Cave Church of Paul the Hermit at the Monastery of St. Paul, Egypt*, ed. William Lyster (New Haven: Yale University Press / American Research Center in Egypt, 2008), 49.

6. Mark R. Cohen, "Jews in the Mamluk Environment: The Crisis of 1442 (A Geniza Study)," *Bulletin of the School of Oriental and African Studies* 47, no. 3 (1984): 425–448.

7. Maurice Martin, "Note sur la communauté copte entre 1650 et 1850," *Annales Islamologiques* 18 (1982): 203; for a contrast between the Ayyubid and Mamluk attitudes toward Copts, see Kurt Werthmuller, "An In-Between Space: An Archival and Textual Study of Coptic Identity and Ayyubid Politics in Egypt, 1171–1250 CE" (PhD diss., University of California Santa Barbara, 2007), 80–83.

8. Winter argues that the Ottoman conquest was especially welcomed by Egypt's Jewish communities (*Egyptian Society*, 199–200). Also see Mark R. Cohen, *Under Crescent and Cross: The Jews in the Middle Ages* (Princeton: Princeton University Press, 1994), 188.

9. For more detail on the devastation, see Muhammad ibn Ahmad ibn Iyas al-Hanafi, *Badāʾiʿ al-Ẓuhūr fī Waqāʾiʿ al-Ḍuhūr*, 5 vols., arranged and introduced by Muhammad Mustafa (Cairo: al-Hayʾa al-Miṣriyya al-ʿĀmma liʾl-Kitāb, 1982), 5:146–180.

10. Winter, *Society and Religion in Early Ottoman Egypt: Studies in the Writings of ʿAbd al-Wahhab al-Shaʿrani* (New Brunswick, NJ: Transaction Books, 1982), 14.

11. The Ottoman state, from its earliest history, had used sürgūn to control unruly tribes and populate new territories. The most famous case of forced relocation follows the conquest of Istanbul in 1453. Mehmed II (1451–1481) used sūrgūn to repopulate his new capital, and this policy continued into the sixteenth century, in the period of the Ottoman conquest of Egypt, as a way of rebuilding the city's prosperity and glory. See Halil İnalcık, "The Policy of Mehmed II toward the Greek Population of Istanbul and the Byzantine Buildings of the City," *Dumbarton Oaks Papers* 23 (1969–1970): 235.

12. Ibn Iyas, *Badāʾiʿ*, 5:232; Iris Habib al-Masri, *Qiṣṣat al-Kanīsa al-Qibṭiyya*, 9 vols. (Alexandria: Maṭbaʿat al-Karnak, 1992 [1975]), 4:8–9. For lists of Egyptians who were deported, see Ibn Iyas, *Badāʾiʿ*, 5:178–179, 5:182–190, 5:229–232.

13. Winter, *Society and Religion*, 18. Attacks against the properties of non-Muslims, including churches, also took place following the Ottoman conquest of the Balkans. In general, see Rossitsa Gradeva, "Ottoman Policy towards Christian Church Buildings," in *Rumeli under the Ottomans, 15th–18th Centuries* (Istanbul: Isis Press, 2004), 339–368. The conservative prescripts regarding non-Muslims and their houses of worship in Egypt were well-articulated, and later regularly followed, by the fourteenth-century Muslim jurist Ibn Taymiyya. See Benjamin O'Keeffe, trans., "Ahmad ibn Taymiyya, Mas'alat al-Kana'is (the Question of the Churches)," *Islamochristiana* 22 (1996): 53–78.

14. Winter, *Society and Religion*, 215, 218. Despite his hatred for non-Muslims, al-Shaʿrani cautioned against unwarranted physical attacks, espousing the traditional Qur'anic understanding that non-Muslims should be humbled but not harmed.

15. Ottoman ideals of justice were embodied in an ancient paradigm commonly dubbed the "circle of equity," whereby the absence/presence of law, strong leadership, military might, and prosperity determined a ruler's ability to protect his people. Boğaç A. Ergene, "On Ottoman Justice: Interpretations in Conflict (1600–1800)," *Islamic Law and*

Society 8, no. 1 (2001): 52–87; Linda T. Darling, "'Do Justice, Do Justice, for That Is Paradise': Middle Eastern Advice for Indian Muslim Rulers," *Comparative Studies of South Asia, Africa and the Middle East* 22, no. 1 (2002): 3–19.

16. See, for instance, A. Fattal, *Le statut legal des non-musulmans en pays d'Islam* (Beirut: Dar El-Machreq, 1995 [1958]); Benjamin Braude and Bernard Lewis, introduction to *Christians and Jews in the Ottoman Empire* (New York: Holmes & Meier, 1982), 1:1–34; Masters, *Christians and Jews*, chapter 1.

17. Barkey, "Islam and Toleration," 16.

18. The Pact of 'Umar was long thought to be an agreement between the second Caliph 'Umar ibn al-Khattab (634–644) and the Christians of Syria, but there is no evidence of its existence prior to the ninth century. It was likely synthesized from a variety of sources before its codification within Islamic legal practice during the Abbasid period. For a detailed discussion of this issue, see Mark R. Cohen, "What Was the Pact of 'Umar? A Literary-Historical Study," *Jerusalem Studies in Arabic and Islam* 23 (1999): 100–157.

19. On Christian ecclesiastical courts, see Bernard Heyberger, *Les chrétiens du Proche-Orient au temps de la Réforme catholique (Syrie, Liban, Palestine, XVIIe–XVIIIe siècles)* (Rome: École Française de Rome, 1994), 69–72. For Muslim-dhimmī interaction in Ottoman courts, see Ronald C. Jennings, *Christians and Muslims in Ottoman Cyprus and the Mediterranean World, 1571–1640* (New York: New York University Press, 1993); Najwa al-Qattan, "Dhimmis in the Muslim Court: Documenting Justice in Ottoman Damascus, 1775–1860" (PhD diss., Harvard University, 1996); and Amnon Cohen, *Jewish Life under Islam.*

20. In the Ayyubid period (1171–1250), Coptic churches were covered with black mud to "reduce them to a proper state of subjugated humiliation." Werthmuller, "An In-Between Space," 73.

21. Violations to these rules were regularly broken in Ottoman Egypt. For the seventeenth century, see court records cited by Galal El Nahal, *The Judicial Administration of Ottoman Egypt in the Seventeenth Century* (Minneapolis: Bibliotheca Islamica, 1979), 56–57. In the eighteenth century, see al-Jabarti *'Ajā'ib*, 2:30; Ahmad Shalabi ibn 'Abd al-Ghani, *Awḍaḥ al-Ishārāt fī man Tawalla Miṣr al-Qāhira min al-Wuzarā' wa'l Bāshāt*, ann. 'Abd al-Rahim 'Abd al-Rahman 'Abd al-Rahim (Cairo: Tawzī' Maktabat al-Khanjī, 1988), 469.

22. This was mostly enforced in bathhouses, where the absence of clothing required distinguishing markers, or during times of persecution. According to Coptic oral traditions, the weight of these crosses caused severe bruising and led to the customary reference to Copts as "blue-necks."

23. Evliya Çelebi, *Seyahatname*, 10 vols., ed. Seyit Ali Kahraman, Yücel Dağlı, and Robert Dankoff (Istanbul: Yapı Kredi Kültür Sanat Yayıncılık, 2008), 10:141.

24. In the earliest days of Ottoman rule, for instance, Egypt's Christians participated in public processions that welcomed new governors to Cairo. In 1519, the Christians marched in this procession, holding candles and taking a prominent place behind Egypt's four religious judges (*quḍāt al-qaḍā' al-arba'a*). The same procession was repeated in 1521 and 1522. See Ibn Iyas, *Badā'i'*, 5:289, 5:384–385, 5:433. Tolerance for Christian religious processions, however, would be subject to customary prohibitions.

25. On the castration of eunuchs by Copts in Upper Egypt, see R. R. Madden's description in *Travels in Turkey, Egypt, Nubia and Palestine*, 2 vols. (London: Henry Colburn, 1829), 2:13–14; Ehud Toledano, "The Imperial Eunuchs of Istanbul: From Africa to the Heart of Islam," *Middle Eastern Studies* 20, no. 3 (1984): 383.

26. Winter, *Egyptian Society*, 205. Although Copts had been paying these taxes for centuries, in the seventeenth century, a Muslim Egyptian writer, Muhammad ibn 'Abd al-Muti' al-Ishaqi al-Manufi, suggested that the Prophet Muhammad would have exempted all Copts from paying the jizya had his son Ibrahim, born from Maryam the Copt, lived. See Ulrich Haarmann, "Regional Sentiment in Medieval Islamic Egypt," *Bulletin of the School of Oriental and African Studies* 43, no. 1 (1980): 58. On collecting taxes from Copts in Jerusalem, see Amnon Cohen, "The Ottoman Approach to Christians and Christianity in Sixteenth-Century Jerusalem," *Islam and Christian-Muslim Relations* 7, no. 2 (1996): 206.

27. Halil İnalcık, "Djizya," *Encyclopedia of Islam*, 2nd ed. (hereafter *EI2*), 2:562–566.

28. Winter, *Egyptian Society*, 210.

29. For a firsthand description of the jizya as it relates to Copts in the seventeenth century, see Vansleb, *The Present State of Egypt*, 175–176. On the taxation of Copts and revolts against authorities in the medieval period, see Mikhail, "Egypt from Late Antiquity to Early Islam," 175–211; on the jizya in the Mamluk period, see el-Leithy, "Coptic Culture and Conversion," 40–52; and for the Ottoman period generally, 'Afifi, *Al-Aqbāṭ fī Miṣr*, 30–41.

30. Vansleb, *The Present State of Egypt*, 175–176. This system, which was widely instituted throughout the Ottoman Empire in 1691, resulted in increased exploitation of non-Muslims, particularly of the lower classes. İnalcık, "Djizya," *EI2* 2:562–566.

31. Ahmad Shalabi, *Awḍaḥ al-Ishārāt*, 590–591; Winter, *Egyptian Society*, 210.

32. Aziz S. Atiya, "John XVII," *Coptic Encyclopedia* 4:1348–1349; *HPEC* III/3, 291.

33. In the late eighteenth century, the English traveler W. G. Browne alleged that the jizya was quite small because so many Copts either were exempted from paying it or were rebellious against tax collectors. Browne writes that there were "many entire villages of Copts in Upper Egypt, several of them are rebellious, and pay nothing . . . [and] the same people [Copts] is very numerous in the towns, but a great proportion of them consists of ecclesiastics, or of patrons in the service of the Beys and both these descriptions are exempt." See Browne, *Travels in Africa, Egypt, and Syria*, 57. Also see 'Afifi, *Al-Aqbāṭ fī Miṣr*, 41.

34. Winter, *Egyptian Society*, 211.

35. Haggai Erlich, *The Cross and the Rover: Ethiopia, Egypt and the Nile* (London: Lynne Rienner, 2002), 59–60.

36. Martin, "Note sur la communauté copte," 206.

37. In the same survey, Jomard estimated the presence of three thousand Jews, five thousand Syrian Christians, five thousand Greeks or Melkites, and two thousand Armenians in Cairo. Some scholars have interpreted Jomard's "ten thousand Copts" as reflecting the total for all of Egypt, although this makes little sense when compared with earlier traveler reports.

38. On problems inherent in Jomard's numbers, see Justin A. McCarthy, "Nineteenth-Century Egyptian Population," *Middle Eastern Studies* 12, no. 3 (1976): 1–39; André Raymond, "La Population du Caire et de l'Égypte a l'époque ottomane et sous Muhammad

'Ali," in *Memorial Ömer Lutfi Barkan*, ed. Robert Mantran (Paris: Librairie d'Amérique et d'Orient Adrien Maisonneuve, 1980), 169–178; and Daniel Panzac, "The Population of Egypt in the Nineteenth Century," *Asian and African Studies* 21 (1987): 11–32. In his reevaluation, McCarthy (6) suggests that Egypt's population in 1800 was 3,835,633 and that Cairo's population was 210,960. Panzac (15) places the figure at closer to 4,500,000 total inhabitants, with Cairo's population being 260,000.

39. Harald Motzki, *Dimma und Égalité: Die nichtmuslimischen Minderheiten Ägyptens in der zweiten Hälfte des 18. Jahrhunderts und die Expedition Bonapartes (1798–1801)* (Bonn: Selbstverlag des Orientalischen Seminars der Universität, 1979), 25.

40. Otto Meinardus, *Christian Egypt: Faith and Life* (Cairo: American University of Cairo Press, 1970), 367, estimated that Copts numbered 2 or 3 million at the time of the Ottoman conquest, and Masters adds that Copts constituted approximately 10 to 15 percent of Egypt's total population during the Ottoman period (*Christians and Jews*, 50).

41. Mikhail, "Egypt from Late Antiquity to Early Islam," 40–41; John Joseph, *Muslim-Christian Relations and Inter-Christian Rivalries in the Middle East* (New York: SUNY Press, 1981), chapter 1. Not much is known about the handful of Syrian Orthodox who lived in Egypt during the Ottoman period, although it is reasonable to infer that they turned to the Coptic patriarch for protection, since their own leadership was based in Tur 'Abdin, a mountainous region near Mardin.

42. The term refers to Ya'qub Barda'i (Jacob Bardai), the religious revivalist who restored anti-Chalcedonian Christianity to Syria in the sixth century following a period of Byzantine persecution. Adrian Fortescue, *The Eastern Churches Trilogy: The Lesser Eastern Churches*, 3 vols. (Piscataway, NJ: Gorgias Press, 2001 [1913]), 2:324. Today, the term "Jacobite" has been rejected by the practitioners of this religious tradition and, while based in Damascus, the Syrian anti-Chalcedonian denomination is known officially as the Syrian Orthodox Church of Antioch.

43. This conflation with Copts might be expected. Syrians in Egypt were so well integrated within the Coptic community that several Coptic patriarchs were Syrian in origin. Johannes den Heijer, "Les patriarches coptes d'origine syrienne," in *Studies on the Christian Arabic Heritage: In Honour of Father Prof. Dr. Samir Khalil Samir S.I. at the Occasion of His Sixty-Fifth Birthday*, ed. R. Y. Ebied, Samir Khalil Samir, and Herman G. B. Teule (Leuven: Peeters, 2004), 45–63.

44. André Raymond, *Artisans et commerçants au Caire au XVIIIe siècle*, 2 vols. (Cairo: Institut Français d'Archéologie Orientale, 1999 [1973–1974]), 2:456.

45. For more on Badr al-Jamali and his importance to Christians in Egypt, see Johannes den Heijer, "Considérations sur les communautés chrétiennes en Égypte fatimide: L'État et l'église sous le vizirat de Badr al-Jamālī (1074–1094)," in *L'Égypte fatimide: Son art et son histoire*, ed. Marianne Barrucand (Paris: Presses de l'Université de Paris-Sorbonne, 1999), 569–578.

46. Kevork Bardakjian, "The Armenian Patriarchate," in Braude and Lewis, *Christians and Jews in the Ottoman Empire*, 1:93.

47. For instance, during the reign of Coptic Patriarch Murqus VI (1646–1656), Armenians in Cairo were granted the use of a small room located above the Church of the Virgin Mary in Harat Zuwayla as a temporary prayer space until their church was

renovated. Coptic Museum Liturgy 312 as cited in al-Masri, *Qiṣṣat al-Kanīsa*, 4:53. Also see Magdi Guirguis, *An Armenian Artist in Ottoman Egypt* (Cairo: American University in Cairo Press, 2008), 49–60.

48. Raymond, *Artisans et commerçants*, 2:500–501.

49. Thomas Philipp, *The Syrians in Egypt, 1725–1975* (Stuttgart: Franz Steiner Verlag, 1985), 5.

50. While maintaining the title of "Patriarch of Alexandria," the Melkite patriarch, like his Coptic correlate, relocated to al-Fustat/Cairo in the medieval era. See Mikhail, "Egypt from Late Antiquity to Early Islam," 282.

51. Within most of the Ottoman Arab world, followers of the patriarch in Constantinople who had earlier used the Melkite moniker would become known simply as "Rūm," meaning Byzantines, Greeks, or simply Orthodox Christians. See Masters, *Christians and Jews*, 50. This terminology can be confusing when looking at other communities in the Ottoman Arab world: in the eighteenth century, the term "Melkite" was revived among the Catholic converts in Syria, who wished to distinguish themselves from the Orthodox followers of Constantinople.

52. Jonathan Shepard, "The Byzantine Commonwealth, 1000–1550," in *The Cambridge History of Christianity*, vol. 5, *Eastern Christianity*, ed. Michael Angold (Cambridge: Cambridge University Press, 2006), 5:34.

53. Raymond, *Artisans et commerçants*, 2:497–498.

54. Winter has suggested that after Copts were weakened by the Mamluk regime, Jewish influence increased disproportionately within state administration and within the economy. Winter, *Society and Religion*, 217. Vansleb confirms the esteemed status of Jews but also notes that Jews eschewed living in Egypt's rural areas due to fear of attacks by the "country-people." See *The Present State of Egypt*, 9–10.

55. See Winter, *Egyptian Society*, 203, 205, 208, 218; Raymond, *Artisans et commerçants*, 2:460. The power of Jewish merchants was so prominent that one European traveler reported in Alexandria that a poor Jew would be forced to submit to the rule of a dozen or so merchants and that if he "refuses to obey them, [he] has no longer any share in trade, and consequently becomes in a little time miserable." Norden, *Travels in Egypt*, 40.

56. Jews lost their positions as they became caught in extortionist schemes by the Egyptian governor ʿAli Bey al-Kabir. For more, see John W. Livingston, "ʿAli Bey al-Kabir and the Jews," *Middle Eastern Studies* 7, no. 2 (1971): 221–228.

57. Raymond, *Artisans et commerçants*, 2:484, and Philipp, *The Syrians in Egypt*, 25. The history of this community has been well documented in Philipp's work.

58. Raymond, *Artisans et commerçants*, 2:490.

59. Holders of berāts paid a 3 percent tax rather than the 10 percent that was required from dhimmīs. See Timur Kuran, "The Economic Ascent of the Middle East's Religious Minorities: The Role of Islamic Legal Pluralism," *Journal of Legal Studies* 33, no. 2 (2004): 499. On capitulations in general, see Maurits H. van den Boogert, *The Capitulations and the Ottoman Legal System: Qadis, Consuls and Beraths in the 18th Century* (Leiden: Brill, 2005).

60. Livingston, "ʿAli Bey Al-Kabir and the Jews," 222.

61. Philipp, *The Syrians in Egypt*, 5.

62. Raymond, *Artisans et commerçants*, 2:456.

63. Maged Mikhail has argued that this rivalry with the Catholic Church progressively altered how the Coptic Church views (and somewhat diminishes) the role and place of St. Peter in its theological doctrines and popular teachings. See Severus (Maged) S. A. Mikhail, "A Reappraisal of the Current Position of St. Peter the Apostle in the Coptic Orthodox Church," *Bulletin of St. Shenouda the Archmandrite Coptic Society* 5 (1998–1999): 55–74.

64. Mikhail, "Egypt from Late Antiquity to Early Islam," 326–327; Mark R. Cohen, *Jewish Self-Government in Medieval Egypt: The Origins of the Office of Head of the Jews, ca. 1065–1126* (Princeton: Princeton University Press, 1980), 74–76; Marlis Saleh, "Government Relations with the Coptic Community in Egypt during the Fatimid Period (358–567 A.H./969–1171 C.E.)" (PhD diss., University of Chicago, 1995), 152–188.

65. On the investiture of patriarchal power by the Mamluk sultans, see C. E. Bosworth, "Christian and Jewish Religious Dignitaries in Mamluk Egypt and Syria: Qalqashandi's Information on Their Hierarchy, Titulature, and Appointment (II)," *International Journal of Middle East Studies* 3, no. 2 (1972), especially 204–207.

66. Bosworth, "Christian and Jewish Religious Dignitaries," 207–210. Regarding the mistrust of Copts as recorded by medieval Muslim writers, see Brian Catlos, "To Catch a Spy: The Case of Zayn al-Din and Ibn Dukhan," *Medieval Encounters* 2, no. 2 (1996): 99–113. For background on the Coptic Church's relations with Ethiopia, see Saleh, "Government Relations," 189–213.

67. Steven Runciman, *The Great Church in Captivity: A Study of the Patriarchate of Constantinople from the Eve of the Turkish Conquest to the Greek War of Independence* (Cambridge: Cambridge University Press, 1968), 176–177.

68. Asterios Argyriou, "Christianity in the First Ottoman Era," in *Christianity in the Middle East*, ed. Habib Badr et al. (Beirut: Middle East Council of Churches, 2005), 609.

69. Yusuf Abudacnus, *The True History of the Jacobites, of Egypt, Lybia, Nubia, etc. and their Origine, Religion, Ceremonies, Lawes, and Customes, whereby you may se how they differ from the Jacobites of Great Britain* (London: R. Baldwin, 1692 [1675]), 6, writes that after the patriarch was chosen by Coptic communal elites, he was "brought to the Bacha or Vice-Roy for that time in Egypt, by whom he is constituted Patriarch of the Jacobites [Copts], and from whom he receives a Grant of his first petition; which is, that he may govern the church, according to the institutions of the Ancestors." On the limited involvement of Ottoman sultans in the internal affairs of their non-Muslim communities, at least until the eighteenth century, see Masters, *Christians and Jews*, 99.

70. Magdi Guirguis, "The Coptic Community in the Ottoman Period," in *Society and Economy in Egypt and the Eastern Mediterranean, 1600–1900: Essays in Honor of André Raymond*, ed. Nelly Hanna and Raouf Abbas (Cairo: American University in Cairo Press, 2005), 203.

71. The best evidence we have of an Ottoman-era Coptic patriarch who actively enforced and reinterpreted Coptic legal codes is in the figure of Yu'annis XIII (1484–1524). For a discussion of his legal stances on marriage, for instance, see el-Leithy, "Coptic Culture and Conversion," 367–382.

72. Claude Sicard, *Oeuvres lettres et relations inédits; Relations et mémoires imprimés; Parallèle géographique de l'ancienne Égypte et de l' Égypte moderne*, 3 vols., ed. Maurice Martin (Cairo: Institut Français d'Archéologie Orientale du Caire, 1982), 2:71. Sicard

mentions that the new patriarch of the Copts (1719) made his tour of the Delta during the spring of that year.

73. Guirguis, "Athār al-Arākhina 'ala Awḍā' al-Qibṭ fi'l-Qarn al-Thāmin 'Āshir," *Annales Islamologiques* 34 (2000): 25 and fn. 8.

74. Mikhail, "Egypt from Late Antiquity to Early Islam," 274–276. Still, some sources hint to their continued role as legal arbitrators, especially in the early Ottoman era. See el-Leithy, "Coptic Culture and Conversion," chapter 9.

75. Jacob Muyser, "Contribution à l'étude des listes épiscopales de l'église copte," *Bulletin de la Société d'Archéologie Copte* 10 (1944): 127, 162.

76. Sicard, *Oeuvres*, 2:72–73. In 1762, Carsten Niebuhr indicated that there had been seventy Coptic bishops at the time of the Arab conquest but only twelve bishoprics remained. Niebuhr, *Travels through Arabia and Other Countries in the East*, trans. Robert Heron, 2 vols. (Beirut: Librairie du Liban, 1978 [1792]), 1:103. For more on the relationship between the bishop of Damietta and Jerusalem, see chapter 4.

77. "Le P. Ch. Rodriguez au P. Général S. J. du Caire, le 25 Janvier 1562," in *Documents inédits pour servir à l'histoire du christianisme en Orient (XVI–XIX siècle)*, ed. Antoine Rabbath, 2 vols. (New York: AMS Press, 1973 [1905–1910]), 1:273–275.

78. Mikhail, "Egypt from Late Antiquity to Early Islam," 322.

79. Sicard, *Œuvres*, 2:72–73. For a comparison with the role of Orthodox bishops in Ottoman Syria, see Carsten-Michael Walbiner, "Bishops and Metropolitans of the Antiochian Patriarchate in the 17th Century (Their Relations to the Muslim Authorities, Their Cultural Activities and Ethnic Background," *ARAM* 10 (1998): 577–587.

80. Richard Pococke, *A Description of the East and Some Other Countries*, 5 vols. (London: W. Bowyer, 1743), 1:70.

81. Vansleb, *The Present State of Egypt*, 160.

82. See documents discussed in chapter 5.

83. Sicard, *Oeuvres*, 2:117.

84. Mikhail, "Egypt from Late Antiquity to Early Islam," 315.

85. Exceptions are found in Coptic manuscripts describing religious rituals and the role of some archons (as deacons) in those rites. See, for instance, Patriarchal Library, MS Liturgy 102, 168v–179v, which details the renovation and consecration of the Church of the Virgin Mary (al-Mu'allaqa) in Old Cairo, and Coptic Museum, Liturgy 128, which narrates the Coptic pilgrimage to Jerusalemin in the early eighteenth century.

86. Mikhail, "Egypt from Late Antiquity to Early Islam," 167, 271.

87. Archbishop Basilios, "Deacon," *Coptic Encyclopedia* 3:885–886.

88. Such was the case in the early modern period. In recent years, however, there has been a visible trend to ordain nearly every monk as a priest, thereby empowering them with greater clerical authority and prestige.

89. See Sicard's description of the four active monasteries at Wadi al-Natrun (St. Macarius, St. Bishuy, al-Baramus, and al-Suryan) in *Oeuvres*, 2:12–18.

90. Sicard, *Oeuvres*, 2:18. He writes, "We have to admit that the life of these good monks is very frugal and austere; but what is admirable, is that they are strong and robust, big, fat, and full of health." For an account of the monks' dietary habits, see Pococke, *A Description of the East*, 1:128.

91. Sicard, *Oeuvres*, 1:27.

92. Ibid., 2:18; see also Charles Sigisbert Sonnini, *Travels in Upper and Lower Egypt undertaken by Order of the Old Government of France* (London: J. Debrett, 1800), 347.

93. Sonnini, *Travels in Upper and Lower Egypt*, 547. This observation is confirmed by earlier travelers. Constantin-François Volney, for instance, wrote, "The Copts have at length expelled their rivals, and as they have been always intimately acquainted with the interior of the country, they are become depositaries of the registers of the lands and tribes." Volney, *Travels through Egypt and Syria in the Years 1783, 1784, and 1785*, 2 vols. (London: Pater-Noster-Row, 1787), 1:79.

94. There are scanty references to Copts who worked for bedouin leaders, particularly in Upper Egypt. In 1714, for instance, Sicard mentions an archon by the name of Jurj Abu Shahata who was a chief accountant for an unnamed bedouin chief. See Sicard, *Oeuvres*, 2:62. Al-Jabarti notes that some Copts worked for the Hawwara, a North African tribe that migrated to Egypt in the fourteenth century and dominated local politics in Upper Egypt until the eighteenth century. He writes that Hawwara shaykhs employed many Coptic accountants and tax collectors who "were at their work day and night." See *'Ajā'ib*, 1:575; 'Afifi, *Al-Aqbāṭ fī Miṣr*, 106.

95. For their historic domination of certain government posts, see Saleh, "Government Relations," 114–117. For the Ottoman period, see 'Afifi, *Al-Aqbāṭ fī Miṣr*, 105–119.

96. Daniel Crecelius, *The Roots of Modern Egypt: A Study of the Regimes of 'Ali Bey Al-Kabir and Muhammad Bey Abu Al-Dhahab, 1760–1775* (Chicago: Bibliotheca Islamica, 1981), 14.

97. Staffa, *Conquest and Fusion*, 234. For the prominent roles bestowed by the Ottoman governor Khayir Bey (1517–1522) to Jews and Christians, see Ibn Iyas, *Badā'i'*, 5: 484–485.

98. Jane Hathaway, *The Politics of Households in Ottoman Egypt* (Cambridge: Cambridge University Press, 1997), 9.

99. Hathaway, "Egypt in the Seventeenth Century," in *The Cambridge History of Egypt*, vol. 2, *Modern Egypt, from 1517 to the End of the Twentieth Century*, ed. M. W. Daly (Cambridge: Cambridge University Press, 1998), 2:38.

100. Winter, *Egyptian Society*, 17. As Crecelius puts it, so "long as the system [iltizām] continued to produce a surplus which was forwarded to Istanbul the central government did little to check the growing dominance that the military units achieved over the administrative system it had established in Egypt." Crecelius, *The Roots of Modern Egypt*, 19.

101. Hathaway "Egypt in the Seventeenth Century," 34–35.

102. Crecelius, *The Roots of Modern Egypt*, 24. The origins of some of these power-holders was the *mamlūk* system, a type of elite military slavery whereby recruits were usually purchased from the region of the Caucasus to join a local grandee's household, given military training, and eventually manumitted. Other beys, however, were Ottoman officials, Muslim converts from Bosnia, and freeborn Turks from Anatolia. See Hathaway, *The Politics of Households*, 11.

103. On the new sources of authority acquired by Egypt's soldiery, see Hathaway, *The Politics of Households*, 46.

104. Abudacnus, *The True History*, 30, affirms that Coptic education emphasized "religion and good manners [and Coptic children] learn to read and write in Arabic and

Coptic tongues. Boys also are wont in these schools to commit to memory the psaltery, and St. Paul's Epistles; they learn for the most part Geometry and Arithmetic, because these two studies are very useful and necessary upon the account of the overflowing of the Nile."

105. 'Afifi, *Al-Aqbāṭ fī Miṣr*, 111–112; Carter Vaughn Findley, *Ottoman Civil Officialdom: A Social History* (Princeton: Princeton University Press, 1989), 51.

106. Stanford J. Shaw, *The Financial and Administrative Organization and Development of Ottoman Egypt, 1517–1798* (Princeton: Princeton University Press, 1962), 341.

107. Winter, *Egyptian Society*, 203. See also Fuad Megally, "Numerical System, Coptic," *Coptic Encyclopedia* 6:1820–1822. This system appears to be quite comparable to the ways that records were kept by Armenian administrators at the imperial mint in Istanbul, who wrote the Ottoman language using Armenian characters. See Hagop Barsoumian, "The Armenian Amira Class of Istanbul" (PhD diss., Columbia University, 1980), 104.

108. This is noted in Egyptian court records from the seventeenth century. El Nahal, *The Judicial Administration*, 56; 'Afifi, *Al-Aqbāṭ fī Miṣr*, 117–119.

109. Shaw, *The Financial and Administrative Organization*, 202, 345.

110. Evliya Çelebi, *Seyahatname*, 10:418.

111. Qasim 'Abdu Qasim, *Ahl al-Dhimma fī Miṣr, al-'Uṣūr al-Wusṭa* (Cairo: Dār al-Ma'ārif, 1977), 29–30.

112. Vansleb, *The Present State of Egypt*, 20; Evliya Çelebi, *Seyahatname*, 10:77, 10:170.

113. In the strife between soldiery during the reign of the Ottoman governor Khidr Pasha (1598–1601), a Copt named Yuhanna al-Binlawi who held the title of *kātib al-khāzīna* (scribe of the treasury) was beheaded, along with other functionaries. See Muhammad bin al-Surur al-Bikri al-Siddiqi, *Al-Nuzha al-Zahiyya fī Dhikr wilāt Miṣr wa'l-Qāhira al-Mu'aziyya*, ann. 'Abd al-Raziq 'Abd al-Raziq 'Isa (Cairo: Al-'Arabī li'l-Nashr wa'l-Tawzī', 1998), 173. Another example emerges from 1660, when a conflict had arisen between Ahmad Bey "the Bosnian," representing the Qasimi faction against a group of rival beys representing the Fiqari faction. During this conflict, a certain Ghitas Bey was killed, and shortly thereafter, his Coptic scribe 'Awad (nicknamed *nuṣrānī al-sanjak*) was poisoned. For more on this conflict, see Winter, *Egyptian Society*, 22. Information on 'Awad is noted by Kamil Salih Nakhla, *Silsilat Tārīkh al-Bābāwāt Baṭāriqat al-Kursī al-Iskandarī* (Wadi al-Natrun, Egypt: Maṭba'at Dayr al-Sayyida al-'Adhrā' Dayr al-Suryān, 2001 [1954]), 4:77.

114. Hathaway, "Egypt in the Seventeenth Century," 37.

115. Ibid., 37–38; Winter, *Egyptian Society*, 22.

116. Staffa, *Conquest and Fusion*, 287.

117. Gradually, as Winter notes, Ottoman governors "spent all their time in the Citadel, as virtual prisoners in their own palace. More and more the leading emirs (beys) dismissed the governors if his policies did not please them, and informed the authorities in Istanbul." Winter, *Egyptian Society*, 20.

118. Michael Winter, "Ottoman Egypt, 1525–1609," in Daly, *The Cambridge History of Egypt*, 2:33. The humiliation of non-Muslims is rooted in the *dhull* prescripts derived from the Qur'an (9:29) and the sharī'a, stipulating that dhimmīs must display deference toward Muslims.

119. Crecelius, *The Roots of Modern Egypt*, 46.

120. For the origins of the Qazdaghli household, see Hathaway, *The Politics of Households*, chapter 4.

121. Hathaway, "Egypt in the Seventeenth Century," 50.

122. Hathaway, *The Politics of Households*, 50–51.

123. According to al-Masri, *Qiṣṣat al-Kanīsa*, 4:95, Yuhanna Abu Masri was the head of the mubāshirs and was a nāẓir (supervisor) over the Church of the Virgin at Harat Zuwayla. He redecorated this church, built up its walls, and paid special attention to its library, making the deacon and archon, Nasim Butrus, the librarian in charge.

124. Damurdashi refers to him as Yuhanna ibn al-Masri and confirms that he held the title of mubāshir al-Ruznāme as far back as the governorate of Isma'il Pasha (1695–1697). See *Al-Durra al-Muṣāna*, 27. The Ruznāme was the principal administrative bureau of the Egyptian treasury, which managed all other departments in the treasury. See Shaw, *The Financial and Administrative Organization*, 340. Magdi Guirguis notes that Abu Masri continued to hold the title of mubāshir for several more years. Guirguis, "Athār al-Arākhina," 27.

125. Shaw, *The Financial and Administrative Organization*, 338.

126. Nakhla, *Silsilat*, 4:95. Nakhla does not specify the exact nature of this post. This is possibly the head of the "Scribes of the Military and Civilian Corps," which included the scribes working for the military regiments as well as those working for the Imperial Treasury. See Shaw, *The Financial and Administrative Organization*, 146.

127. Katkhuda is the Persian word for "steward" and was used in Ottoman Egyptian military regiments to refer to the second officer after the agha. See Hathaway, *The Politics of Households*, 176. Mustahfazan is the common name for Egypt's Janissary corps.

128. This might be Muhammad Kahya Abaza, who is discussed by Hathaway, *The Politics of Households*, 101. For a complete list of these archons and of their titles, see Guirguis, "Athār al-Arākhina," 27–29. In his survey, Guirguis relies mostly on unpublished manuscripts from the Patriarchal Library in Cairo and also from the Monastery of St. Paul.

129. This is cited in an archival document from the Coptic patriarchate, dating from 21 November 1740. See Guirguis, "Idārat al-Azamāt fī Tārīkh al-Qibṭ," 55.

130. Hathaway, *The Politics of Households*, 57, 59; P. M. Holt, *Egypt and the Fertile Crescent, 1516–1922: A Political History* (Ithaca: Cornell University Press, 1966), 91–92.

131. Hathaway, *The Politics of Households*, 75; Guirguis, "Athār al-Arākhina," 28.

132. See Guirguis, "Idārat al-Azamāt fī Tārīkh al-Qibṭ," 54, fn. 27.

133. Hathaway, *The Politics of Households*, 100.

134. Crecelius "Egypt in the Eighteenth Century," in Daly, *The Cambridge History of Egypt*, 74–75. For 'Abd al-Rahman's extensive building program, see al-Jabarti, *'Ajā'ib*, 2:5–9.

135. Crecelius, *The Roots of Modern Egypt*, 75.

136. Hathaway, *The Politics of Households*, 47. For more on the mamlūks, see fn. 102.

137. For a critical discussion of the term "neo-Mamluk beylicate" and its implications, see Hathaway, *The Politics of Households*, 46–51.

138. Crecelius, *The Roots of Modern Egypt*, 27. Muhammad 'Ali deemed the mamlūks a political and military nuisance. On 1 March 1811, he invited the mamlūks to a banquet held at the Cairo Citadel, and as they marched in a procession from the Citadel, he ordered that

they be shot. Those who escaped the massacre or who had not attended the banquet were eventually hunted and killed. See Holt, *Egypt and the Fertile Crescent*, 179.

139. On his working title, see Guirguis, "Athār al-Arākhina," 28. On his status as ʿAli Bey's astrologer, see Volney, *Travels through Egypt and Syria*, 1:135; and Crecelius, *The Roots of Modern Egypt*, 66–67. Al-Jabarti notes that Rizq "attained in ʿAli Bey's days a position no other Copt, as far as we know, had ever achieved." Al-Jabarti, *ʿAjā'ib*, 1:638.

140. Volney, *Travels through Egypt and Syria*, 1:135–136; Al-Jabarti, *ʿAjā'ib*, 2:153; Crecelius, *The Roots of Modern Egypt*, 66–67.

141. Al-Jabarti, *ʿAjā'ib*, 2:192. According to al-Jabarti, in 1786, Hasan Pasha the Kapudan (admiral), who was sent by the sultan to oust the duumvirs, ordered an investigation of all the "waqf endowments of land, incomes, and properties established by al-Muʿallim Ibrahim al-Jawhari on behalf of monasteries and churches. The purpose of all these measures was to extract money and financial compensations." In the same year, he ordered a raid of al-Jawhari's home, which was emptied of "furniture, silver, gold, and china and later sold at auction." See al-Jabarti, *ʿAjā'ib*, 2:205. While al-Jawhari's prominence as a Copt likely incurred greater jealousy and wrath, Hasan Pasha was punishing al-Jawhari and presumably other Coptic archons for their collaboration with Ibrahim and Murad Beys. The beys had, for some years, withheld Egypt's annual taxes from Istanbul and were seen as traitors. See ʿAfifi, *Al-Aqbāṭ fī Miṣr*, 78, 127–128; Hathaway, *The Politics of Households*, 118.

142. Al-Jabarti, *ʿAjā'ib*, 2:437.

143. Ibid., 4:177. Modern hagiographic accounts of the Jawhari brothers are mostly based on stories told in Tawfiq Iskarus, *Nawābigh al-Aqbāṭ*, vol. 2 (Cairo: Maṭbaʿat al-Tawfīq, 1910), 280–312; and Yaʿqub Nakhla Rufayla, *Tārīkh al-Umma al-Qibṭiyya* (Cairo: Metropol, 2000 [1898]), 270–289.

144. Hathaway, *The Politics of Households*, 25.

145. Nakhla, *Silsilat*, 4:62; Guirguis, "Athār al-Arākhina," 44; ʿAfifi, *Al-Aqbāṭ fī Miṣr*, 57–59, 239–241.

146. Hathaway, *The Politics of Households*, 26.

147. Doris Behrens-Abouseif, *Azbakiyya and Its Environs: From Azbak to Ismail, 1476–1879* (Cairo: Institut Français d'Archéologie Orientale, 1985), 67.

148. Al-Jabarti, *ʿAjā'ib*, 4:177.

149. Pococke, *A Description of the East*, 1:73; Vansleb, *The Present State of Egypt*, 222.

150. Raymond, *Artisans et commerçants*, 2:458. The physical proximity of Muslims to non-Muslims is discussed by Galal El Nahal, *The Judicial Administration*, 56, where she notes that in court records pertaining to a particular neighborhood, "it was not uncommon to find Muslims defending a non-Muslim against another Muslim, or to find a non-Muslim bailing a Muslim out of jail, or to find a Muslim man marrying a non-Muslim woman, without the wife changing her religion."

151. Vansleb, *The Present State of Egypt*, 154. On Egypt's agricultural cycle in the seventeenth century, see al-Siddiqi, *Al-Nuzha al-Zahiyya*, 321–328.

152. Eliot Warburton, *The Crescent and the Cross, or Romance and Realities of Eastern Travel* (New York: George P. Putnam, 1848), 95. In the seventeenth century, Vansleb, *The Present State of Egypt*, 242–243, found the town of Isna remarkable in that Copts had a

visible if humble presence. There were two active churches, and all Coptic men of employable age were weavers who worked in what seems to be a guild structure led by two "archpriests."

153. Abudacnus notes that they served as secretaries "to the principal Turks, Chancellors, Quastors, Procurators Regalium muncrum, Commissioners of tithes and Customs, etc. so that they have in their hands the whole Great Sultan's Revenue proceeding out of this country. Others of them are Arithmeticians, or Geometricians, to meet and measure out of the Ground, and to cast up the money yearly going out of Egypt. The Commons amongst them are either Artificers or Servants: Artificers are of the following possessions, goldsmiths, jewelers, shoe-makers, smiths, tailors, masons, engravers, carpenters." Abudacnus, *The True History*, 29.

154. Raymond, *Artisans et commerçants*, 2:456–457. Raymond's research on Coptic *terekes* from the seventeenth and eighteenth century "found neither a tagir [merchant] of coffee, nor a fabric merchant."

155. Raymond, *Artisans et commerçants*, 2:459; Evliya Çelebi, *Seyahatname*, 10:198.

156. For a description of the utter poverty experienced by Copts in the Ottoman period, as recorded in Muslim court records, see Salwa Milad, *Wathā'iq Ahl al-Dhimma fi'l 'Aṣr al-'Uthmānī wa Ahammiyatuha al-Tārīkhiyya* (Cairo: Dār al-Thaqāfa l'il-Nashr wa'l-Tawzī', 1983), 31–32.

157. As Galal El Nahal, *The Judicial Administration*, 39, notes, because the making and consumption of alcohol is deemed illegal by the sharī'a, "disputes related to transactions in alcoholic substances could not be heard in [Muslim] court." Nevertheless, the profession of wine makers (*al-khammār*) was openly recognized in court records; see Milad, *Wathā'iq Ahl al-Dhimma*, 37.

158. Vansleb, *The Present State of Egypt*, 154; Pococke, *A Description of the East*, 1:58.

159. For a brief discussion of Copts and Cairene taverns, see Behrens-Abouseif, *Azbakiyya and Its Environs*, 40.

160. For a decree made in 1730/31, see al-Jabarti, *al-'Ajā'ib*, 1:235.

161. Volney, *Travels through Egypt and Syria*, 1:251.

162. Seventeenth-century court records reveal, according to El Nahal, *The Judicial Administration*, 39, that Janissaries were engaged in the production of *būẓa*, a "beer-like drink."

163. El Nahal, *The Judicial Administration*, 42.

164. Milad, *Wathā'iq Ahl al-Dhimma*, 20–21; El Nahal, *The Judicial Administration*, 44.

165. Pococke, *A Description of the East*, 1:246. On Coptic recourse to Islamic courts in the medieval period see Mikhail, "Egypt from Late Antiquity to Early Islam," 274–276; el-Leithy, "Coptic Culture and Conversion," 412–417.

166. On the coercion of Coptic priests by the laity, particularly with regard to marital disputes, see el-Leithy, "Coptic Culture and Conversion," 362; Guirguis, "Athār al-Arākhina," 43.

167. Vansleb, *The Present State of Egypt*, 76, 141–148.

168. Vansleb was particularly scandalized by the intermingling of the sexes at the Feast of the Epiphany, where men and women frolicked and played "naked" in the water, in the presence of the patriarch and many priests. See *The Present State of Egypt*, 205–207.

169. Al-Jabarti often describes these crises in his chronicle. For the year 1695, he speaks of a great famine that caused an influx of peasants into Cairo and resulted in theft, starvation, cannibalism, and countless deaths. See al-Jabarti, *'Ajā'ib*, 1:43. On the plague and its frequency, see Alan Mikhail, "The Nature of Plague in Late Eighteenth-Century Egypt," *Bulletin of the History of Medicine* 82, no. 2 (2008): 251.

170. Although it is a topic that has yet to be fully studied by Ottoman historians, intracommunal rivalries between Christian laity and clergy occurred with regularity throughout Ottoman lands. See, for example, Richard van Leeuwen, *Notables and Clergy in Mount Lebanon* (Leiden: Brill, 1994), esp. chapters 5 and 6; Runciman, *The Great Church*, chapter 10.

171. John Iskander, "Islamization in Medieval Egypt: The Copto-Arabic 'Apocalypse of Samuel' as a Source for the Social and Religious History of Medieval Copts," *Medieval Encounters* 4, no. 3 (1998): 226; see also el-Leithy, "Coptic Culture and Conversion," 401–412.

172. Historically, as Maged Mikhail notes, the selection of the Coptic patriarch involved multiple groups and interests. Mikhail, "Egypt from Late Antiquity to Early Islam," 280. In the late thirteenth century, the archons of Cairo jockeyed for power by advocating one patriarchal candidate (Yu'annis) against another (Ghubriyal). For a few years and until the death of Ghubriyal in 1274, the two men would swap positions depending on the influence of their supporters and, in one instance, on the interference of the Mamluk sultan. *HPEC* III/3, 228–230.

173. Nakhla, *Silsilat*, 4:53; al-Masri, *Qiṣṣat al-Kanīsa*, 4:21.

174. Nakhla, *Silsilat*, 4:64.

175. Archons were often called *mu'allim* (pl. *mu'allimūn*), a title bestowed on Christians and Jews in Egypt meaning "teacher" or "elder." Winter, *Egyptian Society*, 221.

176. Nakhla, *Silsilat*, 4:74. The "taking" of monks from their monasteries was part of a long-established and at times symbolic ritual that dates to at least late antiquity, a ritual intended to highlight the unassuming nature of the monk-elect-patriarch. Mikhail, "Egypt from Late Antiquity to Early Islam," 288.

177. *HPEC* III/3, 278.

178. *HPEC* III/3, 290, 292.

179. Pococke, *A Description of the East*, 1:245; Sonnini, *Travels in Upper and Lower Egypt*, 356.

180. Mark Swanson characterizes the relationship between archons and higher clergymen best when writing that "while the Coptic Orthodox history records occasional examples of the [archons] becoming sources or rivalry to the ecclesiastical hierarchy, they were also, with great regularity, sources of revitalization and renewal." Swanson, "The Monastery of St. Paul," 46. Conversely, Magdi Guirguis argues that the clergy were the most important source of authority in the sixteenth and early seventeenth centuries and, without explaining his logic, that "civilian notables . . . had no choice but to accept [their] leadership in all matters." See Guirguis, "The Coptic Community in the Ottoman Period," 204.

181. Cited in Guirguis, "The Coptic Community in the Ottoman Period," 204. Guirguis reads this text as a positive indicator of the patriarch's burgeoning authority. On Yu'annis XIII, see in general el-Leithy, "Coptic Culture and Conversion," chapter 9.

182. Gawdat Gabra, "Medieval and Later Inhabitants and Visitors," in *Monastic Visions: Wall Paintings at the Monastery of St. Antony at the Red Sea*, ed. Elizabeth S. Bolman (New Haven: Yale University Press, 2002), 174.

183. For the full inscription, see Sidney H. Griffith, "The Handwriting on the Wall," in Bolman, *Monastic Visions*, 186–187.

184. Before the late fourteenth century, when the Mamluks seized a large amount of lands and properties from the church, the ecclesiastical hierarchy could rely more readily on *awqāf* income. Mikhail, "Egypt from Late Antiquity to Early Islam," 398–399. For a good description of the fund-raising capacity among Christian patriarchs in other Ottoman Arab territories, see the Maronite case as discussed in van Leeuwen, *Notables and Clergy*, 99–100.

185. Abudacnus, *The True History*, 5, writes, "And this only power he [the Coptic patriarch] now possesses, for he is not secure to the things belonging unto the Church, such as Tythes, First-Fruits, Marriage-fees, or Alms which are given by Christians at or near their deathbeds, or those things used to be given such as receive the Sacraments or ordination and confirmation, for concerning these things, he can move no controversy with the subject. For whether he can give, or not give, perform, or not perform what is appointed, it is the same thing, he must wait until his charitable disposition and kindness." Even when church representatives were able to collect tithes, they were often subject to random extortion by local soldiers. In one incident, a Christian monk was arrested and his "chest with deposits belonging to the Christians" was taken. See al-Jabarti, *'Ajā'ib*, 2:200.

186. Colophon to Serial 434, Class 62 in W. E. Crum, *Catalogue of the Coptic Manuscripts in the Collection of the John Rylands Library Manchester* (Manchester: University Press of London, 1909).

187. See an inscription from the eighteenth century discussed by Swanson, "The Monastery of St. Paul," 57, and Gawdat Gabra, "The Coptic and Arabic Inscriptions in the Cave Church," in Lyster, *The Cave Church of Paul the Hermit*, 277, 279, 280.

188. Cited by Guirguis, "Athār al-Arākhina," 30, fn. 40.

189. Lyster, "Reflections on the Temporal World," in Bolman, *Monastic Visions*, 104; Werthmuller, "An In-Between Space," 114–116.

190. Guirguis, *An Armenian Artist*, 80–89. For a sample of the stunning array of icons commissioned by archons and churches during the Ottoman period, see in general *Coptic Icons*, 2 vols. (Cairo: Lehnert and Landrock, 1998).

191. For an eighteenth-century account of the construction of this church, see Gawdat Gabra, "New Research from the Library of the Monastery of St. Paul," in Lyster, *The Cave Church of Paul the Hermit*, 99–105.

192. Sicard, *Oeuvres*, 2:63. Sicard had met Jirjis Abu Mansur during his previous voyage to Cairo, fifteen years prior, when Yu'annis XVI had congregated various bishops and priests in Cairo for the Holy Mayrūn Ceremony. Sicard accompanied then Bishop Murqus of Niqada to this ritual, which according to Coptic sources took place in 1703. In further elaborating on this "patronage" relationship between Abu Mansur and the later bishop of Niqada, Yuhanna, Sicard notes that a large boat filled with sheep, grains, and other foodstuffs was sent to Cairo by the bishop for "his patron" the archon as well as "his patriarch." See Sicard, *Œuvres*, 2:65. On earlier practices, see Vansleb, *The Present State of Egypt*, 102.

193. In the seventeenth century, Evliya Çelebi noted that "all of the *reaya* [tax-payers] in this town are Copts" who occupied approximately eight hundred households. See *Seyahatname*, 10:319.

194. *HPEC* III/3, 286.

195. *HPEC* III/3, 289.

196. For instance, the supervision of the Monastery of St. Antony was given to Yuhanna Yusuf al-Suruji in the mid-eighteenth century. Guirguis, "Idārat al-Azamāt fī Tārīkh al-Qibṭ," 54, fn. 26. Little information exists about the roles of Coptic nāzirs, but we can deduce their functions from the description we have of Muslim nāzirs of pious endowments (awqāf). See Shaw, *The Financial and Administrative Organization*, 43; El Nahal, *The Judicial Administration*, 68–71.

197. *HPEC* III/3, 278–79. The patriarchs' attention to religious rituals and to church properties disputes Magdi Guirguis's assertion that Coptic patriarchs in the eighteenth century "were more interested in money than in spiritual matters; they failed to do their duties towards their church." Guirguis, "The Coptic Community in the Ottoman Period," 211.

198. This is discussed by Guirguis, "Athār al-Arākhina," 40.

199. See al-Masri, *Qiṣṣat al-Kanīsa*, 4:82; Guirguis, "Athār al-Arākhina," 40–41. Mayrūn oil is considered an integral part of the sacrament of Chrismation in the Coptic tradition, and this tradition had not been carried out since 1461. It was performed by notables, with the reported presence of Muslim leaders; the patriarch consecrated this mixture of spices, oil, and perfumes at the patriarchal headquarters in Harat al-Rum.

200. *HPEC* III/3, 282.

201. Winter adds that "a recurrent accusation against the Christians in official [Ottoman and Egyptian] documents was that they dared to flaunt their religion and its symbols, drinking wine, sounding the wooden clappers loudly as a call to prayer and so forth, allegations that were never made against the Jews." Winter, *Egyptian Society*, 220.

202. Al-Masri, *Qiṣṣat al-Kanīsa*, 4:131.

203. Moshe Perlmannn, ed. and trans., *Shaykh Damanhuri on the Churches of Cairo, 1739* (Berkeley: University of California Press, 1975), 10. One wonders why Copts might have been in need of building new churches during this period; a possible explanation is that their population in Cairo was expanding and new houses of worship were in immediate need. Such was the pattern among the Armenians of Istanbul in the late eighteenth and early nineteenth centuries. See Barsoumian, "The Armenian Amira Class of Istanbul," 156.

204. Al-Jabarti, *'Ajā'ib*, 2:199.

205. The Maronite community also offers excellent parallels, but I focus here on two urban and Orthodox Christian communities who provide closer comparisons with the Copts, particularly with Cairo's archons. On the Maronites, see van Leeuwen, *Notables and Clergy*, esp. 101–110.

206. C. G. Patrinelis, "The Phanariots before 1821," *Balkan Studies* 42, no. 1 (2001): 184–185.

207. Runciman, *The Great Church*, 362, 376.

208. Barsoumian, "The Armenian Amira Class of Istanbul," 27–28.

209. Ibid., 29, 141.

210. Ibid., 85.

211. Ibid., 139. As Abraham Marcus notes for the case of eighteenth-century Aleppo, "to reach the top" of local or regional political hierarchies in the Ottoman Empire, "nothing helped . . . if one was not a Muslim." See Marcus, *The Middle East on the Eve of Modernity: Aleppo in the Eighteenth Century* (New York: Columbia University Press, 1989), 68.

CHAPTER 2

1. The idea of hagiographies and martyrologies being used to strengthen Christian communities in the Islamic world has been explored by many. See, for instance, Sidney H. Griffith, "The *Life of Theodore of Edessa*: History, Hagiography, and Religious Apologetics in Mar Saba in Early Abbasid Times," *Orientalia Lovaniensia Analecta* 98 (2001): 147–169.

2. Jason R. Zaborowski, "From Coptic to Arabic in Medieval Egypt," *Medieval Encounters* 14, no. 1 (2008): 36.

3. Most Muslim chroniclers regarded these converts as opportunists and a disgrace to Islam. Some of the new converts continued to be threatened with job insecurity or even death. It is likely that they gradually distanced themselves from the Coptic community to prove that they were loyal to their adopted faith. In general, see Donald P. Little, "Coptic Converts of Islam," in *Indigenous Christian Communities in Islamic Lands Eighth to Eighteenth Centuries*, ed. Michael Gervers and Ramzi Jibran Bikhazi (Toronto: Pontifical Institute of Mediaeval Studies, 1990), 282; Terry Wilfong, "The Non-Muslim Communities," in *The Cambridge History of Egypt*, vol. 1, *Islamic Egypt 640–1517*, ed. Carl F. Petry (Cambridge: Cambridge University Press, 1998), 1:184.

4. For more on Coptic martyrdom in the fourteenth century, see el-Leithy, "Coptic Culture and Conversion," chapter 3.

5. Al-Madrasa al-Salihiyya was built by the Ayyubids during their final years of rule in Egypt. The construction began under al-Malik al-Salih Najm al-Din Ayyub in 1241–1242 and was completed in 1249–1251. In the Mamluk period, it became the "supreme judicial tribunal of the state," where "the four chief justices heard cases referred to them from the lower courts." Carl Petry, *The Civilian Elite of Cairo* (Princeton: Princeton University Press, 1981), 330–331. In the first years of Ottoman rule, most qāḍīs were dismissed, and "all litigation and other legal business" was limited to al-Madrasa al-Salihiyya. See Winter, *Egyptian Society*, 11–12.

6. Ibn Iyas, *Badā'i'*, 5:412–413.

7. Ibid., 5:445–447.

8. Ibid., 5:475–76. This event also took place in 1522.

9. Ahmad Shalabi, *Awḍaḥ al-Ishārāt*, 119–120, 126; Winter, "Ottoman Egypt, 1525–1609," 32–33.

10. On the rebellion and rising inflation, see Winter, *Egyptian Society*, 19; on the resulting pressures against Copts, see al-Masri, *Qiṣṣat al-Kanīsa*, 4:20–28.

11. Winter, *Society and Religion*, 219. Similar complaints had been made by medieval Muslim writers who criticized fellow Muslims for "visiting Coptic monks, and taking the Host and accepting blessing from them." See Subhi Labib, "The Problem of Bid'a in the Light of an Arabic Manuscript of the Fourteenth Century," *Journal of the Economic and Social History of the Orient* 7, no. 2 (1964): 193.

12. Charles Frazee, *Catholics and Sultans: The Church and the Ottoman Empire 1453–1923* (Cambridge: Cambridge University Press, 1983), 24–28, 67–87.

13. Hamilton, *The Copts and the West*, 74–76, 81, talks about the example of Ghubriyal VIII (1587–1603), who signed letters of union in 1594 but did not enforce them. Yu'annis XVI agreed to union in 1684, but his letters were rejected by Rome.

14. Ibid., 76.

15. Ibid., 59–69. Ghubriyal seemed assured that his own authority as patriarch over the Copts would be protected. A manuscript from Coptic archives, which records various "questions and answers" copied from documents found in Ghubriyal's cell after his death, includes instructions to Copts who had abandoned their faith for another Christian sect but who wished to return to the church. The latter are asked to partake in a distinct set of prayers and fasts and to confess their sins before rejoining the community. See Patriarchal Library, MS Theology 294, 14r–16v.

16. Nakhla, *Silsilat*, 4:51–52. The money was needed in order to finance the expedition of Sinan Pasha, Egypt's governor, to subdue a rebellion in Yemen. For more details on this rebellion, see Holt, *Egypt and the Fertile Crescent*, 54–55.

17. Samir Khalil Samir, "Gabriel VII," *Coptic Encyclopedia* 4:1133–1135; al-Masri, *Qiṣṣat al-Kanīsa*, 4:11. The patriarch's fear of persecution is confirmed by a letter he wrote to the Catholic pope in 1563. See Hamilton, *The Copts and the West*, 63.

18. Rufayla, *Tārīkh al-Umma al-Qibṭiyya*, 248–250; Nakhla, *Silsilat*, 4:55–56. Opposing the missionaries was a certain monk from the Monastery of St. Antony named "Ghubriyal" who has been identified by Rabbath as Yu'annis's successor, Ghubriyal VIII. The missionaries nicknamed Ghubriyal "Judas to the Catholics." See Rabbath, *Documents*, 1:208; and for the missionary letter discussing Ghubriyal's involvement, see "Le P. Rodriguez à Mgr Fioribello du Caire, le 7 Avril 1562," in Rabbath, *Documents*, 1:277–285.

19. Hamilton, *The Copts and the West*, 76.

20. Frazee, *Catholics and Sultans*, 149.

21. "Lettera del Console di Francia in Egitto [19 di Marzo del 1610]," published in Vincenzo Buri, "L'Unione della chiesa Copta con Roma sotto Clemente VIII," *Orientalia Christiana* 23, no. 72 (1931): 244–247.

22. Coptic sources mention that the metropolitan of Damietta backed a group of influential archons who wished to legalize polygamy. Murqus, who refused their proposals, was subsequently arrested and beaten by order of the Ottoman governor. The dissenters then chose another patriarch who pronounced that Copts were free to practice divorce and polygamy. Heated conflict ensued, and ultimately Murqus was released, the rebellious faction attacked, their homes destroyed, and "their" patriarch exiled to Upper Egypt. See Nakhla, *Silsilat*, 4:62–63; al-Masri, *Qiṣṣat al-Kanīsa*, 4:32–33.

23. An unidentified manuscript discussed in Guirguis, "The Coptic Community in the Ottoman Period," 207–208.

24. The literature on Christians in the early Islamic era is vast, but on the issue of hagiography as a source of communal distinctiveness and identity, see in particular David H. Vila, "Christian Martyrs in the First Abbasid Century and the Development of an Apologetic against Islam" (PhD diss., St. Louis University, 1999); on the issue of hagiography as fostering a "historical consciousness," see Dennis P. Hupchick, "Orthodoxy and Bulgarian Ethnic Awareness under Ottoman Rule, 1396–1762," *Nationalities Papers* 21, no. 2 (1993): 86–88.

25. Ottoman-era sources rarely focus on Egypt, possibly reflecting the deterioration of an indigenous Egyptian historiographical tradition as well as a decrease in literacy. Winter, *Egyptian Society*, 18–19.

26. While Vaporis defines neo-martyrs by their allegiance to the Byzantine Orthodox Christian creed and by their ethnic identities, Sidney Griffith offers a more general definition of the term, describing neo-martyrdom in the context of the relationship between Christians and Muslims after the Islamic conquests of the seventh century. See Nomikos Michael Vaporis, *Witnesses for Christ: Orthodox Christian Neo-Martyrs of the Ottoman Period, 1437–1860* (Crestwood, NY: St. Vladimir's Seminary Press, 2000); Sidney H. Griffith, "Christians, Muslims, and Neo-Martyrs," in *Sharing the Sacred: Religious Contacts and Conflicts in the Holy Land: First–Fifteenth Centuries CE*, ed. Arieh Kofsky and Guy G. Stroumsa (Jerusalem: Yad Izhak Ben Zvi, 1998), 169.

27. Due to archival restrictions, few original copies of Coptic neo-martyrdoms from the Ottoman era have been made accessible. On 27 December 1523, just a few years after Salib—the focus of this study—was martyred, Mikha'il al-Tukhi was killed. His story is commemorated in St. Macarius Library, MS Hagiography 43. The monk Yuhanna al-Qalyubi was also martyred during the sixteenth century. Reportedly, he was captured by a local ruler who demanded that the monk deny his Christianity. Because he refused to do so, he was tortured and then killed on 6 December 1582. His story is retold by al-Masri in *Qiṣṣat al-Kanīsa*, 4:25. His original martyrology is recorded in Patriarchal Library, MS Liturgy 106(2). Another neo-martyr is Yuhanna al-Namrusi, who was killed in 1563; his martyrdom is recorded in Paris Arabe 153, ff. 445–452, and has been briefly discussed by el-Leithy, "Coptic Culture and Conversion," 54, 257–258. Sidhum Bishay (d. 1844) is the best-known Coptic neo-martyr from the late Ottoman period. A native of Damietta, his story is retold in Bishuy 'Abd al-Masih (Anba Bishuy), *Shahīd Dumyat: Mārī Sidhum Bishay* (Cairo: Maktab al-Nisr li'l-Ṭibā'a, 1987), and 'Abd al-Masih, *Tārīkh Ibrūshiyyat Dumyat* (Cairo: Maktab al-Nisr li'l-Ṭibā'a, 1990), 93–112.

28. Blasphemy among non-Muslims was unusual within Ottoman neo-martyrdom literature. For the Balkans context, Marinos Sariyannis, "Aspects of 'Neomartyrdom'; Religious Contacts, 'Blasphemy' and 'Calumny' in 17th-Century Istanbul," *Archivum Ottomanicum* 23 (2005/2006): 252, remarks that "when Ottoman sources speak of blasphemy, they refer almost always to Muslims who had spoken heretically against Islam; that is, it was far less common for Christians or Jews to be prosecuted for blasphemy in this period."

29. These are Coptic Museum, MS History 475(2), fols. 10r–24v (1550); Paris MS Arabe 152, ff. 90v–108r (sixteenth century); Patriarchal Library, MS History 31(5), ff. 78v–92v (undated); Cairo, Patriarchal Library, MS Liturgy 106(3) (undated, likely sixteenth century); the John Rylands Library, Manchester, MS 433[69], f. 101a (an eighteenth-century hymn, not a hagiography); John Rylands Library, Manchester, MS 435 (1799 entry in a Coptic Difnār). I was able to consult Coptic Museum, MS History 475(2), and Paris Arabe 152; I cite the former because of its clarity and readability.

30. Nakhla, *Silsilat*, 4:39.

31. Vila, "Christian Martyrs in the First Abbasid Century," 109.

32. Elizabeth Zachariadou writes that these stories proliferated because "adherence to the faith was the only possible resistance which the [Orthodox] Church could profess and

preach." Zachariadou, "The Neomartyr's Message," *Bulletin of the Centre for Asia Minor Studies* 8 (1990–1991): 63.

33. Gara, "Neomartyr without a Message," 155.

34. Indeed, some Muslim writers in the sixteenth century, such as Ibn Nujaym al-Misri (d. 1563), saw Coptic Christians as far more "convertible" to Islam than Jews, and some may have been proselytizing among Christians during this period. Winter, *Egyptian Society*, 222.

35. Griffith, "Christians, Muslims, and Neo-Martyrs," 204.

36. Zachariadou, "The Neomartyr's Message," 54–56.

37. Vila, "Christian Martyrs in the First Abbasid Century," 138–139. Christian hagiographies were distinct from of Muslim saints' lives, the latter having little if any liturgical relevance. For more on reading "hagiographic biographies" in the Muslim context, see Josef Meri, *The Cult of Saints* (Oxford: Oxford University Press, 2002), 82–90.

38. Jonathan P. Berkey, "Storytelling, Preaching, and Power in Mamluk Cairo," *Mamluk Studies Review* 4 (2000): 58. Also see, in general, Berkey, *Popular Preaching and Religious Authority in the Medieval Islamic Near East* (Seattle: University of Washington Press, 2001).

39. Nelly Hanna, "The Chronicles of Ottoman Egypt: History or Entertainment?" in *The Historiography of Islamic Egypt (c. 950–1800)*, ed. Hugh Kennedy (Leiden: Brill, 2001), 243, 245. On oral culture in Ottoman Egypt, see Hanna, *In Praise of Books* (Syracuse, NY: Syracuse University Press, 2003), 64–69.

40. On the issue of reading Ottoman-era narratives as texts that are intended to be performed, see, in general, Gabriel Piterberg, "Speech Acts and Written Texts: A Reading of a Seventeenth-Century Ottoman Historiographic Episode," *Poetics Today* 14, no. 2 (1993): 387–418.

41. See Leslie S. B. MacCoull, "Notes on the Martyrdom of John of Phanijoit (BHO 519)," *Medieval Encounters* 6, nos. 1–3 (2000): 75–76.

42. I use this term as explored by Dominick LaCapra in *History and Criticism* (Ithaca: Cornell University Press, 1985), 45–69.

43. On this approach, see the collection edited by Mary A. Suydam and Joanna E. Ziegler, *Performance and Transformation: New Approaches to Late Medieval Spirituality* (New York: St. Martin's Press, 1999).

44. See David Frankfurter, "Hagiography and the Reconstruction of Local Religion," in *The Encroaching Desert: Egyptian Hagiography and the Medieval West*, ed. Jitse Dijkstra and Mathilde van Dijk (Leiden: Brill, 2006), 14.

45. Phokion P. Kotzageorgis, "'Messiahs' and Neomartyrs in Ottoman Thessaly: Some Thoughts on Two Entries in a Mühimme Defteri," *Archivum Ottomanicum* 23 (2005/2006): 230–231.

46. Gara, "Neomartyr without a Message," 157. It is by "sheer luck," she maintains, "that one finds records of trials for apostasy in the surviving court archives."

47. Ibid., 161.

48. Winter, "Attitudes toward the Ottomans," in Kennedy, *The Historiography of Islamic Egypt*, 198. There are no other chronicles dating from this period with which *Badāʾiʿ*

might be compared. See Winter's article for a critical evaluation of this account and for the relationship between Ibn Iyas and the late Mamluk administration.

49. The Upper Egyptian village of Dalja is located southwest of Mallawi and west of the meeting point between Bahr Yusuf and the Nile. Heinz Halm, *Ägypten nach den mamlukischen Lehensregistern*, vol. 1 (Wiesbaden: Reichert, 1979), 113.

50. The text does not specify how he was nailed, but Copts were regularly punished in the Mamluk period by crucifixion. See Maqrizi, *Khiṭaṭ*, 4(2):1074–1075; El-Leithy, "Coptic Culture and Conversion," 107, 182. This continued to be regular practice for the punishment of various criminals in Ottoman Egypt. For incidents in the seventeenth century, see al-Siddiqi, *Al-Nuzha al-Zahiyya*, 193–194, 225.

51. Ibn Iyas, *Badā'i'*, 4:286.

52. Winter, "Attitudes toward the Ottomans," 198. According to Winter, when it suited his views, Ibn Iyas criticized the Mamluk regime; later, however, he would view it as more favorable than the Ottoman rule that replaced it.

53. For more on this lingering "nostalgia" for the Mamluk Empire, see Jane Hathaway, "Mamluk 'Revivals' and Mamluk Nostalgia in Ottoman Egypt," in *The Mamluks in Egyptian and Syrian Politics and Society*, ed. Michael Winter and Amalia Levanoni (Leiden: Brill, 2004), 387–406.

54. In a different context, Boğaç Ergene and I compared the historical accuracy of this text with that of *M.Salib*, specifically with reference to the structure of the Mamluk judicial system. See Armanios and Ergene, "A Christian Martyr under Mamluk Justice: The Trials of Salib (d. 1512) according to Coptic and Muslim Sources," *Muslim World* 96, no. 1 (2006): 115–144.

55. I borrow this phrase from Boğaç Ergene, as used in "Pursuing Justice in an Islamic Context: Dispute Resolution in Ottoman Courts of Law," *PoLAR: Political and Legal Anthropology Review* 27, no. 1 (2004): 56

56. For an analysis and translation of John of Phanijōit's martyrdom, see Jason R. Zaborowski, *The Coptic Martyrdom of John of Phanijōit: Assimilation and Conversion to Islam in Thirteenth-Century Egypt* (Leiden: Brill, 2005); also see, in general, MacCoull, "Notes on the Martyrdom of John of Phanijoit (BHO 519)."

57. De Lacy O'Leary, *The Saints of Egypt* (New York: Macmillan, 1937), 19–20.

58. Al-Ushmunayn is a town (and also a province) on the west bank of the Nile in Upper Egypt. In reference to the thirteenth-century Coptic neo-martyr John of Phanijōit, Leslie MacCoull makes a fascinating observation: she notes that John's origins in al-Ushmunayn might be related to the hagiographer's desire to "convey an Upper Egyptian traditionalist viewpoint to counteract the Cairene cosmopolitanism he regarded as cowardly." See MacCoull, "Notes on the Martyrdom of John of Phanijoit," 78. On al-Ushmunayn, see Ayman Fu'ad Sayyid, "al-Ushmunayn," *EI2* 10:916, and Maurice Martin, "La Province d'Ašmūnayn: historique de sa configuration religieuse," *Annales Islamologiques* 23 (1987): 1–29.

59. *M.Salib*, 12r.

60. Ibid., 13r.

61. Ibid. This description recalls and is likely based on the imprisonment of Paul and Silas in Philippi, as recorded in Acts 16:25–34. For more on the trope of the Virgin Mary dissolving the chains of imprisoned Christians, see Marvin Meyer, "Mary Dissolving More

Chains in Coptic Museum Papyrus 4958 and Elsewhere," in *Coptic Studies on the Threshold of a New Millennium: Proceedings of the Seventh International Congress of Coptic Studies*, ed. Mat Immerzeel, Jacques van der Vliet, and Maarten Kersten (Leuven: Peeters, 2004), 369–376.

62. *M.Salib*, 14r. The inclusion of the Archangel Michael was common in Coptic hagiographies. For a discussion of his role in the martyrdom of St. Victor, for example, see Saphinaz-Amal Naguib, "The Martyr as Witness: Coptic and Coptic-Arabic Hagiographies as Mediators of Religious Memory," *Numen* 41, no. 3 (1994): 242.

63. In 1 Timothy 6:13–14, the phrase "made the noble confession" is used to refer to Jesus' testimony of faith before Pontius Pilate. It is also in the Nicean-Constantinople Creed, which is recited at every liturgical gathering.

64. *M.Salib*, 19v.

65. Ibid.

66. This was precisely the case in the martyrdom of ʿAbd al-Masih, as discussed by Mark N. Swanson, "The Martyrdom of ʿAbd al-Masih, Superior of Mount Sinai (Qays al-Ghassani)," in *Syrian Christians under Islam: The First Thousand Years*, ed. David Thomas (Boston: Brill, 2001), 123.

67. This is a reference to one of Jesus' parables (relating to the laborers in the vineyard) as recorded in Matthew 20:1–16. Here *M.Salib*'s hagiographer glorifies Salib to the same extent as other great martyrs before him.

68. 1 Corinthians 2:9.

69. *Pantocrator* is a Greek word that means "almighty" and is commonly used in Orthodox Christian traditions to refer to God the Father, as in the Nicean Creed, but on occasion it is also used for the Son, as in the icon of Christ Pantocrator.

70. *M.Salib*, 19v–20v.

71. Ibid., 20r–21v. The repetitive offers for Salib to recant mirror Coptic martyrdoms from the fourteenth century. See el-Leithy, "Coptic Culture and Conversion," 129–130.

72. In 1303, Harat Zuwayla became the new headquarters of the Coptic patriarchate, following the Church of Abu Sayfayn in Old Cairo. It would remain the seat of the patriarchate until the transfer to Harat al-Rum in the seventeenth century. See Myriam Wissa, "Harit Zuwaylah," *Coptic Encyclopedia* 4:1207–1209. For more on Yu'annis XIII, see el-Leithy, "Coptic Culture and Conversion," 367–382.

73. This date corrects my earlier miscalculation in Armanios and Ergene, "A Christian Martyr under Mamluk Justice," 122. Incidentally, Salib's story is absent from the modern-day Coptic Synaxarium, but he is commemorated in the Difnār: see De Lacy O'Leary, ed., *The Diphnar (Antiphonarium) of the Coptic Church*, 3 vols. (London: Luzac & Co., 1926), 1:76.

74. Bab Zuwayla was also the execution site for Egypt's last Mamluk sultan, Tumanbay, who was hung at the gate by orders of the conquering Ottoman sultan, Selim I. See Ibn Iyas, *Badāʾiʿ*, 5:175–176.

75. In the gospels, see Mark 3:31–35 and Luke 14:26. Some scholars have challenged the presumption that early Christian hagiographic texts weaken the role of an earthly versus spiritual family. See Susan Ashbrook Harvey, "Sacred Bonding: Mothers and Daughters in Early Syriac Hagiography," *Journal of Early Christian Studies* 4, no. 1 (1996): 27–56; Rebecca Krawiec, "'From the Womb of the Church': Monastic Families," *Journal of Early Christian*

Studies 11, no. 3 (2003): 283–307. Krawiec provides an interesting case of "family-positive" relations (287, 296–301), which contrasts well with *M.Salib*, that of Gregory of Nyssa's fourth-century biography of his sister Macrina.

76. James E. Goehring, *Ascetics, Society, and the Desert* (Harrisburg, PA: Trinity Press International, 1999). In particular, see chapter 4, "The Encroaching Desert: Literary Production and Ascetic Space in Early Christian Egypt," where Goehring (73) argues that in early Christian Egypt, "the city, the product of human achievement and the locus of human habitation, has become symbolically the center of evil. . . . Truth now resides alone in the desert." A good example on the Muslim tradition comes from Heghnar Zeitlian Watenpaugh, "Deviant Dervishes: Space, Gender, and the Construction of Antinomian Piety in Ottoman Aleppo," *International Journal of Middle East Studies* 37, no. 4 (2005): 535–565.

77. See, for instance, the discussion by Robert K. Upchurch of the eleventh-century hagiography of Julian and Basilissa. Unlike Salib's narrative, this eleventh-century legend, modified from an earlier Latin version about late antique martyrs in Egypt, highlights the pressure by Julian's parents to have him marry, the couple's agreement to live a chaste life while married, and later their dual martyrdom. Upchurch comments on the hagiographer's editorialization of the original text, noting that "the couple presents Anglo-Saxon Christians with models of asceticism and orthodoxy he [the narrator] feels are lacking among his flock." See Upchurch, "Virgin Spouses as Model Christians: The Legend of Julian and Basilissa in Ælfric's *Lives of Saints*," *Anglo-Saxon England* 34 (2005): 198. For the influence of Egyptian hagiography on European texts, see *The Encroaching Desert: Egyptian Hagiography and the Medieval West*, ed. Jitse Dijkstra and Mathilde van Dijk (Leiden: Brill, 2006). Familial tensions also appeared in Arab Christian neo-martyrdom literature in the early Islamic centuries. See Vila, "Christian Martyrs in the First Abbasid Century," 110.

78. Compare with Samantha J. E. Riches, "St. George as a Male Virgin Martyr," in *Gender and Holiness: Men, Women and Saints in Late Medieval Europe*, ed. Riches and Sarah Salih (London: Routledge, 2002), 68–77.

79. Curiously, the Archangel Michael is portrayed as a protector of Salib's body regardless of the nature of "physical harm": he not only preserves Salib's chastity but also protects him from death by stoning.

80. *M.Salib*, 17v.

81. Elizabeth A. Clark, "Antifamilial Tendencies in Ancient Christianity," *Journal of the History of Sexuality* 5, no. 3 (1995): 356–380. For a nuanced reading of the role played by "earthly" vs. "spiritual" families in the life of a Christian devotee, see, in general, Krawiec, "'From the Womb of the Church.'"

82. For a discussion of the problems faced by the medieval Coptic Church in dealing with marriage, divorce, and polygamy, see el-Leithy, "Coptic Culture and Conversion," 367–382, 398–401, 422–432.

83. Both Najwa al-Qattan and Rossista Gradeva confirm this trend with regard to Damascus and Sophia, respectively, and Gradeva notes that Christians sought and acquired divorces even as church leaders and Ottoman authorities forbade them. See Najwa al-Qattan, "Dhimmis in Muslim Courts," 434–435; Rossista Gradeva, "Orthodox Christians in the Kadi Courts: The Practice of the Sofia Sheriat Court, Seventeenth Century," *Islamic Law and Society* 4, no. 1 (1997): 57–58. For examples from the Ottoman Jewish community,

see Fatma Müge Göçek and Marc David Baer, "Social Boundaries of Ottoman Women's Experience in Eighteenth-Century Galata Court Records," in *Women in the Ottoman Empire*, ed. Madeline C. Zilfi (Leiden: Brill, 1997), 59.

84. Swanson, "The Martyrdom of 'Abd al-Masīḥ," 122.

85. The absence of reference to these characters' religious affiliation echoes the writings of Habib ibn Hidma Abu Ra'ita, a ninth-century Jacobite Christian. See Vila, "Christian Martyrs in the First Abbasid Century," 65–66.

86. *M.Salib*, 14v.

87. Attacks by "Muslim mobs" are common in the neo-martyr literature. See, for example, Rossista Gradeva, "Apostasy in Rumeli in the Middle of the Sixteenth Century," *Al-Majalla al-Tārīkhiyya al-'Arabiyya li'l-Dirāsāt al-'Uthmāniyya* 22 (2000): 42.

88. This description might reflect a folkloric portrayal of Copts as inherently imbued with magic. The seventeenth-century Ottoman traveler Evliya Çelebi, for instance, remarked of the Copts' seemingly supernatural abilities to read cryptic inscriptions at ancient shrines. See *Seyahatname*, 10:158.

89. Acts 16:25–34. On the function of miracles in neo-martyrdom literature, see Vila, "Christian Martyrs in the First Abbasid Century," 123–125.

90. *M.Salib*, 16v.

91. These findings are quite similar to Gara's analysis of the neo-martyrdom of Ömer Çavuş from 1627, which reveals "a world of complex intercommunal relations that does not fit into the mould of a society rigidly divided along religious lines." See Gara, "Neomartyr without a Message," 173. However, they contrast with the depiction of "inherently" violent Muslim actors found in some Arab neo-martyrdoms under early Islam. See Vila, "Christian Martyrs in the First Abbasid Century," 111.

92. We might compare these motifs, for instance, with the anti-dhimmī sentiment commonly found in Egyptian Muslim texts from the medieval period. As Christopher Taylor has pointed out, many stories about Muslim saints show the triumph of these saints over "their dhimmī antagonists." Taylor, *In the Vicinity of the Righteous: Ziyara and the Veneration of Muslim Saints in Late Medieval Egypt* (Leiden: Brill, 1999), 118–120.

93. Sidney H. Griffith, "Michael, the Martyr and Monk of Mar Sabas Monastery, at the Court of the Caliph 'Abd al-Malik: Christian Apologetics and Martyrology in the Early Islamic Period," *ARAM* 6 (1994): 136.

94. Griffith, "Christians, Muslims, and Neo-Martyrs," 185; Vila, "Christian Martyrs in the First Abbasid Century," 259.

95. Vaporis, *Witnesses for Christ*, 10–11, lists those Balkan martyrs who were victimized in this manner.

96. David Vila points out that even though Peter of Capitolias sought his own martyrdom and was treated fairly by some Muslim characters, the text of his neo-martyrdom still depicts other Muslims as "harsh, violent, cruel and impious." Vila, "Christian Martyrs in the First Abbasid Century," 259.

97. A good comparison could be made here with the trials of Sabbatai Tzevi and his subsequent conversion to Islam, as elucidated by Marc Baer, *Honored by the Glory of Islam: Conversion and Conquest in Ottoman Europe* (Oxford: Oxford University Press, 2008), 127–129. The tradition of an accused blasphemer or apostate being asked to publicly admit

to his crime three times is recurrent in early Christian hagiographies and is also consistent with Islamic legal prescripts. In the Greek Orthodox traditions, a Muslim judge confronting an apostate in neo-martyrdom literature "used every means in his power to persuade the new convert to return to Islam, and allowed him several days to reconsider his decision." See F. W. Hasluck, *Christianity and Islam under the Sultans*, 2 vols. (New York: Octagon Books, 1973 [1929]), 2:456.

98. Armanios and Ergene, "A Christian Martyr under Mamluk Justice," 126–129.

99. One such tale, of the monk Theophanes from Constantinople, says that the hero, "because he was a child-like person, was easily tricked by a group of Muslims to accept the Muslim faith." Theophanes was martyred in 1559 (Vaporis, *Witnesses for Christ*, 76). The martyrdom of John the Tailor (d. 1526) from Ioannina was brought forth partly "because he was quite handsome and a man with great dignity and fearlessness," and therefore "some Muslims were envious of him" (ibid., 64).

100. In that regard, Salib's story correlates well with that of most neo-martyrs in Spain. See, in general, Swanson Edward Colbert, *The Martyrs of Cordoba: A Study of the Sources* (Washington, DC: Catholic University of America Press, 1962).

101. Once again, this seems to be a case of *imitatio Christi*. The gospels in the New Testament, on which many hagiographies are modeled, are rich in imagery of the judicial trials of Jesus prior to his crucifixion. The gospel of Matthew (26:57–66), for example, furnishes a poignant account of the first altercation between Jesus and the Jewish high priest Caiaphas, an exchange retold in the "question-answer" format that later became familiar in the hagiographic genre. Sympathetic judges or rulers can be compared to Pontius Pilate, who reluctantly ordered that Jesus be crucified. On this point, see MacCoull, "Notes on the Martyrdom of John of Phanijoit," 65.

102. *M.Salib*, 17r. Compare this proclamation of faith with that made by the late-eighth-century neo-martyr Rawh al-Qurayshi before the Caliph Harun al-Rashid (763–809), as cited and discussed by Vila, "Christian Martyrs in the First Abbasid Century," 112–114.

103. Vila argues that in the case of Greek neo-martyrdoms of the early Islamic era, the confrontations between martyrs and Muslim officials are "intended to set a pattern for how Christians ought to respond in situations where their own faith is challenged." Vila, "Christian Martyrs in the First Abbasid Century," 277. The tone of *M.Salib*, in general, is far more conservative and reserved. Salib is posited as admirable and exemplary but also somewhat exceptional in his bravery.

104. *M.Salib*, 19v. In the case of Rawh al-Qurayshi, the declaration before Caliph Harun al-Rashid elicited Qurayshi's immediate demise. See Vila, "Christian Martyrs in the First Abbasid Century," 115.

105. According to Hanna Omar, *sabb Allah* involves "denying His Divinity and Oneness, Attributes, Prophets and Messages, or . . . imputing partnership, such as a wife and children to Him. It is also the product of challenging and rejecting His Commands, Prohibitions, and Promises." See Hanna H. Kilany Omar, "Apostasy in the Mamluk Period: The Politics of Accusations of Unbelief" (PhD diss., University of Pennsylvania, 2001), 116.

106. For more on the question of crime and punishment in Salib's case, see Armanios and Ergene, "A Christian Martyr under Mamluk Justice," 126–129, 131–132.

107. Jason Zaborowski confirms that many religious narratives were "hidden texts," available only to the Coptic community and not to the Muslim community at large. See Zaborowski, *The Coptic Martyrdom of John of Phanijōit*, 13, 30.

108. Griffith, "Michael, the Martyr and Monk," 123.

109. Cited in Vaporis, *Witnesses for Christ*, 20. The same provocative tone is also present in the statements of Christian neo-martyrs in ninth-century Muslim Spain; see Kenneth Wolf, *Christian Martyrs in Muslim Spain* (Cambridge: Cambridge University Press, 1988); Jessica A. Coope, *The Martyrs of Cordoba: Community and Family Conflict in an Age of Mass Conversion* (Lincoln: University of Nebraska Press, 1995); and Colbert, *The Martyrs of Cordoba*.

110. See Griffith, "Michael, the Martyr and Monk," 136. One might contrast this point with Tamer el-Leithy's interpretation of the thirteenth-century martyrology of John of Phanijōit, where he notes that the story "sharpens the outlines of religious difference by demonstrating that any middle subject position between Islam and Christianity—be it that of a dissimulating Coptic convert to Islam or even an assimilated Christian—is discreditable and untenable." See "Coptic Culture and Conversion," 7.

111. Kotzageorgis, "'Messiahs' and Neomartyrs in Ottoman Thessaly," 223. Kotzageorgis focuses, in particular, on prophetic texts in his discussion of this concept.

112. Anton Minkov, *Conversion to Islam in the Balkans: Kisve Bahası Petitions and Ottoman Social Life, 1670–1730* (Leiden: Brill, 2004), 193.

113. See N. M. Vaporis, "The Religious Encounter between Orthodox Christianity and Islam as Represented by the Neomartyrs and Their Judges," *Journal of Modern Hellenism* 12–13 (1995/1996): 263.

114. Colbert's research, *The Martyrs of Cordoba*, shows that claims of miraculous preservation of the martyrs' bodies even after their burning is not uncommon. Similarly, the severed head and body of Romanos the Neomartyr (d. 780) were collected by believers from a river and buried in a church in al-Raqqa (northern Syria), where it spawned miracles. Vila, "Christian Martyrs in the First Abbasid Century," 285–286. Earlier Coptic martyrs and some Balkan neo-martyrs were simply burned to death. See Gradeva, "Apostasy in Rumeli," 34–35, 64–65.

115. Christopher Taylor has argued that the "cult of relics" never proliferated in the medieval Islamic world because the blessing or *baraka* "of Muslim saints was not made portable through the translation of their relics." Taylor, "Saints, Ziyara, Qissa in Late Medieval Egypt," *Studia Islamica* 87 (1998): 107. However, the seventeenth-century Ottoman traveler Evliya Çelebi notes that "bones of the martyrs" were prized among Egyptian Muslims; some of these belonged to the men who died while fighting alongside Abu Hurayra (d. 681), one of the Prophet Muhammad's earliest companions. He claims that Copts also collected bones of Muslim saints, and Muslims and Copts venerated these relics during popular celebrations. See Evliya Çelebi, *Seyahatname*, 10:305–306.

116. This point has been explored in detail with regard to the Coptic St. Victor in Naguib's study, "The Martyr as Witness."

117. Hamilton, *The Copts and the West*, 42–46.

118. Ibid., 73.

119. Al-Maqrizi, *Khiṭaṭ*, 4(2):1070–1076.

120. For more on the pursuit of martyrdom among Muslims in the twelfth and thirteenth centuries, see Daniella Talmon-Heller, "Muslim Martyrdom and the Quest for Martyrdom in the Crusading Period," *Al-Masaq: Islam and the Medieval Mediterranean* 14, no. 2 (2002): 131–139.

CHAPTER 3

1. For more on the transformation in early Christian conceptions of piety, see in general Peter Brown, *The Body and Society: Men, Women, and Sexual Renunciation in Early Christianity* (New York: Columbia University Press, 1988).

2. The relationship between holy objects and the rise of shrines centered around the cult of the saints has been addressed in Peter Brown's monumental study *The Cult of the Saints.*

3. Stephen Wilson, introduction to *Saints and Their Cults: Studies in Religious Sociology, Folklore and History* (Cambridge: Cambridge University Press, 1983), 14. Wilson critically engages here with Victor Turner's concept of "liminality" as a passage into a phase, where "previous orderings of thought and behavior are subject to revision and criticism, when hitherto unprecedented modes of ordering relations between ideas and people became possible and desirable." Also see Victor Turner and Edith Turner, *Image and Pilgrimage in Christian Culture: Anthropological Perspectives* (New York: Columbia University Press, 1978), 2.

4. Wilson, *Saints and Their Cults*, 5–16.

5. Otto Meinardus, "A Critical Study on the Cult of Sitt Dimiana and Her Forty Virgins," *Orientalia Suecana* 8 (1969): 54.

6. For a good discussion of the social, political, and economic crises affecting Egypt in the seventeenth century, see Hathaway, "Egypt in the Seventeenth Century," 34–58.

7. Ibid., 40.

8. Patriarchal Library, MS Theology 287, 186v.

9. Ibid., 188v. The monk who complained about the patriarch was named Qudsi. It appears that by the Ottoman period, Coptic patriarchs had lost their ability to earn a steady income. Murqus VI's status can be contrasted with that of Patriarch Yu'annis IV (1189–1286), a "merchant-philanthropist" who gained his wealth from trade with India and "spent it on the poor, never accepting gifts or money while serving as patriarch." See Yaacov Lev, *Charity, Endowments and Charitable Institutions in Medieval Islam* (Gainesville: University Press of Florida, 2005), 37.

10. In a strange twist to this story, his "inheritance deed" was sold at public auction in the presence of the same al-Mu'allim Bishara. See Guirguis, "The Coptic Community in the Ottoman Period," 210.

11. Patriarchal Library, MS Theology 287, 188v–189r. The exact phrase is "ma hājat baṭārika?"

12. Frazee, *Catholics and Sultans*, 99. The new wave of missions in the seventeenth century reflected the Catholic response to the growing Protestant threat in Europe. In

attempting to offset the numbers of converts to Protestantism, the Catholic Church was "trying to recoup its losses by converting the [Orthodox]." See Raphael Demos, "The Neo-Hellenic Enlightenment (1750–1821)," *Journal of the History of Ideas* 19, no. 4 (1958): 528.

13. Hamilton, *The Copts and the West*, 76–81.

14. Patriarchal Library, MS Theology 287, 188r.

15. Vansleb, *The Present State of Egypt*, 174.

16. Guirguis, "The Coptic Community in the Ottoman Period," 211; Guirguis, *An Armenian Artist*, 12.

17. Hagop Barsoumian, "The Dual Role of the Armenian *Amira* Class within the Ottoman Government and the Armenian Millet (1750–1850)," in Braude and Lewis, *Christians and Jews in the Ottoman Empire*, 1:181. The "state" for Copts was represented by those local power-holders in Egypt for whom archons worked and with whom they became closely identified. Parallels can also be derived from the case of eighteenth-century Maronite Khazin leaders, who built churches and monasteries in the Kisrawan region of Mount Lebanon so that they could "enhance their religious prestige and foster the 'Maronization' of the area" vis-à-vis the clergy. See Richard van Leeuwen, "Control of Space and Communal Leadership: Maronite Monasteries in Mount Lebanon," *Revue des Mondes Musulmans et de la Méditerranée* 79–80 (1996): 186.

18. Naguib, "The Martyr as Witness," 228.

19. Papaconstantinou, "Historiography, Hagiography, and the Making of the Coptic 'Church of the Martyrs,'" 80.

20. The Monastery of St. Antony, situated approximately one hundred miles from Cairo, would have been ideal, as it had undergone a revival and restoration in the sixteenth century. The monastery also supplied several patriarchs in the early modern period, dominating control of the church hierarchy. Otto Meinardus, "Dayr Anba Anṭuniyūs: History," *Coptic Encyclopedia* 3:719–729. Other examples of centralizing important Christian manuscripts in one location come from Ottoman Palestine. See Dov Schidorsky, "Libraries in Late Ottoman Palestine between the Orient and the Occident," *Libraries and Culture* 33, no. 3 (1998): 264. Compare this mode of dissemination with the introduction of the printing press in the Levant, which flooded churches and monasteries with thousands of manuscripts. The press was used by the Catholic Church to spread "correct doctrine" to native converts in the region throughout the seventeenth and eighteenth centuries. See Bernard Heyberger, "Livres et pratique de la lecture chez les chrétiens (Syrie, Liban) XVIIe–XVIIIe siècles," *Revue des Mondes Musulmans et de la Méditerranée* ["Livres et lecture dans le monde Ottoman"] (1999): 209–224.

21. Suraiya Faroqhi, *Subjects of the Sultan* (London: I. B. Tauris, 2000), 14. Faroqhi adds that this was a popular way of disseminating literary works well into the nineteenth century.

22. Hanna, *In Praise of Books*, 87–89.

23. For more on the role of Arab Christian scribes, see Heleen Murre-Van Den Berg, "'I the Weak Scribe': Scribes in the Church of the East in the Ottoman Period," *Journal of Eastern Christian Studies* 58, no. 1–2 (2006): 9–26.

24. See Lucy-Anne Hunt, "Manuscript Production by Christians in 13th–14th century Greater Syria and Mesopotamia and Related Areas," *ARAM* 9, no. 1–2 (1997): 298.

25. For example, Coptic Patriarchal Library, MS Biblica 185(7), was copied by Nasrallah Abadir and Ghubriyal Samwil for al-Muʿallim al-Hajj Shanuda Bishay and dedicated to the Church in Harat al-Rum by Anba Athanasius, Bishop of Tij (1788); Coptic Patriarchal Library, MS History 48(4), was copied for al-Muʿallim Ibrahim Salama al-Sayigh al-Tukhi and dedicated to the Monastery of St. Mina at Fum al-Khalij (1726); Coptic Patriarchal Library, MS History 77(2), was dedicated to the Church of St. Mark but was originally copied for al-Muʿallim Dimyan ibn al-Muʿallim Mikha'il (1776); St. Mina Monastery Library, Microfilm 2-58-7-57 was copied for al-Muʿallim Tadrus bin al-Mashikh and al-Muʿallim Habib, and then dedicated to the Church of St. George in Damietta (1854).

26. Katherine Young, introduction to *Women Saints in World Religions*, ed. Arvind Sharma (Albany: State University of New York Press, 2000), 18; for the Coptic context, see Naguib, "The Martyr as Witness," 230–231.

27. Julia M. H. Smith, "Oral and Written: Saints, Miracles, and Relics in Brittany, c. 850–1250," *Speculum* 65, no. 2 (1990): 335.

28. For this study, I consulted numerous editions of Dimyana's hagiography. Her story was published in Girgis Filuthawus ʿAwad, *Mimar al-Shahīda Dimyana* (Cairo: Maṭbaʿat al-Shams al-Ḥadītha, 1948 [1917]). His translation, however, is not consistently accurate. Thus I have chosen to consult the Coptic Museum edition, MS History 549 (*M.Dimyana*), for its completeness and clarity. Extant manuscripts of Dimyana's hagiography from the Ottoman period are divided into three parts. The first part narrates Dimyana's life and death. The second relates the discovery of her relics and the building of a commemorative church at the site of her martyrdom as commissioned by Helena (ca. 250–330), mother of Emperor Constantine (274–337). The last section, which is the most complex and ambiguous, deals little with Dimyana's story and offers an alleged miracle that took place among Copts in the ninth century.

29. This region is on the eastern shore of Lake Burullus in the Nile Delta. The town of Burullus continued to be a Coptic bishopric at least until the eleventh century. It is also considered one of the spots where the Holy Family rested during their flight to Egypt. See Randall Stewart, "Burullus, Al-," *Coptic Encyclopedia* 2:427.

30. This type of reference to the beauty of male and female martyrs is a common feature of Coptic martyrdoms. See Naguib, "The Martyr as Witness," 232.

31. *M.Dimyana*, 47v, my emphasis. A general discussion of commonly atypical mother-daughter relationships in early Christian hagiographies can be found in Harvey, "Sacred Bonding."

32. *M.Dimyana*, 48r. According to the text, this palace was suspended over fifty columns—its roofs inlaid with gold, its walls made of Chinese potsherds, and its floors built from the finest marble. As a final touch, a glorious throne enhanced with jewels was made for Dimyana to sit on.

33. The presence of supportive companions to a martyr was a somewhat unusual theme in Coptic martyrdom texts. See E. A. E. Reymond and J. W. B. Barns, eds., *Four Martyrdoms from the Pierpont Morgan Coptic Codices* (Oxford: Oxford University Press, 1973), 2. On the other hand, medieval Arabic literature often omitted the names of "everyday or common" women, particularly of "slave girls." Fedwa Malti-Douglas, *Woman's Body, Woman's Word: Gender and Discourse in Arabo-Islamic Writing* (Princeton: Princeton

University Press, 1991), 34. But Dimyana's hagiography indicates that these forty virgins were elite women companions; they are referred to in the text as *arbaʿūna ʿadadan min awlād akābir al-madīna bi'l Zaʿfarana* (*M.Dimyana*, 50r).

34. Al-Farama (or Tell al-Farama) is the Arabic name for the classical city of Pelusium, in the northwest corner of the Sinai Peninsula. The Holy Family made a stop here during their flight to Egypt, and many Coptic martyrs hail from this area. See Randall Stewart, "Farama, al-," *Coptic Encyclopedia* 4:1089–1090.

35. Diocletian's demand for loyalty from his governors was a common storyline in Coptic martyrologies. See, for example, the martyrdoms of Saint Colothus, 145; Saints Paese and Thecla, 151–152; and Saint Shenoute and his brethren, 183–184; all in Reymond and Barns, *Four Martyrdoms*. Also see O'Leary, *The Saints of Egypt*, 17–18.

36. Regarding these three saints, see Eric Otto Winstedt, *Coptic Texts on St. Theodore the General (Stratelates, d. c306), on St. Theodore the Eastern (the Oriental) and on Chamoul and Justus* (Amsterdam: APA, 1979).

37. See, in general, Saphinaz-Amal Naguib's discussion of St. Victor in "The Martyr as Witness"; O'Leary, *The Saints of Egypt*, 278–281.

38. O'Leary, *The Saints of Egypt*, 111.

39. *M.Dimyana*, 55r–55v.

40. Willy Clarysse writes that "a very typical feature of Coptic martyrdoms is the bodily restitution of the martyr: after the martyr has been burned in an oven, torn to pieces, after his entrails have fallen to the ground, after he has been declared dead and his ashes are to be thrown into the Nile, an angel comes and restores the body to its full splendor, reuniting the pieces or putting back the entrails into the belly, resuscitating the martyr from death, so that a second and third series of tortures can start all over again." See Clarysse, "The Coptic Martyr Cult," in *Martyrium in Multidisciplinary Perspective*, ed. M. Lamberigts and P. Van Deun (Leuven: Leuven University Press, 1995), 391; and Papaconstantinou, "Historiography, Hagiography, and the Making of the Coptic 'Church of the Martyrs,'" 76–79.

41. Empress Helena gained some renewed cultural prominence during the Ottoman period. In the sixteenth century, when Hürrem, Sultan Suleyman's wife, endowed the construction of a soup kitchen in Jerusalem, she became conflated in popular literature with Helena, who was alleged to have patronized the construction of several buildings in Jerusalem. Amy Singer, *Constructing Ottoman Beneficence: An Imperial Soup Kitchen in Jerusalem* (Albany: State University of New York Press, 2002), chapter 3.

42. *M.Dimyana*, 70v–71r. For more on the reign of this important patriarch, see Davis, *The Early Coptic Papacy*, 47–55.

43. Davis, *The Early Coptic Papacy*, 50–51.

44. Tito Orlandi, "Hagiography, Coptic," *Coptic Encyclopedia* 4:1191–1197.

45. Dimyana's legend circulated in a separate hagiographic form until the 1930s, when it was included in an uncritical publication of the Coptic Synaxarium. See René-Georges Coquin (part 1) and Aziz S. Atiya (part 2), "Synaxarion," *Coptic Encyclopedia*, 7.2171–2190. Coquin and Atiya point out that the earliest renditions of the Coptic Synaxarium (ca. 1300s) refer to one of its authors as "John, bishop of Burullus."

46. Dayr al-Mayma is mentioned twice in St. Dimyana's hagiography: here as the place that contained ancient manuscripts about Dimyana's life, and also as the place where Murqus, Dimyana's father, took her to be baptized when she was one year old. In the medieval era, it seems that Dayr al-Mayma was the most populous monastery in the Delta, but it was likely destroyed sometime before the thirteenth century. See René-Georges Coquin, "Dayr al-Maymah," *Coptic Encyclopedia* 3:837–838.

47. *M.Dimyana*, 46v–48v.

48. According to Reymond and Barns, these clues indicate the "existence of scriptoria, where martyrologies where produced to order and . . . padded out with stock passages to the requisite size." See *Four Martyrdoms*, 2–3.

49. Peter van Minnen, "Saving History? Egyptian Hagiography in Its Space and Time," in Dijkstra and van Dijk, *The Encroaching Desert*, 69–70. Also see O'Leary, *The Saints of Egypt*, 174–175.

50. Naguib, "The Martyr as Witness," 229.

51. Papaconstantinou, "Historiography, Hagiography, and the Making of the Coptic 'Church of the Martyrs,'" 75; Naguib, "The Martyr as Witness," 228, 235, 241.

52. Naguib, "The Martyr as Witness," 235–236.

53. Clarysse, "The Coptic Martyr Cult," 392. Clarysse adds that the public usually enjoyed hearing what stories happened in their own town or in familiar surroundings. Also see Reymond and Barns, *Four Martyrdoms*, 6–7.

54. Suraiya Faroqhi, "An Orthodox Woman Saint in an Ottoman Document," in *Syncretismes et heresies dans l'Orient Seljoukide et Ottoman (XIVe–XVIIIe siècles): Actes du colloque du Collège de France, Octobre 2001*, ed. Gilles Veinstein (Paris: Peeters, 2005), 383–394. Bernard Heyberger contextualizes Hindiyya's life within the politics of Roman Catholic influence and local power struggles in Lebanon, illustrating how early modern Catholic notions of female piety were manifested within an Arab Christian context. See Heyberger, *Hindiyya: Mystique et Criminelle 1720–1798* (Paris: Aubier, 2001); see also Avril M. Makhlouf, "Umm Hindiyya's Syriac Heritage: Religious Life as a Mirror to Liturgy," *Journal of Eastern Christian Studies* 56, no. 1 (2004): 211–223; and Akram Khater, "A Deluded Woman: Hindiyya al-'Ujaimi and the Politics of Gender and Religion in Eighteenth-Century Bilad al-Sham," *Archaeology and History in Lebanon*, no. 22 (2005): 6–20.

55. See, in general, Akram Khater, "'God has called me to be free': Aleppan Nuns and the Transformation of Catholicism in 18th-Century Bilad al-Sham," *International Journal of Middle East Studies* 40, no. 3 (2008): 421–443.

56. Gail Ashton, *The Generation of Identity in Late Medieval Hagiography: Speaking the Saint* (New York: Routledge, 2000), 4.

57. Karen Winstead, *Virgin Martyrs: Legends of Sainthood in Late Medieval England* (Ithaca: Cornell University Press, 1997), 47; Ashton, *The Generation of Identity*, 92–93.

58. See I. Forget, ed., *Synaxarium Alexandrinum*, in *Corpus Scriptorum Christianorum Orientalium*, 47–49 (Louvain-Paris: Carolus Poussielgue Bibliopola, 1905), 140–141; O'Leary, *The Saints of Egypt*, 98.

59. Judith E. Tucker has explored the expected economic, legal, and social roles of husbands and wives in the Ottoman context. See *In the House of Law: Gender and Islamic Law in Ottoman Syria and Palestine* (Berkeley: University of California Press, 1998), 58–67.

60. Dimyana's fierce eloquence can be compared to that of female characters within medieval Arabic literature: as Malti-Douglas notes, women's "dhakā' (wit, intelligence) and 'kayd' (cunning, guile) are the two key, at times overlapping, concepts whose parameters have important civilizational implications for woman's sexuality and her power over discourse." See *Woman's Body*, 32.

61. Jocelyn Wogan-Browne, *Saints' Lives and Women's Literary Culture c. 1150–1300: Virginity and Its Authorizations* (Oxford: Oxford University Press, 2001), 224.

62. Maud McInerney, "Rhetoric, Power and Integrity in the Passion of the Virgin Martyr," in *Menacing Virgins: Representing Virginity in the Middle Ages and Renaissance*, ed. Kathleen Coyne Kelly and Marina Leslie (Newark: University of Delaware Press, 1999), 56.

63. The influence of Greek drama on Coptic martyrologies has been noted by Reymond and Barns, who indicate that supporting characters—be they angels or "the city populace which witnesses the proceedings"—take on the "role of the chorus" typical of a Greek drama. See *Four Martyrdoms*, 2.

64. The importance of sexual purity and virginity as it emerges from Ottoman court records and legal manuals has been well addressed by Başak Tuğ in "Politics of Honor: The Institutional and Social Frontiers of 'Illicit' Sex in Mid-Eighteenth-Century Ottoman Anatolia" (PhD diss., New York University, 2009).

65. Ashton, *The Generation of Identity*, 109.

66. This is in reference to Joel 3:2. "Jehoshaphat" literally means "the lord judges."

67. *M.Dimyana*, 53v–54v.

68. Notably, this trope corroborates gender ideals promoted within traditional Arabic literature whereby female self-expression was ultimately self-destructive and ended in a heroine's "physical downfall." Malti-Douglas, *Woman's Body*, 43.

69. Robert Mills, "Can the Virgin Martyr Speak?" in *Medieval Virginities*, ed. Ruth Evans, Sarah Salih, and Anke Bernau (Toronto: University of Toronto Press, 2003), 202.

70. Leslie Peirce, *Morality Tales: Law and Gender in the Ottoman Court of Aintab* (Berkeley: University of California Press, 2003), 207.

71. Crecelius, "Incidences of Waqf Cases in Three Cairo Courts: 1640–1802," *Journal of the Economic and Social History of the Orient* 29, no. 2 (1986): 179–181; Afaf Lutfi al-Sayyid Marsot, *Women and Men in Late Eighteenth-Century Egypt* (Austin: University of Texas Press, 1995).

72. "Gimyana" does not appear to be a Coptic pronunciation of the Greek name, but more likely a regional, dialectical variation in its articulation. René-Georges Coquin and Maurice Martin confirm that it is "probable" that Gimyana and Dimyana are one and the same, a fact strongly supported by hagiographic evidence in addition to travelers' narratives. See René Georges-Coquin, "Dayr Sitt Dimyanah," *Coptic Encyclopedia* 3:870–872.

73. Al-Maqrizi, *Khiṭaṭ*, 4(2):1047–1051. Al-Maqrizi writes that in the Delta there had been numerous Coptic monasteries but that many of them had been ruined or destroyed, especially during the reign of the Fatimid Caliph al-Hakim (996–1021).

74. Although in the fifteenth century, Dimyana's monastery was not recorded as a pilgrimage site, travelers en route to the neighboring Dayr al-Maghtis may have stopped to get Dimyana's blessing. Pilgrims came to Dayr al-Maghtis in the Coptic month of Bashans (roughly, May) on a day referred to as *'Īd al-Ẓuhūr* or the Feast of the Apparition, when

they celebrated the miraculous sightings of the Virgin Mary. See al-Maqrizi, *Khiṭaṭ*, 4(2):1049; René-Georges Coquin, "Dayr al-Maghtis," *Coptic Encyclopedia*, 3:818–819.

75. Bishuy 'Abd al-Masih, *Tārīkh Ibrūshiyyat Dumyāt*, 48–49. The writer cites an unidentified manuscript dating from 1650 and located in the Church of 'Izbat al-Nakhl in Cairo.

76. Samwil Tawadrus, *Al-Dalīl ila al-Kanā'is wa'l-Adyura al-Qadīma min al-Gīza ila Aswān* (Cairo: Al-Qism, 1990), 59, 64.

77. This is a viable scenario with some precedent, for instance, in the overlapping cults of St. Margaret (Catholic) versus St. Marina (Eastern Orthodox). Wendy R. Larson, "The Role of Patronage and Audience in the Cults of Sts Margaret and Marina of Antioch," in Riches and Salih, *Gender and Holiness*, 23–35.

78. E. L. Butcher, *The Story of the Church of Egypt*, 2 vols. (London: Smith, Elder, & Co., 1975 [1897]), 1:126. The martyrdom of forty monks massacred in the Monastery of St. Catherine was celebrated by the Greek Orthodox on 28 December and 14 January. While these "forty" were not martyred along with St. Catherine, one could argue that the association between Catherine and a set of forty martyrs found its way into Coptic lore. Raithou, a seaport on the Gulf of Clysma near the monastery, also commemorated the massacre of forty monks on the same day as those of St. Catherine's. See Irfan Shahid, "Arab Christian Pilgrimages," in Frankfurter, *Pilgrimage and Holy Space*, 377; see also Meinardus, "A Critical Study," 51. These should be distinguished from the "Forty Martyrs of Sebaste," who were martyred in Lesser Armenia in the year 320 and whose story is commemorated in Eastern Orthodox traditions, including in the Coptic Synaxarium on 13 Baramhut / 9 February.

79. Dimyana's prominence could be related to the demise of the cult of St. Thecla, the most popular female virgin-martyr in late antique Egypt. Stephen Davis suggests that Thecla's cult had faded by the ninth or tenth centuries, possibly because the saint's original Greek identity was never successfully translated into the Egyptian context. The geographic separation between Egypt and Byzantium after the Arab conquests may have led to the end of Thecla's cult, with Dimyana filling the void. As Copts acclimated to Islamic rule, their own local female hagiographic traditions took root and became more popular. Davis, *The Cult of Saint Thecla* (Oxford: Oxford University Press, 2001), 172.

80. See Braude and Lewis, *Christians and Jews*, 1:25–29.

81. See Caroline Williams, "The Cult of 'Alid Saints in the Fatimid Monuments of Cairo," *Muqarnas* 3 (1985): 39–40, 47–48.

82. Alexandra Cuffel writes that "by making Nafisa the [Coptic] woman's last resort, the authors emphasize the ineffectiveness of the holy spaces and relics of other religions besides that of Islam." Cuffel, "From Practice to Polemic: Shared Saints and Festivals as 'Women's Religion' in the Medieval Mediterranean," *Bulletin of the School of Oriental and African Studies* 68, no. 3 (2005): 410. For a partial translation of Nafisa's biography, see Valerie J. Hoffman, "Muslim Sainthood, Women, and the Legend of Sayyida Nafisa," in *Women Saints in World Religions*, ed. Arvind Sharma (Albany: State University of New York Press, 2000), 125–139.

83. On saints and scholars who were buried near her shrine during the Ottoman era, see al-Jabarti, *'Ajā'ib*, 1:46, 1:114, 1:477. Regarding a strange incident or "miracle" that took

place in 1759–1760 surrounding her shrine, see ibid., 1:608–610. Despite evidence of her continued popularity, Yusuf Ragib has argued that her cult declined during the Ottoman period: "Al-Sayyida Nafisa, sa légende, son culte et son cimetière," *Studia Islamica*, no. 44 (1976): 62, fn. 1; 69.

84. Al-Jabarti, *'Ajā'ib*, 2:7.

85. Lutfi, "Coptic Festivals of the Nile," 264. The custom of throwing body parts into the Nile was an ancient tradition, and continues to be seen in the practice of female circumcision. Moreover, abolishing the martyr's feast, according to Lutfi, "cannot be viewed simply as a manifestation of Muslim repugnance at non-Islamic popular practices" but was also linked to the Mamluk state's intent to overtake key Coptic properties and relieve itself of financial ruin. For Maqrizi's description of this feast, see *Khiṭaṭ*, 1:183–185.

86. Lutfi, "Coptic Festivals of the Nile," 68. Also see Mikhail, "Egypt from Late Antiquity to Early Islam," 396–400.

87. Lutfi, "Coptic Festivals of the Nile," 263; El-Leithy, "Coptic Culture and Conversion," 116–126, 360–361.

88. See Christopher Taylor's discussion of the charges leveled against Christians by Ibn Taymiyya and Ibn Qayyim: *In the Vicinity*, 185. Taylor writes that Christians were accused of "tricking ignorant Muslims into venerating Christian tombs, baptizing their children in hopes of prolonging their lives, visiting and making vows to churches and sacred Christian sites, and even seeking communion from priests and monks."

89. Ibid., 57.

90. Here, as Dina Khoury maintains, this move had "mixed results," particularly for female pilgrims: on the one hand, it allowed them to perform their rituals with no male supervision, but on the other, it displaced them from the "sacred spaces of the center." Khoury, "Slippers at the Entrance or behind Closed Doors: Domestic and Public Spaces for Mosuli Women," in Zilfi, *Women in the Ottoman Empire*, 121–122.

91. A Spanish Catholic priest, Antonius Gonzales, describes one of these festivals, celebrating the Nile's rise to completion, at the end of July 1665. The Ottoman governor assumed an active role in these celebrations, which lasted, according to Gonzales, three to four days. See Gonzales, *Voyage en Égypte du Père Antonius Gonzales, 1665–1666*, vol. 1, trans. Charles Libois (Cairo: Institut Français d'Archéologie Orientale du Caire, 1977), 1:356–357.

92. Vansleb, *The Present State of Egypt*, 35.

93. There were some exceptions to this pattern, as seen in the case of Dimyana, whose festival was celebrated on a non-feast day. See Gérard Viaud, "Pilgrimages," *Coptic Encyclopedia* 6:1968–1975.

94. O'Leary, *The Saints of Egypt*, 32.

95. Leslie MacCoull, "Chant in Coptic Pilgrimage," in Frankfurter, *Pilgrimage and Holy Space*, 403. Also see Arietta Papaconstantinou's discussion of these practices in late Byzantine and early Islamic Egypt in *Le Culte des saints en Égypte des Byzantins aux Abbassides* (Paris: CNRS Éditions, 2001), 317–324.

96. MacCoull, "Chant in Coptic Pilgrimage," 404.

97. On the medieval era, see Meri, *Cult of the Saints*, 120.

98. Georgia Frank, "Miracles, Monks, and Monuments: The *Historia Monachorum in Aegypto* as Pilgrims' Tales" in Frankfurter, *Pilgrimage and Holy Space*, 483.

99. Marc Gaborieau, “The Cult of Saints among the Muslims of Nepal and Northern India,” in Wilson, *Saints and Their Cults*, 299. For perceptions of intercession among medieval Muslim chroniclers, see Shaun E. Marmon, “The Quality of Mercy: Intercession in Mamluk Society,” *Studia Islamica* 87 (1998): 125–139.

100. For more on the veneration of saints among Muslims and Jews, see generally Meri, *Cult of the Saints*, as well as his “The Etiquette of Devotion in the Islamic Cult of Saints,” in *The Cult of Saints in Late Antiquity and the Middle Ages: Essays on the Contribution of Peter Brown*, ed. James Howard-Johnston and Paul Antony Hayward (Oxford: Oxford University Press, 1999), 263–288.

101. Brown, *The Cult of the Saints*, chapter 3.

102. Antonius Gonzales, who traveled to Egypt in 1665–1666, mentions a major Muslim pilgrimage to this region by Cairenes. According to Gonzales, thousands of pilgrims went to a mosque located between Cairo and Damietta, likely to the tomb of Ahmad al-Badawi in Tanta, approximately ten to twelve days after the flooding of the Nile. He describes a bustling festival to which pilgrims apparently came not only to honor the saint but also out of a belief that all of their sins would be forgiven. Gonzales, *Voyage en Égypte*, 1:257. Ahmad al-Badawī has been referred to as “the most popular saint of the Muslims in Egypt” for the past seven hundred years. Born in Fez (1199–1200 CE), he eventually settled in Egypt, in the town of Tanta, where he died in 1276. He is venerated at a mosque that was built over his tomb in Tanta. See K. Voller and E. Littmann, “Ahmad al-Badawī,” *EI2* 1:280–281. On Coptic-Muslim veneration in the Delta in recent years, see el-Sayed el-Aswad, “Spiritual Genealogy: Sufism and Saintly Places in the Nile Delta,” *International Journal of Middle Eastern Studies* 38, no. 4 (2006): 501–518; and Otto Meinardus, *Christian Egypt: Ancient and Modern* (Cairo: Cahiers d’Histoire Égyptienne, 1965), 167–182.

103. Niebuhr, *Travels through Arabia*, 1:53. This was also the case in early Christian shrines, as discussed by Brown, *The Cult of the Saints*, 112.

104. Claude Sicard described his motivation to attend the festival as follows: “I have been back for eight days from a voyage made in the isle of the Delta. Here is the reason and a short relation. After the alleged holy fire of Jerusalem there is nothing which is more venerated among Copts than another alleged miracle which is done every year in the Church of Gemiane located in Garbie province of the Delta. There, about May 18, which is the feast day, a multitude of Christians go, from all parts, especially from Cairo and Lower Egypt. I wanted to take part in examining these things up close, to inform and preach in the place of solemnity, to make mission in the heart of the isle Delta.” See Sicard, *Oeuvres*, 2:31.

105. Vansleb, *The Present State of Egypt*, 94–95.

106. Michael Winter talks about the humility shown by the Banu Baghdad bedouin leaders toward a prominent Sufi shaykh at the Ahmad al-Badawi celebration in Tanta. The Banu Baghdad held influence over the Gharbiyya province in the sixteenth century. See Winter, *Society and Religion*, 53–54. Examples of collaboration between leaders at a Christian holy site and local bedouin tribes can also be found in Ottoman Palestine. See Yehoshuʿa Frenkel, “Mar Saba during the Mamluk and Ottoman Periods,” *Orientalia Lovaniensia Analecta* 98 (2001): 115–116.

107. Sicard, *Oeuvres*, 2:34.

108. Vansleb, *The Present State of Egypt*, 96. In 1712, Sicard remarked that the church had twenty-two domes, which were discernible from afar.

109. Vansleb, *The Present State of Egypt*, 96. Vansleb notes that "the chappel where the apparition happens is on the north-side, on the right hand as one enters in, and over against the door."

110. S. H. Leeder, *Modern Sons of the Pharaohs* (New York: Arno Press, 1973 [1918]), 143.

111. Sicard, *Oeuvres*, 2:37.

112. Leeder, *Modern Sons of the Pharaohs*, 144. Giulian Lansing, *Egypt's Princes: A Narrative of Missionary Labor in the Valley of the Nile* (New York: Robert Carter & Br., 1865), 389, also emphasized that there was a great deal of money to be made at this festival.

113. Comparable examples of the economic benefits of these festivals and pilgrimages can be found in Meri, *Cult of the Saints*, 122–123; Winter, *Egyptian Society*, 182–183.

114. Bedouin shaykhs were effectively "masters of much of Egypt's countryside"; the arrangement that allowed the Dimyana festivities to take place each year is impressive, as Winter reports that bedouin shaykhs and their troops were notorious for their violent acts and looting of the region. See *Egyptian Society*, 90–91, 98–99.

115. Vansleb also writes, "On this festival day all the Arabians thereabouts meet here, out of an ancient Custome, to be treated for three days with the revenues of this church: when I was there, they could make up near five hundred horse, and five hundred foot. The horse-men were armed with a lance, the foot-men with a club upon their shoulders, pointed with iron." Vansleb, *The Present State of Egypt*, 98–99. The custom of hospitality to bedouin tribesmen and guests had long-standing roots in the earliest days of Islamic history. Lev, *Charity*, 45.

116. It is more than likely that this was a layman or even an archon, as both Vansleb and Sicard are quick to refer to Coptic religious functionaries by their titles.

117. "Lieutenant governor" is the phrase used by Sicard. It is unclear whether this was a *kahya*—the lieutenant of an Ottoman official.

118. Vansleb, *The Present State of Egypt*, 99–100.

119. Ibid. On the distribution of food as an act of charity and piety in the Ottoman context, see Eyal Ginio, "The Shaping of a Sacred Space: The *Tekke* of Zühuri Şeyh Ahmet Efendi in Eighteenth-Century Salonica," *Medieval History Journal* 9, no. 2 (2006): 287.

120. Leeder, *Modern Sons of the Pharaohs*, 144. In the seventeenth century, Evliya Çelebi, apparently describing the cult of the Coptic martyr Abanub based in Sammanud, in the Gharbiyya province, was astonished by the enormous revenues collected by Coptic clergy during the annual pilgrimage. See *Seyahatname*, 10:407.

121. Lev, *Charity*, 45. While he may have been charitable in handing out coins, Sultan Selim apparently ended the practice of public distribution of food in Cairo; see Winter, *Society and Religion*, 14.

122. As Doris Behrens-Abouseif notes, "charitable endowments made by the Ottoman governors reveal an intelligent religious and social policy which aimed at strengthening ties with the Egyptian population." Behrens-Abouseif, "Patterns of Urban Patronage in Cairo: A Comparison between the Mamluk and the Ottoman Periods," in Haarmann and Philipp, *The Mamluks in Egyptian Politics and Society*, 231. For a comparable case of public charity, see Eyal Ginio, "Living on the Margins of Charity: Coping with Poverty in an Ottoman

Provincial City," in *Poverty and Charity in Middle Eastern Contexts*, ed. Michael Bonner, Mine Ener, and Amy Singer (Albany: State University of New York Press, 2003), 166.

123. Singer, *Constructing Ottoman Beneficence*, 168–169; Oded Peri, "Waqf and Ottoman Welfare Policy. The Poor Kitchen of Hasseki Sultan in Eighteenth-Century Jerusalem," *Journal of the Economic and Social History of the Orient* 35, no. 2 (1992): 167–186.

124. Ginio, "The Shaping of a Sacred Space," 273, 275, 283–290.

125. Van Leeuwen, *Notables and Clergy*, chapter 5.

126. *Sipāhī* (*Sipāhīyūn*) was typically a reference to those cavalry regiments that initially played a significant role in the Ottoman conquest and control of Egypt and were often rebellious and unruly. See Shaw, *The Financial and Administrative Organization*, 196–197, 203, 210.

127. Sicard, *Oeuvres*, 2:37. Violence and robbery were commonplace at Egyptian festivals, particularly those in the Gharbiyya Province. To calm the atmosphere and exercise greater control over the Ahmad al-Badawi festival, the Sufi Shaykh Muhammad al-Shinawi prohibited the organization of processions with drums and flutes, and also used his power to control the robbery and violence that were commonplace on this occasion. Winter, *Society and Religion*, 77.

128. Vansleb, *The Present State of Egypt*, 100–101.

129. Leeder, *Modern Sons of the Pharaohs*, 143. The protection that Dimyana allegedly offered against theft is reminiscent of the stories that circulated in medieval Egypt about Sayyida Nafisa. See Taylor, *In the Vicinity*, 152–153.

130. Leeder's later account (*Modern Sons of the Pharaohs*, 145) is no less skeptical than Vansleb's or Sicard's. On miracles that were related to healing, see Lansing, *Egypt's Princes*, 398–399.

131. Vansleb and Sicard reported that in a neighboring church in the Delta (in the town of Busat al-Nasara), rival apparitions of similar saints occurred in the same month as the Dimyana festival, revealing competition with the Dimyana shrine. Vansleb, *The Present State of Egypt*, 95; Sicard, *Oeuvres*, 2:38.

132. Vansleb, *The Present State of Egypt*, 98. "Porter" is likely St. Victor (Coptic/Arabic, Buqtur). In the eighteenth century, Pococke also reports these "fictive" apparitions, noting that at the convent of "St. Geminiani, [there] is yearly a great resort of Christians for devotion, and much talk of something like spirits, which, as far as I could find, is nothing but the shadow of the people passing, seen by a small hole." See Pococke, *A Description of the East*, 1:129. For a colorful description from the nineteenth century, see Lansing, *Egypt's Princes*, 390, 394–395.

133. Meri, *The Cult of Saints*, 20.

134. Sicard, *Oeuvres*, 2:36.

135. This literally means "blessing." In Christianity and in Islam, God confers this sort of blessing on special individuals and saints, who in turn convey the baraka to believers. See Georges S. Colin, "Baraka," *EI2* 1:1032. For a detailed discussion of baraka within Judaic and Islamic practices, see Meri, "Aspects of Baraka (Blessings) and Ritual Devotion among Medieval Muslims and Jews," *Medieval Encounters* 5 (1999): 46–69.

136. Sicard, *Oeuvres*, 2:35.

137. See comparable examples of lay autonomy and control over public religious practices, as discussed by W. M. Jacob, *Lay People and Religion in the Early Eighteenth Century* (Cambridge: Cambridge University Press, 1996), 89–90.

138. Sicard, *Oeuvres*, 2:37. He was particularly appalled that there was "neither confession nor communion among the Christians in this festival, although two masses were celebrated in all the days." Sicard associated organized sacraments with an authoritative presence of clerical leadership. On drinking at the festival, see Lansing, *Egypt's Princes*, 401, who joked that "surely Bacchus must have been [St. Dimyana's] brother-in-law, or some other very near relative, for in all my residence in the East I have not seen so much drinking as during those few days."

139. Sicard, *Oeuvres*, 2:37. Lansing, *Egypt's Princes*, 391, describes the barrels of wine and ʿaraq that were arranged in various booths and "gave promise of lively times."

140. In the context of Byzantine Egypt, Arietta Papaconstantinou has warned of the "normative tendency of hagiographical literature," as it can mislead historians into "seeing the cult of the saints as a very intellectual or spiritual phenomenon." Papaconstantinou, "The Cult of the Saints: A Haven of Continuity in a Changing World," in *Egypt in the Byzantine World, 300–700*, ed. Roger S. Bagnall (Cambridge: Cambridge University Press, 2007), 352.

141. See Sicard, *Oeuvres*, 2:109. In the context of Muslim practices in medieval Egypt, the association between saints and acts of generosity has been explored in detail by Taylor, *In the Vicinity*, 99–106.

142. For more discussion on gendered spaces in the Ottoman world, see in general Khoury, "Slippers at the Entrance"; and Leslie Peirce, *The Imperial Harem* (Oxford: Oxford University Press, 1993), 6–10.

143. Bernard Heyberger, "Individualism and Political Modernity: Devout Catholic Women in Aleppo and Lebanon between the Seventeenth and Nineteenth Centuries," in *Beyond the Exotic: Women's Histories in Islamic Societies*, ed. Amira Sonbol (Syracuse, NY: Syracuse University Press, 2005), 80. On women in eighteenth-century Levantine convents, see Khater, "'God has called me to be free,'" 431–437.

144. Of course, violations to spatial rules were common: in Ottoman Jerusalem, for instance, elite women moved about town, visiting their relatives and friends and participating in business transactions, while peasants tended to the fields and bought and sold agricultural lands. Dror Ze'evi, "Women in 17th-Century Jerusalem: Western and Indigenous Perspectives," *International Journal of Middle East Studies* 27, no. 2 (1995): 166.

145. For parallel examples of expectations for female behavior among other Ottoman non-Muslims, see Heyberger, *Les chrétiens du Proche-Orient*, 514–516; Ruth Lamden, "Communal Regulations as a Source for Jewish Women's Lives in the Ottoman Empire," *Muslim World* 95, no. 2 (2005): 251–254. Gender boundaries began to erode in the eighteenth-century Ottoman Levant due to the infiltration of a "European style" of entertainment and excess drinking. See Khater, "'God has called me to be free,'" 424.

146. See a discussion of forbidden public spaces for women in Mamluk Egypt in Mounira Chapoutot-Remadi, "Femmes dans la ville mamluke," *Journal of the Economic and Social History of the Orient* 38, no. 2 (1995): 152–158; Huda Lutfi, "Manners and Customs of Fourteenth-Century Cairene Women: Female Anarchy versus Male Sharʿi Order in

Muslim Prescriptive Treatises," in *Women in Middle Eastern History*, ed. Nikki R. Keddie and Beth Baron (New Haven: Yale University Press, 1993), 99–120; Cuffel, "From Practice to Polemic," 413; Meri, *The Cult of the Saints*, 168.

147. Declarations were made by the leading Turkish judge in 1522 against women's public appearances and their right to ride donkeys; see Ibn Iyas, *Badā'i'*, 5:461–462, 467. In 1723, when women were publicly assaulted during the Shamm al-Nasīm festival, similar prohibitions were made; see al-Jabarti, *'Ajā'ib*, 1:95. For a discussion of these rules, see Winter, *Egyptian Society*, 11–12; Winter, *Society and Religion*, 222–223.

148. On the transgression of expected gender boundaries by Egyptian women, see Andreas Tietze, trans. and ed., *Mustafa 'Ali's Description of Cairo of 1599* (Vienna: Verlag der Österreichischen Akademie der Wissenschaften, 1975), 41.

149. Lansing, "A Visit to the Convent of Sittna (Our Lady), Damiane," *Harper's New Monthly Magazine* 28 (1864): 764.

150. Elie Sidawe, "Moeurs et traditions de l'Égypte moderne—Sitti Dimiana sa légende, son mouled," *Bulletin de la Societé de Géographie d'Égypte* 8 (1917): 94. This is reiterated in 'Awad, *Mimar al-Shahīda Dimyana*, 10. He mentions that "whosoever so much as looks at a woman gets a swollen eye." This superstition may have been rooted in a widespread cultural belief, perhaps drawn from a commonly-cited Qur'anic verse (Sūrat al-Nūr, 30) that "the male gaze automatically defiles and dishonors." See Malti-Douglas, *Woman's Body*, 44.

151. Some women were initiated into Sufi orders, and in a few cases, women became Sufi *shaykhas*. Winter, *Society and Religion*, 100–101.

152. Miniatures of such festivities show that "most of the women appear completely veiled in the illustrations, but a careful look at the original miniatures reveals that their faces were covered over later." Derin Terzioğlu, "The Imperial Circumcision Festival of 1582: An Interpretation," *Muqarnas* 12 (1995): 94.

153. Khoury, "Slippers at the Entrance," 117.

154. Gonzales, *Voyage en Égypte*, 1:258–259. Gonzales alleges that married women prostituted themselves to male pilgrims at this festival.

155. Charles Libois, who translated Gonzales's travel writings into French, mentions that we have no other corroboration for this story.

156. Leeder, *Modern Sons of the Pharaohs*, 144.

157. See, in general, Cuffel, "From Practice to Polemic"; and Meri, *Cult of the Saints*, 124. Meri writes, "Although women rarely appear in [medieval] sources, it was not uncommon for Jewish and Muslim women to visit saints' shrines, discuss health problems, seek cures for infertility, and make private visits to a saint."

158. H. S. Haddad, "'Georgic' Cults and Saints of the Levant," *Numen* 16 (1969): 28–30; and for a modern description of some of these fertility rituals performed by women, see David Howell, "Health Rituals at a Lebanese Shrine," *Middle Eastern Studies* 6, no. 2 (1970): 182–184.

159. Al-Jabarti, *'Ajā'ib*, 2:230.

160. This is a small fish that is cured in large quantities of salt, producing a pungent odor. Elie Sidawe describes the scene at Dimyana's festival: "The nauseous odors of decomposition that are released are made more bitter still by the strong heat of the day."

Sidawe, "Moeurs et traditions," 91. Coptic folklore relates that when eaten with boiled eggs (the promise of life) and spring onions (birth), this fish, representing death, historically commemorates the life cycle.

161. It is difficult to assess the status of female Muslim saints during the Ottoman period, but as Yusuf Ragib has noted, Cairo was once home to the largest number of shrines dedicated to female descendants of the Prophet Muhammad through the line of his daughter Fatima and son-in-law ʿAli. However, Ragib indicates that many of these shrines deteriorated over time—following the decline of the Fatimid dynasty—and their status as pilgrimage sites or festival destinations was eradicated over the centuries. The sole exception to this development may have been Sayyida Nafisa's shrine and festival, which are still popular to this day. See, in general, Ragib, "Al-Sayyida Nafisa."

162. As David Frankfurter writes, in the eyes of most believers "the vital martyrs of [early] Egyptian Christianity were 'our' kinsmen, natives of particular villages, persecuted by foreign imperial forces, tried and tortured in 'these' towns along the Nile, and their bones discovered by 'our people.' Such storytelling is very much the process by which a new ideology of religious power is assimilated, situated in the landscape, recognizable to 'us.' And the written versions of these legends served the same intermediary function for the world of the literate. A martyr might be disengaged from his native locale and his relics and supernatural presence reestablished hundreds of miles away, all through careful hagiography." Frankfurter, "Introduction: Approaches to Coptic Pilgrimage," in *Pilgrimage and Holy Space in Late Antique Egypt* (Leiden: Brill, 1998), 36–37.

163. Brown, *The Cult of the Saints*, 67–68.

164. The archon al-Muʿallim Jirjis, son of the late al-Muʿallim Mikha'il al-Faydawi, requested an icon of Dimyana from the prominent eighteenth-century iconographer, Yuhanna the Armenian. The icon was later donated to al-Muʿallaqa (Hanging) Church in Old Cairo. See Guirguis, *An Armenian Artist*, 44; and for an image of this depiction, see *Coptic Icons* 1:100. Two more icons of Dimyana, dating from the Ottoman period, were located in the Church of the Virgin Mary in the Upper Egyptian town of Balyana. See Ashraf Alexandre Sadek, "Two Witnesses of Christian Life in the Area of Balyana," in Gawdat Gabra and Hany N. Takla, eds., *Christianity and Monasticism in Upper Egypt* (Cairo: American University in Cairo Press, 2008), 264. Also see a nineteenth-century icon of Dimyana and the forty virgins, attributed to Anastasi al-Rumi, in *Coptic Icons*, 1:95.

CHAPTER 4

1. For a short, preliminary list of some of the renovated churches, see Guirguis, *An Armenian Artist*, 42, and "Athār al-Arākhina," 33–35. For more information on the revival of the St. Paul Monastery, see Swanson, "The Monastery of St. Paul," 54–57, and Armanios, "Patriarchs, Archons, and the Eighteenth Century Resurgence of the Coptic Community," in Lyster, *The Cave Church of Paul the Hermit*, 61–74.

2. Lyster, "Reviving a Lost Tradition: The Eighteenth-Century Paintings in the Cave Church: Context and Iconography," in *The Cave Church of Paul the Hermit*, 209–231; Tania C. Tribe, "Icon and Narration in Eighteenth-Century Christian Egypt: The Works of

Yuhanna al-Armani al-Qudsi and Ibrahim al-Nasikh," *Art History* 27, no. 1 (2004): 62–94; Guirguis, *An Armenian Artist in Ottoman Egypt.*

3. Hathaway, *The Politics of Households,* 24–27.

4. Suraiya Faroqhi, *Pilgrims and Sultans: The Hajj under the Ottomans, 1517–1683* (London: I. B. Tauris, 1994), 8–10; and Karl Barbir, *Ottoman Rule in Damascus, 1708–1758* (Princeton: Princeton University Press, 1980), especially 108–177 on the significance of the pilgrimage to Ottoman rule in Damascus. For the Ottomans, the attention to Egypt as a pilgrimage center appears to have been military and religious in nature. As Crecelius notes, "it was from Egypt that the holy cities of Mecca and Medina were defended and provisioned and the vital trade routes to Africa and Asia protected." Crecelius, *The Roots of Modern Egypt,* 14.

5. As Faroqhi notes, "The Muslim pilgrim does not necessarily enter the Ka'aba . . . while in most Christian places of pilgrimage, pious visitors are expected to enter the church or shrine." *Pilgrims and Sultans,* 1–2.

6. A good comparison for the increasing participation of lay leaders in preserving religious life and "communal space" among Ottoman Christians comes from the Maronites. See, in general, van Leeuwen, *Notables and Clergy.*

7. Frankfurter, "Introduction: Approaches to Coptic Pilgrimage," 15.

8. As Yehoshu'a Frenkel writes, "Although Jerusalem was a place of worship and pilgrimage to all three biblical religions, members of each of them worshipped and prayed separately: one Jerusalem for the Jews, another Jerusalem for the Christians, and a third one for the Muslims." Frenkel, "Muslim Pilgrimage to Jerusalem in the Mamluk Period," in *Pilgrims and Travelers to the Holy Land,* ed. Bryan F. Le Beau and Menachem Mor (Omaha, NE: Creighton University Press, 1996), 83. For the meaning of Jerusalem to medieval Muslim pilgrims, see Amikam Elad, *Medieval Jerusalem and Islamic Worship: Holy Places, Ceremonies, Pilgrimage* (Leiden: Brill, 1995).

9. Ahmad ibn 'Abd al-Halim Ibn Taymiyya, *Ibn Taimiya's Struggle against Popular Religion, with an Annotated Translation of His Kitāb Iqtidā' as-Sīrat al-Mustaqīm Mukhālafāt Asḥāb al-Jaḥīm,* ann. and trans. Muhammad Umar Memon (The Hague: Mouton & Co., 1976), 77.

10. Herod was in charge of a territory assigned by the Romans; he was therefore a "client-king" of the Romans.

11. In Stephen J. Davis's analysis, Matthew's chapter "carries the reader along on a virtual itinerary of geographical locales, an itinerary marked by biblical signposts." See Davis, "Ancient Sources for the Coptic Tradition," in *Be Thou There: The Holy Family's Journey in Egypt,* ed. Gawdat Gabra (Cairo: American University in Cairo Press, 2001), 134.

12. Ibid., 153.

13. The idea of making a dual pilgrimage to the biblical landscapes of Egypt and Palestine dates back to the late-fourth-century Spanish pilgrim Egeria, who had visited Egypt prior to her pilgrimage to Jerusalem. Over time, as E. D. Hunt notes, the crossroads between Egypt and Palestine became "a path which united the monks of the Egyptian desert and the sacred places around Jerusalem in what amounted to a single devotional landscape when viewed through the pilgrims' 'eyes of faith.'" Hunt, "The Itinerary of Egeria," in *The Holy Land, Holy Lands, and Christian History,* ed. R. N. Swanson (Rochester,

NY: Ecclesiastical History Society, 2000), 38. In what seems to be a less common occurrence among Muslim pilgrims, the Ottoman court poet and pilgrim Nabi (1642–1712) visited both Egypt and Jerusalem, so that he could record descriptions of their holy shrines en route to his pilgrimage to Mecca in 1678. See Menderes Coşkun, "The Most Literary Ottoman Pilgrimage Narrative: Nabi's *Tuhfetü'l-Harameyn*," *Turcica* 32 (2000): 363–388.

14. Descriptions of attacks against pilgrimage caravans to Mecca are frequently noted by al-Jabarti. Among the many examples, see, in the year 1688, al-Jabarti, *'Ajā'ib*, 1:38; in 1695, 1:41; in 1699, 1:47–48; in 1719, 1:191–192; in 1735–1736, 1:273; in 1784, 2:155; and in 1786, 2:221–222.

15. Faroqhi, *Pilgrims and Sultans*, 8–10.

16. An early account of the Syrian pilgrimage to Jerusalem, dating from the thirteenth century but copied and circulated widely in the seventeenth and eighteenth centuries, is the *Ethicon* by Gregory Bar Hebraeus (1226–1286). For the significance of pilgrimage to Syrian Orthodox believers, see Herman Teule, "Syrian Orthodox Attitudes to the Pilgrimage to Jerusalem," *Eastern Christian Art* 2 (2005): 121–125; Andrew Palmer, "The History of the Syrian Orthodox in Jerusalem," *Oriens Christianus* 75 (1991): 16–43; and Sebastian P. Brock, "East Syriac Pilgrims to Jerusalem in the Early Ottoman Period," *ARAM* 18 (2006): 189–201. On Armenians, see Kevork Hintlian, "Travelers and Pilgrims in the Holy Land: The Armenian Patriarchate of Jerusalem in the 17th and 18th Century," in O'Mahony, *The Christian Heritage*, 149–159; and Sergio La Porta, "Grigor Tat'ewac'i's Pilgrimage to Jerusalem," in *The Armenians in Jerusalem and the Holy Land*, ed. R. Ervine, M. Stone, and N. Stone (Leuven: Peeters, 2002), 97–110.

17. 'Afifi, *Al-Aqbāṭ fī Miṣr*, 64–68; Otto Meinardus, *The Copts in Jerusalem* (Cairo: Commission on Oecumenical Affairs of the See of Alexandria, 1960).

18. Oded Peri, *Christianity under Islam in Jerusalem: The Question of the Holy Sites in Early Ottoman Times* (Leiden: Brill, 2001).

19. There are two copies of this narrative, which was originally written by the scribe 'Abd al-Masih, assistant to the patriarch, who accompanied him on the journey. Here, I am using the older version of the manuscript, currently housed in the Coptic Museum in Cairo (Coptic Museum, Liturgy 128). The version from the Patriarchal Library was copied in 1777 by a priest named Jirjis al-Jawhari al-Khanānī, pastor at the Church of the Virgin in Harat al-Rum. See Samir Khalil Samir, "Jirjis al-Jawhari al-Khanānī," *Coptic Encyclopedia* 4:1334–1335.

20. Glenn Bowman, "Pilgrim Narratives of Jerusalem," in *Sacred Journeys: The Anthropology of Pilgrimage*, ed. Alan Morinis (London: Greenwood Press, 1992), 151.

21. Abderrahmane El Moudden, "The Ambivalence of *Rihla*: Community Integration and Self-Definition in Moroccan Travel Accounts, 1300–1800," in *Muslim Travelers: Pilgrimage, Migration, and the Religious Imagination*, ed. Dale F. Eickelman and James P. Piscatori (Berkeley: University of California Press, 1990), 69–84; also see Hala Fattah, "Representations of Self and the Other in Two Iraqi Travelogues of the Ottoman Period," *International Journal of Middle East Studies* 30, no. 1 (1998): 51–76. In general, see Hilary Kilpatrick, "Between Ibn Battuta and al-Tahtawi: Arabic Travel Accounts of the Early Ottoman Period," *Middle Eastern Literatures* 11, no. 2 (2008): 233–248.

22. Alexia Petsalis-Diomidis, "Narratives of Transformation: Pilgrimage Patterns and Authorial Self-Presentation in Three Pilgrimage Texts," *Journeys* 3, no. 1 (2002): 86–88.

23. Meinardus, *The Copts in Jerusalem*, 12.

24. Moshe Gil, "Dhimmī Donations and Foundations for Jerusalem (638–1099)," *Journal of the Economic and Social History of the Orient* 27, no. 2 (1984): 160–161. For more on the Copts under the reign of al-Hakim, see Werthmuller, "An In-Between Space," 54–63.

25. Meinardus, *The Copts of Jerusalem*, 13–14.

26. Ibid., 16; Werthmuller, "An In-Between Space," 74.

27. Meinardus, *The Copts in Jerusalem*, 16–17. Dimitri Rizq, *Qiṣṣat al-Aqbāṭ fi'l-Arḍ al-Muqaddasa* (Cairo: Rābitat al-Quds li'l-Aqbāṭ al-Urthudhuks, 1967), 25–30, considers this move a sign of independence for the Copts and for their properties, both in Jerusalem and the Levant, from the jurisdiction of the Syrian Church at the See of Antioch.

28. Archbishop Basilios, "Jerusalem, Coptic See of," *Coptic Encyclopedia* 4:1324–1329.

29. Meinardus, "The Copts in Jerusalem and the Question of the Holy Places," in O'Mahony, *The Christian Heritage*, 124.

30. Meinardus, *The Copts in Jerusalem*, 29. Germanus was likely exaggerating the dismal status of his church in order to acquire financial assistance from Tsar Ivan.

31. Nakhla, *Silsilat*, 4:61.

32. The leverage that this practice gave the metropolitanate of Jerusalem is illustrated through a later example: Metropolitan Abraam I (1820–1854) was so influential that he succeeded in obtaining the appointment of Kyrillus IV (1854–1861) to the patriarchate. Archbishop Basilios, "Jerusalem, Coptic See of."

33. Amnon Cohen notes that "no attempt, systematic or otherwise, was made by the Ottoman authorities to prevent any of the Christian communities from exercising their historically acknowledged rights of free passage into Jerusalem or to interfere with the practice of their rites in their respective places of worship." Cohen, "The Ottoman Approach," 206.

34. Peri, *Christianity under Islam*, 86–87.

35. Ibid., 87.

36. For more on these points, see ibid., 74–75; Amnon Cohen, "The Ottoman Approach," 209.

37. A. Abdel Nour, "Le réseau routier de la Syrie Ottomane (XVIe–XVIIIe siècles)," *Arabica* 30, no. 2 (1983): 177; Andrew Peterson, "The Archeology of the Syrian and Iraqi Hajj Routes," *World Archaeology* 26, no. 1 (1994): 47–56. On the medieval Muslim pilgrimage to Jerusalem, see Elad, *Medieval Jerusalem*, especially 62–65.

38. Oded Peri, "The Christian Population of Jerusalem in the Late Seventeenth Century: Aspects of Demography, Economy, and Society," *Journal of the Economic and Social History on the Orient* 39, no. 4 (1996): 406–407.

39. Peri, *Christianity under Islam*, 35–38.

40. Kevork Bardakjian, "The Rise of the Armenian Patriarchate of Constantinople," in Braude and Lewis, *Christians and Jews*, 1:95–96.

41. Frazee, *Catholics and Sultans*, 215–216.

42. Abudacnus notes that before arriving in Jerusalem "they are to enter into the City of Gaza and then Catea and Ravilay, in which three mentioned places they are to pay a Toll or Custom to the Turk, such as are Subjects, eight French Crowns, the rest double, to wit, sixteen: Again, when they are come to Jerusalem, four Crowns are to be given by the Subject, eight by the rest." Abudacnus, *The True History*, 27. Moreover, Christian travelers to

Palestine, whether they were merchants or pilgrims, likely paid 30–40 percent more than Jewish travelers. This discrepancy reflects the authorities' estimation of the relative affluence of each community. Amnon Cohen, "The Ottoman Approach," 206.

43. Peri, *Christianity under Islam*, 163–164. We understand from Peri's calculations that from the mid-sixteenth century, pilgrims from Egypt paid the least (84.00 paras), while those from central and western Europe paid the most (327.50 paras). This could mean, following Amnon Cohen, that Copts were the poorest Christian community.

44. Peri, *Christianity under Islam*, 171.

45. As Peri notes, they were left begging in desperation outside the Church of the Holy Sepulchre, pleading with their rich brethren for help; even the Ottoman records indicate that a special category was made in the collection registers for paupers. *Christianity under Islam*, 172.

46. Ibid., 170.

47. Abudacnus, *The True History*, 27.

48. Peri, "The Christian Population of Jerusalem," 408.

49. For a comparable example of the relationship between mother churches and satellite communities in Jerusalem, see Brock, "East Syriac Pilgrims to Jerusalem," 191–192, 196–198.

50. Winter, *Egyptian Society*, 104.

51. Meinardus, *The Copts in Jerusalem*, 34, fn. 157. Ultimately, however, Copts fared much better than their Ethiopian counterparts. In 1640, Jerusalemite Ethiopians came under the charge of the Armenians, and by 1654, they had lost most of their property and ritualistic rights to the Greeks. See Anthony O'Mahony, "Pilgrims, Politics, and Holy Places: The Ethiopian Community in Jerusalem until ca. 1650," in *Jerusalem: Its Sanctity and Centrality to Judaism, Christianity, and Islam*, ed. Lee Levine (New York: Continuum, 1999), 477.

52. Meinardus, *The Copts in Jerusalem*, 34.

53. Shihata Khuri and Niqula Khuri, *Khulāṣat Tārīkh Kanīsat Urushalīm al-Urthudhuksiyya* (Jerusalem: Maṭbaʿat Bayt al-Muqaddas, 1925), 164–165; Frazee, *Catholics and Sultans*, 148.

54. The fact that only one monk represented the Copts during this ceremony, as Maundrell stated in 1697, indicates a diminished presence, although it also testifies to the fact that Coptic attendance was respected by other communities. For an excellent summary of all traveler reports from this period that make mentions of Copts, see Meinardus, *The Copts in Jerusalem*, 31–36.

55. In the eighteenth century, Egypt was the richest province of the Ottoman Empire. For detailed information on Egypt's economic prosperity in this period, particularly as it dramatically contrasted with the seventeenth century, see Şevket Pamuk, *A Monetary History of the Ottoman Empire* (Cambridge: Cambridge University Press, 2000), chapter 11.

56. Published in Georg Graf, "Rede des Abu Ishaq al-Mu'taman Ibn al-ʿAssal: Mit Einladung zur Wallfahrt nach Jerusalem," *Bulletin de la Société d'Archéologie Copte* 7 (1941): 56.

57. The original author is unknown, but the scribe who signs this manuscript is a priest named Nasim Abadir. Patriarchal Library, MS Canon 21, 176r.

58. See T. W. Juynboll, "Farḍ," *EI2* 2:790. For discussion of the infiltration of Muslim theological terminology within Coptic religious discourses, see el-Leithy, "Coptic Culture and Conversion," 434–444.

59. Patriarchal Library, MS Canon 21, 176v. Farḍ is traditionally associated with obligation, whereas sunna is related to a "desirable optional act." See Hava Lazarus-Yafeh's distinction in "Muslim Festivals," *Numen* 25, no. 1 (1978): 54.

60. Patriarchal Library, MS Canon 21, 177r.

61. The Armenian emissaries seem to have been very active, beginning in the sixteenth century, and were referred to as *hraviraks* ("inviters to the Holy Land"). They traveled with a *kontak* (an encyclical) that was read from the altars of various Armenian churches: much like these Coptic sermons, "the kontak described the Holy Places, the economic plight of the patriarchate, solicited funds for the upkeep of the Holy Places, and urged every Armenian believer to perform the holy acts of pilgrimage." See Hintlian, "Travelers and Pilgrims in the Holy Land," 151.

62. The patriarch seems to have been successful in his endeavor: Meinardus notes that in 1782, Copts had managed to enlarge their holdings in Jerusalem and that by the early nineteenth century, they were known to be the rightful owners of the Monastery of St. George.

63. The manuscript does not specify which Muslim factions or groups instigated these threats.

64. Amnon Cohen, "The Ottoman Approach," 209.

65. Peri, "Islamic Law and Christian Holy Sites: Jerusalem and Its Vicinity in Early Ottoman Times," *Islamic Law and Society* 6, no. 1 (1999): 99–100.

66. Patriarchal Library, MS Theology 134, 79r.

67. Yu'annis XVI, or Yuhanna, was the 103rd Patriarch of the See of Alexandria (the official title of Coptic patriarchs), thus he is regularly referred to in the text as "Yuhanna 103."

68. Coptic Museum, MS Liturgy 128, 175v.

69. Ibid., 179r.

70. See my discussion of these titles in chapter 1.

71. The identity of this person is unclear. It might be Isma'il b. 'Iwaz Bey al-Qasimi, who would ascend to the position of *amīr al-ḥajj* in 1711 (Hathaway, *The Politics of Households*, 153); however, it is doubtful that the author would have so easily confused the title of kahya (or katkhuda) with bey.

72. It is probable that this is Muhammad Pasha Kurd Bayram, who was appointed *wāli*, or governor of Jerusalem, Nablus, and Gaza, in 1701. On his appointment, Muhammad Pasha launched several bloody campaigns against bedouin clans that usurped the roads in Gaza. In 1703, the Pasha faced a rebellion in Jerusalem, whose outcome was a period of Jerusalemite self-rule that lasted until 1705. This period resulted in the closing of Jerusalem's gates, which likely ended Muslim and Christian pilgrimage for the duration of the conflict. In 1705, Ottoman authorities sent a military force that regained control of the city; however, the roads through Gaza may not have been opened for pilgrims from Egypt for another few years. See Adel Manna, "Eighteenth- and Nineteenth-Century Rebellions in Palestine," *Journal of Palestine Studies* 25, no. 1 (1994): 52–56.

73. In the Ottoman period, the office of shaykh al-ʿarab was a significant administrative and political position. In Ottoman laws governing Egypt, the shaykh was a tax farmer, an administrator of "public safety, agriculture and public works," and even an army commander. Winter, *Egyptian Society*, 91–92, 95.

74. The pashas who governed Gaza in the late seventeenth and early eighteenth centuries apparently had succeeded, at least for some time, in putting an end to the destructive raids of the bedouins while also maintaining good relations with the Christians and Europeans. Gaza, at that time, had reached its height during the Ottoman period, almost acting as the capital of Palestine with its metropolitan character. See Dominique Sourdel, "Ghazza," *EI2* 2:1056–1057.

75. See Amnon Cohen, "The Army in Palestine in the Eighteenth Century—Sources of Its Weakness and Strength," *Bulletin of the School of Oriental and African Studies* 34, no. 1 (1971): 46.

76. Swanson, "The Monastery of St. Paul," 54–55.

77. Patriarchal Library, MS Liturgy 102, 168v–179v. It was perhaps fitting that both Abu Mansur and Patriarch Yu'annis XVI died around the same time in 1718, when an outbreak of the plague struck Cairo. See the colophon to Patriarchal Library, MS Theology 230.

78. Coptic Museum, MS Liturgy 128, 184r.

79. For more information about this topic in general, see Archbishop Basilios, "Liturgical Instruments," *Coptic Encyclopedia* 5:1469–1475.

80. Suraiya Faroqhi provides a table of payments made to bedouin individuals and to bedouin tribes by Egyptian caravan leaders in the sixteenth and seventeenth centuries. These payments "bought" the protection of the pilgrimage caravan. See Faroqhi, *Pilgrims and Sultans*, 55–56. Bedouins were also used as "desert pilots" who accompanied the caravan in order to navigate the way (ibid., 34).

81. An account by the Moroccan traveler named ʿAbdallah al-ʿAyyashi regarding his pilgrimage in 1663 informs us of the written assurances needed by Muslim pilgrims in order to complete their journey to Jerusalem. As Nabil Matar writes, "In preparation for his voyage, he asked for a letter of introduction from a shaykh who had accompanied him from Medina: it was addressed to the foremost of Gaza's religious scholars, Shaykh ʿAbd al-Qadir bin Qadir. Throughout his journey, ʿAyyashi depended on such letters of introduction in order to ensure him accommodation, religious interaction, and a sense of community and familiarity." See Matar, "Two Journeys to Seventeenth-Century Palestine," *Journal of Palestine Studies* 29, no. 4 (2000): 38.

82. In 1559, Sultan Suleyman had ordered the governor of Egypt to repopulate and install a garrison at the old fortress. The caravan heading to Mecca used this sea route until Gaza, when they turned southeast toward ʿAqaba. See Abdel Nour, "Le réseau routier," 181–182.

83. As Faroqhi writes, "Food for the return journey was sometimes deposited in desert forts protecting the caravan's stopping points. If these supplies were not in the meantime plundered by Bedouins, this was a convenient arrangement." See *Pilgrims and Sultans*, 43.

84. This commander also directly received revenues from the Porte. This position is well described by Shaw, *The Financial and Administrative Organization*, 241–254.

85. Coptic Museum, MS Liturgy 128, 185v–186r. The splitting into two caravans among Copts closely resembles a Muslim tradition that dates to the Mamluk era, when the ḥajj caravan had become too sizable to handle in one procession. In the Ottoman era, this tradition seems to have continued, although the lesser caravan carrying basic supplies for the journey appears to have departed weeks before the second "major" caravan. See Samira Fahmi 'Ali 'Umar, *Imārat al-Ḥajj fī Miṣr al-'Uthmāniyya, 1517–1798* (Cairo: Al-Hay'a al-Miṣriyya al-'Āma li'l-Kitāb, 2000), 165–167.

86. "Al-Qimāma al-Qudsiyya" (lit. "Holy Garbage") was an epithet long used by some Muslims—possibly since the time of the Fatimid Caliph al-Hakim—to refer to this Christian site.

87. This is a likely reference to the village called 'Adiliyya that was located northeast of Cairo, close to Bilbays, which served as a meeting point for the annual ḥajj caravan. It might also refer to an area in northern Cairo near the dome built in 1501 by Sultan al-'Adil Tumanbay over his tomb. Al-Damurdashi, *Al-Durra al-Muṣāna*, 6, fn. 10.

88. A zardakhān is a type of Persian towel.

89. This is north of Harat al-Rum and south of the district of al-Ghawriyya.

90. This Cairene quarter, named after Mamluk Sultan Qansuh al-Ghawri, is located due west of the famous al-Azhar mosque and north of Harat al-Rum.

91. Al-Damurdashi, *Al-Durra al-Muṣāna*, 247 (my translation). Also see Ahmad Katkhuda 'Azaban al-Damurdashi, *Al-Damurdashi's Chronicle of Egypt, 1688–1755: Al-Durra al-Muṣāna fī Akhbār al-Kināna*, trans. and ed. Daniel Crecelius and 'Abd al-Wahhab Bakr Muhammad (Leiden: Brill, 1991), 368–369.

92. Winter, *Society and Religion*, 222.

93. An earlier account of a ḥajj procession in Cairo, recounted by the seventeenth-century Ottoman traveler Evliya Çelebi, may help to shed light on later Muslim concerns over the resemblance: "The high point of the departure ceremony came when the caravan commander appeared on the square of Kara Meydān, which was normally used for military exercises and parades. He was accompanied by a numerous suite of soldiers and officers, while the band played, and the janissaries and other soldiers saluted their commander. The caravan commander then visited the governor of Egypt in his tent, which must have been put up in this place for the occasion. Now artillery was brought to the square, presumably the cannons which the commander was to take along with him on his desert journey. The flag of the Prophet, a major relic, was paraded about the grounds along with the palanquin symbolizing the Sultan's presence, which was to accompany the caravan to Mecca; the palanquin was carried on a camel." Cited in Faroqhi, *Pilgrims and Sultans*, 37–38.

94. This is almost certainly Ibrahim al-Qazdaghli, who became Janissary kahya (regimental officer) in that year and whose leadership of the Qazdaghli household dates from 1748. For more on this character, see Hathaway, *The Politics of Households*, esp. chapter 5, "The Ascendancy of Ibrahim Kâhya al- Qazdağlı and the Emergence of the Qazdağlı Beylicate," 88–106.

95. Reference to the Azahrite shaykhs reminds us that these outspoken leaders of the 'ulamā' were the most privileged and politically powerful within the Muslim religious establishment in Egypt. Winter, *Egyptian Society*, 116.

96. Raymond, *Artisans et commerçants*, 2:455; 'Afifi, *Al-Aqbāṭ fī Miṣr*, 65–66.

97. Raymond, *Artisans et commerçants*, 2:455; 'Afifi, *Al-Aqbāṭ fī Miṣr*, 67–68. The stories of 1748 and 1751 appear so similar and share many details that 'Afifi concludes they likely refer to the same event, and dismisses al-Jabarti's account as error-prone. Al-Jabarti may have copied this story from al-Damurdashi, since, as Peter Holt notes, al-Jabarti often used anecdotal stories from earlier chroniclers. See Holt, "Al-Jabarti's Introduction to the History of Ottoman Egypt," *Bulletin of the School of Oriental and African Studies* 25, no. 1 (1962): 38–51.

98. According to al-Jabarti, Shaykh Muhammad al-Shubrawi (1681–1758) was a descendant of a family of Azharite scholars. He was appointed as the Shaf'i mufti in 1725. He was well learned and highly respected, as demonstrated by the lavish funeral held in his honor at al-Azhar. See al-Jabarti, *'Ajā'ib*, 1:341–42.

99. Shaykh Sidi Muhammad al-Bakri was *shaykh al-sijāda* (head of all Sufi mystical orders). In his obituary, al-Jabarti indicates that there was a close friendship between Shaykh al-Shubrawi and Shaykh al-Bakri. It was al-Shubrawi's habit to visit al-Bakri's home every day before sunrise, sit with him for one hour, and then depart to al-Azhar mosque. Al-Bakri died in 1758. See al-Jabarti, *'Ajā'ib*, 1:362–63. For more discussion on the al-Bakri family, see Afaf Lutfi al-Sayyid Marsot, "The Ulama of Cairo in the Eighteenth and Nineteenth Centuries," in *Scholars, Saints, and Sufis: Muslim Religious Institutions in the Middle East since 1500*, ed. Nikki R. Keddie (Berkeley: University of California Press, 1972), 149–165.

100. Al-Jabarti, *'Ajā'ib*, 1:308.

101. Ibid.

102. Ibid.

103. For more on the ethnic distinctions between Maghribis, Turks, and Egyptians among the 'ulamā', see Winter, *Egyptian Society*, 117–118, and, on tensions between Maghribis and other 'ulamā', 124.

104. Al-Jabarti, *'Ajā'ib*, 1:47–48; Ahmad Shalabi, *Awḍaḥ al-Ishārāt*, 204–205. The incident is discussed in Grehan, "The Great Tobacco Debate in the Ottoman Middle East," 1352–1353.

105. Sonnini, *Travels in Upper and Lower Egypt*, 447, wrote that "being obliged to traverse a considerable part of the city, we had full half a league to go through the streets of Cairo before we reached the castle. The populace, astonished at seeing the Franks [Europeans] treated with such honorable distinction, issued in crowds from their houses as we passed along, lavishing upon us hootings, insults, and the opprobrious epithets of Nazareen and dog. Some of the more moderate contented themselves with pitying the horses on which we rode. 'Unfortunate animals!' exclaimed they, 'what a miserable lot is yours! What crime can you have committed to be thus condemned to carry accursed infidels and dogs!'"

106. As Marsot notes in her discussion of eighteenth-century Cairo, "in Muslim society *vox 'ūlemā'* is legally *vox dei*, and practically *vox populi* for they had it in their power to rouse or placate public opinion—a quality that was fully appreciated by the ruling groups which lay behind much of their political influence." Marsot, "The Political and Economic Functions of the 'Ulemā' in the 18th Century," *Journal of the Economic and Social History of the Orient* 16, pts. 2–3 (1974): 133.

107. Peter Gran, *Islamic Roots of Capitalism: Egypt, 1760–1840* (Syracuse, NY: Syracuse University Press, 1998 [1979]), 67. Additionally, el-Shayyal notes that this revival also took place among eighteenth-century Egyptian Sufis, who "wrote treatises menacing people who slackened in their beliefs"; moreover, it was common "to hear voices raised against those innovations clothed in the mantle of religion and mysticism." El-Shayyal, "Some Aspects of Intellectual and Social Life," 125.

108. Madeline C. Zilfi, *The Politics of Piety: The Ottoman Ulema in the Postclassical Age* (Chicago: Bibliotheca Islamica, 1987), 102, 149. This was also common practice during the Umayyad and Abbasid caliphates.

109. Grehan, "Smoking and Early Modern Sociability," 1367.

110. ʿUmar, *Imārat al-Ḥajj*, 169.

111. Matariyya is a Cairene suburb close to Heliopolis. Historically, it has been considered a holy site by Copts, who believe that it was in this area that the Holy Family took shelter under a sycamore tree. It is also said that Jesus created a well of water here and that Mary used the water to bathe Jesus; at the spot where she bathed him, the water sprouted a balsam tree. The blessing of this "miracle" continued when Copts began using the fragrant balsam plant for making their Mayrūn (Chrismation) oil. See Maqrizi, *Khiṭaṭ*, 1:624–625; Evliya Çelebi, *Seyahatname*, 10:187; and Cornelis Hulsman, "Tracing the Route of the Holy Family Today," in Gabra, *Be Thou There*, 59–60.

112. Stopping to greet the pilgrims was also customary for the ḥajj caravan during the Ottoman period; see al-Jabarti, *ʿAjāʾib*, 1:193.

113. The term *khānqāh* generally refers to a Sufi lodge. This, however, is a likely reference to the town of Al-Khanqah, located about twelve miles northeast of Cairo. A famous lodge called al-Khanqah al-Nasiriyya of Siryaqus, built in 1325 by Sultan Nasir Muhammad bin Qalawun (ruled at various intervals between 1293 and 1341), was once located just west of that town. See al-Maqrizi, *Khiṭaṭ*, 4(2):767, fn. 1. Before the Islamic conquest of Egypt, the town of Siryaqus was renowned for the cult of the Coptic martyr St. Hor, and in the fourteenth century, it continued to have a large Coptic population and a monastery named for the martyr. See John Alden Williams, "The Khanqah of Siryaqus: A Mamluk Royal Religious Foundation," in *In Quest of an Islamic Humanism: Arabic and Islamic Studies in Memory of Mohamed al-Nowaihi*, ed. A. H. Green (Cairo: American University of Cairo Press, 1984), 109.

114. Bilbays is located at a crossroads between the desert and the Delta. It is likely to be a pre-Islamic city, as it is mentioned in ancient Coptic texts, and it is also listed as one of the old Egyptian bishoprics. Not much is known about Bilbays during the Coptic period, but in 1168, the Crusaders occupied this town. Later, in the Mamluk era, Bilbays was restored as a Coptic bishopric. See Randall Stewart, "Bilbeis," *Coptic Encyclopedia* 2:391; Hulsman, "Tracing the Route of the Holy Family Today," 39–41; and Gaston Wiet, "Bilbays," *EI2* 1:1218. There is evidence, moreover, that at least during the seventeenth century, there was a courier route between Cairo and Damascus that went by way of Bilbays. See Faroqhi, *Pilgrims and Sultans*, 41.

115. Al-Salihiyya was a town northeast of Cairo, close to the Mediterranean Sea, which served as a well-known stop for travelers and armies en route to Ottoman Palestine.

116. Coptic Museum, MS Liturgy 128, 188r–188v.

117. As noted, in the Ottoman period, the metropolitan of Jerusalem had jurisdiction over large sections of the Nile Delta, which sometimes included Damietta.

118. Coptic Museum, MS Liturgy 128, 189r. According to Meinardus, the Copts had a Church of St. Mary in Gaza during the first part of the fifteenth century. See *The Copts in Jerusalem*, 22.

119. Copts and Armenians were officially "in communion" as anti-Chalcedonian churches. The closeness of their friendship is captured in a letter from 1808 written by the Coptic Patriarch Murqus VIII to the Armenian patriarch of Jerusalem, Tidrus, resident at the Monastery of Ya'qub. Patriarchal Library, MS Theology 270, 34r–35r.

120. His name is omitted from the text, but it is likely to be Patriarch Chrysanthus Notaras, r. 1707–1731.

121. Runciman, *The Great Church*, 236.

122. Coptic Museum, MS Liturgy 128, 191v.

123. In a later part, the narrator informs us that eleven priests from Egypt accompanied the patriarch to Jerusalem and that there were already, at that time, three priests residing in Jerusalem.

124. This pool of water is known as Siloe, Siloah, or Siloam. It was located outside the south wall of Jerusalem, where Jesus performed the miracle of giving sight to a man born blind (John 9:1–7).

125. Located southeast of the city, Bir Ayyub ("Job's Well") was a major source of water for the city of Jerusalem from the time of the Crusaders until modern times.

126. The ascension of Jesus occurred, according to biblical references, on the fortieth day after Easter Sunday. Tradition designates that this event took place on top of the Mount of Olives outside the Old City of Jerusalem, where Jesus' footprints are embedded in a rock formation and where pilgrims still go to receive blessings.

127. This term has its origins in the Hebrew word "Pesach," which means Passover. Eventually it came to refer to the Passion and death of Christ and later the resurrection and ascension. In the Coptic context, however, all of Holy Week, beginning at Palm Sunday and ending on Good Friday, is considered the week of Pascha. Alfred Cody, "Pascha," *Coptic Encyclopedia* 6:1903–1905.

128. For more on liturgical vestments historically worn by Coptic clergy, see Karel C. Innemée, *Ecclesiastical Dress in the Medieval Near East* (Leiden: Brill, 1992), 90–127.

129. Sicard, in particular, finds the ceremony absurd. See *Oeuvres*, 2:59–62. Also see Colin Morris, *The Sepulchre of Christ and the Medieval West, from the Beginning to 1600* (New York: Oxford University Press, 2005), 315–316. Morris writes that the growing skepticism of Western observers, recorded in travel literature from the thirteenth century onward, served to "alienate further Latin devotion from that of the native Christians . . . and to reduce the celebratory element in their presence at the Holy Sepulchre."

130. Chaldeans are Eastern Christians who are mostly native to Iraq; since the seventeenth century, the Chaldeans have acknowledged union with the Catholic pope in Rome.

131. Abudacnus, *The True History*, 27–28.

132. Peri, *Christianity under Islam*, 118–120.

133. Sicard also discussed the presence of "many" Janissaries around the tomb, noting that they protected the sepulchre from the myriads pressing against it. Sicard, *Oeuvres*, 2:61.

134. Morison, *Relation historique*, 367–370.

135. Sicard, *Oeuvres*, 2:61.

136. These are all names for different parts of ecclesiastical vestments. The akmāmu'l-ithnaynī refers to the "two sleeves" worn by Coptic priests (Innemée, *Ecclesiastical Dress in the Medieval Near East*, 31). The badrashīn derives from the Greek "epitrachelion," which is worn around the neck with two parts hanging down the front of the body (ibid., 46). The burnus is worn over the badrashīn, and in the medieval period, it had a circular shape with an opening for the head. (ibid., 48–49).

137. Coptic Museum, MS Liturgy 128, 198r.

138. In Sicard's narrative, a procession is held before and after the ceremony of the Holy Fire. The order of clergymen in the procession is as follows: Greek, Armenian, Syrian, Coptic, Georgian, and Ethiopian. See Sicard, *Oeuvres*, 2:61.

139. Here, Glenn Bowman's differentiation between Catholic and Orthodox understandings of pilgrimage might be applicable, the former based on the individual experience of the Holy Land and the latter marked by its communal character. Bowman, "Contemporary Christian Pilgrimage to the Holy Land," in O'Mahony, *The Christian Heritage*, 288–309.

140. As Andrew Jotischky notes in the case of the Greek Orthodox pilgrims during the medieval period, "The Holy Land functions as an icon with the capacity to make comprehensible the ideal of this community." Jotischky, "History and Memory as Factors in Greek Orthodox Pilgrimage to the Holy Land under Crusader Rule," in *The Holy Land, Holy Lands, and Christian History*, ed. R. N. Swanson (Rochester, NY: Boydell Press, 2000), 111.

141. In a visit to a remote part of Upper Egypt, Sicard was asked by a group of Coptic scribes why Catholics discount this miracle of "nour"; Sicard answered by disparaging the gullibility of the masses who believe in this miracle and the Eastern Orthodox clerics who perpetuate these beliefs. Sicard, *Oeuvres*, 2:59–60.

142. Lyster, "Reviving a Lost Tradition," 214.

143. In adding to this list, as drawn from Turner's *Image and Pilgrimage in Christian Culture*, and in challenging Turner's classic characterization, Thomas Idinopulos maintains that pilgrimage to the Holy Land is especially unique in its "unpredictable, dramatic, dangerous, and often destructive" quality. Referring to the fanaticism the Holy Land has inspired over the centuries—in the form of crusade or jihad—Idinopulos questions Turner's more hopeful understanding of fellowship as embedded in these spiritual journeys. See, in general, Thomas A. Idinopulos, "Jerusalem: Historical Perspectives on Politics and Religion in the Holy City," *Israel Affairs* 3, no. 2 (1996): 34–49.

144. Bowman, "Pilgrim Narratives of Jerusalem," 153.

145. This custom was not only prevalent among the Copts but was also popular among Syrians, Ethiopians, and Armenians. John Carswell, *Coptic Tattoo Designs*, 2nd ed. (Beirut: American University of Beirut, 1958), xxx. Carswell's study records the designs imprinted on these wooden blocks, which the Razzouk family has owned since the eighteenth century.

146. Ibid. For a pictorial illustration of the souvenirs that Muslim, Christian, and Jewish pilgrims acquire from their pilgrimage to Jerusalem, see Iris Fishof and Noam

Bar'am-Ben Yossef, *Souvenirs de Terre Sainte pour les pèlerins du XIXe et XXe siècle* (Jerusalem: Le Musée d'Israel, 1996).

CHAPTER 5

1. Bernard Heyberger, "Frontières confessionnelles et conversions chez les chrétiens orientaux (XVIIe–XVIIIe siècles)," in *Conversions islamiques: Identités religieuses en Islam méditerranéen*, ed. Mercedes García-Arenal (Paris: Maisonneuve-Larose, 2001), 246.

2. Lucette Valensi, "Inter-Communal Relations and Changes in Religious Affiliation in the Middle East (Seventeenth to Nineteenth Centuries)," *Comparative Studies in Society and History* 30, no. 2 (1997): 253.

3. Masters, *Christians and Jews*, 70. On France's emerging power, see Edhem Eldem, *French Trade in Istanbul in the Eighteenth Century* (Leiden: Brill, 1999), especially chapter 1.

4. Marcus, *The Middle East on the Eve of Modernity*, 47.

5. Ibid.

6. A facsimile of the 1665 berāt is published in Rabbath, *Documents*, 1:504, and is translated into French by Rabbath on 503–505. The 1690 decree is discussed in Masters, *Christians and Jews*, 84.

7. Marcus, *The Middle East on the Eve of Modernity*, 47; Masters, *Christians and Jews*, 82.

8. Masters, *Christians and Jews*, 71.

9. In general, see Heyberger, *Les chrétiens du Proche-Orient*, chapter 15; Khater, "'God has called me to be free,'" 426–427.

10. Marcus, *The Middle East on the Eve of Modernity*, 47. Valensi adds an important observation here regarding the apparent heterodoxy that proliferated during this period, noting, "Conversion is not a univocal operation by which individual X passes from religion A to religion B. First, the conditions that motivate X are varied. Second, the procedures of conversion are similarly varied. Third, the conversion is not always irreversible." Valensi, "Inter-Communal Relations and Changes," 262.

11. These "Greek Catholic" Syrians continued to prosper as French agents following the Capitulation Treaty of 1741, which provided French merchants right of entry to all Ottoman ports, including Egypt's lucrative Mediterranean and Red Sea ports. Philipp, *The Syrians in Egypt*, 16, 23. Philipp (18) points out that even as they employed Syrians in the commercial sector, the French frequently treated the Syrian Catholics "with suspicion and open hostility," and Masters (*Christians and Jews*, 116–118) argues that Syrian migration to Egypt was mostly the result of economic ambition, not religious persecution.

12. Valensi, "Inter-Communal Relations and Changes," 259–260.

13. Masters, *Christians and Jews*, 70–71.

14. Ibid., 74.

15. Ibid., 85; Hamilton, *The Copts and the West*, 88–89.

16. Masters, *Christians and Jews*, 88–95.

17. Ibid., 96–97. Uniate churches were not officially recognized by the Ottoman Porte until 1831.

18. Hamilton, *The Copts and the West*, 56.

19. Ibid., 65.

20. For a copy of the exchange of letters between Pius IV and Ghubriyal VII, see "Pie IV au Patriarche Copte, 16 Aout 1561" in Rabbath, *Documents*, 1:224–225; see Ghubriyal's response through the missionary priest Rodriguez in "Le P. Ch. Rodriguez au Pape Du Caire, le 10 Décembre 1561" in ibid., 1:257–259, and "Le P. Ch. Rodriguez au P. Général S. J. du Caire, le 25 Janvier 1562" in ibid., 1:273–275. Also see Hamilton, *The Copts and the West*, 66.

21. "Documentazione sul primate del Papa," *Studia Orientalia Christiana*, no. 5 (1960): 79.

22. "Letter from Ghubriyal to Clement VIII from 1601," cited in Hamilton, *The Copts and the West*, 75.

23. Ibid., 77.

24. Ibid.

25. The Capuchins are an independent offshoot of the Catholic Franciscan Order.

26. Hamilton, *The Copts and the West*, 84.

27. Ibid., 81.

28. Frazee, *Catholics and Sultans*, 148; Petro B. T. Bilaniuk, "Coptic Relations with Rome," *Coptic Encyclopedia* 2:609–611.

29. Cited in Frazee, *Catholics and Sultans*, 216.

30. Dêtré Jean-Marie, "Contribution à l'étude des relations du patriarche copte Jean XVII avec Rome de 1735 à 1738," *Studia Orientalia Christiana, Collectanea*, no. 5 (1960), 125; Hamilton, *The Copts and the West*, 84–85.

31. Gran, *Islamic Roots of Capitalism*, 4, notes that "French involvement in Egypt, through its merchants' community, missionaries, and local minority groups, was an opening wedge for the expanded penetration of foreign capital into Egypt in the eighteenth century."

32. Dêtré Jean-Marie, "Contribution à l'étude," 130.

33. Sicard, *Oeuvres*, 2:117. Although Sicard refers unsympathetically to the "ignorance of Copts," in reality he was one of the most outspoken advocates of preserving Coptic traditions. As Maurice Martin writes, Sicard "refused to separate the practice of the sacraments by Catholics from that of their original Coptic community and fought long with the Roman authorities in defense of his view." Maurice Martin, "Sicard, Claude," *Coptic Encyclopedia* 7:2136–2137.

34. Hamilton, *The Copts and the West*, 87–88.

35. Ibid., 99; Valensi, "Inter-Communal Relations and Changes," 255.

36. In the modern day Synaxarium of the Coptic Church, within the second entry for 28 Baramhat (24 March)—that concerning Patriarch Butrus VII (1809–1852)—the story is retold about the conversion of the prominent Ghali family from Orthodoxy to Catholicism. It is stated, somewhat paradoxically, that they converted to Catholicism in order to protect the Coptic community from Muhammad 'Ali's policies. See *Al-Siniksār* (Cairo: Maktabat al-Maḥabba, 1978), 84.

37. Native Christians frequently married into Catholic families as a way of partaking in the economic and legal advantages often accorded to Catholic residents within the empire. Valensi writes that "the passage from one church to another could also result from

the micro-strategies of social advancement: The Greeks and Syrians marrying Latins serving the function of intermediaries were not choosing entry into a larger community but, rather, a change in status which allowed them to escape from the Ottoman system." Valensi, "Inter-Communal Relations and Changes," 257.

38. In this period, Syrian Catholics had begun to threaten Coptic and Jewish control of Egypt's financial sector, and by the early nineteenth century Coptic Catholic ascendance to the highest ranks of the Egyptian bureaucracy was visible. After decades of dominating one of the most powerful administrative positions in Egypt, *ra'īs al- kuttāb* (head of the scribes), from 1806 to 1816, the Coptic leadership lost this position to al-Mu'allim Ghali, a Catholic Copt, who was a close ally and friend of the Syrian Catholics in Egypt. Philipp, *The Syrians in Egypt*, 38.

39. Ibid., 19.

40. Issues regarding the marriage of clergy, which is permissible in the Coptic Church but not in Roman Catholicism, created further tensions between the two communities. On the destruction of Coptic manuscripts in the mid-1730s by a Franciscan missionary, see Hamilton, *The Copts and the West*, 87; on this topic in the Ottoman Levant, see Heyberger, "Livres et pratiques de la lecture chez les chrétiens," 211.

41. Cited in Dêtré Jean-Marie, "Contribution à l'étude," 134.

42. As noted, throughout the eighteenth century, sultanic prohibitions were issued against conversion to Catholicism. It is almost certain that Egyptians were aware of these decrees.

43. On these conflicts, see Frazee, *Catholics and Sultans*, 219.

44. Frazee, *Catholics and Sultans*, 219; Bilaniuk, "Coptic Relations with Rome."

45. Dêtré Jean-Marie, "Contribution à l'étude," 145.

46. In the Coptic and Ethiopian Churches, communion wine was traditionally made from the fermented juice of raisins, not from unfermented, freshly pressed grapes.

47. Sonnini, *Travels in Upper and Lower Egypt*, 556.

48. Here we can see that the archons' position mirrored the anti-Catholic sentiments among influential Egyptian elites; French consular reports repeatedly indicate the frequent harassment of Catholic missionaries by local officials. One report notes an incident where 'Ali Bey al-Kabir arrested four Catholic priests and refused to release them until he was paid by their superior. Crecelius, *The Roots of Modern Egypt*, 48.

49. Grehan, "Smoking and 'Early Modern' Sociability," 1362.

50. See "Lettre de P. Eliano à un Père de Rome, Le Caire, 8 Avril 1584," published in Rabbath, *Documents*, 1:305–314. On similar struggles in the Levant, see Heyberger, *Les chrétiens du Proche-Orient*, 365–367, 537–548. As Charles Noel discusses in the context of eighteenth-century Spain, Catholic preachers "measured their success by the number of general confessions, the hours spent at the pulpit, the size of the crowds, praise from local clergy, and the attendance and support of local elites." See Noel, "Missionary Preachers in Spain: Teaching Social Virtue in the Eighteenth Century," *American Historical Review* 90, no. 4 (1985): 871.

51. In Jaffa, concern had arisen over the fact that "the Catholics who followed the Eastern rite [uniates] did not wish to obey their parish priest in the Latin rite for the

practices of Lent, and they continued to eat fish and drink wine." Valensi, "Inter-Communal Relations and Changes," 258.

52. Ibid., 264.

53. For more on Tukhi, see Hamilton, *The Copts and the West*, 95–101; Frazee, *Catholics and Sultans*, 218–219. Although Tukhi was named Bishop of Ansana (Fayyum), he would live most of his life at the Vatican editing Coptic liturgical materials. See Rufayla, *Tārīkh al-Umma al-Qibṭiyya*, 269.

54. Alphonse Mingana, Hans Ludwig Gottschalk, and Derek Hopwood, eds., *Catalogue of the Mingana Collection of Manuscripts*, vol. 2, *Christian Arabic MSS* (Cambridge: W. Heffer, 1933–1985), 98, no. 69, Mingana Chr. Arab. 32. The text reveals little information about its author, although one wonders if it may haven written by Tukhi, who lived in Rome for the latter part of his life and died in 1787. The title of the work, "The Book of Asking Questions," echoes titles of Christian apologetic texts from the early Islamic period. See Vila, "Christian Martyrs in the First Abbasid Century," 81–92.

55. As noted, the name "Jacobite" has historically referred to the anti-Chalcedonian Syrian church based in Antioch, which shares a common theological belief with the Coptic Church. Over the years, however, anti-Chalcedonian communities were often lumped together under "Jacobite," and this term was often used in derogatory ways by Western Catholics.

56. This is a reference to the Egyptian Patriarch Dioscorus (r. 444–454 in Coptic traditions), who rejected, along with his followers, the idea that Jesus had two distinct natures, one divine and one human. His stance represented the anti-Chalcedonian position that Copts were to adopt after 451.

57. *MS.KI*, 77r, my emphasis.

58. Ibid., 16r–17v, my emphasis.

59. Ibid., 114r.

60. Ibid., 86r–87v.

61. In 1714, this complaint was registered by missionary priests in the town of Jirja, who were appalled about the "chaos" inherent within Coptic marriage practices. See Sicard, *Oeuvres*, 2:70.

62. *MS.KI*, 104r.

63. Elizabeth Tingle, "The Sacred Space of Julien Maunoir: The Re-Christianizing of the Landscape in Seventeenth-Century Brittany," in *Sacred Space in Early Modern Europe*, ed. Will Coster and Andrew Spicer (Cambridge: Cambridge University Press, 2005), 243.

64. *MS.KI*, 99r.

65. Khater, "'God has called me to be free,'" 430.

66. *MS.KI*, 104r–105v.

67. Ibid., 108r.

68. Ibid., 109v.

69. Ibid., 110v.

70. Ibid., 111v, my emphasis.

71. MS Franciscan Library, Serial 66, 1. For more advice to priests, see MS Franciscan Library, Serial 66, 2–6, 7–22, 23–34.

72. MS Franciscan Library, Serial 67, 52.

73. For example, after briefly flirting with unification, Butrus VI (1718–1726) would rebuke those Copts who adopted the Catholic faith, explaining to them in his letters why their new faith was considered heretical. See Coptic Patriarchal Library, MS Theology 235, cited in Simayka, *Catalogues*, 2:196.

74. Jirja is a town in Upper Egypt, approximately twenty miles southeast of Suhaj. For its significance in Coptic history, see Randall Stewart, "Jirja," *Coptic Encyclopedia*, 4:1330–1331. Akhmim was one of the major centers of Coptic culture from the fourth to the eighth centuries, and in fact, the "Akhmimic dialect," along with the "Sahidic dialect," constitutes the Upper Egyptian dialect of the Coptic language. See Peter Nagel, "Akhmimic," *Coptic Encyclopedia* (Appendix), A19–A27.

75. During their stay at the monastery, there were approximately twenty-five monks in residence. Meinardus, "Dayr Anba Antuniyus"; Gawdat Gabra, "Perspectives on the Monastery of St. Antony: Medieval and Later Inhabitants and Visitors," in Bolman, *Monastic Visions*, 174.

76. Gabra, "Perspectives," 174.

77. As Gabra notes, "Copts, Syrians, Ethiopians, Franciscans, and perhaps also Armenians visited and lived there at one time or another in the medieval and later periods. . . . Such was its fame and significance within and outside of Egypt that it was a regular destination for study and pilgrimage." See ibid., 175.

78. Monasteries and their libraries served a similar function in other parts of the Arab Christian world, often acting as a hub for serious intellectual and literary production within indigenous Christian communities. See Carsten-Michael Walbiner, "Monastic Reading and Learning in Eighteenth-Century Bilad al-Sham: Some Evidence from the Monastery of al-Shuwayr (Mount Lebanon)," *Arabica* 51, no. 4 (2004): 462–477, and a partial discussion in Schidorsky, "Libraries in Late Ottoman Palestine," 260–276.

79. Nakhla, *Silsilat*, 5:65.

80. When Yu'annis died in 1796, Yusab wrote a homily memorializing the benevolence that this patriarch had shown to his congregation throughout his reign. This is the seventeenth sermon in the collection.

81. Hamilton, *The Copts and the West*, 90; Rufayla, *Tārīkh al-Umma al-Qibṭiyya*, 269.

82. According to Nakhla, he was stunned, for "he found people involved with the heresies of the Roman Catholic Church." Nakhla, *Silislat*, 5:65.

83. Ibid., 5:65.

84. His successor, Murqus VIII (1796–1809), would continue this tradition and similarly used these letters to combat the missionary threat. "Adrāj" is defined by Simayka as "Degrees." However, in a recent article, Samiha Abd al-Shaheed defines them as "letters of recommendation" or *taqlīd* ("tradition"). See "A Catalogue of Unpublished *Durug* from the 17th through 19th centuries in the Coptic Museum," in Immerzeel, van der Vliet, and Kersten, *Coptic Studies on the Threshold of a New Millennium*, 519–528.

85. In my discussion of the *Adrāj*, I have relied on a complete manuscript at the Patriarchal Library in Cairo (MS Theology 134).

86. Coeval missionaries utilized similar language, imparting images of the "battlefield" in their own sermons. In the eighteenth century, "Spanish preachers [like French preachers] . . . often employed the vocabulary and images of the battlefield. They

were soldiers leading the attack on the devil's fortress. Europe 'hummed with traveling missionaries,' summoning the faithful to fight God's cause against sin." Noel, "Missionary Preachers in Spain," 869.

87. Samir Khalil Samir has enumerated from several existing, incomplete manuscripts of *Silāḥ* a total of thirty-four sermons, the order of which seems to be chronological.

88. As Samir writes, these sermons are "very casual, both on account of the language, which is full of grammatical errors and vulgarisms, and on account of the redaction, which contains numerous repetitions and sentences that are often incomprehensible." See Samir, "Yusab Bishop of Jirja and Akhmim," *Coptic Encyclopedia* 7:2360–2362.

89. The most common liturgical readings in the Coptic tradition derive from the Synaxarium (the collection of hagiographies), Homilies (of the "Great Church Fathers"), the Psalmodia (daily hymns and psalms), the Difnār (hymns for saints celebrated on each day of a Coptic month), the Ṭuruḥāt (expositions of biblical readings), and biblical lessons given during matrimonial and burial services. Emil Maher Ishaq, "Lectern," *Coptic Encyclopedia* 5:1434–1435.

90. See Heyberger, *Les chrétiens du Proche-Orient*, 153.

91. For the description of this story, see al-Jabarti, *'Ajā'ib*, 1:79–82. In this moment of catastrophe, Rudolph Peters writes that "the people of Cairo had attributed the calamity that had befallen them to their own impiety and sinfulness. . .. So when a preacher showed them a new way of being pious—a departure from their habitual, mystical religiosity or indifference to religion . . . many must have felt attracted to it." Peters, "The Battered Dervishes of *Bab Zuwayla*: A Religious Riot in Eighteenth-Century Cairo," in *Eighteenth-Century Renewal and Reform in Islam*, ed. Nehemia Levtzion and John Voll (Syracuse, NY: Syracuse University Press, 1987), 104.

92. Zilfi, *The Politics of Piety*, chapter 4.

93. Al-Jabarti, *'Ajā'ib*, 1:206.

94. Heyberger, *Les chrétiens du Proche-Orient*, 355.

95. Patriarchal Library, MS Theology 134, 203r–204v.

96. Ibid., 204v, my emphasis.

97. Ibid., 205v.

98. Valensi, "Inter-Communal Relations and Changes," 256, writes erroneously that "like the Muslims in their mosques, Christians did not tolerate the presence of women in the church."

99. Cairo's medieval Muslim preachers often spoke to "mixed-gender audiences," and sometimes women in the audience responded by "'cry[ing] out like the crying of a pregnant woman at the time of her delivery. At times [women] even throw off their outer garment and stand up.'" Berkey, *Popular Preaching and Religious Authority*, 31. Berkey also notes that women may have even led the sermons.

100. St. Macarius Library, MS Theology 6, 197r–198v.

101. In Ottoman Egypt, diwāns were administrative councils that were held both by the Ottoman governor and by individual households. See Hathaway, *The Politics of Households*, 26, 175.

102. St. Macarius Library, MS Theology 6, 198r–199v. Similarly, Yu'annis complains how people are engaged in excess throughout the day. "From the time of waking until sleeping,

the drinking continues and the stomach is occupied until three, four, or five in the morning. And [people] are working in gluttonous work all day, at one point they eat, and at another they drink coffee, and at another they snuff [tobacco], and at another they drink ʿaraq. This goes on all day . . . particularly among the wealthy." See Patriarchal Library, MS Theology 134, 146r.

103. In the eighteenth century, Muslim religious scholars entered into heated and at times violent arguments over coffee drinking. But the sixteenth-century scholar ʿAbd al-Wahhab al-Shaʿrani found attacks against coffee drinkers to be trivial. As Winter writes, al-Shaʿrani felt that "attention should be paid to serious offenses and not to trifles such as blowing on flutes or drinking coffee, since the ʿulama were, in any case, undecided about their legality." See Winter, *Society and Religion*, 148.

104. Patriarchal Library, MS Theology 256, 145r–145v.

105. Pococke, *A Description of the East*, 1:246. In response to protests, Patriarch Ghubriyal VIII issued an order in 1602 to limit existing Coptic fasts. This is documented in Biblica 203 at the Monastery of St. Antony, as cited by Nakhla, *Silsilat*, 4:59–60.

106. Shaykh al-Shaʿrani admired Coptic monks and in particular respected Coptic traditions of fasting. In one of his writings, he relates the story of a Sufi saint who "esteemed only the Christians' way of fasting, since they ate no meat at all during their fasts, whereas the Muslims ate mutton and poultry." Winter, *Society and Religion*, 220–221.

107. Patriarchal Library, MS Theology 134, 145v. The patriarch goes on to marvel at the fact that divisions in the rules of fasting occur even within one household, therefore creating a "broken home." Once again, these sermons echo medieval Coptic texts that criticized the laity's attitudes toward fasting. In the "Apocalypse of Samuel," the author writes the Christians "will break the fasts which are proper and well-known, and even of those who do fast, some will not complete their fast as is proper, for the sake of gluttony, and they will demand of others that they break their fast with them, for each of them will *create for themselves their own law*" (original emphasis). Cited in Iskander, "Islamization in Medieval Egypt," 226.

108. Using almost identical logic to that used by Yu'annis, Bishop Yusab responds to the sort of criticism raised in *MS.KI* and writes, "I saw other people breaking from what the teachers of the church have arranged in terms of fasting. They see the church fasting, so they [decide] not to fast. They have divided the church into two. . . . there is now separation in the house of God. I saw people fasting the Advent fast, from sixteenth day of Hatur and others eating meat until the first day of Kiyahk. I saw one table split into two, some people eating meat and others fasting." See MS Paris Arabe 4711, 102r.

109. This discourse is similar to accusations made in Aleppo's Islamic courts, in 1726, by Orthodox Christians against dozens of converts who had "turned Frank." See Masters, *Christians and Jews*, 90.

110. Here, Yu'annis's and Yusab's sermons are important in how they reflect the spirit of the times. In eighteenth-century Damascus, for instance, the Antiochian Orthodox priest and historian Mikha'il Breik recorded his own ethical concerns, blaming the "Franks" for undermining, in the words of one historian, the "socio-religious stability of the Orthodox community." Cited in Hayat el-Eid Bualuan, "Mikha'il Breik: A Chronicler and a Historian in 18th century Bilad al-Sham," *Parole de l'Orient* 21 (1996): 264, fn. 34.

111. St. Macarius Library, MS Theology 6, 75r–76v, my emphasis.

112. Ibid., 83v.

113. Ibid., 75r–76v, 168v–168r.

114. Ibid., 75r–76v, 169v. Yusab complained to Yu'annis about the fact that this situation created divisions among husbands and wives: a Catholic wife takes her daughter to be baptized in the Catholic Church, while her Orthodox husband takes his son to be baptized in the Coptic Church. See Patriarchal Library, MS Theology 134, 209v.

115. In Ottoman Acre, for instance, Greek Catholics were known to marry Orthodox and to allow their children to be raised as Orthodox. Valensi, "Inter-Communal Relations and Changes," 259; Heyberger, "Frontières confessionnelles et conversions chez les chrétiens orientaux (XVIIe–XVIIIe siècles)," 250–251.

116. 1 Corinthians 7:14.

117. Patriarchal Library, MS Theology 134, 212r–213v. The biblical reference made by Patriarch Yu'annis is to a Pauline epistle, 1 Corinthians 7:12–16.

118. That women were responsible for preserving a family's religious identity was also a theme in Muslim and Coptic literature of the medieval period. See el-Leithy, "Coptic Culture and Conversion," 193–198, 262–264.

119. Genesis 3:1–20.

120. Guirguis, "Athār al-Arākhina," 43.

121. Owen Bradford and Kwang-Kuo Hwang, "Guilt and Shame in Chinese Culture: A Cross-Cultural Framework from the Perspective of Morality and Identity," *Journal for the Theory of Social Behavior* 33, no. 2 (2003): 128.

122. Al-Jabarti *'Ajā'ib*, 3:123. This incident took place in 1799 during the early days of the French occupation of Egypt and must be read as a double insult to a learned Muslim *'ālim* whose land was occupied by seemingly brutish Frenchmen. Still, it is not difficult to imagine that Jabarti would have deplored such behavior before the French occupation.

123. Patriarchal Library, MS Theology 134, 153v.

124. This sermon was analyzed and translated into English by Maged S. A. Mikhail, "On Cana of Galilee: A Sermon by the Coptic Patriarch Benjamin I," *Coptic Church Review* 23, no. 3 (2002): 66–93.

125. Drunkards are most commonly referred to by both Yu'annis and Yusab as *majānīn* (madmen).

126. If this story were true, then this ḥākim would have been the bey who governed Jirja (as a subprovincial governor), given that the term ḥākim was typically his title.

127. St. Macarius Library, MS Theology 6, 202r–203r. The first part of this passage seems to have been influenced by these sections of Benjamin I's sermon: "Let us keep ourselves from the drunkenness of wine. For any degree of drunkenness is obscene. Is there a man here today who drank, became drunk, and was not moved by wine? When one among (the men) said a sensible word, the drunkard, because of [his] intoxication, said, 'It is not true, you are a liar!' And the devil came into their midst, drunkenness prevailed among them, a dispute began, and they fought with each other [Sir. 31: 29–30]. Some were hurt, others tore their clothes, and some were wounded. The matter was brought before the magistrate, and they were beaten and fined. How unfortunate were those present. They

suffered the same punishment as the drunkard. What did they gain?" See Mikhail, "On Cana of Galilee," 81.

128. Patriarchal Library, MS Theology 134, 74v. An earlier Coptic manuscript from 1699 also outlined strict conduct for Coptic priests: they were forbidden from swearing, laughing, joking, smoking, or acting indecently in any way. They were seen as role models among their parishioners, the text warns, and their behavior would elicit criticism not only from fellow Copts but also from other Egyptians. Patriarchal Library, MS Theology 256, 99r–100r.

129. Patriarchal Library, MS Theology 113, 263r. For more on polygamy as practiced by Copts in the early Islamic and medieval periods, see el-Leithy, "Coptic Culture and Conversion," 382–392.

130. This punishment is referred to as the "defrocking of priests," a process that is similar to the punishment of excommunication in the Coptic Church. See Martin Krause, "Defrocking of Priests," *Coptic Encyclopedia* 3:891. It is doubtful that the "defrocking of priests" was a regular habit in a church that was fighting to keep its parishioners, particularly during those Ottoman centuries in which opportunities to convert to another religion or denomination were real.

131. See critiques from the late seventeenth century in Patriarchal Library, MS Theology 256, 100v–101r, 104r. Yu'annis's astonishment at these practices, which included violations inside places of worship, is similar to existing Muslim admonitions: in 1663, Salim ʿAbdallah al-ʿAyyashi (d. 1679), a Moroccan traveler to Gaza and the Holy Land, was terribly "offended at the sight of Gazans walking through mosques with their shoes on and smoking in the *ṣaḥn* [courtyard]." Matar, "Two Journeys to Seventeenth-Century Palestine," 39.

132. Stephan Dähne, in studying Arabic Christian oratory in Ottoman Syria, has found that Catholic homilies addressing drunkenness eschew any discussion of how immoral conduct would have been seen by broader Muslim society. He writes, "At least a rhetorical question of 'What shall the Muslims think of us?' was expected. [Yet] it seems as if there was no Islamic environment at all for the preacher." Stephan Dähne, "A Christian-Arabic Sermon against the Sin of Drunkenness from the First Half of the 18th Century," *ARAM Periodical* 17 (2005): 228.

133. Patriarchal Library MS Theology 113, 266v–266r.

134. Yusab's willingness to enlist the help of Muslim authorities here can be compared to the enjoinder by the thirteenth-century Patriarch Kyrillus III (1235–1243) to Coptic congregations in Upper Egypt dissuading them "not to appeal to outside powers in their disputes." Cited and discussed by el-Leithy, "Coptic Culture and Conversion," 408–409.

135. St. Macarius Library, MS Theology 5, 177r.

136. This is likely a reference to Abu Zayd al-Hilali, hero of the popular epic "Sīrat Banī Hilāl fī Qiṣṣat Abī Zaid al-Hilalī wa'l-Nāʿisa wa-Zaid al-ʿAjjāj," retold by Malcolm C. Lyons, *The Arabian Epic: Heroic and Oral-Story-telling*, vol. 3, *Texts* (Cambridge: Cambridge University Press, 1995), 295–300. In eighteenth-century Egypt, poetry was often used to communicate social and political conditions. See el-Shayyal, "Some Aspects of Intellectual and Social Life," 126.

137. St. Macarius Library, MS Theology 6, 170r–171r.

138. Al-Jabarti similarly criticized mawlids, condemning the "loose morals," "women mingling with men," "public dancing girls," and prostitution. For an analysis of al-Jabarti's attitudes toward mawlids, see Winter, *Egyptian Society*, 175–184.

139. In earlier Muslim traditions of preaching, for instance, among the most popular themes were "poverty (*al-faqr*) and a renunciation of worldly goods and power." Berkey, *Popular Preaching and Religious Authority*, 45–47.

140. St. Macarius Library, MS Theology 6, 178v–179v. These condemnations bring to mind medieval Coptic literature, such as the Apocalypse of Samuel of Qalamun, which rebuked Christians not necessarily for converting to Islam but for "becoming *like* Muslims and practicing sins in which Muslims supposedly indulged themselves" (original emphasis). Iskander, "Islamization in Medieval Egypt," 225.

141. These condemnations recur in earlier Coptic literature. For the medieval period, see el-Leithy, "Coptic Culture and Conversion," 450–453. Similar criticisms pervaded in the Ottoman Levant. A Melkite (Greek Catholic) deacon attacked the sins of Aleppan Christians, such as "drunkenness . . . consumption of opium . . . [and] emulation of their non-Christian neighbors." Khater, "'God has called me to be free,'" 424.

142. Barsoumian, "The Armenian Amira Class of Istanbul," 81.

143. El-Shayyal, "Some Aspects of Intellectual and Social Life," 126.

144. Ahmad Shalabi, *Awḍaḥ al-Ishārāt*, 596–597; Al-Jabarti repeats the story in *'Ajā'ib*, 1:204–205.

145. As noted in chapter 1, the Copt al-Mu'allim Rizq (d. 1770) served as "astrologer" and personal confidant to 'Ali Bey al-Kabir (1755–1772), Egypt's effective ruler during this period. Condemnations against the practice of magic can also be found in Coptic manuscripts dating back to the seventeenth century. See, for instance, Patriarchal Library, MS Theology 301, 205v–208v (dated 1661–1662).

146. Sicard wrote, "The good bishop thought me so skilled in this art [of alchemy] that I was offered by his nephew, who was a priest, to learn the secret of making gold. I told him everything that I could, for the listening of this uncle and nephew, and that I never studied except the science of salvation and that this was the only science necessary for a clergyman. They were not too happy with my answer and, so that I do not aggravate their resentment, my friends advised me not to stay longer time in the diocese of the prelate." Sicard, *Oeuvres*, 2:65–66.

147. This could be a reference to Acts 16:16–18, where a slave girl who was forced to work as a fortune-teller by her masters was purged of her "satanic" spirits by St. Paul.

148. Patriarchal Library, MS Theology 134, 265r–265v. In an almost identical critique, Bishop Yusab wrote article 15, which addresses the vices committed not at house parties but inside churches. He writes: "We have spoken to you many times before about the habits that you committed such as playing al-ḍā' and al-fanājīn, as well as your bringing poets and adulterers to your weddings, among other habits which are too elaborate to address here. When you brought to the church such immoral habits, anger and fury has occurred to the extent that among you there are those who dare raise their hands [beat another] in the house of God, [the place] which is the foundation of truth and the place of repentance and regret from sin." See St. Macarius Library, MS Theology 6, 181v.

149. Traditionally excommunication could be used in cases such as "a hostile disposition toward one's neighbor," "making young men drunk," "a breach of the precept of sobriety at the Lord's table," "ill treatment of the poor, and offenses against the marriage law." See Krause, "Excommunication," *Coptic Encyclopedia* 4:1079–1080.

150. The delineation of religious from magical practice by Coptic Church authorities can compared to post-Reformation attitudes, as generally discussed in Keith Thomas, *Religion and the Decline of Magic* (New York: Scribner, 1971).

CONCLUSION

1. For more on these political trends, see S. S. Hasan, *Christians versus Muslims in Modern Egypt: The Century-Long Struggle for Coptic Equality* (New York: Oxford University Press, 2003), especially 169–182; and Christiaan van Nispen tot Sevenaer, "Changes in Relations between Copts and Muslims (1952–1994) in the Light of the Historical Experience," in *Between Desert and City: The Coptic Orthodox Church Today*, ed. Pieternella van Doorn-Harder and Kari Vogt (Oslo: Novus Forlag, 1997), 22–34.

2. This is particularly apparent in al-Masri, *Qiṣṣat al-Kanīsa al-Qibṭiyya*; Rufayla, *Tārīkh al-Umma al-Qibṭiyya*; and Manassa Yuhanna, *Tārīkh al-Kanīsa al-Qibṭiyya* (Cairo: Maktabat al-Maḥabba, 1983).

3. Here my conclusions align with Masters's observations that sectarian identities in the Ottoman world, firmly based in religious differentiations, pre-dated but became further heightened in the nineteenth century. Masters, *Christians and Jews*, 133.

4. Bernard Heyberger, "Pour une 'histoire croisée' de l'occidentalisation et de la confessionnalisation chez les chrétiens du Proche-Orient," *MIT Electronic Journal of Middle East Studies* 3 (2003): 37–38.

5. Molly Greene, introduction to *Minorities in the Ottoman Empire* (Princeton: Markus Wiener, 2005), 2.

6. On eighteenth-century Egypt, for instance, Peter Gran has argued that the booming ḥadīth literature produced by the 'ulamā' reveals traces of an "individualist" if wholly lay culture (Gran, *Islamic Roots of Capitalism*, 70–71). Nelly Hanna, studying the literary output of "nonreligious" Muslims in early modern Egypt, cautions against overemphasizing the centrality of religious elites in Ottoman history and encourages instead an examination of a "middle class" whose worldviews were largely secular; see, in general, Hanna, *In Praise of Books*. Following Hanna's argument, Magdi Guirguis has argued that the rise of archons represented the secularization of Coptic culture; see, in general, "The Coptic Community in the Ottoman Period."

7. Dina Khoury, "Who Is a True Muslim? Exclusion and Inclusion among Polemicists of Reform in Nineteenth-Century Baghdad," in *The Early Modern Ottomans*, ed. Virginia H. Aksan and Daniel Goffman (Cambridge: Cambridge University Press, 2007), 258.

8. Ira M. Lapidus, "Islamic Revival and Modernity: The Contemporary Movements and the Historical Paradigms," *Journal of the Economic and Social History of the Orient* 40, no. 4 (1997): 454–455; Masters, *Christians and Jews*, 132.

9. Khater, "'God has called me to be free,'" 423, original emphasis.

10. Masters, *Christians and Jews*, 132.

11. Jak Tajir, *Aqbāṭ wā Muslimūn Mundhu'l-Fatḥ al-'Arabī* (Cairo: Kurrāsat al-Tārīkh al-Miṣrī, 1951), 234.

12. Butcher, *The Story of the Church of Egypt*, 2:366.

13. Al-Masri, *Qiṣṣat al-Kanīsa*, 5:322.

14. Paul Sedra, "Textbook Maneuvers: Evangelicals and Educational Reform in Nineteenth-Century Egypt" (PhD diss., New York University, 2006), 211.

15. This ultimately led to a "textualizing" of the Coptic heritage, as Sedra notes. See Sedra, "Textbook Maneuvers," 198; also see Samir Seikaly, "Coptic Communal Reform: 1860–1914," *Middle Eastern Studies* 6 (1970): 249.

16. Seikaly, "Coptic Communal Reform," 251. The complex struggle that ensued between the clerical leadership and the council, which was often mediated by the government, continued for several decades and is discussed thoroughly in Seikaly's article.

17. Muhammad 'Afifi, "The State and the Church in Nineteenth-Century Egypt," *Die Welt des Islams* 39, no. 3 (1999): 279.

18. These have been closely studied by several scholars. See, for instance, Hasan's discussion, in *Christians versus Muslims in Modern Egypt*, of the "Sunday School Movement" that arose in the 1940s and 1950s; and various articles in van Doorn-Harder and Vogt, *Between Desert and City*.

19. See, in general, Shoshana Felman and Dori Laub, *Testimony: Crises of Witnessing in Literature, Psychoanalysis, and History* (New York: Routledge, 1992).

20. For more on the reinvention of martyrdom in modern Coptic history, see Saphinaz-Amal Naguib, "The Era of Martyrs: Texts and Contexts of Religious Memory," in van Doorn-Harder and Vogt, *Between Desert and City*, 137.

Bibliography

MANUSCRIPTS

St. Macarius Monastery Library, MS Hagiography 16
St. Macarius Monastery Library, MS Hagiography 37
St. Macarius Monastery Library, MS Hagiography 43
St. Macarius Monastery Library, MS Hagiography 71
St. Macarius Monastery Library, MS Theology 5
St. Macarius Monastery Library, MS Theology 6

Coptic Museum, MS History 475
Coptic Museum, MS History 538
Coptic Museum, MS History 549
Coptic Museum, MS Liturgy 128

Dayr Al-Suryan Library, MS Hagiography 272

Franciscan Center of Christian Oriental Studies, Serial 57-1
Franciscan Center of Christian Oriental Studies, Serial 66
Franciscan Center of Christian Oriental Studies, Serial 67

St. Mina Monastery Library, Microfilm 2-23-8-11
St. Mina Monastery Library, Microfilm 2-40-7-39

Mingana Chr. Arab. 32

MS Paris Arabe 152
MS Paris Arabe 153
MS Paris Arabe 4711

Patriarchal Library, MS Biblica 185
Patriarchal Library, MS Canon 21
Patriarchal Library, MS History 31
Patriarchal Library, MS History 48
Patriarchal Library, MS History 60
Patriarchal Library, MS History 77
Patriarchal Library, MS Liturgy 102
Patriarchal Library, MS Theology 113
Patriarchal Library, MS Theology 134
Patriarchal Library, MS Theology 230
Patriarchal Library, MS Theology 256
Patriarchal Library, MS Theology 270
Patriarchal Library, MS Theology 294
Patriarchal Library, MS Theology 301

PUBLISHED PRIMARY SOURCES

Abudacnus, Yusuf. *The True History of the Jacobites, of Egypt, Lybia, Nubia, etc. and their Origine, Religion, Ceremonies, Lawes, and Customes, whereby you may se how they differ from the Jacobites of Great Britain.* Trans. Sir Edwin Sadleir. London: R. Baldwin, 1692 (1675).

'Awad, Girgis Filuthawus. *Mimar al-Shahīda Dimyana.* Cairo: Maṭbaʿat al-Shams al-Ḥadītha, 1948 (1917).

Browne, W. G. *Travels in Africa, Egypt, and Syria from the Year 1792 to 1798.* London: T. Cadell Junior, 1799.

Butcher, E. L. *The Story of the Church of Egypt.* 2 vols. London: Smith, Elder, & Col., 1975 (1897).

Butler, Alfred Joshua. *The Ancient Coptic Churches of Egypt.* 2 vols. Oxford: Clarendon Press, 1884.

Crum, W. E. *Catalogue of the Coptic Manuscripts in the Collection of the John Rylands Library Manchester.* Manchester: University Press of London, 1909.

Curzon, Robert. *Visits to Monasteries in the Levant.* Ithaca: Cornell University Press, 1955 (1851).

Al-Damurdashi, Ahmad Katkhuda 'Azaban. *Al-Damurdashi's Chronicle of Egypt 1688–1755: Al-Durra Al-Muṣāna fī Akhbār al-Kināna.* Translated and annotated by Daniel Crecelius and 'Abd al-Wahhab Bakr. Leiden: Brill, 1991.

———. *Al-Durra al-Mus̩āna fī Akhbār al-Kināna.* Annotated by 'Abd al-Rahim 'Abd al-Rahman 'Abd al-Rahim. Cairo: Institut Français d'Archéologie Orientale du Caire, 1988.

Evliya Çelebi. *Seyahatname.* 10 vols. Ed. Seyit Ali Kahraman, Yücel Dağlı, and Robert Dankoff. Istanbul: Yapı Kredi Kültür Sanat Yayıncılık, 1996–2008.

Gonzales, Antonius. *Voyage en Égypte du père Antonius Gonzales, 1665–1666.* 3 vols. Translated and annotated by Charles Libois. Cairo: Institut Français d'Archéologie Orientale du Caire, 1977.

Graf, Georg. "Rede des Abu Isḥāq al-Mu'taman Ibn al-'Assāl: Mit Einladung zur Wallfahrt nach Jerusalem." *Bulletin de la Société d'Archéologie Copte* 7 (1941): 51–59.

History of the Patriarchs of the Egyptian Church, Known as the History of the Holy Church, vol. 3, part 3: *Cyril II–Cyril V (1235–1894 AD).* Translated and annotated by Antoine Khater and O. H. E. khs-Burmester. Cairo: Société d'Archéologie Copte / Institut Français d'Archéologie Orientale du Caire, 1970.

Ibn 'Abd al-Ghani, Ahmad Shalabi. *Awḍaḥ al-Ishārat fī man Tawalla Miṣr al-Qāhira min al-Wuzarā' wa'l Bāshāt.* Annotated and edited by 'Abd al-Rahim 'Abd al-Rahman 'Abd al-Rahim. Cairo: Tawzī' Maktabat al-Khanjī, 1988.

Ibn Iyas, Muhammad ibn Ahmad. *Badā'i' al-Ẓuhūr fī Waqā'i' al-Ḍuhūr.* 5 vols. Arranged and introduced by Muhammad Mustafa. Cairo: Al-Hay'a al-Miṣriyya al-'Āmma li'l-Kitāb, 1982.

Ibn Taymiyya, Ahmad ibn 'Abd al-Halim. *Ibn Taimiya's Struggle against Popular Religion, with an Annotated Translation of Kitāb Iqtidā' as-Sīrat al-Mustaqīm Mukhālafat Asḥāb al-Jaḥīm.* Annotated and Trans. Muhammad Umar Memon. The Hague: Mouton & Co., 1976.

Al-Jabarti, 'Abd al-Rahman. *'Ajā'ib al-Athār fi'l -Tarājim wa'l-Akhbār.* 4 vols. Ed. Moshe Perlmann and Thomas Philipp. Stuttgart: Franz Steiner Verlag, 1994.

Lansing, Giulian. *Egypt's Princes: A Narrative of Missionary Labor in the Valley of the Nile.* New York: Robert Carter & Br., 1865.

———. "A Visit to the Convent of Sittna (Our Lady), Damiane." *Harper's New Monthly Magazine* 28 (1864): 757–774.

Madden, R. R. *Travels in Turkey, Egypt, Nubia and Palestine in 1824, 1825, 1826, and 1827.* 2 vols. London: Henry Colburn, 1829.

Al-Maqrizi, Taqiyy al-Din Ahmad ibn 'Ali b. 'Abd al-Qadir. *Al-Mawā'iz wa'l-I'tibār fī Dhikr al-Khiṭaṭ wa'l-Athār.* 4 vols. Ed. Ayman Fu'ad Sayyid. London: Al-Furqan Islamic Heritage Foundation, 2002–2004.

———. *Macrizi's Geschichte der Copten (Akhbār Qibṭ Miṣr ma'khūdha min Kitāb al-Mawā'iz wa'l-I'tibār fī Dhikr al-Khiṭaṭ wa'l-Athār).* Trans. Ferdinand Wüstenfeld. New York: Olms, 1979 (1845).

Milad, Salwa, ed. *Wathā'iq Ahl al-Dhimma fi'l 'Aṣr al-'Uthmānī wa Ahammiyatuha al-Tārīkhiyya.* Cairo: Dār al-Thāqāfa l'il-Nashr wa'l-Tawzī', 1983.

Mingana, Alphonse, Hans Ludwig Gottschalk, and Derek Hopwood, eds. *Catalogue of the Mingana Collection of Manuscripts,* vol. 2, *Christian Arabic MSS.* 4 vols. Cambridge: W. Heffer, 1933–1985.

Morison, Antoine. *Relation historique, d'un voyage nouvellement fait au Mont de Sinai et Jerusalem.* Paris: Chez Antoine Dezallier, 1714.

Mustafa 'Ali. *Mustafa 'Ali's Description of Cairo of 1599.* Ed. and trans. Andreas Tietze. Vienna: Verlag der Österreichischen Akademie der Wissenschaften, 1975.

Niebuhr, Carsten. *Travels through Arabia and Other Countries in the East.* 2 vols. Trans. Robert Heron. Beirut: Librairie du Liban, 1978 (1792).

Norden, Frederick Lewis. *Travels in Egypt and Nubia.* London: Lockyer Davis and Charles Reymers, 1741.

Perlmannn, Moshe, ed. and trans. *Shaykh Damanhuri on the Churches of Cairo, 1739.* Berkeley: University of California Press, 1975.

Pococke, Richard. *A Description of the East and Some Other Countries.* 5 vols. London: W. Bowyer, 1743.

Rabbath, Antoine, ed. *Documents inédits pour servir à l'histoire du christianisme en Orient (XVI–XIX siècle).* 2 vols. New York: AMS Press, 1973 (1905–1910).

Raymond, E. A. E., and J. W. B. Barns, eds. *Four Martyrdoms from the Pierpont Morgan Coptic Codices*. Oxford: Oxford University Press, 1973.

Sicard, Claude. *Oeuvres lettres et relations inédits; Relations et mémoires imprimés; Parallèle géographique de l'ancienne Égypte et de l'Égypte moderne*. 3 vols. Ed. Maurice Martin. Cairo: Institut Français d'Archéologie Orientale du Caire, 1982.

Al-Siddiqi, Muhammad bin al-Surur al-Bikri. *Al-Nuzha al-Zahiyya fī Dhikr Wilāt Miṣr wa'l-Qāhira al-Mu'aziyya*. Annoted by 'Abd al-Raziq 'Abd al-Raziq 'Isa. Cairo: Al-'Arabī li'l-Nashr wa'l-Tawzī', 1998.

Sonnini, Charles Sigisbert. *Travels in Upper and Lower Egypt undertaken by Order of the Old Government of France*. London: J. Debrett, 1800.

Thompson, Charles. *Travels through Turkey in Asia, the Holy Land, Arabia, Egypt and Other Parts*. London: J. Newberry, 1767.

Vansleb, Johann Michael. *The Present State of Egypt; or, A New Relation of a Late Voyage into That Kingdom Performed in the Years 1672 and 1673*. Trans. M. D., B. D. London: John Starkey, 1678.

———. *Histoire de l'église d'Alexandrie*. Paris: Chez la Veuve Clousier et Pierre Promé, 1677.

Volney, Constantin-François. *Travels through Egypt and Syria in the Years 1783, 1784, and 1785*. 2 vols. London: G. G. J. and J. Robinson, Pater-Noster-Row, 1787.

Warburton, Eliot. *The Crescent and the Cross, or Romance and Realities of Eastern Travel*. New York: George P. Putnam, 1848.

Zaborowski, Jason R. *The Coptic Martyrdom of John of Phanijōit: Assimilation and Conversion to Islam in Thirteenth-Century Egypt*. Leiden: Brill, 2005.

SECONDARY SOURCES

'Abd al-Masih, Bishuy (Anba Bishuy). *Tārīkh Ibrūshiyyat Dumyat*. Cairo: Maktab al-Nisr li'l-Ṭibā'a, 1990.

———. *Shahīd Dumyāt: Māri Sidhum Bishāy*. Cairo: Maktab al-Nisr li'l-Ṭibā'a, 1987.

Abd El-Shaheed, Samiha. "A Catalogue of Unpublished Durug from the 17th through 19th Centuries in the Coptic Museum." In *Coptic Studies on the Threshold of a New Millennium: Proceedings of the Seventh International Congress of Coptic Studies*, ed. Mat Immerzeel, Jacques van Der Vliet, and Maarten Kersten, 519–528. Leuven: Peeters, 2004.

Abdel Nour, A. "Le réseau routier de la Syrie ottomane (XVIe–XVIIIe siècles)." *Arabica* 30, no. 2 (1983): 169–189.

Abullif, Wadi. "Salib ?–1512. Martire Ch. Copta." In *Santi della Chiesa Copta di Egitto*, vol. 2 of *Bibliotheca sanctorum orientalium*. 2 vols. Roma: Città Nuova Editrice, 1998–1999.

'Afifi, Muhammad. "The State and the Church in Nineteenth-Century Egypt." *Die Welt des Islams* 39, no. 3 (1999): 273–288.

———. *Al-Aqbāṭ fī Miṣr fi'l-'Aṣr al-'Uthmānī*. Cairo: Al-Hay'a al-Miṣriyya al-'Āmma li'l-Kitāb, 1992.

Amélineau, Emile. *Les actes des martyrs de l'église copte, étude critique*. Paris: E. Leroux, 1890.

Anawati, Georges. "The Christian Communities in Egypt in the Middle Ages." In *Conversion and Continuity*, ed. Michael Gervers and Ramzi Bikhazi, 237–252. Toronto: Pontifical Institute of Mediaeval Studies, 1990.

Argyriou, Asterios. "Christianity in the First Ottoman Era, 1516–1650." In *Christianity: A History in the Middle East*, ed. Habib Badr et al., 605–630. Beirut: Middle East Council of Churches, 2005.

Armanios, Febe. "Patriarchs, Archons, and the Eighteenth-Century Resurgence of the Coptic Community." In Lyster, *The Cave Church of Paul the Hermit*, 61–74.

Armanios, Febe, and Boğaç Ergene, "A Christian Martyr under Mamluk Justice: The Trials of Salib (d. 1512) according to Coptic and Muslim Sources." *Muslim World* 96, no. 1 (2006): 115–144.

Ashton, Gail. *The Generation of Identity in Late Medieval Hagiography: Speaking the Saint.* New York: Routledge, 2000.

El-Aswad, El-Sayed. "Spiritual Genealogy: Sufism and Saintly Places in the Nile Delta." *International Journal of Middle Eastern Studies* 38, no. 4 (2006): 501–518.

Atiya, Aziz S. *History of Eastern Christianity.* Notre Dame, IN: University of Notre Dame Press, 1968.

———. "John XVIII." *Coptic Encyclopedia* 4:1350.

Atiya, Aziz S., and René-Georges Coquin. "Synaxarion, Copto-Arabic." *Coptic Encyclopedia* 7:2171–2190.

Ayalon, David. "The Historian al-Jabarti and His Background." *Bulletin of the School of Oriental and African Studies* 23, no. 2 (1960): 217–249.

Baer, Marc. *Honored by the Glory of Islam: Conversion and Conquest in Ottoman Europe.* Oxford: Oxford University Press, 2008.

Barbir, Karl. *Ottoman Rule in Damascus, 1708–1758.* Princeton: Princeton University Press, 1980.

Bardakjian, Kevork B. "The Rise of the Armenian Patriarchate of Constantinople." In *The Central Lands*, vol. 1 of Braude and Lewis, *Christians and Jews in the Ottoman Empire*, 89–100.

Barkey, Karen. "Islam and Toleration: Studying the Ottoman Imperial Model." *International Journal of Politics, Culture and Society* 19, no. 1–2 (2005): 5–19.

Barsoumian, Hagop. "The Dual Role of the Armenian *Amira* Class within the Ottoman Government and the Armenian Millet (1750–1850)." In *The Central Lands*, vol. 1 of Braude and Lewis, *Christians and Jews in the Ottoman Empire*, 171–184.

———. "The Armenian Amira Class of Istanbul." PhD diss., Columbia University, 1980.

Basilios, Archbishop. "Deacon." *Coptic Encyclopedia* 3:885–886.

———. "Jerusalem, Coptic See of." *Coptic Encyclopedia* 4:1324–1329.

———. "Liturgical Instruments." *Coptic Encyclopedia* 5:1469–1475.

———. "Rabitat al-Quds." *Coptic Encyclopedia* 7:2049.

Behrens-Abouseif, Doris. "Patterns of Urban Patronage in Cairo: A Comparison between the Mamluk and the Ottoman Periods." In *The Mamluks in Egyptian Politics and Society*, ed. Ulrich Haarmann and Thomas Philipp, 224–234. Cambridge: Cambridge University Press, 1998.

———. "The Takiyyat Ibrahim al-Kulshani in Cairo." *Muqarnas* 5 (1988): 43–60.

———. *Azbakiyya and Its Environs from Azbak to Isma'il, 1476–1879*. Cairo: Institut Français d'Archéologie Orientale, 1985.

Berkey, Jonathan P. *Popular Preaching and Religious Authority in the Medieval Islamic Near East*. Seattle: University of Washington Press, 2001.

———. "Storytelling, Preaching, and Power in Mamluk Cairo." *Mamluk Studies Review* 4 (2000): 53–73.

Bilaniuk, Petro B. T. "Coptic Catholic Church." *Coptic Encyclopedia* 2:601–602.

———. "Coptic Relations with Rome." *Coptic Encyclopedia* 2:609–611.

Bolman, Elizabeth S., ed. *Monastic Visions: Wall Paintings in the Monastery of St. Antony at the Red Sea*. New Haven: Yale University Press, 2002.

Boogert, Maurits H. van den. *The Capitulations and the Ottoman Legal System: Qadis, Consuls and Beratlıs in the 18th Century*. Leiden: Brill, 2005.

Bosworth, C. E. "Christian and Jewish Religious Dignitaries in Mamluk Egypt and Syria: Qalqashandi's Information on Their Hierarchy, Titulature, and Appointment (II)." *International Journal of Middle East Studies* 3, no. 2 (1972): 199–216.

Bowman, Glenn. "Contemporary Christian Pilgrimage to the Holy Land." In *The Christian Heritage in the Holy Land*, ed. Anthony O'Mahony, 288–309. London: Scorpion Cavendish Ltd., 1995.

———. "Pilgrim Narratives of Jerusalem." In *Sacred Journeys: The Anthropology of Pilgrimage*, ed. Alan Morinis, 149–168. London: Greenwood Press, 1992.

Bradford, Owen, and Kwang-Kuo Hwang. "Guilt and Shame in Chinese Culture: A Cross-Cultural Framework from the Perspective of Morality and Identity." *Journal for the Theory of Social Behavior* 33, no. 2 (2003): 127–144.

Braude, Benjamin, and Bernard Lewis, eds. *Christians and Jews in the Ottoman Empire: The Functioning of a Plural Society*. 2 vols. New York: Holmes & Meier, 1982.

Brock, Sebastian P. "East Syriac Pilgrims to Jerusalem in the Early Ottoman Period." *ARAM* 18 (2006): 189–201.

Brown, Peter. *The Body and Society: Men, Women, and Sexual Renunciation in Early Christianity*. New York: Columbia University Press, 1988.

———. *The Cult of the Saints: Its Rise and Function in Latin Christianity*. Chicago: University of Chicago Press, 1981.

Buri, Vincenzo. "L'Unione della chiesa Copta con Roma sotto Clemente VIII." *Orientalia Christiana* 23, no. 72 (1931): 105–264.

Carswell, John. *Coptic Tattoo Designs*. 2nd ed. Beirut: American University of Beirut Press, 1958.

Catlos, Brian. "To Catch a Spy: The Case of Zayn al-Din and Ibn Dukhan." *Medieval Encounters* 2, no. 2 (1996): 99–113.

Chapoutot-Remadi, Mounira. "Femmes dans la ville mamluke." *Journal of the Economic and Social History of the Orient* 38, no. 2 (1995): 145–164.

Clark, Elizabeth A. "Antifamilial Tendencies in Ancient Christianity." *Journal of the History of Sexuality* 5, no. 3 (1995): 356–380.

Clarysse, Willy. "The Coptic Martyr Cult." In *Martyrium in Multidisciplinary Perspective*, ed. M. Lamberigts and P. Van Deun, 377–395. Leuven, Belgium: Leuven University Press, 1995.

Cody, Alfred. "Pascha." *Coptic Encyclopedia* 6:1903–1905.

Cohen, Amnon. "The Ottoman Approach to Christians and Christianity in Sixteenth-Century Jerusalem." *Islam and Christian-Muslim Relations* 7, no. 2 (1996): 205–212.

———. *Jewish Life under Islam: Jerusalem in the Sixteenth Century*. Cambridge: Harvard University Press, 1984.

———. "The Army in Palestine in the Eighteenth Century—Sources of Its Weakness and Strength." *Bulletin of the School of Oriental and African Studies* 34, no. 1 (1971): 36–55.

Cohen, Mark R. "What Was the Pact of 'Umar? A Literary-Historical Study." *Jerusalem Studies in Arabic and Islam* 23 (1999): 100–157.

———. *Under Crescent and Cross: The Jews in the Middle Ages*. Princeton: Princeton University Press, 1994.

———. "Islam and the Jews: Myth, Counter-Myth, History." *Jerusalem Quarterly*, no. 38 (1986): 125–137.

———. "Jews in the Mamluk Environment: The Crisis of 1442 (A Geniza Study)." *Bulletin of the School of Oriental and African Studies, University of London* 47, no. 3 (1984): 425–448.

———. *Jewish Self-Government in Medieval Egypt: The Origins of the Office of Head of the Jews, ca. 1065–1126*. Princeton: Princeton University Press, 1980.

Colbert, Edward P. *The Martyrs of Cordoba (850–859)*. Washington, DC: Catholic University of America Press, 1962.

Colin, Georges S. "Baraka." *EI2* 1:1032.

Cook, David. *Martyrdom in Islam*. Cambridge: Cambridge University Press, 2008.

Coope, Jessica A. *The Martyrs of Cordoba: Community and Family Conflict in an Age of Mass Conversion*. Lincoln: University of Nebraska Press, 1995.

Coptic Icons. 2 vols. Cairo: Lehnert and Landrock, 1998.

Coquin, René-Georges. "Dayr al-Maghtis." *Coptic Encyclopedia* 3:818–819.

———. "Dayr al-Maymah." *Coptic Encyclopedia* 3:837–838.

———. "Dayr Sitt Dimyanah." *Coptic Encyclopedia* 3:870–872.

Coşkun, Menderes. "The Most Literary Ottoman Pilgrimage Narrative: Nabi's *Tuhfetü'l-Harameyn*." *Turcica* 32 (2000): 363–388.

Courbage, Youssef, and Philippe Fargues. *Christians and Jews under Islam*. Trans. Judy Mabro. London: I. B. Tauris, 1997.

Crecelius, Daniel. "Egypt in the Eighteenth Century." In Daly, *The Cambridge History of Egypt, Volume 2*, 59–86.

———. "Incidences of Waqf Cases in Three Cairo Courts: 1640–1802." *Journal of the Economic and Social History of the Orient* 29, no. 2 (1986): 179–181.

———. *The Roots of Modern Egypt: A Study of the Regimes of 'Ali Bey Al-Kabir and Muhammad Bey Abu Al-Dhahab, 1760–1775*. Chicago: Bibliotheca Islamica, 1981.

Cuffel, Alexandra. "From Practice to Polemic: Shared Saints and Festivals as 'Women's Religion' in the Medieval Mediterranean." *Bulletin of the School of Oriental and African Studies* 68, no. 3 (2005): 401–419.

Dähne, Stephan. "A Christian-Arabic Sermon against the Sin of Drunkenness from the First Half of the 18th Century." *ARAM* 17 (2005): 221–228.

Daly, Martin W., ed. *The Cambridge History of Egypt, Volume 2: Modern Egypt from 1517 to the End of the Twentieth Century*. Cambridge: Cambridge University Press, 1998.

Darling, Linda T. "'Do Justice, Do Justice, for That Is Paradise': Middle Eastern Advice for Indian Muslim Rulers." *Comparative Studies of South Asia, Africa and the Middle East* 22, no. 1 (2002): 3–19.

Davis, Natalie Zemon. "Some Tasks and Themes in the Study of Popular Religion." In *The Pursuit of Holiness in Late Medieval and Renaissance Religion*, ed. Charles Trinkaus, 307–336. Leiden: Brill, 1974.

Davis, Stephen J. *The Early Coptic Papacy: The Egyptian Church and Its Leadership in Late Antiquity*. Cairo: American University in Cairo Press, 2004.

———. "Ancient Sources for the Coptic Tradition." In *Be Thou There: The Holy Family's Journey in Egypt*, ed. Gawdat Gabra, 133–162. Cairo: American University in Cairo Press, 2001.

———. *The Cult of Saint Thecla: A Tradition of Women's Piety in Late Antiquity*. Oxford: Oxford University Press, 2001.

Demos, Raphael. "The Neo-Hellenic Enlightenment (1750–1821)." *Journal of the History of Ideas* 19, no. 4 (1958): 523–541.

Dêtré, Jean-Marie. "Contribution à l'étude des relations du patriarche copte Jean XVII avec Rome de 1735 à 1738." *Studia Orientalia Christiana* 5 (1960): 123–169.

Dijkstra, Jitse, and Mathilde van Djik, eds. *The Encroaching Desert: Egyptian Hagiography and the Medieval West*. Leiden: Brill, 2006.

Doorn-Harder, Pieternella van, and Kari Vogt, eds. *Between Desert and City: The Coptic Orthodox Church Today*. Oslo: Novus Forlag, 1997.

Elad, Amikam. *Medieval Jerusalem and Islamic Worship: Holy Places, Ceremonies, Pilgrimage*. Leiden: Brill, 1999.

Eldem, Edhem. *French Trade in Istanbul in the Eighteenth Century*. Leiden: Brill, 1999.

Ergene, Boğaç A. "Pursuing Justice in an Islamic Context: Dispute Resolution in Ottoman Courts of Law." *PoLAR: Political and Legal Anthropology Review* 27, no. 1 (2004): 51–71.

———. "On Ottoman Justice: Interpretations in Conflict (1600–1800)." *Islamic Law and Society* 8, no. 1 (2001): 52–87.

Erlich, Haggai. *The Cross and the Rover: Ethiopia, Egypt and the Nile*. London: Lynne Rienner, 2002.

Faroqhi, Suraiya. "An Orthodox Woman Saint in an Ottoman Document." In *Syncretismes et hérésies dans l'Orient seljoukide et ottoman (XIVe–XVIIIe siècles): Actes du colloque du Collège de France, Octobre 2001*, ed. Gilles Veinstein, 383–394. Paris: Peeters, 2005.

———. *Subjects of the Sultan: Culture and Daily Life in the Ottoman Empire*. New York: I. B. Tauris, 2000.

———. *Pilgrims and Sultans: The Hajj under the Ottomans, 1517–1683*. London: I. B. Tauris, 1994.

Fattah, Hala. "Representations of Self and the Other in Two Iraqi Travelogues of the Ottoman Period." *International Journal of Middle East Studies* 30, no. 1 (1998): 51–76.

Fattal, A. *Le statut legal des non-musulmans en pays d'Islam*. 2nd ed. Beirut: Dar El-Machreq, 1995.

Felman, Shoshana, and Dori Laub. *Testimony: Crises of Witnessing in Literature, Psychoanalysis, and History*. New York: Routledge, 1992.

Findley, Carter Vaughn. *Ottoman Civil Officialdom: A Social History*. Princeton: Princeton University Press, 1989.

Flemming, Barbara. "Glimpses of Turkish Saints: Another Look at Cami' and Ottoman Biographers." *Journal of Turkish Studies* 18 (1994): 59–73.

Forget, I., ed. *Synaxarium Alexandrinum*. In *Corpus Scriptorum Christianorum Orientalium*, 47, 48, 49, 67, 78, 90. Louvain-Paris: Carolus Poussielgue Bibliopola, 1905–1932.

Fortescue, Adrian. *The Eastern Churches Trilogy*. 3 vols. Piscataway, NJ: Georgias Press, 2001 (1913).

Frank, Georgia. "Miracles, Monks, and Monuments: The *Historia Monachorum in Aegypto* as Pilgrims' Tales." In *Pilgrimage and Holy Space in Late Antique Egypt*, ed. David Frankfurter, 483–505. Leiden: Brill, 1998.

Frankfurter, David. "Hagiography and the Reconstruction of Local Religion in Late Antique Egypt: Memories, Inventions, and Landscapes." In Dijkstra and van Dijk, *The Encroaching Desert*, 13–38.

———. "The Perils of Love: Magic and Countermagic in Coptic Egypt." *Journal of the History of Sexuality* 10, no. 3 (2001): 480–500.

———, ed. *Pilgrimage and Holy Space in Late Antique Egypt*. Leiden: Brill, 1998.

Frazee, Charles. *Catholics and Sultans: The Church and the Ottoman Empire 1453–1923*. Cambridge: Cambridge University Press, 1983.

Frend, W. H. C. "Nationalism and Anti-Chalcedonian Feeling in Egypt." In *Religion and National Identity*, ed. Stuart Mews, 21–38. Oxford: Basil Blackwell, 1982.

Frenkel, Yehoshu'a. "Mar Saba during the Mamluk and Ottoman Periods: The Sabaite Heritage in the Orthodox Church from the Fifth Century to the Present." *Orientalia Lovaniensia Analecta* 98 (2001): 111–118.

———. "Muslim Pilgrimage to Jerusalem in the Mamluk Period." In *Pilgrims and Travelers to the Holy Land*, ed. Bryan F. Le Beau and Menachem Mor, 63–88. Omaha, NE: Creighton University Press, 1996.

Gaborieau, Marc. "The Cult of Saints among the Muslims of Nepal and Northern India." In *Saints and Their Cults*, ed. Stephen Wilson, 291–308. Cambridge: Cambridge University Press, 1983.

Gabra, Gawdat. "The Coptic and Arabic Inscriptions in the Cave Church." In Lyster, *The Cave Church of Paul the Hermit*, 275–285.

———. "New Research from the Library of the Monastery of St. Paul." In Lyster, *The Cave Church of Paul the Hermit*, 99–105.

———. "Perspectives on the Monastery of St. Antony: Medieval and Later Inhabitants and Visitors." In Bolman, *Monastic Visions*, 173–184.

———, ed. *Be Thou There: The Holy Family's Journey in Egypt*. Cairo: American University in Cairo Press, 2001.

Gara, Eleni. "Neomartyr without a Message." *Archivum Ottimanicum* 23 (2005–2006): 155–176.

Gil, Moshe. "Dhimmī Donations and Foundations for Jerusalem (638–1099)." *Journal of the Economic and Social History of the Orient* 27, no. 2 (1984): 156–174.

Ginio, Eyal. "The Shaping of a Sacred Space: The *Tekke* of Zühuri Şeyh Ahmet Efendi in Eighteenth-Century Salonica." *Medieval History Journal* 9, no. 2 (2006): 271–296.

———. "Living on the Margins of Charity: Coping with Poverty in an Ottoman Provincial City." In *Poverty and Charity in Middle Eastern Contexts*, ed. Michael Bonner, Mine Ener, and Amy Singer, 165–184. Albany: SUNY Press, 2003.

Ginzburg, Carlo. *The Cheese and the Worms: The Cosmos of a Sixteenth-Century Miller*. Trans. John and Anne Tedeschi. Baltimore: Johns Hopkins University Press, 1980.

Göçek, Fatma Müge, and Marc David Baer. "Social Boundaries of Ottoman Women's Experience in Eighteenth-Century Galata Court Records." In Zilfi, *Women in the Ottoman Empire*, 48–65.

Goehring, James E. *Ascetics, Society, and the Desert: Studies in Early Egyptian Monasticism*. Harrisburg, PA: Trinity Press International, 1999.

Gradeva, Rossitsa. *Rumeli under the Ottomans, 15th to 18th Centuries: Institutions and Communities*. Istanbul: Isis Press, 2004.

———. "Apostasy in Rumeli in the Middle of the Sixteenth Century." *Al-Majalla al-Tārīkhiyya al-'Arabiyya li'l-Dirāsāt al-'Uthmāniyya* 22 (2000): 29–73.

———. "Orthodox Christians in the Kadi Courts: The Practice of the Sofia Sheriat Court, Seventeenth Century." *Islamic Law and Society* 4, no. 1 (1997): 37–69.

Graf, Georg. *Geschichte der christlichen arabischen Literatur*. 5 vols. Studi e Testi 118, 133, 146, 147, 152. Vatican City: Bibliotheca Apostolica Vaticana, 1944–1953.

Gran, Peter. *Islamic Roots of Capitalism: Egypt, 1760–1840*. Syracuse, NY: Syracuse University Press, 1998 (1979).

Greene, Molly, ed. *Minorities in the Ottoman Empire*. Princeton: Markus Wiener, 2005.

Grehan, James. "Smoking and 'Early Modern' Sociability: The Great Tobacco Debate in the Ottoman Middle East (Seventeenth to Eighteenth Centuries)." *American Historical Review* 111 (2006): 1353–1354.

Griffith, Sidney H. "The Handwriting on the Wall: Monastic Visions." In Bolman, *Wall Paintings in the Monastery of St. Antony at the Red Sea*, 185–194.

———. "*The Life of Theodore of Edessa*: History, Hagiography, and Religious Apologetics in Mar Saba in Early Abbasid Times." *Orientalia Lovaniensia Analecta* 98 (2001): 147–169.

———. "Christians, Muslims, and Neo-Martyrs." In *Sharing the Sacred: Religious Contacts and Conflicts in the Holy Land: First–Fifteenth Centuries CE*, ed. Arieh Kofsky and Guy G. Stroumsa, 163–207. Jerusalem: Yad Izhak Ben Zvi, 1998.

———. "Michael, the Martyr and Monk of Mar Sabas Monastery, at the Court of the Caliph 'Abd al-Malik: Christian Apologetics and Martyrology in the Early Islamic Period." *ARAM* 6 (1994): 115–148.

Guirguis, Magdi. *An Armenian Artist in Ottoman Cairo: Yuhanna Al-Armani and His Coptic Icons*. Cairo: American University in Cairo Press, 2008.

———. "The Coptic Community in the Ottoman Period." In *Society and Economy in Egypt and the Eastern Mediterranean, 1600–1900: Essays in Honor of André Raymond*, ed. Nelly Hanna and Raouf Abbas, 201–216. Cairo: American University in Cairo Press, 2005.

———. "Athār al-Arākhina 'ala Awḍā' al-Qibṭ fi'l-Qarn al-Thāmin 'Ashr." *Annales Islamologiques* 34 (2000): 23–44.

———. "Idārat al-Azamāt fī Tārīkh al-Qibṭ: Namūdhaj min al-Qarn al-Thāmin 'Ashr." *Annales Islamologiques* 33 (1999): 45–59.

Haarmann, Ulrich. "Regional Sentiment in Medieval Islamic Egypt." *Bulletin of the School of Oriental and African Studies* 43, no. 1 (1980): 55–66.

Haarmann, Ulrich, and Thomas Philipp, eds. *The Mamluks in Egyptian Politics and Society.* Cambridge: Cambridge University Press, 1998.

Haddad, H. S. "'Georgic' Cults and Saints of the Levant." *Numen* 16, no. 1 (1969): 21–39.

Halm, Heinz. *Ägypten nach den mamlukischen Lehensregistern.* 2 vols. Wiesbaden: Reichert, 1979–1983.

Hamilton, Alastair. *The Copts and the West 1439–1822: The European Discovery of the Egyptian Church.* Oxford: Oxford University Press, 2006.

———. "An Egyptian Traveler in the Republic of Letters: Josephus Barbatus or Abudacnus the Copt." *Journal of the Warburg and Courtauld Institutes* 57 (1994): 123–150.

Hanna, Nelly. *In Praise of Books: A Cultural History of Cairo's Middle Class, Sixteenth to the Eighteenth Century.* Syracuse, NY: Syracuse University Press, 2003.

———. "The Chronicles of Ottoman Egypt: History or Entertainment?" In Kennedy, *The Historiography of Islamic Egypt,* 237–250.

Harvey, Susan Ashbrook. "Sacred Bonding: Mothers and Daughters in Early Syriac Hagiography." *Journal of Early Christian Studies* 4, no. 1 (1996): 27–56.

Hasan, S. S. *Christians versus Muslims in Modern Egypt: The Century-Long Struggle for Coptic Equality.* New York: Oxford University Press, 2003.

Hasluck, F. W. *Christianity and Islam under the Sultans.* 2 vols. New York: Octagon Books, 1973 (1929).

Hathaway, Jane. "Mamluk 'Revivals' and Mamluk Nostalgia in Ottoman Egypt." In *The Mamluks in Egyptian and Syrian Politics and Society,* ed. Michael Winter and Amalia Levanoni, 387–406. Leiden: Brill, 2004.

———. "Rewriting Eighteenth-Century Ottoman History." *Mediterranean Historical Review* 19, no. 1 (2004): 29–53.

———. "Egypt in the Seventeenth Century." In Daly, *The Cambridge History of Egypt, Volume* 2, 34–58.

———. *The Politics of Households in Ottoman Egypt.* Cambridge: Cambridge University Press, 1997.

Heijer, Johannes den. "Les Patriarches Coptes d'Origine Syrienne." In *Studies on the Christian Arabic Heritage: In Honour of Father Prof. Dr. Samir Khalil Samir S.I. at the Occasion of His Sixty-Fifth Birthday,* ed. R. Y. Ebied, S. Khalil Samir, and Herman G. B. Teule, 45–63. Leuven: Peeters, 2004.

———. "Considérations sur les communautés chrétiennes en Égypte fatimide: L'État et l'église sous le vizirat de Badr al-Jamālī (1074–1094)." In *L'Égypte fatimide: Son art et son histoire,* ed. Marianne Barrucand, 569–578. Paris: Presses de l'Université de Paris–Sorbonne, 1999.

———. "Recent Developments in Coptic-Arabic Studies (1992–1996)." In *Ägypten und Nubien in spätantiker und christlicher Zeit* (Proceedings of the Sixth International Congress of Coptologists, Münster, 20–26 July 1996), vol. 2, ed. Stephen Emmel, 49–64. Wiesbaden: Reichert, 1999.

———. "Coptic Historiography in the Fatimid, Ayyubid and Early Mamluk Periods." *Medieval Encounters* 2, no. 1 (1996): 67–98.

Heyberger, Bernard. "Individualism and Political Modernity: Devout Catholic Women in Aleppo and Lebanon between the Seventeenth and Nineteenth Centuries." In *Beyond the Exotic: Women's Histories in Islamic Societies*, ed. Amira Sonbol, 71–88. Syracuse, NY: Syracuse University Press, 2005.

———. "Pour une 'histoire croisée' de l'occidentalisation et de la confessionnalisation chez les chrétiens du Proche-Orient." *MIT Electronic Journal of Middle East Studies* 3 (2003): 36–49.

———. "Frontières confessionnelles et conversions chez les chrétiens orientaux (XVIIe–XVIIIe siècles)." In *Conversions islamiques: Identités religieuses en Islam méditerranéen*, ed. Mercedes García-Arenal, 245–258. Paris: Maisonneuve-Larose, 2001.

———. *Hindiyya: Mystique et criminelle 1720–1798*. Paris: Aubier, 2001.

———. "Livres et pratiques de la lecture chez les chrétiens (Syrie, Liban) XVIIe–XVIIIe." *Revue des Mondes Musulmans et de la Méditerranée* ("Livres et lecture dans le monde ottoman") (1999): 209–224.

———. *Les chrétiens du Proche-Orient au temps de la Réforme catholique (Syrie, Liban, Palestine, XVIIe–XVIIIe siècles.)* Rome: École Française de Rome, 1994.

Hintlian, Kevork. "Travelers and Pilgrims in the Holy Land: The Armenian Patriarchate of Jerusalem in the 17th and 18th Century." In *The Christian Heritage*, ed. Anthony O'Mahony, Göran Gunner, and Kevork Hintlian, 149–159. London: Scorpion Cavendish, 1995.

Hoffman, Valerie J. "Muslim Sainthood, Women, and the Legend of Sayyida Nafisa." In *Women Saints in World Religions*, ed. Arvind Sharma, 125–139. Albany: State University of New York Press, 2000.

Holt, P. M. *Egypt and the Fertile Crescent, 1516–1922: A Political History*. Ithaca: Cornell University Press, 1966.

———. "Al-Jabarti's Introduction to the History of Ottoman Egypt." *Bulletin of the School of Oriental and African Studies* 25, no. 1 (1962): 38–51.

Howell, David. "Health Rituals at a Lebanese Shrine." *Middle Eastern Studies* 6, no. 2 (1970): 179–188.

Hulsman, Cornelis. "Tracing the Route of the Holy Family Today." In Gabra, *Be Thou There*, 31–132.

Hunt, E. D. "The Itinerary of Egeria." In *The Holy Land, Holy Lands, and Christian History*, ed. R. N. Swanson, 34–54. Rochester, NY: Ecclesiastical History Society, 2000.

Hunt, Lucy-Anne. "Cultural Transmission: Illustrated Biblical Manuscripts from the Medieval Eastern Christian and Arab Worlds." In *The Bible as Book: The Manuscript Tradition*, ed. John L. Sharpe III and Kimberly van Kampen, 123–136. London: British Library, 1998.

———. "Manuscript Production by Christians in 13th–14th Century Greater Syria and Mesopotamia and Related Areas." *ARAM* 9, nos. 1–2 (1997): 289–336.

———. "Churches of Old Cairo and Mosques of al-Qahira: A Case of Christian-Muslim Interchange." *Medieval Encounters* 2, no. 1 (1996): 43–66.

Hupchick, Dennis P. "Orthodoxy and Bulgarian Ethnic Awareness under Ottoman Rule, 1396–1762." *Nationalities Papers* 21, no. 2 (1993): 75–93.

Idinopulos, Thomas A. "Jerusalem: Historical Perspectives on Politics and Religion in the Holy City." *Israel Affairs* 3, no. 2 (1996): 34–49.

İnalcık, Halil. "The Policy of Mehmed II toward the Greek Population of Istanbul and the Byzantine Buildings of the City." *Dumbarton Oaks Papers* 23 (1969–1970): 229–249.

———. "Djizya." *EI2* 2:562–566.

Innemée, Karel C. *Ecclesiastical Dress in the Medieval Near East.* Leiden: Brill, 1992.

Irwin, Robert. "The Image of the Byzantine and the Frank in Arab Popular Literature of the Late Middle Ages." *Mediterranean Historical Review* 4, no. 1 (1989): 226–242.

Ishaq, Emil Maher. "Lectern." *Coptic Encyclopedia* 5:1434–1435.

Isidhiros (Anba). *Al-Kharīda al-Nafīsa fī Tārīkh al-Kanīsa.* 2 vols. Cairo: Maṭbaʿat Qāʿid Khayr, 1964.

Iskander, John. "Islamization in Medieval Egypt: The Copto-Arabic 'Apocalypse of Samuel' as a Source for the Social and Religious History of Medieval Copts." *Medieval Encounters* 4, no. 3 (1998): 219–227.

Iskarus, Tawfiq. *Nawābigh al-Aqbāṭ.* 2 vols. Cairo: Maṭbaʿat al-Tawfīq, 1910–1913.

Jacob, W. M. *Lay People and Religion in the Early Eighteenth Century.* Cambridge: Cambridge University Press, 1996.

Jennings, Ronald C. *Christians and Muslims in Ottoman Cyprus and the Mediterranean World, 1571–1640.* New York: New York University Press, 1993.

Jomier, Jacques. "Bulāk." *EI2* 1:1299.

Joseph, John. *Muslim-Christian Relations and Inter-Christian Rivalries in the Middle East: The Case of the Jacobites in an Age of Transition.* New York: SUNY Press, 1981.

Jotischky, Andrew. "History and Memory as Factors in Greek Orthodox Pilgrimage to the Holy Land under Crusader Rule." In *The Holy Land, Holy Lands, and Christian History*, ed. R. N. Swanson, 110–122. Rochester, NY: Ecclesiastical History Society, 2000.

Keddie, Nikki R., and Beth Baron, eds. *Women in Middle Eastern History.* New Haven: Yale University Press, 1993.

Kennedy, Hugh, ed. *The Historiography of Islamic Egypt (c. 950–1800).* Leiden: Brill, 2001.

Khater, Akram. "'God has called me to be free': Aleppan Nuns and the Transformation of Catholicism in 18th-Century Bilad al-Sham." *International Journal of Middle East Studies* 40, no. 3 (2008): 421–443.

———. "A Deluded Woman: Hindiyya al-ʿUjaimi and the Politics of Gender and Religion in Eighteenth-Century Bilad al-Sham." *Archaeology and History in Lebanon*, no. 22 (2005): 6–20.

El Khawaga, Dina. "The Political Dynamics of the Copts: Giving the Community an Active Role." In *Christian Communities in the Arab Middle East: The Challenge of the Future*, ed. Andrea Pacini, 172–190. Oxford: Clarendon Press, 1998.

Khoury, Dina Rizk. "Who Is a True Muslim? Exclusion and Inclusion among Polemicists of Reform in Nineteenth-Century Baghdad." In *The Early Modern Ottomans*, ed. Virginia H. Aksan and Daniel Goffman, 256–274. Cambridge: Cambridge University Press, 2007.

———. "Slippers at the Entrance or Behind Closed Doors: Domestic and Public Spaces for Mosuli Women." In Zilfi, *Women in the Ottoman Empire*, 105–127.

Khuri, Shihata, and Niqula Khuri. *Khulāṣat Tārīkh Kanīsat Urushalīm al-Urthudhuksiyya.* Jerusalem: Maṭbaʿat Bayt al-Muqaddas, 1925.

Kilpatrick, Hilary. "Between Ibn Battuta and al-Tahtawi: Arabic Travel Accounts of the Early Ottoman Period." *Middle Eastern Literatures* 11, no. 2 (2008): 233–248.

———. "Brockelmann, Kahhala & Co: Reference Works on the Arabic Literature of Early Ottoman Syria." *Middle Eastern Literatures* 7, no. 1 (2004): 33–51.

Kotzageorgis, Phokion P. "'Messiahs' and Neomartyrs in Ottoman Thessaly: Some Thoughts on Two Entries in a Mühimme Defteri." *Archivum Ottomanicum* 23 (2005–2006): 219–232.

Kramers, Johannes Hendrik. "Al-Maḥalla al-Kubra." *EI2* 5:1221.

Krause, Martin. "Defrocking of Priests." *Coptic Encyclopedia* 3:891.

———. "Excommunication." *Coptic Encyclopedia* 4:1079–1080.

Krawiec, Rebecca. "'From the Womb of the Church': Monastic Families." *Journal of Early Christian Studies* 11, no. 3 (2003): 283–307.

Kuran, Timur. "The Economic Ascent of the Middle East's Religious Minorities: The Role of Islamic Legal Pluralism." *Journal of Legal Studies* 33, no. 2 (2004): 475–515.

Labib, Subhi. "The Problem of Bid'a in the Light of an Arabic Manuscript of the Fourteenth Century." *Journal of the Economic and Social History of the Orient* 7, no. 2 (1964): 191–196.

LaCapra, Dominick. *History and Criticism*. Ithaca: Cornell University Press, 1985.

Lamden, Ruth. "Communal Regulations as a Source for Jewish Women's Lives in the Ottoman Empire." *Muslim World* 95, no. 2 (2005): 249–263.

Langdon, Martin Telles, and Cawthra Mulock. *The Icons of Yuhanna and Ibrahim the Scribe*. London: Nicholson and Watson, 1946.

Lapidus, Ira M. "Islamic Revival and Modernity: The Contemporary Movements and the Historical Paradigms." *Journal of the Economic and Social History of the Orient* 40, no. 4 (1997): 444–460.

Larson, Wendy R. "The Role of Patronage and Audience in the Cults of Sts. Margaret and Marina of Antioch." In *Gender and Holiness: Men, Women and Saints in Late Medieval Europe*, ed. Samantha J. E. Riches and Sarah Salih, 23–35. New York: Routledge, 2002.

Lazarus-Yafeh, Hava. "Muslim Festivals." *Numen* 25, no. 1 (1978): 52–64.

Leeder, S. H. *Modern Sons of the Pharaohs*. New York: Amo Press, 1973 (1918).

Leeuwen, Richard van. "Control of Space and Communal Leadership: Maronite Monasteries in Mount Lebanon." *Revue des Mondes Musulmans et de la Méditerranée* 79–80 (1996): 183–199.

———. *Notables and Clergy in Mount Lebanon: The Khāzin Sheikhs and the Maronite Church (1736–1840)*. Leiden: Brill, 1994.

El-Leithy, Tamer. "Coptic Culture and Conversion in Medieval Cairo, 1293–1524 A.D." PhD diss., Princeton University, 2005.

Lev, Yaacov. *Charity, Endowments, and Charitable Institutions in Medieval Islam*. Gainesville: University Press of Florida, 2005.

Levin, Eve. "Dvoeverie and Popular Religion." In *Seeking God: The Recovery of Religious Identity in Orthodox Russia, Ukraine, and Georgia*, ed. Stephen K. Batalden, 29–52. DeKalb: Northern Illinois University Press, 1993.

Levine, Lee, ed. *Jerusalem: Its Sanctity and Centrality to Judaism, Christianity, and Islam*. New York: Continuum, 1999.

Little, Donald P. "Coptic Converts to Islam during the Bahri Mamluk Period: Conversion and Continuity." In Gervers and Bikhazi, *Indigenous Christian Communities*, 263–288.

Littmann, Enno, and K. Voller. "Aḥmad al-Badawī." *EI2* 1:280–281.

Livingston, John W. "'Ali Bey al-Kabir and the Jews." *Middle Eastern Studies* 7, no. 2 (1971): 221–228.

Louca, Anouar. "Ya'qub et les lumières." *Revue des Mondes Musulmans et de la Méditerranée*, nos. 52–53 (1989): 63–76.

Lutfi, Huda. "Coptic Festivals of the Nile: Aberrations of the Past?" In *The Mamluks in Egyptian Politics and Society*, ed. Thomas Philipp and Ulrich Haarmann, 254–282. Cambridge: Cambridge University Press, 1998.

———. "Manners and Customs of Fourteenth-Century Cairene Women: Female Anarchy versus Male Shar'i Order in Muslim Prescriptive Treatises." In *Women in Middle Eastern History*, ed. Nikki R. Keddie and Beth Baron, 99–120. New Haven: Yale University Press, 1993.

Lyons, Malcolm C. *The Arabian Epic: Heroic and Oral Story-telling*. 3 vols. Cambridge: Cambridge University Press, 1995.

Lyster, William, ed. *The Cave Church of Paul the Hermit at the Monastery of St. Paul, Egypt*. New Haven: Yale University Press / American Research Center in Egypt, 2008.

———. "Reviving a Lost Tradition: The Eighteenth-Century Paintings in the Cave Church: Context and Iconography." In Lyster, *The Cave Church of Paul the Hermit*, 209–231.

———. "Reflections on the Temporal World." In Bolman, *Monastic Visions*, 103–126.

MacCoull, Leslie. "Chant in Coptic Pilgrimage." In Frankfurter, *Pilgrimage and Holy Space*, 403–413.

———. "Notes on the Martyrdom of John of Phanijoit (BHO 519)." *Medieval Encounters* 6, nos. 1–3 (2000): 58–79.

Makhlouf, Avril M. "Umm Hindiyya's Syriac Heritage: Religious Life as a Mirror to Liturgy." *Journal of Eastern Christian Studies* 56, no. 1 (2004): 211–223.

Malti-Douglas, Fedwa. *Woman's Body, Woman's Word: Gender and Discourse in Arabo-Islamic Writing*. Princeton: Princeton University Press, 1991.

Manna, Adel. "Eighteenth- and Nineteenth-Century Rebellions in Palestine." *Journal of Palestine Studies* 25, no. 1 (1994): 51–66.

Marcus, Abraham. *The Middle East on the Eve of Modernity: Aleppo in the Eighteenth Century*. New York: Columbia University Press, 1989.

Marsot, Afaf Lutfi al-Sayyid. *Women and Men in Late Eighteenth-Century Egypt*. Austin: University of Texas Press, 1995.

———. "The Ulama of Cairo in the Eighteenth and Nineteenth Centuries." In *Scholars, Saints, and Sufis: Muslim Religious Institutions in the Middle East since 1500*, ed. Nikki R. Keddie, 149–165. Berkeley: University of California Press, 1972.

Martin, Maurice. "La Province d'Ašmūnayn: Historique de sa configuration religieuse." *Annales Islamologiques* 23 (1987): 1–29.

———. "Note sur la communauté copte entre 1650 et 1850." *Annales Islamologiques* 18 (1982): 193–215.

———. "Sicard, Claude." *Coptic Encyclopedia* 7:2136–2137.

———. "Vansleb (Wansleben), Johann Michael." *Coptic Encyclopedia* 7:2299.

Al-Masri, Iris Habib. *Qiṣṣat al-Kanīsa al-Qibṭiyya*. 9 vols. Alexandria: Maṭba'at al-Karnak, 1992 (1975).

Masters, Bruce. *Christians and Jews in the Ottoman Arab World: The Roots of Sectarianism.* Cambridge: Cambridge University Press, 2001.

Matar, Nabil. "Two Journeys to Seventeenth-Century Palestine." *Journal of Palestine Studies* 29, no. 4 (2000): 38.

McCarthy, Justin A. "Nineteenth-Century Egyptian Population." *Middle Eastern Studies* 12, no. 3 (1976): 1–39.

McInerney, Maud. "Rhetoric, Power and Integrity in the Passion of the Virgin Martyr." In *Menacing Virgins: Representing Virginity in the Middle Ages and Renaissance*, ed. Kathleen Coyne Kelly and Marina Leslie, 50–70. Newark: University of Delaware Press, 1999.

McPherson, J. W. *The Moulids of Egypt (Egyptian Saints-Days).* Cairo: Nile Mission Press, 1941.

Meinardus, Otto. *Two Thousand Years of Coptic Christianity.* Cairo: American University in Cairo Press, 2002.

———. "The Copts in Jerusalem and the Question of the Holy Places." In O'Mahony, *The Christian Heritage*, 112–128.

———. "Dayr Anba Antuniyus." *Coptic Encyclopedia* 3:719–729.

———. *Christian Egypt: Faith and Life.* Cairo: American University of Cairo Press, 1970.

———. "A Critical Study on the Cult of Sitt Dimiana and Her Forty Virgins." *Orientalia Suecana* 8 (1969): 45–68.

———. *Christian Egypt, Ancient and Modern.* Cairo: American University in Cairo Press, 1965.

———. *The Copts in Jerusalem.* Cairo: Commission on Oecumenical Affairs of the See of Alexandria, 1960.

Meri, Josef W. *The Cult of Saints among Muslims and Jews in Medieval Syria.* Oxford: Oxford University Press, 2002.

———. "Aspects of Baraka (Blessings) and Ritual Devotion among Medieval Muslims and Jews." *Medieval Encounters* 5 (1999): 46–69.

———. "The Etiquette of Devotion in the Islamic Cult of Saints." In *The Cult of Saints in Late Antiquity and the Middle Ages: Essays on the Contribution of Peter Brown*, ed. Paul Antony Hayward and James Howard-Johnston, 263–288. Oxford: Oxford University Press, 1999.

Meyer, Marvin W., and Richard Smith. "Mary Dissolving More Chains in Coptic Museum Papyrus 4958 and Elsewhere." In *Coptic Studies on the Threshold of a New Millennium: Proceedings of the Seventh International Congress of Coptic Studies*, ed. Mat Immerzeel, Jacques van der Vliet, and Maarten Kersten, 369–376. Leuven: Peeters, 2004.

———, eds. *Ancient Christian Magic: Coptic Texts of Ritual Power.* Princeton: Princeton University Press, 1999.

Mikhail, Alan. "The Nature of Plague in Late Eighteenth-Century Egypt." *Bulletin of the History of Medicine* 82, no. 2 (2008): 249–275.

Mikhail, Maged S. A. "Egypt from Late Antiquity to Early Islam: Copts, Melkites, and Muslims Shaping a New Society." PhD diss., University of California Los Angeles, 2004.

———. "On Cana of Galilee: A Sermon by the Coptic Patriarch Benjamin I." *Coptic Church Review* 23, no. 3 (2002): 66–93.

Mikhail, Severus (Maged) S. A. "A Reappraisal of the Current Position of St. Peter the Apostle in the Coptic Orthodox Church." *Bulletin of St. Shenouda the Archmandrite Coptic Society* 5 (1998–1999): 55–74.

Mills, Robert. "Can the Virgin Martyr Speak?" In *Medieval Virginities*, ed. Ruth Evans, Sarah Salih, and Anke Bernau, 187–213. Toronto: University of Toronto Press, 2003.

Minkov, Anton. *Conversion to Islam in the Balkans: Kisve Bahası Petitions and Ottoman Social Life*. Leiden: Brill, 2004.

Minnen, Peter van. "Saving History? Egyptian Hagiography in Its Space and Time." In Dijkstra and Dijk, *The Encroaching Desert*, 57–91.

Morris, Colin. *The Sepulchre of Christ and the Medieval West, from the Beginning to 1600*. New York: Oxford University Press, 2005.

Motzki, Harald. *Dimma und Égalité: Die nichtmuslimischen Minderheiten Ägyptens in der zweiten Hälfte des 18. Jahrhunderts und die Expedition Bonapartes (1798–1801.)* Bonn: Selbstverlag des Orientalischen Seminars der Universität, 1979.

El Moudden, Abderrahmane. "The Ambivalence of *Rihla*: Community Integration and Self-Definition in Moroccan Travel Accounts, 1300–1800." In *Muslim Travelers: Pilgrimage, Migration, and the Religious Imagination*, ed. Dale F. Eickelman and James P. Piscatori, 69–84. Berkeley and Los Angeles: University of California Press, 1990.

Muʿjizāt wa Ẓuhūrāt al-Shahīda al-ʿAfīfa Dimyana. Cairo: Al-Anba Ruways al-Ufst, 2000.

Müller, C. Detlef G. "John of Parallos, Saint." *Coptic Encyclopedia* 5:1367–1368.

Murre-Van Den Berg, Heleen. "'I the Weak Scribe': Scribes in the Church of the East in the Ottoman Period." *Journal of Eastern Christian Studies* 58, nos. 1–2 (2006): 9–26.

Muyser, Jacob. "Contribution à l'étude des listes épiscopales de l'église copte." *Bulletin de la Société d'Archéologie Copte* 10 (1944): 115–176.

Naguib, Saphinaz-Amal. "The Era of Martyrs: Texts and Contexts of Religious Memory." In van Doorn-Harder and Vogt, *Between Desert and Church*, 121–141.

———. "The Martyr as Witness: Coptic and Copto-Arabic Hagiographies as Mediators of Religious Memory." *Numen* 41 (1994): 223–254.

El Nahal, Galal H. *The Judicial Administration of Ottoman Egypt in the Seventeenth Century*. Chicago: Bibliotheca Islamica, 1979.

Nakhla, Kamil Salih. *Silislat Tārīkh al-Bābawāt Baṭārikat al-Kursī al-Iskandari*. 5 vols. Wadi al-Natrun, Egypt: Maṭbaʿat Dayr al-Sayyida al-ʿAdhrāʾ, Dayr al-Suryan, 2001 (1954).

Nispen tot Sevenaer, Christiaan van. "Changes in Relations between Copts and Muslims (1952–1994) in the Light of the Historical Experience." In van Doorn-Harder and Vogt, *Between Desert and Church*, 22–34.

Noel, Charles. "Missionary Preachers in Spain: Teaching Social Virtue in the Eighteenth Century." *American Historical Review* 90, no. 4 (1985): 866–892.

O'Keeffe, Benjamin, trans. "Ahmad ibn Taymiyya, Mas'alat al-Kana'is (The Question of the Churches)." *Islamochristiana* 22 (1996): 53–78.

O'Leary, De Lacy. *The Saints of Egypt*. London: Macmillan, 1937.

———, ed. *The Diphnar (Antiphonarium) of the Coptic Church*. 3 vols. London: Luzac & Co., 1926.

O'Mahony, Anthony. "Pilgrims, Politics, and Holy Places: The Ethiopian Community in Jerusalem until ca. 1650." In *Jerusalem: Its Sanctity and Centrality to Judaism, Christianity, and Islam*, ed. Lee Levine, 467–481. New York: Continuum, 1999.

Omar, Hanna H. Kilany. "Apostasy in the Mamluk Period: The Politics of Accusations of Unbelief." PhD diss., University of Pennsylvania, 2001.

Orlandi, Tito. "Hagiography, Coptic." *Coptic Encyclopedia* 4:1191–1197.

———. "Literature, Coptic." *Coptic Encyclopedia* 5:1450–1460.

———. "Literature, Copto-Arabic." *Coptic Encyclopedia* 5:1460–1467.

Pacini, Andrea, ed. *Christian Communities in the Arab Middle East: The Challenge of the Future*. Oxford: Clarendon Press, 1998.

Palmer, Andrew. "The History of the Syrian Orthodox in Jerusalem." *Oriens Christianus* 75 (1991): 16–43.

Pamuk, Şevket. *A Monetary History of the Ottoman Empire*. Cambridge: Cambridge University Press, 2000.

Panzac, Daniel. "The Population of Egypt in the Nineteenth Century." *Asian and African Studies* 21 (1987): 11–32.

Papaconstantinou, Arietta. "The Cult of the Saints: A Haven of Continuity in a Changing World." In *Egypt in the Byzantine World, 300–700*, ed. Roger S. Bagnall, 350–367. Cambridge: Cambridge University Press, 2007.

———. "Historiography, Hagiography, and the Making of the Coptic 'Church of the Martyrs' in Early Islamic Egypt." *Dumbarton Oaks Papers* 60 (2006): 65–86.

———. *Le culte des saints en Égypte des Byzantins aux Abbassides*. Paris: CNRS Éditions, 2001.

Patrinelis, C. G. "The Phanariots before 1821." *Balkan Studies* 42, no. 1 (2001): 177–198.

Peirce, Leslie. *Morality Tales: Law and Gender in the Ottoman Court of Aintab*. Berkeley: University of California Press, 2003.

———. *The Imperial Harem: Women and Sovereignty in the Ottoman Empire*. Oxford: Oxford University Press, 1993.

Peri, Oded. *Christianity under Islam in Jerusalem: The Question of the Holy Sites in Early Ottoman Times*. Leiden: Brill, 2001.

———. "Islamic Law and Christian Holy Sites: Jerusalem and Its Vicinity in Early Ottoman Times." *Islamic Law and Society* 6, no. 1 (1999): 97–111.

———. "The Christian Population of Jerusalem in the Late Seventeenth Century: Aspects of Demography, Economy, and Society." *Journal of the Economic and Social History on the Orient* 39, no. 4 (1996): 398–421.

———. "Waqf and Ottoman Welfare Policy: The Poor Kitchen of Hasseki Sultan in Eighteenth-Century Jerusalem." *Journal of the Economic and Social History of the Orient* 35, no. 2 (1992): 167–186.

Perlmann, Moshe. "Notes on Anti-Christian Propaganda in the Mamluk Empire." *Bulletin of the School of Oriental and African Studies* 10, no. 4 (1942): 843–861.

Peters, Rudolph. "The Battered Dervishes of Bab Zuwayla: A Religious Riot in Eighteenth-Century Cairo." In *Eighteenth-Century Renewal and Reform in Islam*, ed. Nehemia Levtzion and John Voll, 93–115. Syracuse, NY: Syracuse University Press, 1987.

Peterson, Andrew. "The Archeology of the Syrian and Iraqi Hajj Routes." *World Archaeology* 26 (1994): 47–56.

Petry, Carl F. *Protectors or Praetorians? The Last Mamluk Sultans and Egypt's Waning as a Great Power*. Albany: State University of New York Press, 1994.

———. *Twilight of Majesty: The Reigns of the Mamluk Sultans al-Ashraf Qaytbay and Qansuh al-Ghawri in Egypt*. Seattle: University of Washington Press, 1993.

———. *The Civilian Elite of Cairo in the Later Middle Ages*. Princeton: Princeton University Press, 1981.

Petsalis-Diomidis, Alexia. "Narratives of Transformation: Pilgrimage Patterns and Authorial Self-Presentation in Three Pilgrimage Texts." *Journeys* 3, no. 1 (2002): 84–109.

Philipp, Thomas. *The Syrians in Egypt: 1725–1975*. Stuttgart: Franz Steiner and Verlag Wiesbaden, 1985.

Piterberg, Gabriel. "Speech Acts and Written Texts: A Reading of a Seventeenth-Century Ottoman Historiographic Episode." *Poetics Today* 14, no. 2 (1993): 387–418.

La Porta, Sergio. "Grigor Tat'ewac'i's Pilgrimage to Jerusalem." In *The Armenians in Jerusalem and the Holy Land*, ed. R. Ervine, M. Stone, and N. Stone, 97–110. Leuven: Peeters, 2002.

Qasim, Qasim 'Abdu. "Al-Waḍ' al-Ijtimā'ī li'l-Aqbāṭ fī 'Aṣr Salāṭīn al-Mamālīk." *Al-Tārīkh wa'l-Mustaqbal* 3 (1989): 151–170.

———. *Ahl al-Dhimma fī Miṣr, al-'Uṣūr al-Wusṭa*. Cairo: Dār al-Ma'ārif, 1977.

Al-Qattan, Najwa. "Dhimmis in the Muslim Court: Legal Autonomy and Religious Discrimination." *International Journal of Middle East Studies* 31, no. 3 (1999): 429–444.

———. "Dhimmis in the Muslim Court: Documenting Justice in Ottoman Damascus, 1775–1860." PhD diss., Harvard University, 1996.

Ragib, Yusuf. "Al-Sayyida Nafisa, sa légende, son culte et son cimetière." *Studia Islamica* 44 (1976): 61–86.

Raymond, André. *Artisans et commerçants au Caire au XVIIIe siècle*. 2 vols. Cairo: Institut Français d'Archéologie Orientale, 1999 (1973–1974).

———. "La population du Caire et de l'Égypte a l'époque ottomane et sous Muhammad 'Ali." In *Memorial Omer Lutfi Barkan*, ed. Robert Mantran, 169–178. Paris: Librairie d'Amerique et d'Orient Adrien Maisonneuve, 1980.

Richards, Donald S. "Dhimmi Problems in Fifteenth-Century Cairo: Reconsideration of a Court Document." *Studies in Muslim-Jewish Relations* 1 (1993): 127–163.

Riches, Samantha J. E. "St. George as a Male Virgin Martyr." In *Gender and Holiness: Men, Women and Saints in Late Medieval Europe*, ed. Samantha J. E. Riches and Sarah Salih, 65–85. New York: Routledge, 2002.

Rizq, Dimitri. *Qiṣṣat al-Aqbāṭ fī'l-Arḍ al-Muqaddasa*. Cairo: Rābitat al-Quds li'l-Aqbāṭ al-Urthudhuks, 1967.

Rufayla, Ya'qub Nakhla. *Kitāb Tārīkh al-Umma al-Qibṭiyya*. Cairo: Metropol, 2000 (1898).

Runciman, Steven. *The Great Church in Captivity: A Study of the Patriarchate of Constantinople from the Eve of the Turkish Conquest to the Greek War of Independence*. Cambridge: Cambridge University Press, 1968.

Sadek, Ashraf Alexandre. "Two Witnesses of Christian life in the Area of Balyana." In *Christianity and Monasticism in Upper Egypt*, ed. Gawdat Gabra and Hany N. Takla, 253–268. Cairo: American University in Cairo Press, 2008.

Saleh, Marlis. "Government Relations with the Coptic Community in Egypt during the Fatimid Period (358–567 A.H. / 969–1171 C.E.)." PhD diss., University of Chicago, 1995.

Samir, S. Khalil. "Gabriel VII." *Coptic Encyclopedia* 4:1133–1135.

———. "Jirjis al-Jawhari al-Khanānī." *Coptic Encyclopedia* 4:1334–1335.

———. "Yusab, Bishop of Jirja and Akhmim." *Coptic Encyclopedia* 7:2360–2362.

Saperstein, Marc. "The Sermon as Oral Performance." In *Transmitting Jewish Traditions: Orality, Textuality, and Cultural Diffusion*, ed. Yaakov Elman and Israel Gershoni, 248–277. New Haven: Yale University Press, 2000.

Sariyannis, Marinos. "Aspects of 'Neomartyrdom': Religious Contacts, 'Blasphemy' and 'Calumny' in 17th-Century Istanbul." *Archivum Ottomanicum* 23 (2005/2006): 249–262.

Sayyid, Ayman Fu'ad. "Al-Ushmunayn." *EI2* 10:916.

Schidorsky, Dov. "Libraries in Late Ottoman Palestine between the Orient and the Occident." *Libraries and Culture* 33, no. 3 (1998): 260–276.

Sedra, Paul. "Textbook Maneuvers: Evangelicals and Educational Reform in Nineteenth-Century Egypt." PhD diss., New York University, 2006.

Seikaly, Samir. "Coptic Communal Reform: 1860–1914." *Middle Eastern Studies* 6 (1970): 247–275.

Shahid, Irfan. "Arab Christian Pilgrimages." In Frankfurter, *Pilgrimage and Holy Space*, 373–392.

Sharkey, Heather J. *American Evangelicals in Egypt: Missionary Encounters in an Age of Empire*. Princeton: Princeton University Press, 2008.

Shaw, Stanford. *The Financial and Administrative Organization and Development of Ottoman Egypt, 1517–1798*. Princeton: Princeton University Press, 1962.

El-Shayyal, Gamal el-Din. "Some Aspects of Intellectual and Social Life in Eighteenth-Century Egypt." In *Political and Social Change in Modern Egypt: Historical Studies from the Ottoman Conquest to the United Arab Republic*, ed. P. M. Holt, 117–132. London: Oxford University Press, 1968.

Shepard, Jonathan. "The Byzantine Commonwealth, 1000–1550." In *The Cambridge History of Christianity, Vol. 5: Eastern Christianity*, ed. Michael Angold, 3–52. 9 vols. Cambridge: Cambridge University Press, 2006.

Shoshan, Boaz. *Popular Culture in Medieval Cairo*. Cambridge: Cambridge University Press, 1993.

Sidawe, Elie. "Moeurs et traditions de l'Égypte moderne—Sitti Dimiana sa légende, son mouled." *Bulletin de la Societé de Géographie d'Égypte* 8 (1917): 75–99.

Simayka, Murqus. *Fahāris al-Makhṭūṭāt al-Qibṭiyya wa'l-'Arabiyya al-mawjūda bi'l-Mathaf al-Qibṭi wa'l-Dār al-Baṭriyarkiyya wa-Ahamm Kanā'is al-Qāhira wa'l-Iskandariyya wa-Adyirat al-Quṭr al-Miṣrī*. 2 vols. Cairo: Government Press, 1939.

Singer, Amy. *Constructing Ottoman Beneficence: An Imperial Soup Kitchen in Jerusalem*. Albany: State University of New York Press, 2002.

Al-Siniksār. Cairo: Maktabat al-Maḥabba, 1978.

Smith, Julia. "Oral and Written: Saints, Miracles, and Relics in Brittany, c. 850–1250." *Speculum* 65, no. 2 (1990): 309–343.

Soetens, Claude. "Origine et developpement de l'église copte catholique." *Irenikon* 65, no. 1 (1992): 42–62.

Sourdel, Dominique. "Ghazza." *EI2* 2:1056–1057.

Staffa, Susan Jane. *Conquest and Fusion: The Social Evolution of Cairo A.D. 642–1850*. Leiden: Brill, 1977.

Stewart, Randall. "Archon." *Coptic Encyclopedia* 1:229.

———. "Bilbeis." *Coptic Encyclopedia* 2:391.

———. "Burullus, Al-." *Coptic Encyclopedia* 2:427.

———. "Farama, al-." *Coptic Encyclopedia* 4:1089–1090.

———. "Jirja." *Coptic Encyclopedia* 4:1330–1331.

Suydam, Mary A., and Joanna E. Ziegler, eds. *Performance and Transformation: New Approaches to Late Medieval Spirituality*. New York: St. Martin's Press, 1999.

Swanson, Mark N. "The Martyrdom of 'Abd al-Masih, Superior of Mount Sinai." In *Syrian Christians under Islam: The First Thousand Years*, ed. David Thomas, 107–129. Boston: Brill, 2001.

———. "The Monastery of St. Paul in Historical Context." In Lyster, *The Cave Church of Paul the Hermit*, 43–60.

Tajir, Jak. *Aqbāṭ wa Muslimūn mundhu'l-Fatḥ al-'Arabī*. Cairo: Kurrāsat al-Tārīkh al-Miṣrī, 1951.

Talbot, Alice-Mary. *Women and Religious Life in Byzantium*. Burlington, VT: Ashgate, 2001.

Talmon-Heller, Daniella. "Muslim Martyrdom and the Quest for Martyrdom in the Crusading Period." *Al-Masaq: Islam and the Medieval Mediterranean* 14, no. 2 (2002): 131–139.

Tamura, Airi. "Ethnic Consciousness and Its Transformation in the Course of Nation-Building: The Muslim and the Copt in Egypt, 1906–1919." *Muslim World* 75, no. 2 (1985): 102–114.

Tawadrus, Samwil. *Al-Dalīl ila al-Kanā'is wa'l-Adyura al-Qadīma min al-Gīza 'ila Aswān*. Cairo: Al-Qism, 1990.

Taylor, Christopher S. *In the Vicinity of the Righteous: Ziyara and the Veneration of Muslim Saints in Late Medieval Egypt*. Leiden: Brill, 1999.

———. "Saints, Ziyara, Qissa, and the Social Construction of Moral Imagination in Late Medieval Egypt." *Studia Islamica* 87 (1998): 103–120.

Terzioğlu, Derin. "Man in the Image of God in the Image of the Times: Sufi Self-Narratives and the Diary of Niyāzī-i Miṣrī (1618–94)." *Studia Islamica* 94 (2002): 139–165.

———. "The Imperial Circumcision Festival of 1582: An Interpretation." *Muqarnas* 12 (1995): 84–100.

Teule, Herman. "Syrian Orthodox Attitudes to the Pilgrimage to Jerusalem." *Eastern Christian Art* 2 (2005): 121–125.

Thomas, Keith. *Religion and the Decline of Magic*. New York: Scribner, 1971.

Tingle, Elizabeth. "The Sacred Space of Julien Maunoir: The Re-Christianizing of the Landscape in Seventeenth-Century Brittany." In *Sacred Space in Early Modern Europe*, ed. Will Coster and Andrew Spicer, 237–258. Cambridge: Cambridge University Press, 2005.

Toledano, Ehud R. "The Imperial Eunuchs of Istanbul: From Africa to the Heart of Islam." *Middle Eastern Studies* 20, no. 3 (1984): 379–390.

Tribe, Tania C. "Icon and Narration in Eighteenth-Century Christian Egypt: The Works of Yuhanna al-Armani al-Qudsi and Ibrahim al-Nasikh." *Art History* 27, no. 1 (2004): 62–94.

Tritton, A. S. *The Caliphs and Their Non-Muslim Subjects*. London: Frank Cass and Company, 1970 (1930).

Trossen, Jean-Pierre. *Les Relations du patriarche copte Jean XVI avec Rome (1676–1718): Thèse de Doctorat*. Luxembourg: Imprimerie Hermann, 1948.

Tucker, Judith. *In the House of Law: Gender and Islamic Law in Ottoman Syria and Palestine*. Berkeley: University of California Press, 1998.

Tuğ, Başak. "Politics of Honor: The Institutional and Social Frontiers of 'Illicit' Sex in Mid-Eighteenth-Century Ottoman Anatolia." PhD diss., New York University, 2009.

Turner, Victor, and Edith Turner. *Image and Pilgrimage in Christian Culture: Anthropological Perspectives*. New York: Columbia University Press, 1978.

'Umar, Samira Fahmi 'Ali. *Imārat al-Ḥajj fī Miṣr al-'Uthmāniyya, 1517–1798*. Cairo: Al-Hay'a al-Miṣriyya al-'Āma li'l-Kitāb, 2000.

Upchurch, Robert K. "Virgin Spouses as Model Christians: The Legend of Julian and Basilissa in Ælfric's *Lives of Saints*." *Anglo-Saxon England* 34 (2005): 197–217.

Valensi, Lucette. "Inter-Communal Relations and Changes in Religious Affiliation in the Middle East (Seventeenth to Nineteenth Centuries)." *Comparative Studies in Society and History* 30, no. 2 (1997): 251–269.

Vaporis, Nomikos Michael. *Witnesses for Christ: Orthodox Christian Neo-Martyrs of the Ottoman Period, 1437–1860*. Crestwood, NY: St. Vladimir's Seminary Press, 2000.

———. "The Religious Encounter between Orthodox Christianity and Islam as Represented by the Neomartyrs and Their Judges." *Journal of Modern Hellenism* 12–13 (1995/1996): 257–325.

Viaud, Gérard. "Pilgrimages." *Coptic Encyclopedia* 6:1968–1975.

———. *Les pèlerinages coptes en Égypte*. Cairo: Institut Français d'Archéologie Orientale du Caire, 1979.

Vila, David H. "Christian Martyrs in the First Abbasid Century and the Development of an Apologetic against Islam." PhD diss., St. Louis University, 1999.

Vycichl, Werner. "Magic." *Coptic Encyclopedia* 5:1499–1509.

Walbiner, Carsten-Michael. "Monastic Reading and Learning in Eighteenth-Century Bilad al-Sham: Some Evidence from the Monastery of al-Shuwayr (Mount Lebanon)." *Arabica* 51, no. 4 (2004): 462–477.

Watenpaugh, Heghnar Zeitlian. "Dervishes: Space, Gender, and the Construction of Antinomian Piety in Ottoman Aleppo." *International Journal of Middle East Studies* 37, no. 4 (2005): 535–565.

Werthmuller, Kurt. "An In-Between Space: An Archival and Textual Study of Coptic Identity and Ayyubid Politics in Egypt, 1171–1250 CE." PhD diss., University of California Santa Barbara, 2007.

Wilfong, Terry G. "The Non-Muslim Communities: Christian Communities." In *The Cambridge History of Egypt, Vol. 1: Islamic Egypt 640–1517*, ed. Carl F. Petry, 175–197. 2 vols. Cambridge: Cambridge University Press, 1998.

Williams, Caroline. "The Cult of 'Alid Saints in the Fatimid Monuments of Cairo." *Muqarnas* 3 (1985): 39–60.

Williams, John Alden. "The Khanqah of Siryaqus: A Mamluk Royal Religious Foundation." In *In Quest of an Islamic Humanism: Arabic and Islamic Studies in Memory of*

Mohamed al-Nowaihi, ed. A. H. Green, 109–119. Cairo: American University of Cairo Press, 1984.

Winstead, Karen. *Virgin Martyrs: Legends of Sainthood in Late Medieval England*. Ithaca: Cornell University Press, 1997.

Winter, Michael. "Attitudes toward the Ottomans." In Kennedy, *The Historiography of Islamic Egypt*, 195–210.

———. "Ottoman Egypt, 1525–1609." In Daly, *The Cambridge History of Egypt, Volume 2*, 1–33.

———. *Egyptian Society under Ottoman Rule, 1517–1798*. New York: Routledge, 1992.

———. *Society and Religion in Early Ottoman Egypt: Studies in the Writings of ʻAbd al-Wahhab al-Shaʻrani*. London: Transaction Books, 1982.

Wissa, Myriam. "Harit Zuwaylah." *Coptic Encyclopedia* 4:1207–1209.

Wogane-Browne, Jocelyn. *Saints' Lives and Women's Literary Culture c. 1150–1300: Virginity and Its Authorizations*. Oxford: Oxford University Press, 2001.

Wolf, Kenneth. *Christian Martyrs in Muslim Spain*. Cambridge: Cambridge University Press, 1988.

Young, Katherine. Introduction to Sharma, *Women Saints in World Religions*, 1–38.

Yuhanna, Manassa. *Tārīkh al-Kanīsa al-Qibṭiyya*. Cairo: Maktabat al-Maḥabba, 1983.

Zaborowski, Jason R. "From Coptic to Arabic in Medieval Egypt." *Medieval Encounters* 14, no. 1 (2008): 15–40.

Zachariadou, Elizabeth A. "The Neomartyr's Message." *Bulletin of the Centre for Asia Minor Studies* 8 (1990–1991): 51–63.

Ze'evi, Dror. "Women in 17th-Century Jerusalem: Western and Indigenous Perspectives." *International Journal of Middle East Studies* 27, no. 2 (1995): 157–173.

Zilfi, Madeline C. *The Politics of Piety: The Ottoman Ulema in the Postclassical Age*. Chicago: Bibliotheca Islamica, 1987.

———, ed. *Women in the Ottoman Empire: Middle Eastern Women in the Early Modern Era*. Leiden: Brill, 1997.

Index